THE PARENTAL LEAVE CRISIS: TOWARD A NATIONAL POLICY

EDITED BY EDWARD F. ZIGLER
AND MERYL FRANK

The Parental Leave Crisis

Toward a National Policy

Yale University Press
New Haven and London

Designed by Nancy Ovedovitz and set in Baskerville type by Rainsford Type. Printed in the United States of America by Vail-Ballou Press, Binghamton, N.Y.

Library of Congress Cataloging-in-Publication Data
The Parental leave crisis
 Includes index.
 1. Parental leave—Government policy—United
States. 2. Parental leave—Government policy.
I. Zigler, Edward, 1930–   II. Frank, Meryl.
HD6065.P37 1987   331.25'76   87–10729
ISBN 0–300–03984–0 (alk. paper)

The paper in this book meets the guidelines for permanence and durability of the Committee on Production Guidelines for Book Longevity of the Council on Library Resources.

10   9   8   7   6   5   4   3   2   1

*To Bernice Weissbourd, whose work
has led the way for all who would support
our nation's families.*

Contents

Contributors

Joseph Allen, The Clinical Research Training Program, Laboratory for Social Psychiatry, Massachusetts Mental Health Center and the Harvard Medical School

Jay Belsky, Associate Professor, Department of Individual and Family Studies, The Pennsylvania State University

T. Berry Brazelton, M.D., Associate Professor of Pediatrics, Harvard Medical School

Urie Bronfenbrenner, Jacob Gould Schurman Professor of Human Development and Family Studies, Cornell University

Barbara Butler, Research Associate, Program for the Study of Family Owned Businesses, School of Organization and Management, Yale University

Ellen A. Farber, Assistant Professor of Psychology, State University of New York at Buffalo

Meryl Frank, Director, Infant Care Leave Project, The Bush Center in Child Development and Social Policy, Yale University

Thomas J. Gamble, Director, Edmund L. Thomas Children's Center, Erie, Pennsylvania

Sheila B. Kamerman, Professor of Social Work, School of Social Work, Columbia University

Thomas H. Kean, Governor of the State of New Jersey

Susan Muenchow, Acting Director, Governor's Constituency for Children, State of Florida

Mary Piccirillo, Assistant Director, Office of Government and Community Affairs, School of Medicine, Yale University

Peggy Pizzo, Research Associate, National Center for Clinical Infant Programs, Washington, D.C.

Joseph H. Pleck, Henry R. Luce Professor of Families, Change and Society, Wheaton College, Norton, Massachusetts

Patricia Schroeder, Member of the House of Representatives, Washington, D.C.

Kathyrn T. Young, Acting Associate Director, The Bush Center in Child Development and Social Policy, Yale University

Edward F. Zigler, Sterling Professor of Psychology and Director, The Bush Center in Child Development and Social Policy, Yale University

Staff Members of and Special Consultants to the Bush Center in Child Development and Social Policy, Yale University: Marguerite Alejandro-Wright, Barbara A. Emmel, Johanna Freedman, Robin Harwood, Robyn Lipner, Kathleen Makuen, Randy Sheinberg, and Janis Wasserman

Acknowledgments

We would like to thank the Bush Foundation of St. Paul, Minnesota, for their support of the Yale Bush Center Infant Care Leave Project from its inception. Their generous support made this work possible and helped to bring another pressing issue affecting our nation's families to the forefront of the nation's social policy agenda. We would also like to express our appreciation to the United States Department of Health and Human Services for their support. Specifically, we would like to acknowledge Dorcas Hardy and James Kissco of the Department of Health and Human Services for having the foresight to encourage the Bush Center to pursue research on this topic.

Our work would not have received the attention it was due were it not for the continued support and the intellectual contribution of Irving Harris, who recognized the need to inform the public about issues affecting children in order for these issues to be thoughtfully considered and properly assessed by our nation's families and policy makers. Mr. Harris also deserves our acknowledgment as an active member of the Advisory Committee on Infant Care Leave.

The work of the Advisory Committee on Infant Care Leave helped to refine and direct the research which eventually led to the chapters of this volume. The expert contributions of T. Berry Brazelton and Sally Provence were vital to the Committee's understanding of the parent-infant relationship. Sheila Kamerman's broad knowledge and deep understanding of the issues associated with infant care leave were truly invaluable, as were Wendy Williams's enthusiasm and her ability to find the central point of an issue. Wilbur Cohen, Julius Richmond, and JoAnn Gasper brought to the Committee their significant experience and knowledge of both social policy and the national policy process. Urie Bronfenbrenner lent to the Project and the Committee not only his expertise on the family system, but also his strong interest in the policy issues which affect the family. Blandina Cardenas Ramirez added the perspective of her area expertise, that of social policy making and the experience of minorities in American society. An important contribution to our knowledge concerning child development was provided by Jerome Kagan and Bettye Caldwell.

In addition to the contributions of the Advisory Committee members we wish to acknowledge the thoughtful and consistent work of George Silver, and the ongoing contribution of S. Lynn Kagan. We are also grateful to our editors at Yale University Press, Jeanne Ferris and Judith Calvert, for their support and encouragement.

It is near impossible to express the depth of our gratitude to the staff of the Yale Bush Center. Their commitment to this project was unending, and often lasted into the small hours of the night. Specifically, we would like to acknowledge Mary Lang and Johanna Freedman for their contributions to the Project, text of this book, and the well-being of the editors. We would also like to thank Adria DeBenedetto, Joyce Downing, Bettye Faison, Marisa Moolick, and Claudia Pilato for their assistance. Barbara Emmel deserves special praise for her expert work on the original chapters of the book. Her contributions went above and beyond the call of duty, and a better book is the result.

We would like to recognize Beth Pedersen of Copenhagen, Denmark, whose contribution led to the recognition of the lack of sufficient support for employed families with infants in the United States, and Vanessa Spence of Kingston, Jamaica, for her encouragement, her support and her keen ability to challenge assumptions. We would like to acknowledge Mollie Bayroff for setting high standards and insisting on our meeting them. We would also like to thank Steven Gabel for his assistance with every aspect of the preparation of this book, and for the example he sets.

Finally, we thank our families, Bernice and Scott Zigler, Al and Ricky Frank, and Steven Gabel for their unending support, and Isaac Roberto Gabel-Frank for perfect timing.

Introduction

EDWARD ZIGLER, MERYL FRANK, AND BARBARA EMMEL

In recent years, American society has experienced a rapid and lasting change in the composition of the family and the work force. The traditional family, in which the father works outside the home and the mother remains at home, primarily to care for the children, has been replaced by two-paycheck and single-parent families. Today, many mothers return to the work force after their children are born and before they enter school, either by choice or out of necessity. In fact, mothers of children under three years of age are considered the fastest growing segment of the work force.

The problems associated with the care of children of working parents, including issues of day care and latch-key children, and the balance between work and family responsibilities have become the focus of considerable national attention. However, the problems of a subgroup of working parents, those with infants under one year of age, have to date received only scant attention. With nearly one-half of all married mothers of infants participating in the work force, the issue of the problems working families face is not an insignificant one. Often these mothers had worked before the birth of their child, needed or choose to continue working for financial reasons, or were required by employers to return to work as soon as possible after delivery. The phenomenon of large numbers of very young infants in day care is so new that researchers have only now begun to address this issue (Belsky 1986; Zigler and Hall, in press; Phillips et al., in press). More analysis is required to understand the conflicting needs of all involved: parents, whose work schedules may cut into their time with the infant; infants, who need care that supports their healthy development in the early months of life; and employers, who are dependent on responsible and available employees, no matter what their family status.

Mothers who must return to work shortly after delivery report that they are often unhappy at leaving their young infants so soon after birth, especially for a full day (Brazelton 1986). Infants may be detrimentally affected by day care if it fails to meet their unique needs (Gamble and Zigler 1985). Fathers, more aware of their important roles as nurturers of their children, are now asking for more time with their newborns. In their dual roles of worker and family member, parents of today are often forced to return to work before they have time to feel comfortable with their infants or to establish the newly required patterns of family functioning.

Families deal with the conflict between work and family responsibilities in individual ways. Nonetheless, the problems that these families face have their origins in the structure of our society and must be solved on a structural level, not on a family-by-family basis. Resolution of this issue is essential to society's well-being, for conflict between family needs and work force demands carries the potential for further fragmentation of the family. Time for parenting in the period immediately following an infant's birth may be essential in the development not only of the infant, but of the whole family system as well (Bronfenbrenner 1979).

Changes in the composition of the work force have created a substratum of related issues concerning child care and the world of work. There is a growing need for more comprehensive care programs and for qualified caregivers who are cognizant of and responsive to a young infant's needs. For parents who wish to remain at home with their young infants both job security and career advancement are factors that may limit their desire or ability to take a leave. Further, day-to-day conflict between work and family concerns arise when parents must return to work before they feel ready to leave the young infant; these conflicts can affect both work performance and family dynamics.

Concerns of employers also come into play, especially when they involve costs, job performance, and management issues. Until recently, there has been little analysis of the issues that arise when parents must work during the early months of an infant's life. The phenomenon of large numbers of working mothers with very young children has come about so rapidly that researchers recognize the potential for a variety of related problems. This change has occurred almost before our nation has had the time to realize its impact, understand the range of issues it raises, and generate solutions for the problems faced by working families.

Thus no uniform policy has emerged, in either the private or the public sector, to support working families in meeting the demands on their time and energy that arise during the period surrounding the birth and early growth of a new infant. Many mothers are expected to return to work even before they are physically, no less emotionally, able to; this return may take place within a matter of days or weeks. Fathers are typically granted no more than a few days, if any time at all; the father's need to be at home during the first months after birth as the entire family adjusts to the new member is little recognized by the general public. The nation's response to the influx of working mothers has been for individuals and employers to create a hodgepodge of policies surrounding the circumstances of childbirth and the parents' return to work. These policies can range from extremely supportive to extremely limited, depending on an employer's needs and concerns.

Against this background of rapid change and the need for more information, the Bush Center in Child Development and Social Policy at Yale University conceived in 1983 of a project to study the impact on families and children of the lack of leave time and support for parenting in the early months of an infant's life.

The Project focused on several key areas of investigation. The first task was to establish what had previously been only an intuition, that changes in the composition of the work force and the family were having an adverse effect on working families with infants. A survey of seven hundred Connecticut mothers was inititated, as were several reviews on parent and infant needs in the early months postpartum. Having established that working families with infants were in need of support, time to recover from birth, and time to nurture the new family, the investigators were clear about the second task. This task was to determine specifically what sort of support was necessary and what sort of support was currently available. Project staff and consultants subsequently undertook studies of existing leave policies, both at home and abroad.

Research on existing policies revealed an important void in American leave practices: the lack of any uniform policy of parental leave. Research pointed to the fact that many parents of infants had no option but to return to the workplace before physically or emotionally ready to do so, forcing these parents to find alternative care for their young infants. The third task of the project was to evaluate the nation's infant day care, and the effect the varying quality of care may have on our nation's infants. Finally, once it had been clearly established that a need existed for parental leave, the project focused upon solutions: the cost, financing mechanisms, and legal ramifications of a national infant care leave policy.*

Early in the project an advisory committee was formed. Composed

---

*Since the beginning of this project, the Bush Center has used the term *infant care leave* to emphasize the time that families need with very young infants. The term infant care leave, however, is becoming interchangeable with *parental leave* or *family leave* as a result of legislation introduced in Congress first as the Parental and Medical Leave Act and later as the Family and Medical Leave Act.

of leading scholars from the field of child development, pediatrics, law, social policy, as well as representatives from business, labor and the federal government, the members of this committee were to critique the project's research and propose a set of national policy recommendations (see chapter 21 for a discussion of the committee and its recommendations).

During its two-year tenure, the committee considered research on the well-being of infants and their families, the demographic features of the family and the work force, infant care preferences of parents, and the quality and appropriateness of infant day care. In addition, the committee reviewed an array of American public- and private-sector infant-care-leave policy initiatives, as well as leave policies instituted in nations throughout the world. The committee also had the opportunity to examine research on financing and implementation mechanisms and the costs and legal ramifications of leave policy options.

The advisory committee examined the various issues raised from the vantage point of the well-being of the family. The study concentrated on the period of the first year of an infant's life. Within this period, the project focused on the problems working parents have integrating their various roles and responsibilities. Although the arrival of an infant usually engenders positive feelings in new parents, this time is also a stressful and demanding one for families (Brazelton 1986). The advisory committee felt that this first year would be even more stressful for first-time parents who may be uncertain in their parental roles, still new to their employee responsibilities, and worried about both. Both mothers and fathers may feel fragmented by the numerous roles they must play, and they may feel uncertain of those roles even as they try to carry them out. By and large, women are still expected to be the primary caregiver/nurturer even when they must also help the family earn a living—yet the support systems necessary for them to carry out both roles are not in place. Fathers are expected and may want to take on more caregiving duties, but are neither given the time nor support by the workplace to do so. Both parents are expected to be more active, more successful, more knowledgeable about all that they do—and to do it all in an ever more compact amount of time. The project was intended to create an overview of those factors which affect the family's well-being during this period: what parents and infants need in their first months of life together, how a leave could resolve work-family conflicts during this period, and what kind of infant day care could best serve the infant.

By November 1985, the advisory committee made public its recommendations (chapter 21), which, in turn, were based on the work that eventually became the chapters in this book. The following statements represent the findings upon which the recommendations are based.

1. Fifty percent of all mothers of infants under one year of age are now working outside the home.
2. Irrespective of the changing demographics of the family and the workplace, the family remains the primary base for the well-being and development of children.
3. The majority of parents work because of economic necessity. The employed mother's salary is vital to the basic well-being of her family.
4. Families need time to adjust to the entrance of a new family member. Mothers must physically recover from pregnancy, labor, and childbirth, and parents require time to adjust to the demands of new parenthood. The estimates of the length of time needed vary according to individual health and family needs.
5. A growing number of American families do not have the means to finance leaves of absence from work in order to care for their infants.
6. More than two-thirds of the nations in the world, including almost all industrialized nations, have some provisions for parents of infants to take paid, job-protected leaves of absence from the workplace for physical recovery from labor and birth and to care for their newborn infants.
7. In the United States, federal policy prohibits discrimination in employment on the basis of pregnancy. Federal policy requires that employers grant leaves to women unable to work because of pregnancyand childbirth on the same basis that they grant leaves for short-term disabilities of any kind if they grant short-term disability. Federal policy does not mandate that employers establish new disability benefits or provide leave to parents to care for newborn infants.

WHAT AN INFANT CARE LEAVE WOULD PROVIDE

Following a review of what parents want and what they and their infants need, and of the various strategies open to employers and parent-employees to meet those needs, the Infant Care Leave Advisory Committee recommended that our nation provide all workers with the option of a six-month leave. The leave would be paid at 75% of salary up to three months, with an option for an additional three months of unpaid leave. This central recommendation was based on the consensus that it was important for parents and infants to have a foundation upon which a healthy relationship could be established. Further, such a leave would benefit parents and infants in a number of other ways, all of which would assist family well-being.

Although the term *infant care leave* implies a focus on the infant's needs, all members of the family benefit from this time together. Mothers would benefit by having sufficient time to recover from the physical and emotional demands of birth and from the fatigue surrounding the adjustment to a very young infant. At the same time that this period of adjustment initiates the parent-infant relationship, it also places a demand on the mother's energy and emotions. The success of this beginning can be eclipsed by an early return to work, which competes with the mother's attention to and time for the young infant. Ellen Farber et al. found that mothers frequently felt they had to return to work before they were emotionally and physically ready; that they were preoccupied at work with concerns about their infant; and that they felt something special had been disrupted by a too early return to work (chapter 9). In his discussion of work-related disruption of the stages of growth that a parent and infant go through together in this early period (chapter 3), T. Berry Brazelton identifies the three stages of emotional distancing parents experience when they feel they cannot meet their child's needs (denial, projection, detachment). A leave time not only permits the mother to recover physically from childbirth, but also permits both parents to begin to feel secure and competent in their parenting roles. Both parents need this emotional recovery time and support for their growth as parents.

When parents are given time to spend with their infants, they are laying foundations for their infant's future growth as well as immediate well-being. They are able to establish patterns of communication and patterns of caring and response. For the infant, these patterns create a sense of security and love—that they are cared for, and that someone is there for whom they are especially important. It is in these early months that the foundations for a child's social and emotional development are laid; the patterns of parent-child interaction in the early months help establish a sense of self and self-worth, both in childhood and in later life. Too often, the demands that an early return to work may make on a parent are disruptive to achieving these patterns. Leave time represents an opportunity for parent and child to start off on the right foot by developing a secure relationship and family unit.

An infant care leave further supports the family, in that it delays the infant's entry into a substitute-care setting. This delay is beneficial because it allows the parents and infant time to establish a healthy relationship, one which can help the infant adjust to this change. The process by which a parent and an infant build an identity together—by which they come to know, respond to, and trust each other—can take place without disruption, and can provide a strong emotional base for the infant once he enters a substitute care setting.

Further, a leave period would permit parents to take the time necessary to seek out and evaluate an appropriate care environment for their child, once they must return to work. This environment has important implications for the well-being of both parents and infants. For infants, it becomes a new set of conditions, with different caregiver patterns and responses. It presents a new world with which the infant must learn to interact, and from which the infant will learn. For parents, it represents ideally a place of care and safety for their infant while they are at work. Because parents have an emotional investment in the quality of care their infant will receive, their own sense of competence, both at home and at work, may well be affected by their perceptions of the caregiver and environment to which they have entrusted their infant.

It is important to remember that even when infants do not enter day care until four or six months of age, their care is still *infant* day care, which involves special requirements. Parents need to be sure that the infant's needs are being met, and that their own concerns about the infant are understood and addressed by the caregivers. When the caregivers are interested in the child's growth and overall family interaction, and when the caregivers and parents exchange openly and freely about the child's day, his or her accomplishments and needs, then all concerned feel more secure in what is happening while the parents are at work. With more and more younger children as its clients, day care has become part of the family's support system. For this reason, the advisory committee recommended that standards for day care, as well as a greater understanding of the role day care can play in supporting the family, be given more national attention.

Because a leave provides the time for parents to respond to the infant, grow in their identities as parents, and establish routines and patterns of interaction, they are also strengthened in their ability to attend to work tasks when they do return. Early research shows that when parents are given support for substantial leave time (three months or longer), they are willing to make a greater commitment to the employer in return, are less likely to need to take sick days out of concern and anxiety over the new infant, and are often energized and strengthened by the sense that they have taken care of family matters to their satisfaction (Catalyst 1981; Kamerman 1980; Kamerman and Kahn 1981).

THE CHAPTERS OF THE BOOK

The chapters of this book are arranged according to a perceived relationship between two concerns: that parents need time with their newborn infants to establish patterns of trust and integrate family relationships; and that the quality of day care infants receive contributes both to their own development as well as to that of the total family system. These two foci are interrelated, because time for parent-infant interaction in the early months helps prepare the infant for the upcoming daily separations and reunions; and also because day care can play a role in supporting the family. Further, leaves for parenting can help families achieve an adequate quality of life, measured not only in economic terms, but also in familial satisfaction. The seven sections of the book address the parent-child relationship, with each section focused on one particular aspect of what working parents face in the first year of their child's life.

In part I, two such aspects are examined: the need that exists today for an established national infant-care-leave policy, and the conditions of the past that have led to the formulation of leave policies for mothers who work. In chapter 1, Frank and Lipner focus on the development of infant-care-leave policies in other nations, and they trace the history of protective leaves for mothers, both in the United States and in other countries. In chapter 2, Freedman examines the current demographics of the work force and deals with such questions as where infants and mothers and fathers are shortly after the infant's birth. Because the work force has been changing so rapidly, the figures are startling: over 50% of women with children under one year of age are now at work, and the figures are increasing yearly. The first part of the book is concluded in chapter 3, where Brazelton draws on his wealth of clinical experience to explore the four stages of growth of infants in their first four months of life, the need for a caring adult who is both invested in and able to guide those stages, and the three stages of emotional response experienced by parents who have been denied involvement in this four-month period.

Because so many infants are currently being placed into day care at very young ages, part II examines to what extent the infant's needs are being met. Harwood begins this section in chapter 4 with a look at infants' and parents' needs, and she asks whether day care and substitute caregivers can successfully meet those needs. In chapter 5, Gamble and Zigler examine research on the effects of out-of-home care on very young infants, and they postulate, on the basis of that evidence, what the special needs of infants in day care are. Belsky presents two current and conflicting views about infant day care in chapter 6: (1) that it is harmful to the infant's emotional development; and (2) that it aids the infant's growth by providing more contact with peers and more outside stimulation and interests. He examines the basis for and validity of each of these views. In chapter 7, Young and Zigler examine the existing state and federal standards for the group care of infants and toddlers, and they assess each state's performance against the withdrawn Federal Infant Day Care Requirements of 1980. The federal standards themselves are critically reviewed, and the authors conclude with a delineation of three policy steps that need to be taken to insure better quality care for infants.

What a family needs to get off to a good start, and how parents feel about the growing conflict between their work and parenting roles, provides the basis for part III. In chapter 8, Bronfenbrenner discusses the relationship between family and society, and he outlines the systems of support that he believes families need to become healthy and fully functioning units. In chapter 9, Farber et al. report on a research project in which 200 mothers were interviewed to determine what leave and child-care arrangements were available to them. The authors also reported on how these women felt about issues related to a leave (such as whether they would take advantage of a six-month period at home if it were offered). In chapter 10, Pleck examines what kinds of leave are currently available to men and whether such leaves are encouraged by employers, or viewed as harmful to men's careers. His analysis of the existing leave policies for men in Sweden and their utilization patterns reveals both the biases felt toward male workers who take leave and the desire of those men to be supported in their family role by a leave.

Part IV involves a consideration of existing support for leave by both business and government. Chapters 11, 12, and 13 examine the leave practices of the public sector, large firms, and midsize and small firms, respectively. In chapter 11, Makuen notes that no uniform policy exists for leave by employees of the federal government. Instead, federal employees are subject to a highly arbitrary guideline where leave is "up to the discretion of the supervisor." State employee policies vary dramatically; in most states, no guidelines exist. Sheinberg, in chapter 12, examines the role industry has taken in leading the way toward increasingly supportive leave practices, primarily in order to retain and support highly valued and trained workers. Such practices in large firms are establishing a standard against which other leave policies may be measured; nevertheless, they tend to be accessible only to a small segment of the parent population, those who are employed by firms hiring more than a specified number of employees. In chapter 13, Butler and Wasserman find that, among smaller and midsize firms, practices range from nonexistent to highly supportive, with the existence of an actual leave policy dependent on an informed and community-minded management. Where no formal policy exists, they find that firms may be discriminatory in their practices, offering widely differing leave times to different employees.

Although eighty-one of the world's countries have some form of national leave policy, the United States stands alone among industrialized nations in its lack of a formal policy recognizing a social responsibility toward the well-being of the family. In looking at the leave policies of

other countries, part V provides a background of experience against
which to measure U.S. efforts to formulate such a national policy. In
chapter 14, Kamerman presents an overview of leaves offered in other
countries, both in terms of length of leave time and financial support.
In chapter 15, Allen examines the policies of major European countries
and the nature of their implementation: who pays for the leave (government or business); the effect of leave on employer-employee relationships; and the attitudes toward social responsibility reflected in such
support by businesses. In chapter 16, Pizzo examines the policies of third
world nations as they attempt to integrate a recognition of the family
into emerging industrial practices.

As the United States attempts to formulate its own national infant-
care-leave policy it faces legal, financial, and political challenges, and
these issues are examined in part VI. In chapter 17, Piccirillo delineates
the history of women's protective legislation, the legal precedents for a
leave policy, and the current debate about whether special treatment or
equal treatment of the sexes should form the basis for such a policy. In
chapter 18, Frank looks at the various financial mechanisms for implementing a national infant-care-leave policy; this study examines both the
national cost of such a leave and the financial effects of its implementation on various agents, such as government, industry, and families. In
chapter 19, Schroeder addresses the need for recognizing the federal
responsibility for such a leave, and she outlines the various stages such
legislation must pass through before it becomes law. In chapter 20, Kean
describes the experiences of New Jersey's disability program and the
various factors and decisions that go into the state's efforts to implement
a state-wide leave policy.

Finally, part VII looks to the future. Chapter 21 presents the recommendations of the Bush Center Advisory Committee on Infant Care
Leave. The conclusion, by Zigler and Frank, reviews those factors which
any policy formulation and implementation must take into consideration: the increasing need for out-of-home care for young infants; how
such a policy will work in actuality; who is responsible for cost; and what,
ideally, we can expect from an enlightened and sound infant-care-leave
policy.

Conclusion

The issues of infant care leave and infant day care are both intimately related
to the quality of family life in America today. The increase of the number of
two-paycheck families is a result of the need for families to have two incomes
in order to maintain a comfortable standard of living. In addition to economic survival, however, quality of life includes time for families apart from

work. Although the changes brought about by the dramatic increase of mothers in the work force have been cited, they need not have a negative impact. Yet, without recognition of the support required to meet the changing needs of a society in which two-paycheck families will soon predominate, the family will continue to struggle with conflicting financial need and personal interests. Mothers and fathers need recognition of their parenting roles in the form of a nationally-mandated leave, which provides for and supports those roles. Infant day care is a reality, yet the consequences of out-of-home care for infants have not yet been fully explored, and licensing standards for good quality care have not yet been mandated. With the absence of either time to parent or satisfactory care for their children, working parents are in effect penalized for what is a necessity: to earn money to support their families and to care for their children. A nationally-mandated infant care leave would address a key aspect of the work-family conflict that many parents face: the need for a family to have time to establish the early patterns of trust and caring necessary for the healthy development of all family members. If society in turn is to benefit from well-integrated and empowered families, it itself must see that a national policy of infant care leaves becomes a reality.

REFERENCES

Belsky, J. September 1986. Infant day care: a cause for concern? *Zero to three.* Vol. 6, no. 5, pp. 1–7.

Brazelton, T. B. 1985. *Working and Caring.* Boston: Addison-Wesley.

Bronfenbrenner, U. 1979. *The Ecology of Human Development: Experiments by Nature and Design.* Cambridge: Harvard University Press.

Catalyst. 1981. Parental leaves for child care. *Career and Family Bulletin,* no. 2.

Gamble, T., and Zigler, E. 1986. Effects of infant day care: another look at the evidence. *American Journal of Orthopsychiatry* 56: 26–42.

Kamerman, S. B. 1980. Maternity and parental benefits and leaves: an international review. *Impact on Policy Series,* Columbia Center for the Social Sciences.

Kamerman, S. B., and Kahn, A. J. 1981. *Child Care, Family Benefits, and Working Parents: A Study in Comparative Policy.* New York: Columbia University Press.

Phillips, D., McCartney, K., and Scarr, S. Child care quality and children's social development. Yale University, Bush Center in Child Development and Social Policy. Typescript.

Zigler, E., and Hall, N. W. In press. Day care and its effects on children. an overview for pediatric health professionals. *Journal of Development and Behavioral Pediatrics.*

PART I

Mothers at Work:
Past and Present

ONE

History of Maternity Leave in Europe and the United States

MERYL FRANK AND ROBYN LIPNER

The debate over the need and desirability of infant care leave is often based on the assumption that this type of policy responds to the recent phenomenon of mothers of infants working outside the home. A review of the history of maternity legislation, however, reveals that neither the problem nor the proposed solutions are new. What is new is the rationale for adoption of such policies, which would allow either parent a leave of absence from work to care for a newborn. An infant-care-leave policy seeks to address the issues of stability and emotional development of the family: that mothers and fathers and infants need a period together immediately after birth to adjust to, grow into, and establish their new roles and identities.

The concept of maternity leave, on the other hand, which allows a *mother* time to rest after giving birth has a long history. In fact, such leaves were commonplace in preindustrial and preliterate societies where the "natural" role of mothers as caretakers and nurturers and the physical health of the infant were primary concerns. In their survey of 202 such societies, for example, Jiminez and Newton found two central rationales for the custom of permitting a leave of absence from work following childbirth (1979). The first acknowledged the need for rest following childbirth and was tied closely to a consideration of the health of the mother and infant. The second involved religious beliefs which suggest that following childbirth women are unclean or possess evil spirits. Although reasons for adopting a maternity or parental leave in industrial society continue to focus on the health of mothers and infants, taboos against women working after childbirth have been replaced by others that are based on cultural mores rather than religious ones. More powerful motivating forces, such as national population or industrial policy, are behind efforts to affect women's employment following childbirth.

Recent theorists have credited the widespread adoption of maternity legislation over the past century to the women's movement in Europe (Hewlett 1986). They contend that the European women's movement was more willing to focus on the condition and needs of working mothers than was their American counterpart, whose leaders have been chastised for focusing on legal equality, rather than the equality of results represented by such policies as maternity legislation. However, there is little evidence to support the claim that the women's movements differed in their direction or philosophy. In fact, during the important years of leave policy development in Europe both the American and European women's movements followed similar courses of activity. During the first stage of maternity policy development in the late nineteenth century, women's movement organizations in both Europe and the United States had distinct elements of support for and opposition to protective maternity legislation. They were also allied in their support of improved working conditions and in their concern for infant and child health. Later, in the second stage of policy development, during the period between the two World Wars, both movements were dedicated to the extension of equality under the law and to women's suffrage (Bell and Offen 1983). Yet the influence of the women's movement alone would not have been sufficient to warrant national and then international action on the issue.

On the contrary, the fate of maternity legislation seems to be more closely tied to movements to improve working conditions in the early industrial period (initiated by women's organizations, public health advocates, etc.); to the power and influence of socialist parties and labor unions; and to reaction to the massive economic and military destruction of the two wars. In Europe, this combination of influences played a major role in the adoption of extensive welfare states in which maternity leaves and insurance were included as a matter of policy.

THE ADOPTION OF MATERNITY LEGISLATION IN EUROPE

Work and maternity became an issue of public debate as European nations moved into the industrial age. Industrialization was marked by the movement away from agriculture, fishing, and forestry and into manufacturing and commercial endeavors. The factory replaced the household as the center of production, with the result that earned wages became the economic base of society.

By 1851, 45% of all working women in England and 27% of those in France were employed in manufacturing (Tilly and Scott 1978). Married women made up a small proportion of this population, although it has been suggested that the number of working mothers was greatly underestimated because of the sporadic nature of their work lives (Tilly and Scott 1978). Nonetheless, married women with small children were expected to contribute to the family wage, and most of these women developed a system of providing income outside of full-time labor force participation. Then, as now, many married women with very young children worked as temporary or casual laborers, entering and exiting the work force according to family circumstances.

Infants of working mothers were most often cared for by elderly relatives or older siblings. When no relatives were available, women would hire older women to care for their infants for a fee. In France, England, Austria, and Belgium during the 1840s and 1850s, day nurseries were established to care for the infants of working women (Tilly and Scott 1978; Wilson 1977). Whether they were cared for by relatives, older women, or day nurseries, however, the infants of working mothers suffered. As a result of ignorance about the immaturity of infants' digestive systems and the properties of sterilization, the incidence of mortality rates among these infants, who were bottlefed animal milk or soup, was appreciably higher than those breastfed by their mothers. Doctors felt that if women could be induced to breastfeed their infants several months longer, then the rate of infant deaths would decrease (Tilly and Scott 1972; Hewitt 1958). The following comment describes one medical officer's observations:

> The result of the enquiry [on infant mortality] approaches unanimity only on one point, but on that point we submit that the medical evidence is conclusive, viz, the great damage and loss of life caused by the employment of suckling women as they are now employed in factories... our correspondents who see no evidence of increased mortality reside chiefly in country districts or in parts of the country where suckling women do not generally work. (Hewitt 1958)

Concern about the health of mothers who work long hours in dirty, hot factories and about the effects of their employment on the health of their infants is central to the development of leave legislation. In fact, this concern, coupled with the belief that women's natural and proper place was at home, led to the first measures to "protect" working mothers from the workplace by prohibiting them from working for several weeks surrounding childbirth. A report published in Britain illustrated this concern well:

> The law, as it stands, prohibits the employment of mothers in factories and workshops during the first month after childbirth. It is so worded that

it is hard to enforce, but, at best, it is a law for the mother and not for the child. If the child is to be saved, we must extend the present period of prohibition until gradually this system of employment dies. Gradually, then, the proper balance would be restored; the mother would serve her children and her husband by her presence in the home, not by her presence in the factory. In that way she best serves the State; and while she passes from her place in the factory to her place in the home, the State should, directly or indirectly, protect her, should see that she suffers no loss. The employer who withdraws her from the service of her home for his own service should insure her against the loss of those wages he has taught her to lean upon—sometimes forced her to lean upon. And the State should take charge: the children of the State are the business of the State; if it neglects that business there is nothing that will atone. (Tilly and Scott 1978)

The movement toward maternity protection and, later, toward maternity leave was further fueled by the growing influence of socialists agitating for workers' rights and improved working conditions, and, some have argued, labor's desire to force women out of competition with men for wages. In 1890, for example, the Swiss and German governments were urged by Social Catholics in those countries to regulate industrial work and to promote worker protection in order to diminish the appeal of socialism (Bell and Offen 1983). The intergovernmental congress drew up resolutions and stimulated action abroad toward protective legislation, generally, and unpaid maternity leave, specifically (Bell and Offen 1983).

Maternity protection was first introduced as part of Bismarck's German social insurance program. In 1883, the Reichstag approved the first proposal to establish a national compulsory sickness insurance scheme for all industrial workers. This insurance scheme marked the initiation of a series of social programs, including the Imperial Industrial Code of 1891, which was the first effort to legislate maternity leave (Quataert 1979). The code set maximum workday hours and mandated that employers could not employ a woman within four weeks of childbirth. The code was amended first in 1903 to provide a six-week "rest," and then again in 1911 to grant women a two-week paid leave before delivery.

Bismarck's revolutionary social insurance system was discussed and debated widely throughout the European nations. Although it was not imitated exactly, many of the issues and solutions it established were used as a springboard for policy within other nations (Flora and Heidenheimer 1981). Toward the end of the nineteenth century, private and public activity toward maternity insurance was brewing in many countries. One English factory owner is reported to have instituted a six-week paid leave financed through a simple insurance system (Wilson 1977).

In England, like Bismarck's Germany, the first steps toward maternity leave were protective in character. The Act of 1891 and the Factory and Workshop Act of 1895 (Hewitt 1958; Tilly and Scott 1978) forbade employers from employing mothers within four weeks of their giving birth. By the turn of the century, it had become increasingly clear that if women were to be kept from working in the weeks following childbirth, they would require some sort of financial support. Miss Squires, a factory inspector, described this reality well in 1906:

> Disastrous as are the consequences in so many instances of the early return to work, one can neither be surprised nor blame the mothers who take the risk of them rather than accept what seems to them the only alternative. Insurance of some kind against this recurring event seems a necessary adjunct to the enforcement of the law. (Hewitt 1958)

It was not until 1911, however, that the English first attempted to insure maternity leaves. Before the outbreak of World War I, France and Italy had also established maternity insurance for working mothers.

Debate about worker protection in Russia predates the establishment of the Soviet Union in 1917. In the wake of mass unrest an act was passed in 1903 to provide what was essentially an employer liability law, but it was so limited and weak that dissatisfaction quickly mounted and a law was enacted in 1912 to provide cash benefits in case of occupational accident, illness, or maternity. Employers were responsible only for payments resulting from occupational accidents, and not for any of the costs of providing coverage. Unfortunately, only one quarter of the Russian work force was covered under the law's provisions. In 1912 this law was attacked by an exiled Lenin at the sixth All-Russian Congress of the Russian Social Democratic Party in Prague. Lenin pronounced that it was the responsibility of the state to provide a comprehensive system of insurance. He contended that a social insurance system must contain the following principles:

1. It should provide assistance in all cases of incapacity, including old age, accidents, illness, or death of breadwinner, as well as maternity and birth benefits.
2. It should cover all wage earners and their families.
3. The benefits should equal full earnings and all costs should be borne by employers and the state.
4. There should be uniform insurance organizations (rather than by risk) of territorial type and under the full management of insured workers. (Rimlinger 1971)

Only five days after the Bolshevik seizure of power, the new government issued a social security program predicated on Lenin's principles. In 1922, maternity leave was granted by the Labor Code at the full wage rate for that occupation. Women doing physical labor were entitled to a leave of six weeks before and six weeks after giving birth. In addition, all working mothers and wives of insured workers received supplementary benefits, including a nursing grant at 25% of the local wage for nine months (Rimlinger 1971).

War temporarily put a halt to demands for maternity insurance throughout Europe, yet it also intensified the conditions that brought the issues to the forefront. Both Allied and Central governments were forced to mobilize the female labor force for the war efforts (Bell and Offen 1983), thus tying women's rights as workers to national conditions more strongly than ever. Following the war, interest in maternity insurance grew, but the rationales for adopting such policies changed markedly. War had devastated the populations and economies of the continent. As a result, women were called upon to serve their nations in two capacities: as rebuilders of the nations' economy and as rebuilders of its population. Fear of the loss of industrial and military strength manifested itself in hysteria over population depletion and what some called "racial suicide" (Bell and Offen 1983). The fear of a weakened population base coupled with the migration of colonials to some European nations brought about a flurry of pronatalist maternity policies, designed to encourage women to bear more children.

The year 1919 brought maternity protection to the international arena with the ratification of the International Labor Organization's *Maternity Protection Convention*. The Convention, adopted by the General Conference of the ILO convened in Washington, D.C., by the United States, advocated that a woman

1. shall not be permitted to work during the six weeks following her confinement;
2. shall have the right to leave her work if she produces a medical certificate stating that her confinement will probably take place within six weeks;
3. shall, while she is absent from her work . . . be paid benefits sufficient for the full and health maintenance of herself and her child, provided either out of public funds or by means of a system of insurance . . . and as an additional benefit shall be entitled to free attendance by a doctor or certified midwife.

In addition, the Convention also provided two nursing breaks during work hours for breastfeeding mothers (ILO Convention, No. 3, 1919).

Following the ILO Convention, and urged by fears of left-wing momentum and depopulaion, several European countries immediately instituted maternity protection legislation. Of those nations taking action, only six countries (France, Greece, Norway, Rumania, Spain, and Switzerland) provided legislation that protected the new mother's right to return to work after the leave period. Nine of the countries that instituted policies in 1919 (Czechoslovakia, Germany, Great Britain, Italy, The Netherlands, Norway, Poland, Rumania, and Switzerland) provided payment of some sort of replacement wage through an insurance scheme (ILO, Revision of Maternity Protection Convention 1919 (No. 3), 1952).

Worldwide economic depression further exacerbated the need for such action. The activities of both right- and left-wing parties gave strength to the movement for maternity protection. The argument for workers' rights by left-wing parties resulted in the development and expansion of the welfare states in general and in a more liberal maternity policy. Right-wing nationalist parties' doctrine of racial superiority, particularly in Germany and Italy, manifested itself in a policy which forced women out of some segments of the work force and glorified early marriage and motherhood (Reimer and Fout 1980).

In Sweden, as in many other European nations, maternity leave was introduced as an instrument of population policy. The Swedish Population Commission was established in 1935 to promote early marriage and to increase the birth rate. Its goals were to be achieved by "reducing expenses which families incur to raise, nurture and care for children" (Kamerman and Kahn 1978). The Commission work resulted in legislative reforms that made motherhood more attractive, including maternity leave, which was instituted in 1937.

The pronatalist and nationalist bent to maternity legislation continued during the course of World War II. Lord Beveridge's Report on Social Insurance and Allied Services, the cornerstone of the British welfare state, is but one example of this influence:

> That attitude of the housewife to gainful employment outside the home is not and should not be the same as that of the single woman. She has other duties... Taken as a whole the Plan for Social Security puts a premium on marriage in the place of penalizing it... In the next thirty years housewives as Mothers have vital work to do in ensuring the adequate continuance of the British Race and of the British Ideals in the World. (1945)

Another flurry of action toward maternity leave occurred during the late 1940s and early 1950s, most significantly when the new Eastern European Socialist nations adopted Soviet-type maternity policies. Their action was tied to their ideological commitment to women in the work force and, moreover, to their need to rebuild and industrialize after the

war. In the nations of Eastern Europe, which suffered heavily during
the war, pronatalism was an explicit part of their industrial, employment,
and social policy. Yugoslavia and Hungary, which had ratified the ILO
Convention in 1927 and 1928, respectively, liberalized their legislation.
Bulgaria in 1951, the Ukraine and Czechoslovakia in 1956, and Rumania
in 1958 all ratified the ILO Convention. It is interesting to note that
during the same period of the 1950s, the ILO was prompted to reexamine
its Maternity Protection Convention, and this led to several revisions in
1952.

The 1952 Convention on Maternity Protection provided six weeks of
compulsory leave after childbirth, but the remaining twelve weeks of
leave were recommended for either the period prior to confinement or
following the end of the compulsory, postnatal leave "as may be pre-
scribed by national laws or regulations." This revision also recommended
that cash benefits to women during maternity leave should be at least
two-thirds of the woman's previous earnings, but that employers should
not be "individually liable" for the cost of benefits. This provision was
emphasized in 1952 because experience had shown that individual *employer* liability for maternity benefits resulted in employment discrimination against women ("Convention concerning Maternity Protection,"
revised 1952, Article 5, ILO). Governments were excepted individually
for certain categories of occupations: agriculture, private domestic work,
women wage earners working at home, ocean transportation, and "certain categories of non-industrial occupations" (Article 7).

Leave legislation was generally expanded and liberalized throughout
the 1960s and the 1970s following intense debate over the rationale for
adoption of maternity leave policies, over the results of these policies,
and over sex roles. It was not until 1974 that a major change in the
character and scope of European leave policies was introduced in Sweden—parenthood insurance or parental leave—allowing either parent a
leave of absence from work to care for a newborn child (Kamerman and
Kahn 1978). Finland and Norway have since adopted parental leave
policies.

THE ADOPTION OF MATERNITY LEGISLATION IN THE UNITED STATES

The early development of maternity policies and legislation in the United
States reflects a rationale and set of assumptions similar to those in
Europe. From the late nineteenth century, both Congress and the courts
treated women as a special category to be protected by laws that limited
the amount of time and the nighttime hours women could work. Progressive reformers such as the Women's Trade Union League (WTUL)
and the National Consumers League (NCL) fought hard throughout the

1910s and 1920s to establish and maintain protective laws for women in an effort to improve working conditions. Underlying the reformers' efforts was a persistent belief that working women were physically frail and unable to bargain effectively on their own behalf for better working conditions. Dr. Alice Hamilton, who became the leading expert in the United States on industrial diseases, eloquently defended protective legislation for women, but was against equal rights: "I must," she claimed, "as a practical person, familiar with the great, inarticulate body of working women, reiterate my belief that they are largely helpless, that they have very special needs which unaided they cannot attain." (Rothman 1978; Ware 1981)

Yet even with a growing social reform movement, labor's attempt to win the eight-hour day for all workers was largely defeated by the turn of the century. The American Federation of Labor (AFL) had also become skeptical about what could be accomplished through legislative reform. Many of the stronger trade and craft unions had negotiated successfully for better conditions on their own behalf. But for women, who were largely unorganized in the early part of the twentieth century, protective legislation seemed like the perfect answer (Ratner 1986). Conditions were squalid, wages low, and hours long and arduous. Moreover, few unions were much interested in organizing women workers. By 1912, thirty-four states had enacted measures to restrict women's working hours, with Wisconsin being the first (Kamerman, et al. 1983). Half a century later, forty states and the District of Columbia had laws on maximum daily or weekly hours directed only at women in one or more occupations or industries (U.S. Department of Labor 1976).

The arguments that reformers stressed to secure protective legislation for women elaborated the differences between men and women. Consistent with conventional thinking about the division of labor between the sexes, Josephine C. Goldmark of the National Consumers League wrote that "women as *women* should have certain safeguards secured by law . . . is a proposition adopted and acted upon by all states" (Collins 1983). Clara Beyer, a researcher for the Women's Bureau in 1923, characterized women's labor as typically filling "the gap between school and marriage" (Rothman 1978). Yet, by distinguishing women from other workers, both Goldmark and Beyer contributed to the belief that women were largely marginal workers with special frailties whose participation in the labor force was, at best, temporary. Nothing so brilliantly captured the arguments on behalf of protective legislation as did the famous *Brandeis Brief*, written jointly by Louis Brandeis and Josephine C. Goldmark on behalf of laundress and labor activist Emma Gotcher, in the landmark case of *Muller v. Oregon* (1908). Supported by a wealth of data, they argued that the "[l]ong hours of labor are dangerous for women primarily because of their special physical organization" (Collins 1983, p. 295). Similarly, they demonstrated—with evidence from nine different authorities—that "[t]he evil effect of overwork before as well as after marriage upon childbirth is marked and disastrous" (Collins 1983). Thus, only by being protected as wives and mothers could women find protection as workers.

Not everyone agreed, however. The debate over protective labor legislation erupted after the passage of the suffrage amendment in 1920. The National Women's Party (NWP), a small but vocal group, began to question the impact that these laws had on working women and whether they promoted or hindered women's advancement. The NWP championed legislation granting equal rights, not special protection. One party leader insisted that "[p]rotection, no matter how benevolent in motive, unless applied alike to both sexes, amounts to actual penalization" (Rothman 1978). "The pleas of special protection for women only," declared an editorial in *Equal Rights*, the party's official publication, "is based [*sic*] on the assumption that the maternal function incapacitates women from free competition in the industrial field. This takes for granted motherhood as a constant corollary for womanhood" (Rothman 1978).

The protective ideology made woman's maternal role sacrosanct and received broad support from feminists and reformers alike. In 1921, Congress enacted the Sheppard-Towner Act, "the first federally funded health care program to be implemented in the United States" (Rothman 1978). Its goal was straightforward: "to reduce the infant and maternal mortality rate by providing the states with matching federal funds for prenatal and child health centers" (Rothman 1978). The clinics, staffed almost entirely by women, were to provide preventive care for mothers and their babies. The Sheppard-Towner clinics were enormously successful in promoting child welfare. Moreover, they almost literally invented the field of public health by gathering experts and scientists together to form community-based programs and well-baby clinics. Yet, in spite of their success, or more probably because of it, the American Medical Association fought to repeal the Sheppard-Towner Act and take over the public health services that the clinics had been providing. Opponents of Sheppard-Towner convinced Congress that pregnancy and child welfare were not social problems but medical ones that could only be dealt with through education and research. In 1929, the physicians defeated Sheppard-Towner (Rothman 1978).

In addition to justifying progressive legislation like the Sheppard-Towner Act and because of its emphasis on woman's central role as mother, the protective ideology also perpetuated a deep ambivalence in American society over whether married women, especially those with children, should work outside their homes. Common belief held that married women should not work. One author, writing in 1916, stated: "The American family standard has always been a bread-winning father, and a mother occupying herself with care of her children. Any deviation from this custom is cause for comment. Pride on the part of our native workmen serves to keep their wives out of the ranks of wage earners" (Williams 1977). In the 1920s, the new ideals of motherhood and childhood demanded that a woman be actively involved in her child's education and care, while at the same time fulfilling the role of wife-companion. Popular literature reinforced the notion that a woman's proper place was at home, and that if she worked it was because of economic necessity rather than for autonomy. Their "labor force participation was a direct extension of their family roles" (Wandersee 1981).

In spite of public opinion, the actual number of married women in the work force increased throughout the 1920s. Their number rose 40%, with the most perceptible growth in the twenty to thirty-five age group. Married women grew from 21% to 28% of all female workers. But protective legislation made no provision for pregnant workers or working mothers; rather, common practice allowed a woman to stay in the work force only until her first pregnancy (Scharf 1980). How successfully women combined family and work "remained a question that was to be answered by each woman alone" (Scharf 1980). These growing numbers, however, fueled the opposition to women working, and the attack was two pronged. First, opponents argued that woman abrogated her social responsibilities for childrearing; and second, she competed economically with men and single women for scarce jobs (Scharf 1980). Married working women were seen "as a menace to the race...accountable for the falling birthrate, declining parental responsibility and decadence in home and family life" (Kamerman et al. 1983).

The Depression only exacerbated this trend. By early 1931, New York Assemblyman Arthur Swartz, among others, announced that the employment of married women was reprehensible and admonished "our federal, state and local governments [to] cooperate to remove these undeserving 'parasites' " (Scharf 1980). The attack against married women working outside the home became a political issue in the 1930s, first in state and local governments and later in the federal government, where a bill was eventually introduced that stipulated that married persons were to be the first discharged if their spouses were also government employees. In what became Section 213 of the 1932 Economy Act, the *married persons clause* passed as part of a larger appropriations bill. Although the NWP and other women's groups, as well as Labor Secretary Frances Perkins, vigorously opposed the bill, it was supported by the American public, which overwhelmingly rejected the idea of married women working. From an opinion poll George Gallup concluded that he had never seen the respondents "so solidly unified in opposition as on any subject imaginable including sin and hay fever" (Scharf 1980). By the time Section 213 had its first anniversary, 1,505 married persons had been discharged, and 186 had resigned to protect a spouse's position. The Women's Trade Union League, the Business and Professional Women's Club, the League of Women Voters, and the General Federation of Women's Clubs joined together successfully to seek the repeal of Section 213. At the same time that they argued against the futility of dismissing a handful of women to solve the economic crises, these women's groups "emphasized the self-denial and family-oriented values for working wives... virtues that precluded the personal desire to work and the satisfaction that one derived from employment" (Scharf 1980). In spite of this victory, the battleground against working wives shifted to the states, where by 1939, twenty-six state legislatures had proposed "married person clauses of their own" (Scharf 1980). A few states did not even wait for legislation to pass before dismissing employees. Two land grant colleges refused to hire married women, and a third replaced its married dean of women on the grounds that "marriage itself was for a woman an adequate career" (Scharf 1980). Teaching, long a professional haven for women, had become bitterly hostile to married women. A National Education Association study for 1930 and 1931 found that 77% of all school systems refused to hire wives, and 63% dismissed teachers who got married (Huckle 1981). Married women who were allowed to continue their jobs were usually given a choice between resignation and dismissal when they became pregnant.

Most of the New Deal programs discriminated against women. The National Industrial Recovery Act (NIRA) instituted an unequal pay scale based on sex. One quarter of the National Recovery Act's (NRA) 465 codes established lower rates for women, and these ranged from 14% to 30% below what men received (Scharf 1980). The one program that was potentially most helpful to women was the Federal Emergency Relief Act (FERA), whose mandate was to provide jobs for the unemployed as well as emergency nursery schools for "children of needy, unemployed families or neglected or underprivileged homes" (Marver and Larson 1978). This was the federal government's first commitment to day care, and at their peak New Deal programs funded 1,900 childcare centers serving 75,000 children. Yet FERA was primarily a "jobs" bill, and as employment increased at the end of the 1930s and federal funds were withdrawn, childcare centers quickly disappeared (Marver and Larson 1978). In fact, women received only 8% of FERA funds (Scharf 1980), and even the one provision of the act that offered the most potential for women—Section 7(a), which established the legal right to collective bargaining—depended on public attitudes and union commitment to women's working conditions in order to be implemented successfully.

Only with the war effort in the 1940s did working women regain some of the status that they lost in the 1930s. In spite of overt discrimination, 22% of all women worked outside the home at the end of the 1930s. By 1944 that number had climbed to 31.5%, or nearly one-third of the female population over fourteen. Between 1941 and 1944 alone the number of women in the work force increased by 36%. In 1944, more than sixteen million women made up one-third of the nation's labor force; and of these, 9.4 million were married. For the first time, out of a desperate need for wartime workers, the nation had to come to terms with married women in the work force and how these women were to continue with their familial responsibilities (Gregory 1974).

World War II is generally considered a watershed for working women. The federal government did an about-face: it launched a highly so-phisticated recruitment campaign designed to attract housewives into the war industries by demonstrating the similarity between common household tasks and industrial ones such as welding, joining, and riv-eting. "Rosie the Riveter" called upon women to fulfill their patriotic duty to serve their country, to support "our boys" overseas, and to work in industry. Yet, in spite of tremendous propaganda efforts, new female recruits made up less than 40% of the wartime women workers (Gregory 1974). The remainder were part of the labor force before Pearl Harbor, working in low-status and low-paying jobs. Wartime work offered higher salary, better benefits, union protection, and prestige.

In addition to recruitment, the federal government for the first time looked at employer practices affecting pregnant women. In an effort to provide some nationwide guidelines for employers, the Women's Bureau issued uniform standards for maternity care for employed women. The standards noted that "a woman who is expecting a child should give first consideration to her own health and to plans for safeguarding the health and care of the child. Nevertheless, some women who are pregnant or who have young children may find it necessary to work" (U.S. Depart-ment of Labor 1942). Furthermore, the report—in the spirit of the protective ideology—issued recommendations for prenatal care, a work-day limited to eight daytime hours, rest periods, six weeks of prenatal leave, two months of postnatal leave, and restrictions in occupation or type of work—for example, no lifting, continuous standing, or exposure to toxic substances (Kamerman et al. 1983).

The Women's Bureau's recommendations for maternity leave rep-resented a significant break with past practice of dismissals, calling in-stead on employers to provide leave takers with job protection and seniority rights. But as a 1942–43 study done by the Children's Bureau on actual employer practices demonstrated, the practical situation for women improved only marginally. Leave often became mandatory and unpaid, and it was unrelated to physical, economic, or family needs. Reinstatement often meant returning to work at a lower level with lower pay or the loss of seniority and accrued pension benefits. Although employers often explained that the reason for mandatory leaves was for the "protection" of the mother and the fetus, one researcher noted that it was primarily for "aesthetic and moral" qualms: Employers believed it was "not nice" for obviously pregnant women to be at work because it had a "bad effect" on male employees (Silverman 1943).

In addition to the problems posed by pregnancy, the federal government faced the enormous task of integrating into the work force these six million new female entrants, many of whom were already mothers. A plethora of government agencies sprang up to help accommodate their concerns, from recruitment and job training to equal pay for equal work. But as the number of women with small children entering the work force continued to grow, childcare and housing needs became an overriding concern, not only for the mothers who desperately needed services, but also for employers who wanted to retain trained workers. The Children's Bureau played a significant role in securing federal funds under the Communities Facilities Act and the Lanham Act, which together helped to finance over three-thousand childcare centers and, at their peak, aided some 130,000 children. By the later years of the war there were 1.5 million children under age six who had mothers in the work force. The existing day-care centers could not begin to meet this need (Gregory 1974), but, oddly enough, in the 1940s the public debate concerning child care was not about the lack of centers, but about whether the women who used these centers were abandoning their roles as nurturers (Rothman 1978).

At the end of the war, in 1945, the Federal Works Agency, which oversaw wartime funding for child care, terminated 2,800 centers with very little public outcry (Marver and Larson 1978). And in spite of the propaganda campaign exhorting them to stay home, women continued to work. Between 1940 and 1950 their numbers rose slightly, from 27% to 31% of all women (Rothman 1978). At the same time, many women lost their high paying union jobs to returning G.I.s and went back to low-paying, low-status "female" jobs, because the Selective Service Act of 1940 had entitled veterans to reinstatement in their former jobs after discharge from the military. The unions did very little to help women keep their jobs or seniority; if anything, they manipulated job definitions so that women, because of existing protective labor laws, would be unable to perform them. Traditional attitudes about a woman's proper place prevailed; and women who continued to work did so because of economic necessity, meeting their childcare needs through an informal network of relatives and neighbors (Marver and Larson 1978).

For the majority of women, however, the move was not to lower paying jobs but to new homes in suburbia made easily available through Veterans Administration (VA) loans. In their own way, the 1930s and 1940s had been an aberration: first women were pushed out of the labor force and then they were propelled to return to it because of the war. The 1950s in many ways resembled the 1920s, when the ideal role for a woman had been the wife-companion of her husband (Rothman 1978). As one historian has argued, "The war was not so much a transforming experience as an interruption, after which women returned to pursue an inherited role" (Hartman 1976). For the next fifteen years, women attempted to fulfill this role of the wife-companion, but for many the experience resulted in frustration and anger (Hartman 1976).

Expanded opportunities in the labor force, the increasing numbers of women with college degrees, and the isolation of suburbia began to undermine this model; in its place "a notion of woman as a person began to filter through" (Rothman 1978). By 1961, the Citizen's Advisory Council on the Status of Women, established by President John F. Kennedy, assumed a broad mandate to "examine the needs and changing position of American women to make recommendations to eliminate barriers to their full participation in the economic, social, civil and political affairs of the nation" (Rothman 1978). By the middle of the decade the Council had collected voluminous material documenting sexual discrimination; it also noted the unwillingness of the Equal Employment Opportunity Commission (EEOC) to enforce Title VII of the Civil Rights Act of 1964 which prohibited discrimination on the basis of sex in the same manner as it prohibited racial discrimination.

The Council's failure to act goaded feminist critics to establish their own association. In 1966, these women founded the National Organization for Women (NOW), with the pledge to "take action to bring women into full participation in the mainstream of American society now" (Rothman 1978). To do so, the NOW feminists "moved from politics to the media, from compromise to confrontation, becoming the first civil rights organization for women" (Rothman 1978). Their agenda encompassed a broad mandate from eliminating barriers in the workplace to ending discrimination in higher education. The women's movement began to focus on issues of equality for women as individuals and workers, not as wives and mothers. In the charter of their first convention, they called for job-protected maternity leave for working women.

The federal government had also turned its attention to pregnant workers. In 1963, the President's Commission on the Status of Women set up two task forces to look specifically at the problem of maternity benefits for working women. The Commission recommended that employers, unions, and the government should explore the best means of providing a paid maternity leave, or comparable insurance benefits, for a least six months without forfeiting reemployment or seniority rights (Rothman 1978). These recommendations, however, did not evolve into legislation calling for employers to grant women maternity leave, paid or unpaid.

The passage of the Civil Rights Act a year later provided another avenue for expanding rights and protections for pregnant workers, although initially feminists did not hold out much hope for success. The inclusion of the word "sex" in the 1964 Civil Rights Act had been a ploy to kill the bill altogether, but once it had been amended to include women, feminists and legislators rallied to keep the issue of sex discrimination recognized in the final version of the bill. Moreover, because discrimination based on sex was added at the last moment, the record contained none of the usual debate over the meaning Congress intended this particular legislation to have. Title VII of the Civil Rights Act prohibits discrimination on the basis of sex with respect to "compensation, terms, conditions, or privileges of employment," but early versions of EEOC guidelines did not mention pregnancy disability. In fact, in 1966 the EEOC took the position that denial of disability benefit coverage to pregnant employees comparable to male and nonpregnant employees did not constitute sex discrimination (Kamerman et al. 1983).

In 1972, the EEOC reversed itself and issued a statement claiming that disabilities resulting from "pregnancy, miscarriage, abortion, childbirth, and recovery therefrom are, for all job-related purposes, temporary disabilities" and must be treated in the same fashion as other short-term disabilities with regard to leave, health or disability insurance, seniority, and reemployment (Guideline on Discrimination Because of Sex 1979). It is generally thought that continued congressional debate to broaden the Civil Rights Act in the years following its enactment contributed to the EEOC's policy reversal. Between 1964 and 1972, Congress had "made more explicit and more central the significance of the legislative protections against sex discrimination" (Kamerman et al. 1983).

Following the EEOC's lead, twenty-two states and the District of Columbia passed legislation requiring coverage for pregnancy and pregnancy-related disabilities similar to that provided for other temporary disabilities (Meyer 1978). This was in sharp contrast to the thirty-five states that only a decade before had explicitly excluded pregnant women from eligibility for benefits (Kamerman et al. 1983). But the battle had not been won. In 1976, in spite of the consistency of lower court rulings and the increasing number of states to adopt language making discrimination on the basis of pregnancy illegal, in *General Electric Co. v. Gilbert* (429 U.S. 125 [1976]) the Supreme Court ruled that a company's disability benefits plan was not discriminatory under Title VII because it failed to cover pregnancy-related disabilities. One year later, in a related case, *Nashville Gas v. Satty* (434 U.S. 137 [1977]), the Court ruled that employers may refuse sick pay to women employees who are unable to work due to pregnancy and childbirth, but that they may not divest those women of their accumulated seniority merely because they take maternity leave (Congressional Quarterly, Inc. 1979).

To counteract the Supreme Court decision in *Gilbert*, and that part of *Satty* that denied pregnant female employees the right to sick pay, a coalition of women, civil rights, church, and organized labor groups pushed Congress to override the Supreme Court, "fearing a further erosion of the 1964 Civil Rights Act guarantees of equality to women workers" (Simpson 1979, p. 13). Wendy Williams, professor of law at Georgetown University and one of the authors of the Pregnancy Discrimination Act, commented that "[l]urking between the lines of the Gilbert decision is the outdated notion that women are only supplemental or temporary workers—earning 'pin money' or waiting to return home to raise children full time" (Simpson 1979). The *Gilbert* decision made it clear that the arguments used throughout the twentieth century to support protective laws for women would be the very same ones used to exclude them from equal protection under the law. As Sue Ross, codirector of the Campaign to End Discrimination Against Pregnant Workers, explained so succinctly before the Senate hearings on the Pregnancy Discrimination Act (PDA): "Employers use women's role as child-bearers as the central justification of and support for discrimination against women workers. Thus, discrimination against women workers cannot be eradicated unless the root discrimination, based on pregnancy and childbirth, is also eliminated" (U.S. Senate 1977a).

The passage of the PDA heralded the end to the *Muller* era and marked an important turning point in women's fight for equality. By amending the PDA to Title VII of the Civil Rights Act of 1964, Congress made explicit what for many years had been an implicit policy. The PDA confirmed the 1972 EEOC guidelines and what the lower courts had been saying all along. Moreover, by challenging the Supreme Court, women won the basic right to be treated equally under the law as individuals and workers, rather than as wives and mothers. At the same time, their victory provided basic protection related to their own physical condition before and after childbirth. More important, instead of being based on the special protection rhetoric of the past, these new rights would be grounded in the civil right's language of the 1960s. By the close of the 1970s, a national maternity policy had thus been established. It did not

emerge from a coherent set of policy agendas advanced by the government; rather "it emerged as an issue in sex discrimination and then a
response to it" (Kamerman et al. 1983).

Yet the PDA does not address the broad issues of maternal and child
health or the development of the family as a unit as do the most comprehensive policies of other countries. In fact, the PDA only provides
protection for women who work for employers offering disability insurance benefits, and roughly only 40% of all women receive the type
of maternity leave benefits that guarantee a job-protected leave with
partial wage replacement (Kamerman et al. 1983). Only 65% of employees overall receive coverage under a temporary disability plan.
Nevertheless, the PDA laid the groundwork for further legislation.

Congress is currently considering legislation that would guarantee not
only mothers but also all American workers the right to a job-protected
leave of up to six months because of a serious medical condition, including pregnancy. This provision emanates directly from the (PDA) and
assures that men and women be treated similarly in their inability to
work. The bill also goes far beyond the (PDA) to address the needs of
new families and children by entitling parents to a job-protected leave
to care for newborn, newly-adopted, or seriously ill children for up to
four months. These leaves would be unpaid, but would provide for the
continuation of medical benefits, guarantee job reinstatement, and protect pension, seniority, and other benefits. Although far short of its
European counterparts, this legislation nevertheless represents a significant advance for women and men who—in spite of the PDA—remain
vulnerable to the discretionary policies of employers and supervisors, in
both the public and private sectors.

Conclusion

In this survey of the history of maternity leave in Europe and the United
States we have brought attention to the various rationales for the adoption of or failure to adopt leave policies. The rationales that fuel legislative efforts seem to change character over time. Yet the factors leading
to the development of leave policies in each nation share certain elements
that seem essential.

Central to the discussion is the influence of left-wing parties and labor
unions demanding an expansion of the social welfare state. It is also
clear that the effects of war on the size of the population and the health
of the economy heighten the sense of the value of motherhood and
birth. These combined factors seem to have been necessary conditions
for the early adoption of maternity leave policies in the industrialized
world. The United States, having experienced neither of these essential
factors, has been less likely to feel the need to address its social, labor,

or population problems with maternity policies. However, the changing demographics of the American work force in recent years and the subsequent need to support American families may finally prove to be sufficient justification for enactment of an infant-care-leave policy.

REFERENCES

Bell, S. G. and Offen, K. (eds.) 1983. *Women, The Family and Freedom.* Stanford: Stanford University Press.

The Beveridge Report on Social Insurance and Allied Services. 1942.

Collins, R. K. L. March 1983. Looking back on *Muller* v. *Oregon. American Bar Association Journal,* 69:294–98.

Flora, P., and Heidenheimer, A. 1981. *The Development of the Welfare State in Europe and America.* New Brunswick, New Jersey: Transaction Books.

Gregory, C. W. 1974. *Women in Defense Work During World War II: An Analysis of the Labor Problem and Women's Rights.* New York: Exposition Press.

Hartman, H. May 1976. Women's work in the United States. *Current History.* 70:215–19.

Hewitt, M. 1958. *Wives and Mothers in Victorian Industry.* London: Barrie and Rockliff.

Hewlett, S. 1986. *A Lesser Life.* New York: William Morrow.

Huckle, P. March 1981. The womb factor: pregnancy policies and employment of women. *Western Political Quarterly* 34:114–26.

International Labor Office (ILO). 1980. *Selected Standards and Policy Statements of Special Interest to Women Workers, Adopted under the Auspices of the International Labor Office.* Geneva: International Labor Office.

International Labor Office (ILO). 1952. *Revision of the Maternity Protection Convention 1919 (No. 3).* Geneva: (ILO).

Jimenez, M., and Newton, N. Sept. 1979. Activity and work during pregnancy and the postpartum period: a cross cultural study of 202 societies. *American Journal of Obstetrics and Gynecology* 135(2):171–76.

Kamerman, S., and Kahn, A. 1978. *Family Policy: Government and Families in Fourteen Countries.* New York: Columbia University Press.

Kamerman, S., Kahn, A. J., and Kingston, P. 1983. *Maternity Policies and Working Women.* New York: Columbia University Press.

Marver, J. D., and Larson, M. A. 1978. Public policy toward child care in America: a historical perspective. *Child Care and Public Policy.* Lexington, Mass.: Lexington Books.

Meyer, M. 1978. *Women and Employee Benefits.* New York: Conference Board Report No. 752.

Quataert, J. 1979. *Reluctant Feminists in German Social Democracy 1885–1917.* Princeton, New Jersey: Princeton University Press.

Ratner, R. S. March–April 1986. The paradox of protection: maximum hours legislation in the United States. *International Labour Review* 119:187–88.

Reimer, E., and Font, J. 1980. *European Women: A Documentary History 1878–1945.* New York: Shocken Books.

Rimlinger, G. 1971. *Welfare Policy and Industrialization in Europe, America, and Russia*. New York: John Wiley & Sons.

Rothman, S. 1978. *Woman's Proper Place: A History of Changing Ideals and Practices, 1870 to the Present*. New York: Basic Books.

Scharf, L. 1980. *To Work and To Wed: Female Employment, Feminism and the Great Depression*. Westport, Conn.: Greenwood Press.

Silverman, C. August 1943. Maternity policies in industry. *The Child* 8(2):20–24.

Simpson, P. Spring 1979. A victory for women. *Civil Rights Digest* 2:13–21.

1980. *The Supreme Court and Individual Rights. Congressional Quarterly*. Washington, D.C.

Tilly, L., and Scott, J. 1978. *Women, Work and Family*. New York: Holt, Rinehart and Winston.

United States Congress. Testimony, April 6, 1977. *Report of the Hearings of the Committee on Education and Labor before the Subcommittee on Employment Opportunities*. Washington, D. C.: Government Printing Office.

U.S. Senate. Testimony, 1977. *Report of the Hearings of the Subcommittee on Labor of the Committee on Human Resources*. Washington, D.C.: Government Printing Office.

U.S. Department of Labor. Women's Bureau. 1942. *Standards for Maternity Care and Employment of Mothers in Industry*. Washington, D.C.: Government Printing Office.

U.S. Department of Labor. Women's Bureau. 1976. *State Labor Law in Transition: From Protection to Equal Status for Women*. Washington, D.C.: Government Printing Office.

Wandersee, W.D. 1981. *Women's Work and Family Values, 1920–1940,* Boston: Harvard University Press.

Ware, S. 1981. *Beyond Suffrage: Women in the New Deal*. Boston: Harvard Universiy Press.

Wilson, E. 1977. *Women and the Welfare State*. London Tavistock.

TWO

The Changing Composition of the Family and the Workplace

JOHANNA FREEDMAN

It has become commonplace to note that we are living through a period of rapid social change. American infants today are born into families radically different from those in which their parents were raised. Norman Rockwell's charming scenes of American family life, replete with images of extended families gathered around a groaning board at Thanksgiving or pert housewives sending their husbands off to work with a loving peck on the cheek, now characterize less than one-third of all families with children (Hayes 1980). At the center of change is the radical reconstruction (some would say, destruction) of American families. What, then, do families look like today? How have they changed? What do they need? I will focus primarily on young families, since this is the group undergoing the most rapid and extreme alteration, in order to paint a clear picture of the new American family.

A short overview reveals the following data. Maternal employment has increased dramatically. The divorce rate has skyrocketed 700% since 1900 (Keniston 1977), to the point where half of all children born in the 1970s will spend part or all of their childhood in a one-parent family (Bloomfeshbach 1986). An upsurge in the rate of unwed mothers also contributes to this trend—even though no one can say to what extent, since the phenomenon is outpacing the census takers. These statistics characterize the majority of American homes and cut across class and race boundaries, although their effects are most profound among low-income groups. Using national data, Urie Bronfenbrenner has demonstrated the injurious effects of these trends on the quality of human life in America. The past several decades have seen an increase in infant mortality, a decrease in student achievement, a rise in rates of children killed by homicide and suicide, and enormously augmented rates of juvenile delinquency (Bronfenbrenner 1975).

There is also evidence that most American families are worse off economically than they were in the early 1970s (Joint Economic Committee 1985). As reported by Representative David Obey of Wisconsin, a family with children living at the middle income level lost income at an annual rate of almost $300 over each of the past eleven years, and this trend has worsened significantly in the past five years. The greatest loss of income was among the very poor, who lost 34% of their already meager income.

Families are responding to this crisis by working harder. The number of workers in households with children has grown 20%—twice the rate of families with no children (Joint Economic Committee 1985). But even in these households, for families in the lower income levels, especially minority families, incomes have declined severely. Wages have fallen at 1% per year, and the supplementary income of second wage earners is often less than the median wage for part-time work (Joint Economic Committee 1985).

What do these families look like? Where are their members?

WHERE'S MOMMY?

One place she's *not* is at home. Of all the demographic changes in America today, the most often cited is the rapid influx of mothers of young children into the out-of-home work force. Sixty-two percent of mothers are paid employees (Joint Economic Committee 1986). This represents a ten-fold increase since World War II (Hayes 1980) and the trend is continuing.

The reality is that women are entering the work force as never before. In 1960, only 35% of American women were in the labor force; today, that ratio is 55%. They hold 44% of all available jobs, and since 1980, women have taken 80% of the new jobs created in the economy. If this pace continues, women will make up most of the work force by the end of the century (Hacker 1986).

The fastest-growing subgroup of working mothers has children under one-year-old. In 1975, of 28% of mothers of infants, less than 1% were employed. In 1984, that figure had reached 48%—an increase of 40% (Hayghe 1984; Klein 1985; O'Connell and Rogers 1983; Department of Labor 1982). This point is revealed more starkly by the following statistics:

• From 1970 to 1981, the number of women in the labor force increased from 31.5 to 46.7 million. These numbers represent a growth in labor-force participation by women from 43% to 52%.

- For the same period, the rate for working mothers (husband present) increased from 41% to 52%; for single mothers (divorced, separated, widowed, or never-married), the change was from 53% to 61%.
- Since 1970, the labor-force-participation rate of mothers (husband present) with children under six has grown from 30% to 49%; for single mothers, it grew from 47% to 54%.
- The participation rate of mothers (aged eighteen to forty-four) with children one year old has expanded from 37% to 48% (Department of Labor 1982).

These data tell us that more children have mothers who are working than ever before. It is also estimated that 80% of women in the work force are of childbearing age, and that 93% of them will become pregnant at some time during their working life. Already, in 1984, more than half of all mothers with children under six, and nearly half of all mothers with children under one year of age, were in the labor force. Some of the figures to follow may be startling, but they are signs of family stresses to come.

Marital Status
- In 1981, more than four million mothers, one out of every four, were single. Except for never-married mothers, the labor-force-participation rate was higher in every other category of single motherhood than that for married mothers.
- The sharpest increase occurred among divorced mothers. The rise went from 1.3 million women (23%) in 1970 to 3.5 million (37%) in 1981 (O'Connell and Rogers 1983).

Race
- In 1981, 50% of all black children were likely to be living with one parent compared to 15% of white children (U.S. Bureau of the Census 1982).
- In 1981, proportionately more black children (59%) had working mothers than white children (53%) (U.S. Bureau of Labor Statistics 1983).
- Black women were more likely to use group care (21%) than white women (14%) (U.S. Bureau of the Census 1982).

Economic Status
- In 1983, the mean annual income for families with two working parents was $31,032. Without the mother's salary, it was $24,433. In a single-parent, female-headed family, it was $8,887. The mean income

of black families was 15% to 43% less (National Commission on Working Women 1984).

* two-thirds of women working full-time earn less than $10,000.
* two-thirds of persons living below the poverty line are women (House Select Committee on Children, Youth, and Families 1984).

Fertility Trends
* Between June 1979 and June 1980, the fertility rate was 114.8% and 60% for the group aged twenty-five to twenty-nine and thirty to thirty-four, respectively.
* In the past eight years, women over age 30 who were having children doubled from 57,000 to 104,000. This rate was even higher among highly educated women who live in large cities and are more likely to be in the higher ranks of business (Catalyst 1982).
* Between March 1980 and March 1981, the number of working mothers increased by 600,000 to reach 18.4 million. Mothers with children under six were responsible for 60% of that gain. Within that group, women between the ages of twenty-five and thirty-four made the greatest increases.
* Since 1970, the number of children with working mothers has grown by 6.2 million in spite of a 6.6 million decline in the children's population (Grossman 1983).

Simply put, the above facts reiterate that the number of families headed by single women continues to grow. Women are now marrying later, becoming mothers later, and having fewer children. Even as mothers, however, they are much less likely to leave the labor force because, increasingly, they are the sole source of support of their families. Single black women have fewer options when it comes to the choice between work and family.

Why this sudden shift in women's work? Not so long ago, men dominated the public sphere, and women were relegated to the private sphere—today, whatever their marital status, more than 52% of the work force is female (U.S. Department of Labor, Bureau of Labor Statistics 1983b).

The reasons for this shift in the composition of the labor force are complex, involving changes in the social, political, and sexual mores of America, as well as profound alteration in the economy. Only one-third of the population will be able to sustain a family of four comfortably on one paycheck (Hayes 1980). Additionally, our era has come to be characterized by the *feminization of poverty*. Whereas in 1960 the majority of poor individuals were in families with a male household head, by 1980 less than one-third were. As of 1980, half of all people in poverty were in families with a female head of household. Between 1970 and 1983, the number of one-parent families doubled, while the number of two-parent families dropped by 4.1%. In the same period, about 90% of one-parent families were maintained by the mother (U.S. Department of Labor, et al. 1984).

In 1984, of more than four million mothers, one out of every four was single (U.S. Bureau of the Census 1985). Experts predict that one out of every three families, possibly even one out of two will be headed by a single parent in 1990 (Gelman, et al. 1985). In 1950, 4% of all families were headed by a never-married mother. Today, that figure has reached over 18.4% (National Center for Health Statistics 1984). Births to unmarried adolescents increased by almost one-third in the last decade (House Select Committee on Children, Youth, and Families 1982) and the rate continues to increase. The rate is still higher among blacks— 55.3% of all black families were headed by a never-married mother in 1980. These women, generally young and uneducated, with childcare schedules to juggle, have little hope of earning a living wage. Almost one-third cannot work because of childcare demands (Hayghe 1986; U.S. Bureau of the Census 1982). Even when these women are able to enter an unwelcoming labor market, they often have a difficult time finding a steady position. In March 1983, the unemployment rate for single mothers (with preschoolers) who were actively seeking work was 23%, compared with 15% for mothers whose youngest child was of school age. The unemployment rate for mothers in married-couple families was less than half that of mothers maintaining families. Among those who somehow manage to find work, labor-market returns are poor. Half of all families maintained by the mother alone are below the poverty level; the rate reaches almost 70% among black families (Hayghe 1984). Cuts in social action, publicly-funded employment, and training programs have made the picture bleaker. The Vocational Education Act, CETA, and WIN have all been cut. Similarly, support services which served women and their families have been decimated (Fleming 1986).

The reasons for this are many—women's work patterns, though more stable than in the past, are still largely determined by family-composition changes which affect the well-being of their children, a relatively unimportant factor for men (U.S. Department of Labor, Women's Bureau 1983). Women workers must often interrupt or reduce their work to care for children.

More than 20% of women who work do so part-time. One survey reported that 48% of the female respondents cited "parental responsibilities" as their most important reason for working part-time (House Select Committee on Children, Youth, and Families 1984). The economic consequences of these responsibilities are serious. Part-time jobs are often low paying and without fringe benefits, have greater turnover and more difficult working conditions, and provide less opportunity for training or career advancement (House Select Committee on Children, Youth and Families 1984). Furthermore, women's salaries often fall farther behind men's between the ages of twenty-five and thirty-five, years crucial for both career building and childbearing.

A second, more subtle cause of the economic lag that women experience is a form of job segregation based on sex. The many reasons for this include both socialization factors, which lead women to aspire to positions deemed suitable for their sex, and structural features of the male-dominated world of employment, which limit opportunities open to women (Gerson 1986). In addition, women have only recently begun to join trade unions, whose members tend to have wages one-third higher than other workers. Part of this is a consequence of women's exile to the so-called "pink collar ghetto" of service jobs, which have traditionally been less organized than most manual (and more male-dominated) trades (U.S. Bureau of Labor Statistics 1984). Finally, many employers have continued to pay women as secondary wage earners, in spite of their new status as primary wage earners. The fierce competition among women for the few positions open to them has also acted to depress women's wages (U.S. Department of Labor, et al. 1984; Pennard and Mervosh 1985). These causes have acted synchronously to ensure that most women are in low-level poor-paying positions.

In fact, at present, only 7% of employed women in America work in managerial positions, and only 10% earn more than $20,000 per year (U.S. Department of Labor, et al. 1984). In 1984, one-quarter of all women in full-time jobs earned less than $10,000 (U.S. Bureau of the Census 1985). In the same year, the median earnings of a woman who worked full-time were $14,479, while similarly employed men earned $23,218 (U.S. Bureau of the Census 1985). A woman with four years of college still earns less than a male high school drop-out (Hewlett 1986). In spite of a perception that roles for women in our society have changed, and in spite of advertisements and magazine articles that hail the New Woman, even executive and professional women are failing to close the wage gap. Although women hold twice as many executive and professional positions today compared to a decade ago (National Committee on Pay Equity 1982), the gap between wages for male and female executives has actually widened. In 1960, female managers earned 58% of male wages; in 1980, they earned 55% (Bureau of the Census 1983). In fact, the wages of white women *entering* the job market were three percentage points farther behind comparable white male wages than in 1970. In addition, women are simply not making it into the upper echelons of management. While women represent half of all entry-level managers, and one-fourth of all those in middle management, they account for only 1% or 2% of upper management (Pennard and Mervosh 1985). This is "despite the growth of affirmative action and educational gains by women" (*New York Times* 1984). In short, women are in the job market by necessity, and they are left in necessity by their jobs.

WHERE'S DADDY?

Where are fathers in the midst of this change? Are they helping at home to offset women's increased work load outside the home? Answer: No. In two-parent families in which the mother is at home, the father spends only 20% to 25% as much time with his children as does his wife (Lamb, et al., in press; Pleck 1983). Many studies show that fathers assume essentially no responsibility for child care (Lamb 1986). Seven percent of married women rely on the father as principal caregiver, as against 2% unmarried women (U.S. Bureau of the Census 1982). In two-parent families in which both parents are employed outside the home, the percent of time that fathers spend with their children is higher (Lamb, et al., in press; Pleck 1983), averaging 33% of their wives involvement (Golinkoff and Ames 1979; Kotelchuk 1975; Lewis and Weinraub 1974). This figure, however, is more an artifact of the *decreased* amount of time employed mothers spend with their children than an actual increase in the time fathers spend with them. In fact, even when both parents are employed thirty or more hours per week, the amount of responsibility assumed by fathers appears to be "as negligible" as when mothers are unemployed (Lamb 1986). This is not to say that fathers do not care; when they are offered the opportunity to care for their infants, fathers do so with the same attention and affection generally that mothers give (Lamb, et al., 1985; Pleck, Lamb, and Levine 1985).

Stimulated by the pioneering work of Rapoport and Rapoport (1965) and Kantor (1977), it has become widely recognized that paid work and family roles are interconnected and mutually influence each other. Yet fathers have so long been relegated to the role of breadwinner that even now, with such views becoming increasingly maladaptive, they are unable to define themselves as parents. This point is perhaps most poignantly made by the fact that 25% of all men and 35% of younger men believe in what has been termed *a family of limited liability*. Specifically, they would not remain in an unsuccessful marriage "for the sake of the children" (*Playboy Report on American Men* 1979). Eased divorce laws facilitate these attitudes. As mentioned, the divorce rate has increased nearly 700% since 1900 (Keniston 1977), and almost half of all children of divorce never see their fathers (Furstenberg and Nord 1985); fewer men seek custody of their children than they did even ten years ago, and only one-third of custodial mothers receive child support. Divorced men are more likely to be up to date on their car payments than their child support commitments (Yee 1980).

If mom's at work and dad's at work, who's taking care of baby? The answer seems to be everyone and no one.

WHERE'S BABY?

Infants, like their parents, are not home. A recent report by Robert Klein (1985) reports that the employment rate for mothers of children under one year old was 40.8%, a figure that represents an increase of 40.4% since 1977. With only a minority of these parents entitled to a leave to care for their infants, most are forced to find substitute care for their children soon after they are born.

At present, early child care has the following profile:

- In June 1982, 17% of the care for the youngest preschool-age child of employed mothers was provided by a grandparent. Other relatives provided 12% of the care.
- 40% of care to children under five years of unmarried mothers was provided by the grandmother or another relative.
- As of June 1982, 26% of working mothers of children age three to four used group care. Twelve percent of mothers of children aged one to two used group care. Only 5% of the mothers of children under one year used group care.
- 14% of families used the father as principal caretaker. Among these fathers, 71% were themselves employed and 24% were unemployed but looking for work (U.S. Bureau of the Census 1982).

What does this out-of-home care look like?

Family Day Care

By far the largest group of children in substitute care in America can be found in family day care (56%; U.S. Bureau of the Census 1982). Although such care takes place in private homes, it differs from *in-home care* in that the children in one home, typically four to six in number, are unrelated to each other. Infants constitute the fastest growing fraction of users of this kind of care, as parents attempt to find a homelike center to replace what they have no time to provide. In spite of the large numbers of children enrolled in such care, the vast majority of family day-care homes are unlicensed and unregulated (Ruopp and Travers 1982; Young and Zigler 1986). As a consequence, very little can be ascertained about the quality of such care. The research that exists suggests that the majority of family centers are mediocre, barely meeting the physical needs of the infants, but going no further. These centers are used because they are, unfortunately, far more affordable than good care.

Day-Care Centers

Approximately 18% of American children in nonmaternal care attend day-care centers. Although centers serve a relatively small proportion of children, this type of arrangement tends to be the most highly visible. The centers fall into two subcategories: for-profit centers, including large chains like KinderCare, and not-for-profit centers such as those run by churches, community centers, and employers. Little is known to date about whether the quality of care differs between for-profit and non-profit childcare centers. Center care tends to be less expensive than having a private sitter at home, because resources are distributed among a larger group. Centers are also more likely to base fees on a sliding scale, or to offer discounts for parents who enroll more than one child. Yet, although half of these centers cater to poor, usually single-parent families and have been publicly subsidized, they have been severely affected by the budget cuts of the Reagan administration. Title XX funding has been cut 21% since 1980 (Children's Defense Fund 1985), and this has forced many centers to reduce the number of children enrolled.

For those who want to have their infants cared for at home, qualified congenial people are difficult to find, and although excellent caregivers can be found, there is little stability in such a system. Many are uncomfortable about advertising widely for such a person, preferring to find someone through friends. In addition, a good nanny or sitter may be difficult to keep, because such arrangements are often informal, and also because parents are unlikely to be able to offer much in the way of employment benefits. Many of these caregivers are students, or recent immigrants who cannot get jobs elsewhere and who may or may not speak the family's language (Fallows 1985). Changes in school schedule or in work status may suddenly leave parents with no caregiver. There is also no back-up if the sitter is ill or has to be absent for some other reason, usually with little advance warning. In such cases, parents must struggle to make alternative arrangements, or must themselves miss work to care for their children.

In-Home Care

According to the most recent U.S. Bureau of Census figures for day-care use (1982), 26% of the children of working parents are in home care in which one person, a relative or a nonrelative, comes to the children's home to care for them, or in which one child is taken to the caregiver's home to receive individual care. By far the smallest portion of this group, about 6% (Fallows 1985), are cared for by regular sitters, nannies, or housekeepers. The remainder are cared for by grandparents, fathers, or other relatives, or by the mother herself, taking turns with someone else. The advantages of home care are obvious. Children are in a familiar environment and receive the personal attention their parents cannot provide.

There are reasons that this arrangement is uncommon, however (Fallows 1985; Scarr 1984). First, it is far more costly. To have one person caring for one child, or one family's children, is expensive. Second, and predictably enough, the pool for such caregivers is small and unreliable, as they are forced through necessity and familial economic needs to seek higher wages than the often below-minimum-wage scale that child care offers (U.S. Department of Labor 1986).

Patchwork Arrangements

Approximately one-third of all children are cared for in multiple informal arrangements over the course of a single day. Many parents are forced to this "solution" because they cannot find high-quality day care or, more often, because they simply cannot afford it.

Conclusion

Clearly, the present state of affairs is untenable. Those who claim that the decimation of families is rending the social fabric are, however, incorrect. It is society that is failing American families. The patchwork systems of support that are based on past rather than present realities and the structural obstacles to family survival are injuring the nucleus of our social system. Families are combating enormous fiscal and social odds in their attempts to stay together. They deserve support in this endeavor, for both practical and moral reasons. Families are, in Urie Bronfenbrenner's words, "the best method we have for making and keeping human beings human" (see chapter 8). If that is a social value— and it must be, if we are to survive as a society—we must do what we can to ensure that families survive. The first weeks of life are very important for establishing family bonds and family responsibilities. Though economic reality may dictate that parents must work, we must use our economic prowess as a country for more than bombs and budgets. We must use it to enable the American family to survive. A paid infant care leave would do much toward making this possibility a reality.

Parental leave is not just for children. It is for working mothers. It is for fathers, so that they can at least take their rightful place in the family system. It is for families, so that all members will be part of a healthy environment. And it is for people without children, so that the economy can run smoothly. As a result of changes in the American socioeconomic system, infant care leave is no longer a luxury. It has become an essential part of a much larger national picture, and it must be reckoned with as an important social issue.

REFERENCES

Bronfenbrenner, U. 1975. Ecology of child development. *Proceedings of the American Philosophical Society* 119:439–69.

Catalyst. 1982. *Disability and Parental Leave: The Corporate Role*. Unpublished manuscript.

Children's Defense Fund. 1985. *A Children's Defense Budget*. Analysis of the President's Budget for Fiscal Year 1986.

Fallows, D. 1985. *A Mother's Work*. Boston: Houghton Mifflin.

Fleming, A. 1986. The American Wife. *The New York Times Magazine*, October 26:30–36.

Furstenberg, F., and Nord, C. 1985. Parenting apart: Patterns of childbearing after mental disruption. *Journal of Marriage and the Family*: 874.

Gelman, D., Greenberg, N., Coppola, U., Burgower, B., Doherty, S., Anderson, M., and Williams, E. 1985. Playing both mother and father. *Newsweek*. July 15:42–50.

Gerson, K. 1986. *Hard Choices: How Women Decide About Work, Career, and Motherhood*. Irvine: University of California Press.

Golinkoff, R., and Ames, G. 1979. A Comparison of fathers' and mothers' speech with their young children. *Child Development* 50:28–32.

Grossman, A. 1983. *Children of Working Mothers*. U.S. Department of Labor, Bureau of Labor Statistics, Bulletin 2158. Washington, D.C.: Government Printing Office.

Hacker, A. 1986. Women at work. *The New York Review*. August, 26–32.

Hayghe, H. 1984. Working mothers reach record numbers in 1984. Research summaries. Monthly Labor Review. U.S. Department of Labor Statistics, December. Washington, D.C.

Hayes, C., Ed. 1980. *Work, Family, and Community: Summary of an Ad Hoc Meeting*. Washington, D.C.: National Academy of Service.

Hewlett, S. 1986. *The Myth of Women's Liberation*. New York: William Morrow.

House Select Committee on Children, Youth, and Families. 1984. *Children, Youth and Families: 1983*. A year end report of the Select Committee on Children, Youth, and Families. Washington, D.C.

Joint Economic Committee. 1985. *Family Income in America*. Washington, D.C.

Joint Economic Committee. 1986. *Family Income in America*. Washington, D.C.

Kantor, R. 1977. *Work and Family Life in the United States: A Critical Review and Agenda for Research and Policy*. New York: Columbia University Press.

Keniston, K. 1977. *All our Children. The American Family Under Pressure*. New York: Harcourt Brace Jovanovich.

Klein, R. 1985. Caregiving arrangements by employed women with children under 1 year of age. *Developmental Psychology* 21(3):403–06.

Kotelchuk, M. 1975. Father caretaking characteristics and their influence on infant father interaction. Paper presented to the American Psychological Association, Chicago, September.

Lamb, M. 1986. The changing roles of fathers. M. Lamb, ed. *The Father's Role.* New York: John Wiley & Sons.

Lamb, M., Pleck, J., Charnov, E., and Levine, J. In Press. The role of the father in child development: The effects of increased paternal involvement. P. Lahey and A. Kazdin, eds. *Advances in Clinical Child Psychology*, vol. 8. New York: Plenum.

Lewis, M., and Weinraub, M. 1974. The Father's role in the social network. M. Lamb, ed. *The Role of the Father in Child Development.* New York: John Wiley & Sons.

National Center for Health Statistics 1984. *Monthly Vital Statistics Report*, vol. 33, no. 6, Supplement. September 28.

National Commission on Working Women. 1984. *Working Mothers and Their Families. A Fact Sheet.* Washington, D.C.

National Committee on Pay Equity. 1982. *The Wage Gap: Myths and Facts.* Washington, D.C.

New York Times. January 11, 1984.

O'Connell, M., and Rogers, C. 1983. *Child Care Arrangements for Working Mothers*: June 1982 Current Population Reports, Series P–23, no. 129. Washington, D.C.

Pennard, K., and Meroosh, E. 1985. Women at work. The big push for higher wages. *Business Week.* January 28:80–85.

The Playboy Report on American Men. 1979. *A Study of the Values, Attitudes and Goals of U.S. Males, 18–49 Years Old.* New York: Louis Harris.

Pleck, J. 1983. Husband's paid work and family roles: Current research issues. H. Lopata and J. Pleck, eds. *Research in the Interweave of Social Roles*, vol. 3. *Families and Jobs.* Greenwich, Conn.: JAI Press.

————. 1986. Employment and fatherhood: Issues and innovative policies. M. Lamb, ed. *The Father's Role.* New York: John Wiley & Sons.

————, Lamb, M., and Levine, J. 1985. Facilitating future change in men's family roles. R. Lewis and M. Sussman, eds. *Men's Changing Roles in the Family.* New York: Haworth.

Rapoport, R., and Rapoport, R., 1965. Work and family in contemporary society. *American Sociological Review* 30:381–94.

Ruopp, R., and Travers, U. 1982. Janus faces day care: Perspective on quality and cost. E. Zigler and E. Gordon, eds. *Day Care: Scientific and Social Policy Issues.* Boston: Auburn House.

Scarr, S. 1984. *Mother Care/Other Care.* New York: Basic Books.

U.S. Bureau of the Census. 1982. Trends in child care arrangements of working mothers. *Current Population Reports*, no. 117. Washington, D.C.

————. 1983. *American Women: Three Decades of Change.* Washington, D.C.

————. 1985. Money, income, and poverty status of families and persons in the U.S. *Current Population Reports*, series P–60. Washington, D.C.

U.S. Department of Labor, Bureau of Labor Statistics. 1983a. More than half of all children have working mothers. *Children of Working Mothers*. Bulletin 2158. Washington, D.C.

———. 1983b. *Women at Work: A Chartbook*. Bulletin 2168. Washington, D.C.

———. 1986. Personal Correspondence with author.

———, U.S. Department of Commerce, Bureau of Census, the Small Business Administration, Office of the Secretary, and Women's Bureau. 1984. *Twenty Facts on Women Workers*. Washington, D.C.

U.S. Department of Labor, Women's Bureau. 1983. *Time of Change: Handbook on Women Workers*. Washington, D.C.

Yee, L. 1980. What really happens in child support cases: An empirical study of the establishment and enforcement of child support orders in the Denver District Court. *Denver Law Journal* 57:21–26.

Young, K., and Zigler, E. 1986. Infant and toddler day care: Regulations and policy implications. *American Journal of Orthopsychiatry* 56:43–55.

THREE

Issues for Working Parents*

T. BERRY BRAZELTON

In 1981, more than half the mothers in the United States were employed outside the home (U.S. Senate 1982). By 1990, it is predicted that 70% of children will have two working parents. The number has been increasing each year since World War II, and ten times as many mothers of small children work now as did in 1945. No longer is it culturally unacceptable for mothers to have jobs. In fact, the practice has become so widespread that many mothers at home feel that they "should" be working. There is a general feeling that: (a) unless she works, a woman is missing out on an important part of life; and (b) taking care of a home is not sufficiently rewarding work. These feelings create unspoken pressures on women today, making new mothers wonder when they should return to their job or begin to look or train for one. At each domestic frustration, at each spurt in their baby's independence, new mothers are apt to question whether their baby's need to have them at home outweighs their own need for an occupation outside the home.

At the same time, there is still a strong bias against mothers leaving their babies in substitute care unless it is absolutely necessary. In the back of each mother's mind these conflicting pressures lead to a nagging question: Is it really all right for mothers to work? Indeed, this troubling question is a reflection of the age-old, commonly cherished image of the "perfect mother"—a woman at home taking care of her children.

Moreover, the loss of the extended family has left the nuclear family unsupported during a period when strong cultural values have been overshadowed by broad social issues (such as nuclear war, ecological misuse, and overpopulation) that parallel the more personal issue of changing roles for women and for men. As each sex begins to face

*This article was originally published in the *American Journal of Orthopsychiatry* 56(1): January 1986, and it is reprinted here by permission.

squarely the unforeseen anxieties of dividing the self into two important roles—one geared toward the family, the other toward the world—the pressures on men and women are enormous and largely uncharted by earlier generations. It is no wonder that many new parents are anxiously overwhelmed by these issues as they take on the important new responsibility of creating and maintaining a stable world for their baby.

We do not have enough studies yet to know about the issues for the infant. The studies that we do have are likely to be biased, or based on experiences in special, often privileged populations (Gamble and Zigler 1986; Kessen et al. 1970). We need to know when it is safest for the child's future development to have to relate to two or three caregivers; what will be the effects of a group care situation on a baby's development; when babies are best able to find what they need from caregivers other than their parents; when parents are best able to separate from their babies without feeling too grieved at the loss. In a word, we need information on which to base general guidelines for parents, for it could be that the most subtle, hard-to-deal-with pressure on young adults comes indirectly from society's ambivalent and discordant attitudes, which create a void of values in which the building and nurturing of a family become very difficult.

Another serious threat to the new family is posed by the very instability of its future as a family. Largely because of divorce (U.S. Senate 1982), 58% of children in the U.S. will have spent a significant part of their lives in a single-parent home. Half of the marriages of the 1970s will split up in the 1980s. The U.S. family is in serious trouble.

Because of the realignments that necessarily occur with the advent of the new member, the old ties and the previous adjustments to the family's integrity are likely to be shaken—for better or for worse. The "work of pregnancy" for each parent has been documented by Bibring (1961) and others (Brazelton 1983). The powerful ambivalence of pregnancy forces parents to reshape their lives and even their adjustment to each other. The self-questioning that leads to worry about having an impaired baby is common to women during this time and represents the depth of their anxious ambivalence as they attempt to "make it" to the new level of nurturing and caring for the coming baby. Yet these forces can also serve to strengthen relations with other members of the family. But this cannot be left to chance: supportive, sensitive interventions during pregnancy must be offered to stressed parents.

Relatively minor and inexpensive adjustments on the part of the medical system—such as prepared childbirth, participation of the father, presenting the baby to the mother and father at delivery (Klaus and Kennel 1970)—can increase the opportunities for *bonding* to the baby. Although this is likely to be only a first step toward fostering attachment and significantly enhancing the possibilities for the baby's optimal development, it is a most important step. These simple interventions in an otherwise rather unwelcoming pathological medical system seem to enhance the parents' image of themselves as vital to their baby and to each other. Thus, they further the likelihood that the parents' positive self-image will be passed on to the baby.

In my work in pediatric primary care, the parents I see in a prenatal interview are generally predisposed to share their concerns about themselves and the well-being of their future baby. As they talk to me, they share the passion and the work of making the future adjustment to parenthood with either the hoped-for normal or the dreaded impaired infant. However, when both parents anticipate the pressures of having to return to work "too early" (in their own words, "before three months"), they seem to guard against talking about their future baby as a person and about their future role as parents. Instead, their concerns are expressed in terms of adjusting to time demands, to schedules, to lining up the necessary substitute care. Very little can be elicited from them about their dreams of the baby or their vision of themselves as new parents. Perhaps they are already defending themselves in anticipation of the pain of separating too early from the new baby.

Efforts to involve the father in the birth process, to enhance his sense of paternity and empowerment as he adjusts to his new role, should be increased. Having the father involved in labor and delivery can significantly increase his sense of himself as a person who is important to his child and to his mate. Several investigators have shown that increased participation of fathers in the care of their babies, increased sensitivity to their baby's cues at one month, and significantly increased support of their wives can result from the rather simple maneuver of sharing the newborn baby's behavior with the new father at three days, using the Neonatal Behavioral Assessment Scale (NBAS) (Beal 1984). Ensuring the father's active participation is likely to enhance his image of himself as a nurturing person and to assist him toward a more mature adjustment in his life as a whole. With these gains in mind, we would do well to consider a period of paid paternity leave, which might serve both symbolically and in reality as a means of stamping the father's role as critical to his family.

Supporting the mother in her choices about delivery and in adjusting to the new baby seems even more critical for those new mothers who must return to work. If the mother can be awake and in control of delivery, if she can have the thrill of cuddling her new infant in the delivery room, if she can have the choice of rooming in with her baby and of sharing her baby's behavior with a supportive professional, she is likely to feel empowered as a new mother.

WORK OF ATTACHMENT

The efforts of the medical system to enhance parental bonding to a new baby are certainly important to parents who must return to work, but bonding is not a magical assurance that the relationship will go well thereafter. The initial adjustment to the new baby at home is likely to be extremely stressful to all new parents. Most have had little or no experience with babies or with their own parents as they nurtured a smaller sibling. They come to this new role without enough knowledge or participational experience. The generation gap makes it difficult for them to turn back to parents or extended family for support. Professional support is expensive and difficult to locate. The mother (and father) is likely to be physically exhausted and emotionally depressed for a period after delivery. The baby is unpredictable and has not developed a reliable day-night cycle of states of sleep and waking. Crying at the end of the day often serves as a necessary outlet and discharge for a small baby's nervous system after an exciting but overwhelming day. This crying can easily be perceived as a sign of failure in parenting by harassed, inexperienced parents, and the crying that starts as a fussy period is then likely to become a colicky, inconsolable period at the end of every day over the next three months. Any mother is bound to feel inadequate and helpless at this time. She may wish to run away and to turn over her baby's care to a "more competent person." If she must go back to work in the midst of this trying period, she is unlikely to develop the same sense of understanding and competence with regard to her baby as she might if she had been able to stay at home and to "see it out." When this period of regular crying at the end of the day mercifully comes to an end at about twelve weeks, coincident with further maturation of the nervous system, mothers tell me that they feel relieved and as though they had finally "helped" the baby learn to adjust to its new environment. They claim to have a sense of having learned to cope with the baby's negativism over these months; their feelings of anger, frustration, and inadequacy during the infant's fussy period are replaced by a sense of mastery. And since the baby is now vocalizing, smiling, and cooing responsively at the end of every day, they report that they feel they have "taught" the baby to socialize in more acceptable ways. They feel that "at last the baby is mine, and is smiling and vocalizing for me." There is likely to be a significant difference in a mother's feelings of personal achievement and intimacy with her baby if she has had to leave this adjustment to another caregiver in order to return to work before the end of the three-month transition.

In research on the development of reciprocal communication between parents and small babies, my colleagues and I have been impressed with the necessity for the development of a reciprocal understanding of each other's rhythms of attention and nonattention that develop between parents and baby over the first four months and enable them to communicate more and more complex messages in clusters of behavior. Such behavior does not demand verbal communication, but involves important elements of affective and cognitive information and forms the base for the infant's learning about the world (Brazelton et al. 1974). Thus, in an important period of intense communication between parent and infant, the parent provides the baby with affective and cognitive information, and with the opportunity to learn to exert controls over the internal homeostatic systems needed to pay attention to its surroundings. The four stages of learning about these controls provide infants with a source of learning about themselves and provide the mother and father with an important opportunity for learning the ingredients of a nurturant role with their baby (Brazelton and Als 1979). These early experiences of learning about each other are the basis for their shared emotional development in the future and are critical as anlages for the infant's future ego.

MOTHER'S ROLE

The most important role of the adults seems to be that of helping infants to form a regulatory base for their immature psychological and motor reactions (Als 1978; Brazelton et al. 1975). The most important rule for maintaining an interaction seems to be that a mother develop a sensitivity to her infant's capacity for attention and the infant's need for withdrawal—partial or complete—after a period of attending to her. Short cycles of attention and inattention seem to underlie all periods of prolonged interaction. Although in the laboratory setting we thought we were observing continuous attention to the mother on the part of the infant, stop-frame analysis subsequently revealed the cyclical nature of the infant's looking and not-looking. Looking-away behavior reflects the need of infants to maintain some control over the amount of stimulation they can take in during such intense periods of interaction. This is a homeostatic model, similar to the type of model that underlies all the physiological reactions of the neonate, and it seems to apply to the immature organism's capacity to attend to messages in a communication system (Brazelton et al. 1974).

An essential component of this regulatory system or reciprocal interaction between parent and infant is the basic rhythm of attention-inattention that is set up between them (Brazelton et al. 1974). A mother must respect her infant's needs for the regulation that this affords or she will overload the infant's immature system and the infant will need to protect itself by turning her off completely. Thus, she learns the infant's capacity for attention-inattention early, in order to maintain her infant's attention. Within this rhythmic, coherent configuration, mother and infant can introduce the mutable elements of communication. Smiles, vocalizations, postures, and tactile signals all are such elements. They can be interchanged at will as long as they are based on rhythmic structure (Brazelton et al. 1975). The individual differences of the baby's needs for such a structure set its limits. The mother then has the opportunity to adapt her tempo within these limits. If she speeds up her tempo, she can reduce the baby's level of communication. If she slows down, she can expect a higher level of engagement and communicative behavior from her infant (Brazelton et al. 1974; Stern 1974). Her use of tempo as a means of entraining the baby's response systems is probably the basis of the baby's learning about his† own control systems. In this process of variability, the baby learns the limits of his control systems, and he also learns about basic self-regulation and adaptation.

In addition, by using a systems approach to understand the nonverbal message, we found that each behavioral message or cluster of behavior from one member of the dyad acts as a disruption of the system, which must then be reorganized. The process of reorganization affords the infant and the parent a model for learning—learning about the other as well as learning about oneself within this regulatory system. An *appropriate* or attractive stimulus creates a disruption and reorganization that are different from those that are the result of an intrusive or *inappropriate* stimulus. Each serves a purpose in this learning model (Brazelton 1983).

An inspection of the richness of such a homeostatic model, which provides each participant with an opportunity to turn off or on at any time in the interaction, demonstrates the fine-tuning available and necessary to each partner of the dyad for learning about the other. The individual actions that may be introduced into the clusters that dominate the interaction become of real, if secondary, importance. In this way, a smile or a vocalization may be couched within several other actions to form a signaling cluster. In effect, the individual piece of behavior is not the necessary requirement for a response: the cluster is. The basic rhythm, the *fit* of clusters of behavior, and the timing of appropriate clusters to produce responses in an expectable framework become the

†I use *his* here only to distinguish from the female mother.

best prediction of real reciprocity in parent-infant interaction (Brazelton et al. 1975).

STAGES OF REGULATION

We have identified the following four stages of regulation and of learning within this system over the first four months of life (Brazelton and Als 1979):

1. Infants achieve homeostatic control over input and output systems (that is, they can both shut out and reach out for single stimuli, but then achieve control over their physiological systems and states).

2. Within this controlled system, infants can begin to attend to and use social cues to prolong their states of attention and to accept and incorporate more complex trains of messages.

3. Within such an entrained or reciprocal system, infants and parents begin to press the limits of (a) infant capacity to take in and respond to information, and (b) infant ability to withdraw to recover in a homeostatic system. Sensitive adults press infants to the limits of both of these and allow infants time and opportunity to realize that they have incorporated these abilities into their own repertoires. The mother-infant *games* described by Stern (1974) are elegant examples of the real value of this phase as a system for affective and cognitive experiences at three and four months of age.

4. Within the dyad or triad, the baby is allowed to demonstrate and incorporate a sense of autonomy. (This phase is perhaps the real test of attachment.) At the point where the mother or nurturing parent can indeed permit the baby to be the leader or signal giver, when the adult can recognize and encourage the baby's independent search for and response to environmental or social cues and games and allow the baby to initiate the games or to reach for and play with objects, the small infant's own feeling of competence and of voluntary control over its environment is strengthened. This sense of competence is at a more complex level of awareness and is constantly influenced by the baby's feedback systems. We see this at four to five months in normal infants during a feeding, when the infant pauses to look around and to process the environment. When a mother can allow for this and even foster it, she and the infant become aware of the baby's burgeoning autonomy. In psychoanalytic terms, the infant's ego development is well on its way (Brazelton 1983)!

This model of development is a powerful one for understanding the reciprocal bonds that are set up between parent and infant. It allows for flexibility, disruption, and reorganization. Within its envelope of inter-action, one can conceive of a rich matrix of different modalities for communication, individualized for each pair and critically dependent on the contribution of each member of the dyad or triad. There is no reason that each system cannot be shaped in different ways by each of its participants, but each must be sensitive and ready to adjust to the other member in the envelope. And at successive stages of development, the envelope will be different—richer, we would hope.

I regard these observations as evidence for the first stages of emotional and cognitive awareness in the infant and in the nurturing *other*. A baby is learning about himself and developing an ego base. The mother and father who are attached to and intimately involved with this infant are both consciously and unconsciously aware of parallel stages of their own development as nurturers (Brazelton 1983).

In these four stages of learning about each other the participants are learning as much about social communication as they are about themselves. Learning about the internal control system becomes the experimental base for internalizing a kind of early ego function for the small infant. As infants achieve homeostasis and then go on to learn about a less-than-balanced state of expectation and excitement within a nurturant envelope, they learn about the control systems and the capacities for emotional experience with which they are endowed. They are experiencing emotion. As they learn to elicit and then to reply to the nurturant adults around them, they learn the importance of communication and even the experiencing of emotion in the other. Thus, they are experiencing the ingredients of affect within themselves and learning to demonstrate and to enrich their responses to the external world in order to elicit affect in others.

As they engage, respond to, and enlarge upon the adult's responses, infants learn from adults how to produce an affective environment—one that is appropriate and necessary for learning about themselves and about their world. Thus, infants are learning to fuel both sources of energy—that from within and that from without. They learn about causality within the emotional sphere. They begin to internalize controls that are necessary for experiencing emotion but also learn what is necessary for producing emotional responses from others. By the end of the fourth month, infants can "turn on" or "turn off" those around them with an actively controllable set of responses. They have begun to learn how to manipulate their own experience and their own world. The emotions that they are experiencing and registering unconsciously by this age can be consciously manipulated as well. Up to this point, they have been learning about their own emotions within the envelope of attachment (Bowlby 1973; Brazelton 1983) but now the anlages for detachment and autonomy are also surfacing, and the precursors for the infant's superego are already apparent.

In summary, the precursors for ego function, the anlages of emotional experience in an older child, are observable in the behavior of the infant (and the fetus). The experience of completing an anticipated act of social communication closes a feedback cycle. Infants add a further source of fuel toward development by entraining the nurturant environment around them, within which they can learn more quickly a sense of self and the mastery of complex inner control mechanisms as well as social response systems. Thus, early experience provides the base for precursors of future emotion and permits us to conceptualize how experience can be represented in the memory of infants and how it can shape them toward future responses.

These early experiences, when they are repeated, and when they are accompanied by a behavioral representation of recognition in the infant, must be considered potential anlages of future ego development or of cognitive patterns. These early reactions are likely to become, as Greenacre (1941) put it, the "precursors for future response patterns." Successful patterns in early infancy will probably be repeated, be learned, and eventually become preferred patterns in the older infant. In this way, behavior that represents reactions of the infant becomes a precursor for future development. But what if the infant is deprived of this opportunity for learning about himself?

An understanding of the infant's development within any particular developmental line—such as that of affect or emotional development—must include the interaction between this and other developmental lines. The responses of the infant's neurological and physical systems are at the core of any development of emotions. The immaturity of these systems limits the infant's potential for developing clearly definable emotions in the early months, but as they mature the base for future emotional experience emerges. As infants learn to cope with stimuli from the outside world, they experience a sense of achievement, and the feedback system that is activated may give them an inner representation of mastery (White 1959). Although this terminology is *adultomorphic* and probably represents mechanisms that are more consciously experienced in an older child or adult, it seems to me that the concepts of mastery and learning do fit the anlage of experiences on which the infant begins to build.

The central nervous system (CNS), as it develops, drives the infant toward maturation and mastery of self and world. Any internal equilibrium is tested and upset by the imbalance that is created as the CNS matures. Hence, maturation and an increase in differentiation of infant skills and potential become forces that drive the infant to reorganize and "relearn" control systems. Each step is a new opportunity for mastery and for learning new feedback systems.

There are two sources fueling this maturation. Feedback loops that close on completion of an experience after an anticipated performance affect the baby from within. As each step is mastered, anticipation has generated energy that becomes realized and is available as the step is completed, and this liberated energy drives the infant toward the next developmental achievement. In this way, a sense of mastery (White 1959) is incorporated by the developing infant. Meanwhile, a second important source of energy fuels and enhances each experience. When it is nurturant, the environment tends to entrain responsive behavior to the behavior of the infant. Not only do parents register recognition and approval of an infant's achievement, but they add a salient, more developed signal to their approval. This signal, coupled with positive reinforcement, both fuels the infant and leads him to match the adult's expectation. For example, when an infant vocalizes with an "Ooh," a parent will add, "Oh yes!" to it. The parent couples an added experience with open approval of the infant's production. Thus parents offer the infant positive reinforcement and added stimulus. This fuels the infant to go on (Als 1978).

These two sources of energy—one from within, the other from without—are in balance under ideal conditions, and both provide the energy for future development. The infant's recognition of each of these sources, as he or she masters a developmental step, is often unconscious, but it adds to a preconscious recognition of mastery. This internal representation and the closure of the loops of mastery of steps in autonomic and CNS control must become the precursors of emotional as well as of cognitive recognition, both of which contribute to the infant's developing ego.

When either of these are deficient, the infant's development of affective and cognitive stages can be impaired. This occurs when an infant is at risk for CNS or autonomic deficits (such as one whose autonomic system is too labile or too sluggish, or one whose threshold for intake of stimuli is too low and is thus overwhelmed by each stimulus); or when the environment is inappropriately responsive to the infant (either under- or over-responsive). Thus, the internal and external feedback systems become intertwined from the first, since each is dependent on the infant's genetic capacities for overt and internalized reactions. They both fuel the infant's development and place limits on it.

When parents are deprived too early of this opportunity to participate in the baby's developing ego structure, they lose the opportunity to understand the baby intimately and to feel their own role in the development of these four stages. The likelihood that they will feel cheated of the opportunity for their own development as nurturing adults is great.

When a new mother must share her small baby with a secondary caregiver, she will almost inevitably experience a sense of loss. Her feeling of competition with the other caregiver may well be uppermost in her mind. But beneath this conscious feeling of competition there is likely to be a less-than-conscious sense of grief. Lindemann (1944) described a syndrome, which he labeled a grief reaction, that seems to fit the experiences that mothers of small babies describe when they leave them in substitute care. They are apt to feel sad, helpless, hopeless, inadequate to their babies. They feel a sense of loneliness, of depression, of slowed-down physical responses, and even of somatic symptoms. To protect themselves from these feelings, they are likely to develop three defenses (Brazelton 1985). These are healthy, normal, and necessary defenses, but they can interfere with the mother's attachment to her baby if they are not properly evaluated. The younger the baby and the more inexperienced the mother, the stronger and more likely are these defenses. They are correlated with the earliness with which she returns to work:

1. Denial. A mother is likely to deny that her leaving has consequences— for the child or for herself. She will distort or ignore any signals in herself or in the baby to the contrary. Mothers who obviously know better will not visit their baby's day care center "because it is too painful." This denial may be a necessary defense against painful feelings but it may distort a mother's capacity to make proper decisions.
2. Projection. Working parents will have a tendency to project the important caregiving issues onto the substitute caregivers. Responsibility for both good and bad will be shifted, and often sidestepped.
3. Detachment. Not because she doesn't care but because it is painful to care and to be separated, the mother will tend to distance her feeling of responsibility and of intense attachment.

These three defenses are commonly necessary for mothers to handle the new feelings engendered by separating from a small baby. For example, imagine the feelings of a mother who arrives to pick her baby up from the day-care center at the end of a working day. The baby has saved up all his important feelings and now blows up in a temper tantrum when the mother arrives. At that point, someone in the day-care center turns to her and says, "He never cries like that with me, dear."

These conflicting emotions need to be faced by new parents and understood by them in order to prevent costly adjustments which are not in the family's best interests. We need to prepare working parents for their roles in order to preserve the positive forces in strong attachments—to the baby and to each other. We certainly must protect the period in which the attachment process is solidified and stabilized by new parents. With the new baby, this is likely to demand at least four months in which the new mother can feel herself free from the competing demands of the workplace. Since most young families cannot afford a period of unpaid leave, and since the workplace is not inclined to provide such a period, it seems critical at this time to work toward a nationally subsidized policy for paid leave to care for a new baby. National recognition of this need would be a symbolic recognition of the value of the family, as well as a means to heighten the emphasis on strong ties within the family at a time when the national trend toward divorce and instability of attachments has proven especially costly to our children (Hetherington 1981; Wallerstein and Kelly 1975). As a nation, we can no longer afford to ignore our responsibilities toward children and their families.

STRENGTHENING THE FAMILY

All of the evidence that we have concerning pregnancy, labor and delivery, and the development of attachment between parents and their young infants demonstrates that this is an important time to aid and support families in creating a sense of mutual understanding, trust, and love. If we provide new parents with information on the needs of their infant and how best to meet those needs early in the relationship, and if we give parents a feeling that this is a time when they are needed as nurturers, we can help to reinforce their attachment both to the baby and to each other, and thus strengthen the family as a whole. The family is our future, for from well-integrated, caring family systems come content and well-adjusted children, who grow to become the responsible and productive adults of the future.

First and foremost in strengthening the family system is a recognition of a parent's need to be with an infant and to have the time to grow successfully into the role of parent. Society needs to provide the full, free choice for a parent to be at home to nurture a new infant for a significant time, if that parent so desires. Thus, at a national level, a paid leave for a three-month period at least, and preferably for four months, is a necessity for working women. If we also want men to be involved with their future families, we must provide a one-month paid leave for them—to allow new fathers time to get to know their infants and to adjust to their new role as father. If a mother, father, and infant are to take the crucial steps together to become a family unit, they need both the time, the social, and the financial support to do so. Yet few families can afford to have one or both parents at home for many months without salary or health benefits; therefore a parental leave is a social matter that requires a national mandate.

Once the government has established a parental leave policy (with pay), we should expect industry to follow suit by reconsidering its role in the lives of the parents of young families. Such programs as flextime, job sharing, part-time options for new parents, and industry-provided care for employees' children help send a message of support and encouragement to the employee whose role as worker is increasingly at odds with his or her role as parent. Industries that are already providing these supports for the family are finding that they themselves are benefiting from a stronger integration between the two key areas of a parent's life, work and family. With such supports, employees are showing a predictable increase in output, increased allegiance, and decreased attrition. The decreased stress on workers in juggling family and work obligations increases their energy for investing in their jobs (Strideright, et al. 1985). Industries that are not alert to these programs and their success need to be informed not only of the increase in employee satisfaction and productivity, but also of the greater social impact such supports can have.

Second only in importance to a paid maternity/paternity leave is a serious look at our existing day-care system. Since over half of the mothers of children under six are in the work force in this country, it is critical that we examine what kind of environment they are able to provide for their children during the workday. Optimal and affordable substitute child care must exist as a supplement to family care. When parents have to work outside the home, we must ensure that their children are cared for in a nurturing, stimulating environment. Although this issue may be more critical for very young children, as a result of their more complete dependence on others, we know that the number of supervised day-care centers and family day-care homes is woefully inadequate to serve the needs of all involved—the developing infant, the absent parent, the family unit itself.

Research that has looked into the development of infants and toddlers in substitute care has resulted in everything from warnings of potential emotional damage (Ainsworth 1979; Egeland and Sroufe 1981; Farber and Egeland 1982; Fraiberg 1977; Gamble and Zigler 1986; Schwartz 1983) to reports of potential emotional gains. Most studies to date have not found negative consequences (Belsky et al. 1982; Caldwell et al. 1970; Clarke-Stewart et al. 1980; Kagan 1982), but they have tended to be flawed in several ways. In general, they have investigated development only in the short-term; they have studied middle-class families in well-funded, regulated day-care centers; and their outcome measures have often failed to include aspects of the child's total development. Certainly, for millions of children, substitute care as it now exists may not be optimal, and we shall not understand fully the consequences for another generation. Yet day care does not have to be a negative force. Quality day care can and does function to make the family system work better, when the center is run properly—as some are. Day care which supports and strengthens the family as a whole needs to become the standard rather than the exception.

A portrait of such day care might be as follows. There is at least one adult to care for every three infants, and not less than one adult for every four toddlers. Its caregivers are mature, sensitive, trained adults who spend an appropriate amount of time with each baby to assure reciprocal and caring communication. Safety and intellectual stimulation are provided by thoughtful, developmentally-appropriate programs. Not only would parents be urged to participate actively in their babies' care, but the centers would provide opportunities for education, for peer support groups, and for the nurturing supports of parenting that have been lost to nuclear families through the demise of the extended family. Thus, with quality day care, both families and their small children could benefit.

Such a day-care system will not come about by magic. It must have government support and subsidies to attract the kind of highly-trained and caring person to whom we can safely entrust our children. The child care now available to over 50% of working mothers is grossly inadequate. Poor and vulnerable parents, especially, are often unable to find and afford quality care and must leave their small children in dangerously inadequate circumstances. Physical, as well as sexual, abuse and neglect can easily occur under such conditions.

Quality training for caregivers is essential, if we are to make day care part of our social strength rather than a social weakness. But training and commitment will not exist without a financial upgrading of the profession. At present, infant caregivers are too often not only untrained and unsupervised, but also grossly underpaid. Until we provide our caregivers with recognition and salary, we cannot expect professional work. For day care to function at the highest level of quality, professional supervision, involvement, and training need to be mandated at the local, state, and national levels (Zigler and Butterfield 1968; Zigler and Trickett 1978). The National Association for Education of Young Children is ready to institute a program for supervising quality assessment of day-care centers. It cannot do so, however, without financial support from the government. Parents cannot afford to carry the burden alone of responsibility for upgrading daycare.

Our future generations are at stake. Over the past forty years, Spitz, Bowlby, Harlow, and many subsequent researchers have pointed to the importance of providing a nurturing environment for small children. We must provide safeguards to protect the development of these children. These safeguards are costly, and necessitate government subsidies. Our responsibility as mental health and childcare professionals requires that we work toward development of a national policy with a national subsidy.

REFERENCES

Ainsworth, M. 1979. Attachment as related to mother-infant interaction. *Advances in the Study of Behavior*, vol. 9. J. Rosenblatt, et al., eds. New York: Academic Press.

Als, H. 1978. Assessing an assessment. *Organization and Stability of Newborn Behavior: Commentary on the Brazelton Neonatal Behavioral Assessment Scale*, A. Sameroff, ed. Monographs of the Society for Research in Child Development. 43(177):14–29.

Beal, J. 1984. The effect of demonstration of the father-infant relationship. Paper presented to the International Conference in Infant Studies, New York.

Belsky, J., Steinberg, L., and Walker, A. 1982. The ecology of day care. *Childrearing in Nontraditional Families*. M. Lamb, ed. Hillsdale, N.J.: Erlbaum.

Bibring, G., Dwyer, T., and Valenstein, A. 1961. A study of the psychological processes in pregnancy. *Psychoanal. Stud. Child* 16:9–72.

Bowlby, J. 1973. *Attachment and Loss*, vol. 2. New York: Basic Books.

Braun, S., and Caldwell, B. 1973. Emotional adjustment of children in day care who enrolled prior to or after the age of three. *Early Child Development and Care* 2:13–21.

Brazelton, T. 1973. The Neonatal Behavioral Assessment Scale. *Spastics International Medical Publications*, London: Heinemann (Philadelphia: Lippincott, 1984).

Brazelton, T. 1983. Precursors for the development of emotions in early infancy. *Theory, Research, and Experience*, vol. 2. R. Pluchik, ed. New York: Academic Press.

Brazelton, T. 1985. *Working and Caring*. Boston: Addison-Wesley.

Brazelton, T., and Als, H. 1979. Four early stages in the development of mother-infant interaction. *Psychoanal. Stud. Child* 34:349–69.

Brazelton, T., Koslowski, B., and Main, M. 1974. The origins of reciprocity: The early mother-infant interaction. *The Effect of the Infant on Its Caregiver*. M. Lewis and L. Rosenblum, eds. New York: John Wiley & Sons.

Brazelton, T., et al. 1975. Early mother-infant reciprocity. *Parent-Infant Interaction*. Ciba Foundation Symposium 33. Amsterdam: Elsevier.

Caldwell, B., et al. 1970. Infant day care and attachment. *American Journal of Orthopsychiatry* 40:397–412.

Clarke-Stewart, K., et al. 1980. Development and prediction of children's sociability from 1 to 2 1/2 years. *Developmental Psychology* 16:290–302.

Egeland, B., and Sroufe, L. 1981. Attachment and early maltreatment. *Child Development* 52:44–52.

Farber, E., and Egeland, B. 1982. Developmental consequences of out-of-home care for infants in a low income population. *Day Care: Scientific and Social Policy Issues.* E. Zigler and E. Gordon, eds. Boston: Auburn House.

Fraiberg, S. 1977. *Every Child's Birthright: In Defense of Mothering.* New York: Basic Books.

Gamble, T., and Zigler, E. 1986. Effects of infant day care: another look at the evidence. *American Journal of Orthopsychiatry* 56:26–42.

Greenacre, P. 1941. *The Predisposition to Anxiety: Trauma, Growth, and Personality,* (Parts I and II). New York: International Universities Press.

Hetherington, M. 1981. Children and Divorce. *Parent-Child Interaction: Theory, Research, and Prospect.* R. Henderson, ed. New York: Academic Press.

Kagan, J. 1982. *Psychological Research on the Human Infant: An Evaluation Summary.* New York: W. T. Grant Foundation Publications.

Kessen, W., Haith, M., and Salapatek, P. 1970. Human infancy: a bibliography and guide. *Carmichael's Manual of Child Psychology,* vol. 1. W. Mussen, ed. New York: John Wiley & Sons.

Klaus, M., and Kennell, J. 1970. Mothers separated from their newborn infants. *Pediat. Clin. N. A.* 17:1015.

Lindemann, E. 1944. Grief. *American Journal of Psychiatry* 101:141.

Rutter, M. 1981. Social-emotional consequences of day dare for preschool children. *American Journal of Orthopsychiatry* 51:4–28.

Schwartz, P. 1983. Length of day care attendance and attachment behavior in eighteen-month-old infants. *Child Development* 54:1073–78.

Stern, D. 1974. The goal and structure of mother-infant play. *Journal of the American Academy of Child Psychiatry* 13:402–21.

U. S. Senate. 1982. *American Families: Trends and Pressures.* Joint Hearings before the Subcommittee on Children and Youth and the Committee on Labor and Public Welfare (Sept).

Wallerstein, J., and Kelly, J. 1975. The effect of parental divorce: experiences of the preschool child. *J. Amer. Acad. Child Psychiat.* 14:600–16.

White, R. 1959. Motivation reconsidered: the concept of competence. *Psychol. Fev.* 66:297–333.

Zigler, E., and Butterfield, E. 1968. Motivational aspects of changes in IQ test performance of culturally deprived nursery school children. *Child Development* 39:1–14.

Zigler, E., and Trickett, P. 1978. IQ, social competence, and evaluation of early childhood intervention programs. *Amer. Psycho.* 33:789–98.

PART II

The Newborn Infant:
At Home and in
Out-of-Home Settings

FOUR

Parental Stress and
the Young Infant's Needs

ROBIN HARWOOD

PARENT-INFANT INTERACTION AND INFANT STIMULATION LEVELS

In the early months of the infant's life the mother and father do more than tend to their infant's physiological needs. They also hold their infant, smile, gaze, jiggle, vocalize, talk to, and caress him or her. The infant in turn gazes back or looks away, soon returns the smile, vocalizes, and moves arms and legs in response to the sights and sounds of other people. During the first year of life, the infant will accomplish more than physical growth and motor development. He or she will also learn basic patterns of human social communication and begin to develop a sense of self-worth and efficacy, the capacity to love other people, and a belief that the world is an understandable and enjoyable place. This process begins at birth when the consistent and appropriate responsiveness of an adult to an infant's signals builds in the infant the beginnings of trust and delight in the world.

Each partner contributes to this process. Indeed, some researchers have suggested that a primary function of early parent-infant interactions is the mutual regulation of stimuli (Brazelton, Koslowski, and Main 1974; Stern 1974). *Stimuli* denote the arousal of the baby through any of the senses: through light, noise, movement, colors, faces, voices, toys, hunger, wet diapers, uncomfortable clothing, mouthed objects, tastes, and odors. Babies learn about their world through such stimulation and are fascinated by it. They can only absorb so much at a time, however, and when they have had enough, they fuss, cry, turn away, or fall asleep. One of the tasks of parenting an infant is to provide enough stimulation for the infant to remain interested in the world during times of alertness, while at the same time screening out elements of the environment that might be overstimulating. In turn, the infant sends the parent signals when he or she is either overstimulated, or ready to begin interacting again. The parent, then, must be able to read the infant's signals and to respond to them appropriately.

Some researchers have suggested that there is an optimal range of stimulation in which the infant is best able to grow and thrive socially and emotionally. Belsky, Rovine, and Taylor have hypothesized that too much as well as too little interaction might be detrimental to the beginnings of trust and confidence in the infant (1984). Using a standardized procedure called the Strange Situation (Ainsworth and Wittig 1969), these authors found that both very high and very low levels of reciprocal interaction and stimulation throughout the first year (the infants were tested at one, three, and nine months) correlated with insecure attachment behavior at twelve months. Parents, then, need to be sensitive not only to the baby's readiness for play or social interaction, but also to those times when the baby has had enough. It is the parents' ability to respond appropriately that helps set the stage for the infant to develop a sense of trust and confidence.

Studies comparing infants' performance on the Neonatal Behavioral Assessment Scale (NBAS) at two to three days after birth with the nature of the mother-infant interaction at three months substantiate this relationship between parental ability to screen stimulation and infant responsiveness. Penman, Meares, Baker, and Milgrom-Friedman report that newborn infants "who were more socially responsive and attentive to stimuli had mothers with a greater capacity for screening out redundant stimuli" (1983). In a study of 134 mother-infant pairs, Osofsky (1976) similarly found that more alert and responsive infants had more responsive and sensitive mothers, and that the better the mother's presentation of the stimuli during the NBAS, the better the infants responded to them. The regulation of stimuli is thus a mutual process, involving contributions from both parent and infant.

Crying

Crying is one of the infant's primary signals. It is present from birth, it is loud, and by its very nature it demands response even when other signals might be overlooked. Most studies have considered the infant's cry to be a signal of distress, and have understood the termination of crying to indicate relief from distress. As a consequence, most studies on crying have focused on the relationship between parental responsiveness to crying and various measures of infant well-being. Bell and Ainsworth found that prompt, consistent, and appropriate responsiveness was associated with a decline in both frequency and duration of infant crying during the first three months of life (1972). Stayton and Ainsworth (1973) linked responsiveness to crying throughout the first year of life to an anxiety-security dimension in infant reactions to brief, everyday separations: infants whose mothers had been consistently responsive to their cries displayed little distress over brief, everyday separations at one year, whereas infants whose mothers had not been consistently and appropriately responsive to their cries throughout the first year were more likely to be anxious during brief separations. Ainsworth and her colleagues also linked maternal responsiveness to secure attachment behavior in the Strange Situation at twelve months (Ainsworth, Blehar, Waters, and Wall 1978). In a critical examination of this literature, although Lamb and his colleagues (1984) concluded that further research on the topic is needed, these authors noted that the literature has consistently found a link between parental sensitivity and secure attachment behavior.

Thoman, Acebo, and Becker found that consistency in caretaking patterns during the first two to five weeks of life (as measured by the time regularly allocated for certain daily activities) is also linked to low levels of crying during social attention (1983). The authors understood this as an indicator of the degree of equilibrium in the parent-infant relationship, with high levels of equilibrium reflecting consistency in caretaking patterns. Thus, factors which have been found to relate to lower levels of infant distress, as measured through duration and frequency of crying, are prompt and appropriate responsiveness to infant crying and consistency of caretaking patterns.

Attachment and Separation

During the first eight to twelve weeks of life, the infant's sociability is undiscriminating. He or she smiles at and looks with interest at all faces and can be comforted by any pair of arms. Between the ages of two and four months, the infant begins to distinguish between familiar and unfamiliar faces. Kagan suggests that novelty is particularly arousing for the four- to twelve-month-old infant, who is just beginning to form mental schemas of the world (1983). While infants enjoy moderate amounts of novelty, too much of it can be a potent stressor, resulting in protest, pulling away, or crying.

From birth, the infant's cry signals discomfort or tension, but at about six to seven months of age, the infant also begins to cry when he or she is separated from the person or people who have been primarily involved with his or her care. In America, this is usually the mother, and the majority of studies of infants' responses to separation have used mother-infant pairs. Crying at separation coincides with the infant's increased capacity for memory, a capacity which also gives rise to the normal phenomenon known as *stranger anxiety* (Fox, Kagan, and Weiskopf 1979; Kagan and Hamburg 1981), and thus marks the advent of new cognitive abilities. That infants will cry at the departure of a specific person is a signal that a new milestone in social and emotional development has been reached: he or she has formed a primary attachment to another person. At this point, the infant will actively maintain proximity to this person, will preferentially seek out this person for comforting when distressed, and will protest separation from this person (Bowlby, 1969). The older infant's experience of security within an attachment relationship has been linked in several studies (Arend, Gove, and Sroufe 1979; Londerville and Main 1981; Matas, Arend, and Sroufe 1978; Pastor 1981; Waters, Wippman, and Sroufe 1979) to the possession of culturally valued qualities such as "a tendency toward exploration, autonomy, and sociability, as well as a reasonable compliance to parental requests" (Kagan 1983).

There is some evidence that, for the seven- to twelve-month-old infant, separation from familiar caregivers is in itself upsetting (Bowlby 1969). For the seven-to-twelve-month-old, then, caregiver *continuity* is of particular importance. However, during the first six months of life, a period which constitutes the preattachment and attachment formation phases, what may be even more important than caregiver continuity is a predictable routine and responsive, sensitive *caretaking*. Kagan, for example, notes that "partial transformations of established schemata alert the infant, lead to the inhibition of motor and vocal responses and, on occasion, produce crying. It is reasonable to suppose that frequent changes in feeding and sleeping routines could produce the state of uncertainty" (1983). From this perspective, extreme unpredictability may be more upsetting to the infant in the first few months of life than moderate amounts of separation.

In fact, there is some evidence that moderate amounts of separation involving regular contact with nonparental caregivers do not necessarily interfere with the development of a secure attachment relationship when high-quality substitute care arrangements are used (Brookhart and Hock 1976; Kagan, Kearsley, and Zelazo 1977; Jacobson and Wille 1984; Ragozin 1980; Schwartz 1983). Schwartz suggests that, under these circumstances, moderate amounts of separation may be integrated into the infant's cognitive schema and expectations (1983). Additionally, other researchers have attempted to separate the effects of change in routine from the effects of maternal work status, and they have also concluded that separation can be part of a predictable environment (Owen, Easterbrooks, Chase-Lansdale, and Goldberg 1981; Thompson, Lamb and Estes, 1982).

Gamble and Zigler have suggested that stress in the parents' lives is one factor that may diminish a parent's ability to be responsive to the infant's cues (1986). They point to studies which have found relationships between out-of-home care and insecure parent-infant attachments among lower income families using out-of-home care arrangements of varying quality (Egeland and Sroufe 1981; Vaughn, Egeland, Sroufe, and Waters 1979; Vaughn, Gove, and Egeland 1980). The mother's assessment of her situation as highly stressful may be one factor in determining which babies are adversely affected by circumstances surrounding a mother's early return to work and the advent of substitute care arrangements.

Premature and Ill Infants

High-risk infants include those who are premature and/or suffer from neurophysiological deficits, perinatal illnesses, or low birthweight. These groups may be in particular need of caregiver sensitivity and environmental predictability in their early months of life. Premature infants are not as well adapted to normal caregiving practices as are full-term infants. They are less able to give clear cry signals (Lester, in press), and they sometimes exhibit disorganized sleep patterns which make it difficult for the parent to judge the infant's relative state of alertness (Dreyfus-Brisac 1974). Moreover, the premature infant's cries may differ in quality from the cries of a healthy, full-term infant, sounding more urgent and aversive. This quality can galvanize caregiver responsiveness, or it can dismay an already anxious parent; for the stressed parent in a nonsupportive environment, the cry can be irritating and overwhelming (Lester, in press). Some parents may experience feelings of inadequacy in caring for these infants, and this can hamper their ability to respond sensitively and appropriately to their infants (Stengel 1982).

Because premature and ill infants are separated by necessity from their parents following birth, often spending weeks in a neonatal intensive care unit, they have been the focus of research on the long-term effects of early separation on the development of the parent-infant bond, asking whether allowing mothers to have high-contact with their full-term or preterm infants in the first hours or days of life will produce long-lasting benefits in the parent-child relationship. Klaus and Kennell (1976) reported that low-income mothers whose contact with their full-term infants began within one hour of the child's birth seemed more interested in their infants throughout the first year of life; they also found that these infants fared better developmentally than did mother-infant pairs who did not experience such early contact. However, researchers who have studied the effects of early contact on parent-infant bonding, using middle-class mother-infant pairs that included both preterm and full-term babies, have failed to replicate these findings. Several studies showed that by one year of age the low-contact mother-infant pairs in which the infants were premature could not be differentiated either from high-contact pairs where the infants were premature or from full-term infant-mother pairs (Leifer, Leiderman, Barnett, and Williams 1972; Seashore, Leifer, Barnett, and Leiderman 1973; Sostek, Scanlon, and Abramson 1982).

Studies investigating the effects of early parent-infant separation on later quality of attachment have found that, by the age of one year, preterm and seriously ill full-term infants who had spent ten or more days in a neonatal intensive care unit showed the same proportion of secure to insecure parent-infant attachments as a control sample of healthy, full-term infants who did not experience early separation (Chang, Thompson, and Fisch, 1982; Rode, Chang, Fisch, and Sroufe, 1981). Rode and her colleagues concluded that "attachment patterns are influenced by maternal-infant interactions over a period of time and provide evidence for the resiliency of infants in their formation of at-tachment patterns" (1981, p. 188).

The parent's ability to provide consistent and responsive care once again becomes a key mediating factor, because parents who experience prolonged separation from their infants often report feelings of guilt and incompetence in handling their infants during the early months (Sostek, et al., 1982). Given a minimum of other stressors, these feelings of distress and inadequacy gradually give way to normal parent-infant interactions, and by the age of one year, the preterm infant is likely to be doing as well as full-term mother-infant pairs who did not experience early prolonged separation. When these feelings of inadequacy are com-plicated by other factors, such as poverty and low social support, how-ever, the effects of early separation on the mother's sense of adequacy in caring for her child may be more long-lasting, and early contact may be of particular benefit to them (Leiderman 1983; Lamb 1983).

Other infants who may be in particular need of caregiver sensitivity during the early months of life include infants suffering from neuro-physiological deficits, perinatal illnesses, low birthweight, or physical ab-normalities. Like premature infants, they may spend extended periods of time in the neonatal intensive care unit. Further, they may present special adjustment needs for the entire family and frequently demand a great deal of parental time and energy. As a group, then, these infants are in greater need of caregiver sensitivity than healthy, full-term infants. Some parents, in turn, may need to be assured a nonstressful environ-ment in order to give these infants the extra care and attention they need to thrive, as well as to deal with the stressful circumstances often surrounding the hospitalization of an infant.

Less Robust Infants

Some infants may be relatively robust to less sensitive caretaking, whereas others may not (Crockenberg, 1981; Waters, Vaughn, and Egeland

1980). In a study of factors associated with the development of and change in quality of attachment over time in a low-income sample, Egeland and Farber found that there were some infants who, although falling within normal ranges, nonetheless had more difficulty than others in meeting the developmental demands of the neonatal period (1984). With sensitively responsive caretakers, these infants were doing well by one year of age, but with less competent caretaking, these infants were more likely to develop insecure attachment relationships.

These infants may be the same ones Gunnar (in press) found to be more highly reactive to routine hospital procedures such as undressing, weighing, and measuring. These infants may need higher amounts of caregiver sensitivity and environmental predictability during their early months, as they appear to be more easily overstimulated than other infants.

Researchers also suggest that boys in general may be more vulnerable throughout the early years of life (Gamble and Zigler 1986; Rutter 1982, 1983). In particular, Egeland and Farber (1984) found that boys seemed more vulnerable than girls to factors associated with being reared in a nonintact family. A majority of boys from intact homes were securely attached at one year, and a majority of boys from nonintact homes were insecurely attached at one year. This was not true for female infants. Although it is not clear what factors associated with intact as opposed to nonintact families impact on boys but not girls, the literature suggests at this point that boys may in general be more vulnerable to early environmental variations than are girls.

In summary, all infants need a certain amount of caretaker responsiveness and environmental predictability. Some infants, however, need more than others if they are to meet the challenges of their first months of life with optimal success. Parents, in turn, vary in terms of their own abilities to provide an infant with sensitive, responsive caretaking and a reasonably predictable environment. In the next section, I will examine factors which may help or hinder a parent's ability to provide an infant with sensitive caretaking and a predictable routine.

STRESS IN THE EARLY POSTPARTUM MONTHS

Perceptions of Stress

The transition to parenthood, coupled with juggling of multiple roles (worker, spouse, homemaker, parent), is a stressful period of time for many people (Belsky and Rovine 1984; Dohrenwend, Krasnoff, Askenasy, and Dohrenwend 1978; Rossi 1968). In fact, in a study of over 2,500 adults, Dohrenwend et al. found that the birth of the first child was listed as the sixth most stressful life event out of a list of 102 events (1978).

The early postpartum months are viewed as potentially stressful for several reasons: (1) The physical events surrounding pregnancy and delivery can be difficult; (2) the newborn infant requires a great deal of direct care and attention; (3) there is a disruption of established life patterns and routines; (4) the addition of a new member changes existing relationships within the family; (5) an infant's arrival can cause financial stress; and (6) if the infant is the first-born, both mother and father are confronted with the psychological task of assuming a new role—that of parent (Belsky and Rovine, 1984). If the mother chooses not to return to work, these events are usually accompanied by a reduction in income; if she does return to work, scheduling patterns and caregiving arrangements may become one more demand on time.

At issue in the debate about work and parenting is to what extent the mother's early return to work is associated with stress and to what degree stress is in turn related to decreased caregiver sensitivity or greater environmental unpredictability. Early return is defined as anytime between two and six weeks after an infant's birth. The argument linking work with quality of caregiving proceeds as follows: sensitive caretaking demands a great deal of parental energy; a parent under stress has less energy to give to the task of parenting; thus, a parent under stress may be less able to provide an infant with sensitive caregiving and a reasonably predictable environment. The added assumption is that a mother who is working is more likely to feel stressed than a mother who is not working. For example, mothers who feel forced to return to work early solely out of economic necessity may feel that their needs and their family's needs are being compromised. However, such an interpretation of work as stress may not be accurate in all situations. For some mothers, work may be an important source of self-esteem, and an extended leave from their jobs would be experienced as a loss. But the parent who feels stressed by the combined demands of home and parenting may be less able to provide an infant with sensitive caretaking and a reasonably predictable routine.

Stress and Caregiving

Sorce and Emde found that a mother's emotional availability promoted infant exploration and confidence in the face of novel, unpredictable events; conversely, the infants of mothers who were emotionally unavailable in an unfamiliar setting (they were instructed to spend the time reading, and not to respond to their infants' bids for attention) exhibited less pleasure and less exploration (1981). The findings of this study suggest a relationship between the emotional availability of the caretaker and infant well-being. This leads to the question of whether a parent under stress is likely to be less responsive to an infant's cues.

The literature suggests a relationship between high levels of perceived stress and decreased sensitivity to infant cues. Crockenberg found that mothers who reported low social support at three months postpartum were observed to be more unresponsive to infant crying than mothers who reported high social support (1981). In this study, the degree of social support was defined by the amount of stress the mother reported she felt. In other words, a mother was considered to have low social support when she felt that her needs exceeded her degree of support. Thus, perceived stress was a key ingredient in this study's findings. How a mother perceived her infant also contributed to the quality of her caregiving. Both Crnic et al. (1983, 1984) and Campbell (1979) found that if a mother thought of her nine-month-old baby as difficult, she was less responsive to the infant's cues. Nover, Shore, Timberlake, and Greenspan similarly found that maternal expectations and perceptions translated into specific maternal behaviors (1984). Together, these findings suggest that a mother's feelings of stress and dissatisfaction may hinder her ability to be appropriately responsive to her infant.

Stress and Work Status

Does an early return to work necessarily bear a one-to-one relationship with the degree of perceived stress? Put more simply, are working mothers of infants more likely to feel overwhelmed by multiple and competing demands on their time than nonworking mothers? The literature on role combination and interrole conflict suggests that the relationship between work status and stress is not direct, but rather is mediated by a variety of individual and situational resources and variables.

The literature suggests that role combination does not necessarily lead to higher levels of peceived stress. Baruch and Barnett (1986) studied multiple role involvement in 238 women aged thirty-five to fifty-five. They found that role occupancy per se was unrelated to well-being, except that occupying the role of paid worker significantly predicted self-esteem. These researchers concluded that role quality rather than quantity was key to understanding the relationship between multiple role involvements and psychological well-being in women. Ivancevich and Matteson looked at employed and nonemployed middle-class mothers (1982). They found that, in general, nonemployed women were "more stressed by children, domestic work conditions, and roles issues" than employed women (p. 994), which argues against the idea that combining job, homemaking, and child care necessarily results in high stress and low satisfaction. Similarly, Alpert, Richardson, and Fodaski found that nonworking mothers tended to rate conflicting demands between needs of self and needs of child as more stressful than working mothers (1983). Jiminez and Newton studied the relationship between reported job commitment and emotions in the third trimester of pregnancy and at six weeks postpartum in 120 first-time mothers (1982). They found that women who scored high in job commitment "had more favorable psychological and emotional experiences in the first pregnancy and post-partum period on some measures" (p. 157). In a survey of 711 Detroit adults, Verbrugge found that multiple roles had no special effects on health (1983). Finally, Barnett compared employed and nonemployed mothers of preschool children on two indexes of well-being (self-esteem and satisfaction with one's current role patterns), and found no differences between the two groups (1982).

A related question is whether the infants of working mothers are more likely to show insecure attachment behavior than those of non-working mothers. Again, the literature suggests that the relationship between work status and quality of parent-child relationship is not direct, but is mediated by other individual and situational resources and variables.

Owen, Easterbrooks, Chase-Lansdale, and Goldberg looked at the quality and stability of attachment in first-born infants whose mothers worked, were nonemployed, or changed employment status (1984). A high proportion of all these infants (85%) displayed secure attachment behavior in the Strange Situation at both twelve and twenty months; stability of attachment classification between the two assessments was also high (78%). Moreover, the proportion of stable to unstable attachments was comparable across the work status groups. The authors concluded that maternal full-time work, part-time work, or nonemployment can all be components of a stable home environment. Schubert, Bradley-John-son, and Nuttal looked at the quality of interactive behavior (visual contact, vocalization, touch, and responsiveness) among employed and nonemployed mothers of fifteen- to seventeen-month-old infants (1980). They found no negative effects attributable to maternal employment on the quality of mother-infant communication. Both of these studies employed middle-class, married mothers. On the other hand, when Vaughn et al. (1980) used a lower socioeconomic sample, they found that infants whose mothers returned to full-time work prior to the infant's first birthday showed a high percentage of insecure attachments. However, these mothers were more likely to be single parents, to report higher levels of perceived stress, and to be faced with other environmental stresses. It is likely that these factors mediated the differential impact of maternal work status.

Overall, these findings are consistent with a stress and coping para-digm, which considers individual and situational resources and variables to be central in determining whether or not a person finds a given life event to be stressful (Lazarus and Folkman 1984).

WORK STATUS, PARENTING, AND STRESS: MEDIATING FACTORS

Spouse Support

One mediating factor of stress which has received a great deal of attention is spouse support. In a review of the sociological literature, Kessler and Essex reported that role strains are in general less damaging for the married than for the unmarried, even after adjusting for variations in intimacy within the marriage (1982). Berkowitz and Perkins, in a study of stress among farm women, used self-report measures to assess stress symptoms, husband support, farm and home task loads, and perceived role conflict between home and farm responsibilities (1984). They found that although actual work loads did not predict stress, low husband support did. Moreover, role conflict was associated not with actual home or farm task loads, but with low husband support. They concluded that "the degree of involvement in different roles and the potential conflicts between them may not be as important as the 'psychological climate' in which role duties are performed" (p. 164).

Looking specifically at stress associated with the transition to parenthood, Crnic et al. found that emotional support from the spouse (but not from friends) had much to do with positive postpartum adjustment (1983, 1984). Although this suggests that spouse support can moderate the effects of stress, they noted that the long-term predictability of support and stress measures for maternal attitudes was low; concurrent relationships among spouse support, stress, general life satisfaction, and satisfaction with parenting were strong, but these relationships were not stable over time, due to changing life circumstances. Cutrona also examined social support, stress, and depression among middle-class, first-time mothers during pregnancy, at two weeks, eight weeks, and one year postpartum (1984). She found that social support appeared to alleviate stress, particularly at the eight-week assessment; but this was not true at the highest levels of stress, suggesting that support may ease depression only up to a certain level of perceived stress. Paykel, Emms, Fletcher and Rassaby found that life stress and marital discord together predicted postpartum depression, such that only women with both high stress and discorded marriages became depressed (1980).

The effects of spouse support on parental sensitivity to infant cues in the early postpartum months are less clear. Crnic et al. found that intimate support correlated with affect ratings of mothers' responses to their infant's cues (1983, 1984). On the other hand, neither social support variables nor stress were related to a mother's ability to foster socio-emotional or cognitive growth.

Again, these studies all used stable, intact, middle-class families, and the findings may not be applicable to other families. Moreover, it is not clear how *spouse support* was defined in these studies—was this actual help with caring for the infant or with household tasks? Or was it the degree of emotional intimacy and overall marital satisfaction? Belsky, Gilstrap and Rovine found that while father-infant interaction was positively related to husband-wife interactions, there was little relation between mother-infant and spousal interaction (1984). Goth-Owens et al. also found consistent relationships between marital satisfaction scores and parenting behaviors for fathers but not for mothers (1982). They suggest that "the determinants of the behavior of mothers and fathers may differ. In the absence of specific socialization into a caregiving role, fathers' caregiving style may become organized and develop primarily in the context of their relationship with their spouses" (p. 187).

Personal Factors

While spouse support is one of the most frequently studied variables in relation to perceived stress, other factors also play a mediating role. Hetherington points to personal resources such as finances, educational level, and overall physical health; individual variables such as temperament, coping styles, skills, intelligence, self-esteem, attitudes, age, sex, and past experience; and family resources such as cohesion, adaptability, communication, and problem-solving skills (1984). Elman and Gilbert, in a study of coping strategies in married professional women with children, found that personal resources such as self-esteem and career engagement, as well as spouse and social support, were associated with lower role conflict and greater coping effectiveness (1984). Kazak and Linney examined life satisfaction in a sample of divorced, middle-income working mothers; they found that a perception of competence as a self-supporter was the strongest predictor of life satisfaction, indicating the importance of self-esteem variables (1983). Myers-Walls studied coping strategies in the balancing of multiple role responsibilities among married, middle-class women at two months postpartum (1984). Successful coping during this time period was related not only to greater marital satisfaction and harmony, but also to the use of identifiable coping strategies which allowed fewer changes in living patterns and personal behavior following the birth of the first child, as well as more positive reactions to the changes that did occur.

The importance of attitude variables is further demonstrated in research by Hock and her colleagues. They found that working mothers tended to perceive less infant distress at separation and were less apprehensive about substitute caregivers than nonemployed mothers (Hock 1978; Hock et al. 1980). On the other hand, Hock found that working mothers who believed that only they could properly care for their infants, also tended to have infants who exhibited more frequent and intense negative reunion behavior (1980). Hock suggested that the mother's *satisfaction* with her work status may have a greater effect on the quality of the mother-infant relationship than does her work status itself.

Pilstrang (1984) further implicates maternal attitudes in the effects of work status on perceived stress. She found few overall differences between working and nonworking mothers in their experiences of new motherhood, but significant relationships between prenatal work involvement and postpartum work status (1984). Women who were highly involved with their work and who returned to work shortly after giving birth tended to have more positive experiences of motherhood than those women who had been highly involved with their work, but chose to stay home out of a belief that this was best for their infants. Among women who were less involved with their work, those who did not work following the birth of their infants reported greater satisfaction with motherhood than those who returned to work early for financial reasons. She concluded that leaving work may be construed as a loss or a gain, and that women who sense it as a loss may have less positive experiences of motherhood. This confirms Hock's suggestion that the degree of congruence between postpartum work status, maternal career salience, and beliefs about infant needs may affect maternal satisfaction and the perceived stressfulness of combining work and parenting responsibilities.

Hock, Gnezda, and McBride used self-report measures to assess attitudes toward employment and motherhood both in the maternity ward and at three months postpartum in a sample of 317 first-time mothers of healthy infants (1984). All mothers were from middle-class, intact homes. Of these women, 88% had been employed during pregnancy, and 66% indicated at the time of parturition that they would like to return to work within a year, with the mean projected reentry time being twelve weeks postpartum. When assessed in the maternity ward, a majority of these women scored high on the Exclusive Maternal Care Scale (59% felt that only they could best meet their children's needs); 77% agreed that motherhood was the major way of fulfillment in a woman's life, and 69% expressed a preference for staying home over working full-time. Although these findings were less typical of older, more educated women in the sample, Hock et al. suggested that "traditional attitudes toward motherhood continue to be well-rooted in our society" (p. 429). The high percentage of mothers who felt that only they could best meet their infant's needs, and who would prefer to stay at home, conflicts with the fact that 66% of them intended to reenter the work force before their infants were one-year old. These findings suggest a

discrepancy between beliefs about infant needs and labor force participation among many women.

There is also one further note on the methodological problems in the
study of stress and coping. Dohrenwend et al. pointed out that most
measures of stress confound aspects of environmentally-induced life
stress with symptoms of psychological distress and disorder (1984). It is
therefore difficult to determine whether the person or the situation is
primarily responsible for the degree of perceived stress. Research by
Hock serves to explain this insight in terms of our topic. Hock found
that a personality variable she called *susceptibility to stress*—characterized
by poor self-confidence, depression, and poor performance in stressful
conditions—was negatively related to adaptive attitudes and feelings of
competence in perceiving and meeting infant needs (1980). Morgan and
Hock studied psychosocial variables and the career patterns of women
with young children; they concluded that "women who report becoming
disorganized under stress may be more likely to avoid attempts to combine work and family life" (1984, p. 384). In other words, the direction
of causality in relationships obtained between perceived stress and maternal attitudes is not clear. It may be that higher levels of stress pre-
dispose a mother to feel more dissatisfied with parenting; or it may be
that a mother who feels unsure of her mothering abilities is more susceptible to the hassles of daily life; a third possibility is that some other
variable gives rise to both a greater susceptibility to stress and lower
perceived competence in meeting infant needs.

In light of the present research, it is possible to draw three tentative
conclusions: (1) The transition to parenthood is a major life event which
many people may find stressful. (2) Higher levels of perceived stress
appear to be associated with lower levels of caretaker sensitivity and
responsiveness to infant cues. (3) Relative levels of perceived stress in
managing both work and parenting responsibilities during the early
postpartum months tend to vary with the presence or absence of a variety
of individual and situational resources. In addition to factors such as
spouse support, the mother's level of work involvement, and beliefs
about infant's needs, several others deserve mention: socioeconomic status, educational level, overall physical health, intelligence, age, self-esteem, styles of coping, problem-solving skills, previous experiences,
number of other children, and the infant's own temperament and capacities (Hetherington 1984). Any of these factors can affect an individual's ability to combine the demands of work and parenting.

WORK, PARENTING, AND STRESS: VULNERABILITY FACTORS

There are three groups of families that may be especially vulnerable to
stress during the early months of an infant's life: single-parent families,

low-income families, and families in which the mother is experiencing a serious postpartum depression.

Weinraub and Wolf noted that many studies of single parenting confound the effects of parental status with the socioemotional effects of divorce, separation, or death, and with the material effects which frequently accompany loss of income and change in living arrangements (1983). In an attempt to separate these factors, the investigators studied a group of working mothers of preschool children who had been single for at least two years and matched them on several demographic variables with a sample of married working mothers. They were particularly interested in whether or not mothers raising their children alone face more life stress, have more difficulty coping, and have fewer social supports than married mothers.

Some of the findings were more surprising than others. As might be expected, the married mothers tended to report less conflict between meeting their own needs for emotional support and meeting the needs of their children. In single-parent families, the mother's increased social contacts correlated with reduced maternal nurturance and lower maternal control. The authors also found that the single parents worked longer hours, faced more potentially stressful life changes, and tended to be more socially isolated. Aside from these predictable variances and except in the area of household chores, single parents did not differ from married mothers in how difficult they found coping with the demands of their lives. Further, no differences in parent-child interactions were found between the two groups of women.

A more significant factor is given in the authors' conclusion that "with adequate financial resources, and with maturity, vocational competence, and personal resourcefulness, single parents may be as successful" as married mothers in combining work and parenting (p. 1309).

Colletta (1983b) also interviewed divorced and married mothers at both middle- and lower-income levels to determine how family stress varied with family structure. She concluded that income rather than marital status was the key factor in family stress, with low-income divorced mothers reporting the highest levels of stress. Crnic et al. (1984) similarly found that mothers who were young, unmarried and receiving some form of public assistance were more likely to report greater stress and less social support.

It appears that the relationships among work, single parenting and stress are not simple, but once again depend on a variety of individual and situational resources and variables. Key among these variables may be socioeconomic status: the single, low-income mother is less likely to possess financial, personal and social resources which would serve as buffers against stress. The middle-income single parent, however, may also be more vulnerable to stress than married parents, particularly if the transition to parenthood is associated with other life stressors. For some of these women, a curtailed work schedule without financial loss may significantly reduce the stressfulness of this time period, thus enabling them to provide the infant with more sensitive and responsive caregiving. For others, the sense of competence, self-esteem and social support gained through a job they value may mitigate against a complete or extended absence from the work force; many of these women may find part-time work most beneficial. For all single parents who maintain some presence in the work force, adequate and affordable daycare arrangements close to home or work may be particularly important in reducing stress.

Finally, research indicates that the period of time surrounding pregnancy and childbirth places many women at increased risk for depression. O'Hara, Neunaber and Zekoski (1984) looked at predictor variables for postpartum depression among ninety-nine married, middle-class women who were followed from their second trimester until nine weeks postpartum. The authors found that the level of depression during pregnancy and scores on several scales of stressful life events proved the strongest predictors of depressive symptomatology during the postpartum period. They concluded that the postpartum period does not represent a time of significantly greater risk for depression than does pregnancy; however, they reported a higher rate of diagnosed major depressions (RDC) in this sample than normally obtained among non-puerperal women (9% prepartum and 12% postpartum, as compared to roughly 6% among women aged eighteen to twenty-four years).

Colletta (1983a) studied young mothers (aged fifteen to nineteen years) and found that depression varied with marital status, education, and maternal age, and that was related to hostile, indifferent, and rejecting patterns of mother-infant interaction. Depressed mothers had lower levels of marital adjustment and more extensive postpartum concerns. Paykel et al. also found an interaction between life stress and marital discord as predictors of postpartum depression (1980).

Livingood, Daen and Smith studied the effects of depression on mother-infant interactions and found that depressed mothers provided lower levels of unconditional positive regard and gazed less at their infants while holding them (1983). Cohn and Tronick investigated the reactions of three-month-old infants to simulated maternal depression (1983). Infants whose mothers simulated depression showed greater disorganization in their behavior than infants in the normal condition, who cycled between monitoring of mothers, brief positive "flashes," and play. This suggests that the depressed mother may be unable to provide the dyadic engagement thought to be essential to the mutual regulation of stimuli in early mother-infant interactions.

Together, these findings indicate that: (1) depression may seriously interfere with mother's ability to provide sensitive and responsive caregiving for her newborn infant; and (2) the most significant predictor of postpartum depression appears to be level of depression during pregnancy. This, in turn, relates to a variety of factors, including stressful life events, marital status and discord, and personality variables such as previous depression history and dysfunctional self-control attitudes.

In summary, it is clear that individual and situational resources and variables can mediate the impact of potentially stressful life events. Further, there is a relationship between perceived stress and attitudes toward and satisfaction with parenting. These variables, in turn, relate to caregiver sensitivity and responsiveness to infant cues. Although the direction of causality among these variables is uncertain, it seems likely that some mothers may find combining work with parenting in the early postpartum months more stressful and difficult than other mothers.

In particular, women with low work involvement and strong beliefs about the importance of exclusive maternal care may find that working during this period increases their level of perceived stress. Conversely, women with high work involvement who feel that they must stay at home to care for their infants may be more likely to find the early postpartum months stressful than those who return to work early. Other groups of parents who may find this period of time particularly stressful include: single mothers, low-income women, women who are experiencing a postpartum depression, and parents of premature, ill, or disabled infants. Since perceived stress may influence quality of caregiving more than does the actual number of demands, the best option for parents is one that reduces overall stress for each individual family. A policy for infant care leave would provide an important option which would reduce overall stress and thus promote the well-being of a large number of families.

REFERENCES

Ainsworth, M., Blehar, M., Waters, E., and Wall, S. 1978. *Patterns of Attachment: A Psychological Study of the Strange Situation*. Hillsdale, New Jersey: Erlbaum.

Ainsworth, M., and Wittig, B. 1969. Attachment and exploratory behavior of one year olds in a strange situation. B. M. Foss, ed. *Determinants of Infant Behavior*, vol. 4. New York: Methuen.

Alpert, J., Richardson, M., and Fodaski, L. 1983. Onset of parenting and stressful events. *Journal of Primary Prevention* 3(3):149–59.

Arend, R., Gove, F., and Sroufe, L. A. 1979. Continuity of individual adaptation from infancy. *Child Development* 50:950–59.

Barnett, R. 1982. Multiple roles and well-being: A study of mothers of preschool age children. *Psychology of Women Quarterly* 7(2):175–78.

Baruch, G., and Barnett, R. 1986. Role quality, multiple role involvement, and psychological well-being in midlife women. *Journal of Personality and Social Psychology*, 51:578–85.

Bell, S., and Ainsworth, M. 1972. Infant crying and maternal responsiveness. *Child Development* 43:1171–90.

Belsky, J., and Rovine, M. 1984. Social-network contact, family support, and the transition to parenthood. *Journal of Marriage and the Family* 46:455–62.

Belsky, J., Gilstrap, R., and Rovine, M. 1984. The Pennsylvania infant and family development project, I: Stability and change in mother-infant and father-infant interaction in a family setting at one, three, and nine months. *Child Development* 55:692–705.

Belsky, J., Rovine, M., and Taylor, D. 1984. The Pennsylvania infant and family development project III: The origins of individual differences in infant-mother attachment: Maternal and infant contributions. *Child Development* 55:718–28.

Berkowitz, A., and Perkins, H. 1984. Stress among farm women: Work and family as interacting systems. *Journal of Marriage and the Family* 46:161–66.

Bowlby, J. 1969. *Attachment and Loss, 1*. New York: Basic Books.

Brazelton, T. B., Koslowski, B., and Main, M. 1974. The origins of reciprocity: The early mother-infant interaction. M. Lewis and L. Rosenblum, eds. *The Effect of the Infant on Its Caregiver*. New York: John Wiley & Sons.

Brookhart, J., and Hock, E. 1976. The effects of experimental contexts and experiential background on infants' behavior toward their mothers and a stranger. *Child Development* 47:333–40.

Campbell, S. 1979. Mother-infant interaction as a function of maternal ratings of temperament. *Child Psychiatry and Human Development* 10(2):67–76.

Chang, P. N., Thompson, T., and Fisch, R. 1982. Factors affecting attachment between infants and mothers separated at birth. *Journal of Developmental and Behavioral Pediatrics* 3(2):96–98.

Cohn, J., and Tronick, E. 1983. Three-month old infants' reaction to simulated maternal depression. *Child Development* 54:185–93.

Colletta, N. 1983a. The situation of divorced mothers and their children. *Journal of Divorce* 6(3):19–31.

Colletta, N. 1983b. A study of young mothers. *Journal of Genetic Psychology* 142(2):301–10.

Crnic, K., Greenberg, M., Ragozin, A., Robinson, N., and Basham, R. 1983. Effects of stress and social support on mothers and premature and full-term infants. *Child Development* 54:209–17.

Crnic, K., Greenberg, M., Robinson, N., and Ragozin, A. 1984. Maternal stress and social support: Effects on the mother-infant relationship from birth to eighteen months. *American Journal of Orthopsychiatry* 54(2):224–35.

Crockenberg, S. 1981. Infant irritability, mother responsiveness, and social support influences on the security of infant-mother attachment. *Child Development* 52:857–65.

Cutrona, C. 1984. Social support and stress in the transition to parenthood. *Journal of Abnormal Psychology* 93(4):378–90.

Dohrenwend, B. S., Krasnoff, L., Askenasy, A., and Dohrenwend, B. P. 1978.

Exemplification of a method for scaling life events: The PERI life events scale. *Journal of Health and Social Behavior* 19:205–29.

Dohrenwend, B. S., Dohrenwend, B. P., Dodson, M., and Shrout, P. 1984. Symptoms, hassles, social supports, and life events: Problem of confounded measures. *Journal of Abnormal Psychology* 93(2):222–30.

Dreyfus-Brisac, C. 1974. Organization of sleep in prematures: Implications for caregiving. M. Lewis and L. Rosenblum, eds. *The Effect of the Infant on Its Caregiver*. New York: John Wiley & Sons.

Egeland, B., and Sroufe, L. A. 1981. Attachment and early maltreatment. *Child Development* 52:44–52.

Egeland, B., and Farber, E. 1984. Infant-mother attachment: Factors related to its development and changes over time. *Child Development* 55:753–71.

Elman, M., and Gilbert, L. 1984. Coping strategies for role conflict in married professional women with children. *Family Relations* 33:317–27.

Fox, N., Kagan, J., and Weiskopf, S. 1979. The growth of memory during infancy. *Genetic Psychology Monographs* 99(1):91–130.

Gamble, T., and Zigler, E. 1986. Effects of infant day care: Another look at the evidence. *American Journal of Orthopsychiatry* 56:26–42.

Goth-Owens, T., et al. 1982. Marital satisfaction, parenting satisfaction, and parenting behavior in early infancy. *Infant Mental Health Journal* 3(3):187–98.

Gunnar, M. (In press.) Human developmental psychoneuroendocrinology: A review of research on neuroendocrine responses to challenge and threat in infancy and childhood. To appear in M. Lamb, A. L. Brown, and B. Rogoff eds., *Advances in Developmental Psychology*, vol. 4. Hillsdale, New Jersey: Earlbaum.

Hetherington, E. M. 1984. Stress and coping in children and families. A. B. Doyle, D. Gold, and D. Moskowitz, eds. *Children in Families under Stress. New Directions for Child Development*, no. 24. San Francisco: Jossey-Bass.

Hock, E. 1978. Working and nonworking mothers with infants: Perceptions of their careers, their infants' needs, and satisfaction with mothering. *Developmental Psychology* 14(1):37–43.

Hock, E. 1980. Working and nonworking mothers and their infants: A comparative study of maternal caregiving characteristics and infant social behavior. *Merrill-Palmer Quarterly* 26(2):79–101.

Hock, E., Christman, I. K., and Hock, M. 1980. Factors associated with decisions about return to work in mothers of infants. *Developmental Psychology* 16(5):535–36.

Hock, E., Gnezda, M. T., and McBride, S. 1984. Mothers of Infants: Attitudes toward employment and motherhood following birth of the first child. *Journal of Marriage and the Family* 46:425–31.

Ivancevich, J., and Matteson, M. 1982. Occupational stress, satisfaction, physical well-being, and coping: A study of homemakers. *Psychological Reports* 50:995–1005.

Jacobson, J., and Wille, D. 1984. Influence of attachment and separation experience on separation distress at 18 months. *Developmental Psychology* 20(3):477–84.

Jiminez, M., and Newton, N. 1982. Job orientation and adjustment to pregnancy and early motherhood. *Birth: Issues in Perinatal Care & Education* 9(3):157–63.

Kagan, J. 1983. Stress and coping in early development. N. Garmezy and M. Rutter, eds. *Stress, Coping, and Development in Children*. New York: McGraw-Hill.

Kagan, J., and Hamburg, M. 1981. The enhancement of memory in the first year. *Journal of Genetic Psychology* 138(1):3–14.

Kagan, J., Kearsley, R., and Zelazo, P. 1977. The effects of infant day care on psychological development. *Evaluation Quarterly* 1(1):109–42.

Kazak, A., and Linney, J. 1983. Stress, coping, and life change in the single-parent family. *American Journal of Community Psychology* 11(2):207–20.

Kessler, R., and Essex, M. 1982. Marital status and depression: The importance of coping resources. *Social Forces* 61(2):484–507.

Klaus, M., and Kennell, J. 1976. *Maternal-infant bonding*. St. Louis: C. V. Mosby.

Lamb, M. 1983. Early mother-neonate contact and the mother-child relationship. *Journal of Child Psychology and Psychiatry and Allied Disciplines* 24(3):487–94.

Lamb, M., Thompson, R., Gardner, W., Charnov, E., and Estes, D. 1984. Security of infantile attachment as assessed in the "strange situation": Its study and biological interpretation. *The Behavioral and Brain Sciences* 7:127–71.

Lazarus, R., and Folkman, S. 1984. *Stress, Appraisal, and Coping*. New York: Springer Publishing.

Leifer, A., Leiderman, P. H., Barnett, C., and Williams, J. 1972. Effects of mother-infant separation on maternal attachment behavior. *Child Development* 43:1203–18.

Leiderman, P. H. 1983. Social ecology and childbirth: The newborn nursery as environmental stressor. N. Garmezy and M. Rutter, eds. *Stress, Coping, and Development in Children*. New York: McGraw-Hill.

Lester, B. (In press.) A biosocial model of infant crying. To appear in L. Lipsett, ed., *Advances in Infant Behavior and Development*.

Levine, S. 1983. A psycho-biological approach to the ontogeny of coping. N. Garmezy and M. Rutter, eds. *Stress, Coping, and Development in Children*. New York: McGraw-Hill.

Livingood, A., Daen, P., and Smith, B. 1983. The depressed mother as a source of stimulation for her infant. *Journal of Clinical Psychology* 39(3):369–75.

Londerville, S., and Main, M. 1981. Security of attachment, compliance, and maternal training methods in the second year of life. *Developmental Psychology* 17(3):289–99.

Matas, L., Arend, R., and Sroufe, L. A. 1978. Continuity of adaptation in the second year: The relationship between quality of attachment & later competence. *Child Development* 49:547–56.

Morgan, K., and Hock, E. 1984. A longitudinal study of psychosocial variables affecting the career patterns of women with young children. *Journal of Marriage and the Family* 46:383–90.

Myers-Walls, J. 1984. Balancing multiple role responsibilities during the transition to parenthood. *Family Relations* 33:267–71.

Nover, A., Shore, M., Timberlake, E., and Greenspan, S. 1984. The relationship of maternal perception and maternal behavior: A study of normal mothers and their infants. *American Journal of Orthopsychiatry* 54:210–23.

O'Hara, M., Neunaber, D., and Zekoski, E. 1984. Prospective study of postpartum depression: Prevalence, course, and predictive factors. *Journal of Abnormal Psychology* 93(2):158–71.

Osofsky, J. 1976. Neonatal characteristics and mother-infant interaction in two observational situations. *Child Development* 47:1138–47.

Owen, M., Easterbrooks, N.A., Chase-Lansdale, L., Goldberg, W. 1984. The relation between maternal employment status and the stability of attachments to mother and to father. *Child Development* 55:1894–1901.

Pastor, D. 1981. The quality of mother-infant attachment and its relationship to toddler's initial sociability with peers. *Developmental Psychology* 17(3):326–35.

Paykel, E., Emms, E., Fletcher, J., and Rassaby, E. 1980. Life events and social support in puerperal depression. *British Journal of Psychiatry* 136:339–46.

Penman, R., Meares, R., Baker, K., and Milgrom-Friedman, J. 1983. Synchrony in mother-infant interaction: A possible neurophysiological base. *British Journal of Medical Psychology* 56(1)1–7.

Pistrang, N. 1984. Women's work involvement and experience of new motherhood. *Journal of Marriage and the Family* 46:433–47.

Ragozin, A. 1980. Attachment behavior of day-care children: Naturalistic and laboratory observations. *Child Development* 51:409–15.

Řode, S., Chang, P. N., Fisch, R., and Sroufe, L. A. 1981. Attachment patterns of infants separated at birth. *Developmental Psychology* 17(2):188–91.

Rossi, A. 1968. Transition to parenthood. *Journal of Marriage and the Family* 30:26–39.

Rutter, M. 1982. Epidemiological-longitudinal approaches to the study of development. W. A. Collins, ed. *The Concept of Development: Minnesota Symposia on Child Psychology*, vol. 15. Hillsdale, New Jersey: Erlbaum.

Rutter, M. 1983. Stress, coping, and development: Some issues and some questions. N. Garmezy and M. Rutter, eds. *Stress, Coping, and Development in Children*. New York: McGraw-Hill.

Schubert, J., Bradley-Johnson, S., and Nuttal, J. 1980. Mother-infant communication and maternal employment. *Child Development* 54:1073–78.

Schwartz, P. 1983. Length of day-care attendance and attachment behavior in eighteen-month-old infants. *Child Development* 54:1073–78.

Seashore, M., Leifer, A., Barnett, C., and Leiderman, P. H. 1973. The effects of denial of mother-infant interaction on maternal self-confidence. *Journal of Personality and Social Psychology* 26:369–78.

Sorce, J., and Emde, R. 1981. Mother's presence is not enough: Effect of emotional availability on infant exploration. *Developmental Psychology* 17(6):737:45.

Sostek, A., Scanlon, J., and Abramson, D. 1982. Postpartum contact and maternal confidence and anxiety: A confirmation of short-term effects. *Infant Behavior and Development* 5(4):323–29.

Stayton, D., and Ainsworth, M. 1973. Individual differences in infant responses to brief, everyday separations as related to other infant and maternal behaviors. *Developmental Psychology* 9(2):226–35.

Stengel, T. 1982. Infant behavior, maternal psychological reaction, and mother-infant interactional issues associated with the crises of prematurity: A selected review of the literature. *Physical and Occupational Therapy in Pediatrics* 2(2–3):3–24.

Stern, D. 1974. Mother and infant at play: The dyadic interaction involving facial, vocal, and gaze behaviors. M. Lewis and L. Rosenblum, eds. *The Effect of the Infant on Its Caregiver*. New York: John Wiley & Sons.

Thoman, E., Acebo, C., and Becker, P. 1983. Infant crying and stability in the mother-infant relationship: A systems analysis. *Child Development* 54:653–59.

Thompson, R., Lamb, M., and Estes, D. 1982. Stability of infant-mother attachment and its relationship to changing life circumstances in an unselected middle-class sample. *Child Development* 53:144–48.

Vaughn, B., Egeland, B., Sroufe, L. A., and Waters, E. 1979. Individual differences in infant-mother attachment at 12 and 18 months: Stability and change in families under stress. *Child Development* 50:971–75.

Vaughn, B., Gove, F., Egeland, B. 1980. The relationship between out-of-home care and the quality of infant-mother attachment in an economically disadvantaged population. *Child Development* 51:1203–14.

Verbrugge, L. 1983. Multiple roles and physical health of women and men. *Journal of Health and Social Behavior* 24(1):16–30.

Waters, E., Wippman, J., and Sroufe, L. A. 1979. Attachment, positive affect, and competence in the peer group: Two studies in construct validation. *Child Development* 50:821–29.

Waters, E., Vaughn, B., and Egeland, B. 1980. Individual differences in infant-mother attachment relationships at age one: Antecedents in neonatal behavior in an urban, economically disadvantaged sample. *Child Development* 51:208–16.

Weinraub, M., and Wolf, B. 1983. Effects of stress and social supports on mother-child relationships in single- and two-parent families. *Child Development* 54:1297–1311.

FIVE

Effects of Infant Day Care:
Another Look at the Evidence

THOMAS J. GAMBLE
AND EDWARD ZIGLER

During the past three decades, the most striking demographic change in our society has been the increased number of women working outside the home. A majority of mothers with school-age children are now in our nation's work force, and more are expected to enter in the future. Current estimates indicate that, by 1990, 75% of all American mothers will work (Urban Institute 1982). A major consequence of this development is that more and more children are being placed into various types of day care, and, given our relatively long experience with school and preschool nurseries, the effects of out-of-home care for children above the age of three years are not particularly worrisome.

The last decade or so, however, has witnessed a phenomenon that can only be termed a new social form. Infants as young as three weeks of age are now being placed into day care as a result of recent economic and social changes. Infant day care is currently the fastest growing type of supplemental care in our nation (Jones and Prescott 1982). Yet the very newness of this trend means that little is known about the effects of out-of-home care on the short- and long-term development of the very young. That both parents and large numbers of professionals are concerned about this issue is reflected in a growing number of empirical and theoretical papers. Some prominent workers have highlighted the potentially damaging effects of infant day care, while equally prominent workers have asserted that such care is essentially benign (Caldwell 1970;

*This article was originally published in the *American Journal of Orthopsychiatry* 56(1): January 1986, and it is reprinted by permission.

Kagan et al. 1978; Ricciuti 1976; Rutter 1981). This argument, which has become rather heated, would appear to be resolvable through empirical efforts.

Several reviews have now assessed studies of the effects of infant day care (Belsky and Steinberg 1982; Belsky et al. 1982; Kagan et al. 1978; Rutter 1981). A common conclusion is that there are no strikingly negative psychological consequences accruing to infants who experience regular nonparental care. Nonetheless much of the research conducted to date is limited in an important way: the majority of studies have been conducted on stable middle-class families using high-quality centers (Belsky and Steinberg 1978; Martin 1981; Ruopp and Travers 1982; Rutter 1981). Since few parents have access to these settings, and since family stability cannot be assumed, the conclusion that infant day care has few negative consequences cannot be safely generalized to the situations that most infants really experience.

Our purpose here is to analyze the evidence concerning the effects of infant day care on children's socioemotional development. We will pay close attention to methodology, since this is often a problem in research with infants, and since faulty methodology can cast doubt on the most definitive findings. We will also attempt to place the issue within the broader theoretical context of the effects of attachment and early experience on later social development. Another dimension is added by considering how family situations and the child's gender mediate the putative effects of infant day care.

EARLY EXPERIENCE AND HUMAN DEVELOPMENT

Over the past three decades there has been a major change in our understanding of the human infant (Kagan 1982; Kessen et al. 1970). Once viewed as passive and inactive, the infant is now seen as a complex, capable organism with an active role in its own development. In spite of this new concept of the baby, there are still two antithetical views of the nature of change in the infant's behavior, as well as two opposing models of how the environment delivers its impact.

Nature vs. Nurture

Consonant with the predeterministic and maturational views of old, one school of thought views the infant as biologically canalized, responding dynamically to environmental events in an effort to remain on a pre-established developmental trajectory. This view has been adopted by many developmental psychologists (Kagan 1982; Kagan and Klein 1973; Kessen et al. 1970), but its earliest and fullest treatment is found in the work of the biologist, C. H. Waddington (1962;1971). Of interest for the effects of infant day care is how theorists in this camp would interpret negative environmental events, such as a lack of sensory or social stimulation. They might argue that since the child has a biological blueprint that determines development, the child is already buffered against negative encounters and should display considerable resiliency to these situations. Indeed, the concepts of resilience and invulnerability to negative experiences have become popular in current literature (Clarke and Clarke 1976; Kagan and Klein 1982; Werner and Smith 1982).

In a quite different school of thought, the infant is viewed as making substantial use of the caretaking environment to construct novel schemas which will guide future social and cognitive interactions. This approach emphasizes the delicacy and complexity of early interactions and their importance to later development (Brazelton et al. 1974; Brunner 1977; Stern 1974). In this model, negative experiences are viewed with more alarm, on the grounds that any deprivation is potentially damaging to the process of development.

These two views of the nature of the developing child represent the extremes of current developmental thought, of course. These brief summaries can do little more than present caricatures of the more subtle views underlying these theories. However, there is a captivating simplicity attending these descriptions which, if left unexamined, could all too easily lead to premature conclusions about the likely effects of variations in the early caretaking environment.

To put these either/or positions in perspective, we begin with a statement by Ann Clarke, who is a highly visible advocate of the neomaturational viewpoint: "To argue that anything as complex as human behavior and experience must have multifactoral origins demanding a systems analysis is today a statement of the obvious" (1984, p. 33). Although Clarke did not elaborate a scheme for the proposed systems analysis, such an approach might begin with conceptualizing the child as a system of subsystems that are intricately coevolved and that are constantly in a state of interaction with each other. For example, the child's cognitive and personality subsystems may develop at different rates in different fashions, but they operate synergistically to determine performance.

One of our major theses is that the subsystems involved in human development are differentially sensitive to environmental variation (Zigler 1978; Zigler and Butterfield 1968; Zigler and Triclett 1978). Some may be highly sensitive to environmental influences; others may be relatively impervious to them. Such subsystems will be referred to as *robust* or *resilient*. The point is that the demonstration of robustness in one subsystem cannot automatically be generalized to other important subsystems in development.

The potential value of a more differentiated view of development becomes clear when one notes how much effort has been expended in investigating only one of many integral subsystems, namely that of cognition. Although there are those who argue otherwise, there is strong evidence supporting the consensus that intelligence is more influenced by internal than external factors. Neomaturationists, then, have made their case for the relative unimportance of early experience in general by concentrating on a subsystem that natural selection has buffered against the effects of environmental variations (Jensen 1983; Kagan and Klein 1973; Scarr-Salaptek 1976).

Even though the subsystem underlying intellectual development is probably a poor candidate for the demonstration of sensitivity to environmental variation, other subsystems may well be highly influenced by environmental events, including those that subsume social interaction, motivation, and personality development. Evidence for the greater openness of these subsystems to environmental influences is found in the lower ratios for heredity that are reported for socioemotional as opposed to intellectual variables (Scarr and Kidd 1983). So, neither the maturationists nor the environmentalists are either all right or all wrong.

Models of Environmental Impact

To understand how environmental variation influences different subsystems, it is helpful to draw upon two models of environmental impact. In the threshold model, environments that fall below a minimum standard can weaken the potential development of the biologically-determined trait in question, but variations above this threshold have little discernible effect. To illustrate the point, a baby comes equipped with a goal for adult height. Given minimal nutrition and health requirements, this height will be realized. An "enriched" diet will not alter this stature, but prolonged nutritional deficits will cause the person to fall short of the innate goal. There is considerable evidence that the threshold model is also valid for intellectual development (Clarke 1984; Jensen 1978; Zigler et al. 1984), because a deplorable environment can thwart a child from attaining his or her full intellectual potential, but above this threshold variations in environment have little influence. Given our current state of knowledge, however, it would be inappropriate to apply the threshold model to other subsystems of behavior, which may be more sensitive to relatively small variations in the environment.

Traits in the socioemotional domain are perhaps better described by an additive model, in which chances for developmental damage increase as a function of the number and magnitude of negative environmental encounters. For example, we hypothesize that a socially impoverished day care center poses some risk to an infant's social subsystem and that the risk for damage increases if the child who experiences poor infant day care also comes from a highly stressed home environment, or one without a father, to suggest but two additional factors. We feel that the weight of the evidence gathered on the effects of infant day care supports such a model. In reviewing this evidence, we will focus on two subsystems of socioemotional development: parent-infant attachment and social relations with peers and unfamiliar adults.

EFFECTS OF INFANT DAY CARE ON PARENT-CHILD ATTACHMENT

Two fundamental questions regarding the effects of out-of-home care on parent-infant attachment have been posed by Rutter (1981). The first is whether such care can redirect primary attachment from the parent to the substitute caregiver. Current evidence indicates that the formation of a primary attachment to one's parents is a robust phenomenon. The possibility that substitute or supplementary care in infancy can prevent the formation of primary attachments to parents, or cause them to be directed elsewhere, seems small indeed (Fox 1977; Kagan et al. 1978; Konner 1982; Rutter 1981). Konner, in fact, called the development of parental attachment a putative universal of the second half of the first year of life (Konner 1982). It takes place under the most varied childrearing conditions: among the Kung, whose parenting involves twenty-four-hour physical contact between mother and infant in a dense social context; among infants of Israeli kibbutzim, where mother-infant contact occurs only in the afternoons and on weekends; and across diverse childrearing practices in the U.S. (Kagan, et al. 1978).

The second issue identified by Rutter has to do with individual differences in the quality of attachment. In order to address this question, we must be more specific about how attachment behavior can be measured. The only validated and reliable instrument for the assessment of parent-infant attachment available is the Strange Situation (Ainsworth 1982; Ainsworth et al. 1978). The technique is based upon a series of situations involving the infant, one parent, and a stranger. Separations from and reunions with the parent, in the presence and absence of the stranger, are staged in such a way that stress on the part of the infant is increased. The infant's conduct during the reunion episodes is scored in a standardized fashion.

From their investigations, Ainsworth and her colleagues identified three patterns of attachment (1978). *Secure* attachments (type *B*) are characterized by proximity and contact-seeking during the reunion episode, coupled with independent play while the parent is in the room. *Anxious avoidant* attachments (type *A*) describe infants who avoid the parent during reunion and who have conflict during free play. *Anxious ambivalent* children (type *C*) mix anger and resistance to the parent during reunion with proximity and contact seeking. They seek contact, but seem unable to be comforted by it.

As with most attempts to gauge infant behavior, the Strange Situation is far from perfect as an assessment device, but, the instrument has now been subjected to searching analysis and its usefulness has not been seriously undermined (Lamb et al., in press.). Since it appears to be the best measure available, we have limited our review of infant day care and parent-child attachment to those studies that have used the Strange Situation.

Unfortunately, not all studies have used the Strange Situation in an appropriate fashion. As has been pointed out by Schwartz (1983), several investigators (Blehar 1974; Moskowitz et al. 1977; Portnoy and Simmons 1977; Portnoy and Simmons 1978; Roopnairene and Lamb 1979) have used the instrument to assess attachment in children three years of age and older. There is, however, no reason to believe that the situations it poses can distinguish variations in attachment for children so far past infancy. Ainsworth herself suggested that the instrument is inappropriate for children above the age of twenty months (1982). Hence, the fact that all of these studies, with the exception of Blehar (1974), report no effect of out-of-home care on quality of attachment must be interpreted critically. In order to gain a legitimate sense of the effects of infant group care on attachment, we must look to those studies that made appropriate use of the assessment device.

Studies Showing No Effect

Blanchard and Main assessed attachment in twenty-one children between twelve and twenty-one months of age (1979). These middle-class children had been in a high quality day-care center for a substantial length of time (on the average of twelve months). They found that quality of attachment was not affected by hours per week in day care; further, avoidance at reunions with mother was negatively correlated with number of months in care to a significant degree. They concluded that the children who had been in day care longer had had time to make positive socioemotional adjustments to regular maternal absence. Another possibility, which Blanchard and Main may not have entertained, is that length of time in day care is positively associated with age, and that age is negatively associated with the sensitivity of the Strange Situation as a guide to quality of attachment.

Brookhart and Hock also studied children of an appropriate age, ten-to twelve-months old, including eighteen home-reared and fifteen day-care infants (1976). They found no significant effects attributable only to the condition in which the child was reared. The authors concluded that "this important finding suggests that early experience when characterized globally as day care or home rearing does not affect [mother-child attachment]" (p. 338). This study too was methodologically flawed, because the separation and reunion episodes were staged in the infant's home rather than at an unfamiliar location. It cannot reasonably be expected that children will be very upset by brief maternal separations in their own homes.

Studies of Types of Attachment

The picture to this point is one of consistent but methodologically-flawed evidence in favor of the quality of parent-infant attachment in spite of variations in type of care. None of the studies reviewed so far has distinguished between secure (type *B*) and anxious-avoidant (type *A*) or anxious-ambivalent (type *C*) attachments. Ethological attachment theory predicts that regular parental absence would lead to anxious-avoidant behavior. Thus, a breakdown of attachment types would offer more significant evidence concerning the effects of out-of-home care.

One such breakdown was performed by Schwartz, who studied infants from middle-class intact families (1983). Seventeen infants were in full-time substitute care, sixteen were in part-time care, and seventeen were home-reared. Those in the first two groups had been placed in care before they were nine months of age. Schwartz found that the full-time day-care group displayed the most avoidant behavior during the final reunion episode of the Strange Situation. The next highest degree of avoidance was found in the part-time care group, although their scores did not differ significantly from those of the home-reared infants. These results, then, suggest an effect of infant day care when specific patterns of attachment behavior are considered.

More detailed evidence was obtained by Vaughn, Gove, and Egeland (1980). These researchers selected three parent-infant groups, defined by mothers who returned to work prior to their infant's first birthday (*Early Work*), those who started work when the infants were between twelve and eighteen-months old (*Late Work*), and a group who did not use substitute care during the first eighteen months (*No Work*). This study was unique in a number of ways. In addition to being specific about particular patterns of attachment, it was not limited to the high-quality, university-based day care typical of many studies. Further, it involved a lower socioeconomic (SES) sample selected with unusual care. For example, tests of twenty-nine potential differences among the three groups were conducted to gauge pretreatment comparability, although this still cannot completely eliminate the possibility of inherent group differences.

Attachment was assessed at twelve and eighteen months using Ainsworth's Strange Situation. As predicted, there was a significant relationship between work status and attachment classification at both ages. At twelve months, all the infants in the Early Work group who were not securely attached (47%) fell into the anxious-avoidant category (A). at eighteen months, this group still contained a disproportionate number of type A attachments. Interestingly, when the two anxious attachment types (A and C) were collapsed, there were no significant differences among the three groups. Hence, if Vaughn et al. had not attended to type of attachment, their results would have shown limited effects of infant day care.

Farber and Egeland extended the Vaughn et al. study by adding a twenty-four month assessment (1982). To their credit, Farber and Egeland did not attempt to use the Strange Situation with two-year-olds. Instead, they chose a procedure which was more developmentally appropriate for that age group, namely a problem-solving task requiring cooperation between parent and child. They found that the boys in the Early Work group showed less enthusiasm for the task, were less compliant, and had higher negative affect scores than those in the No Work group. Nonetheless, the investigators concluded that their overall results showed only minimal effects of early day-care experience on parent-infant attachment.

Different conclusions were derived by Vaughn, Deane, and Waters (in press), who reanalyzed the Farber and Egeland data. They found that the effects of early day care were indeed long lasting, but could only be properly understood when attachment history and early care experience were considered together. Specifically, they found that among the two-year-olds who had been assessed as secure at eighteen months, those who entered day care prior to one year exhibited less optimal behavior on the problem-solving task than did the No Work group. In fact, they fared no better than did those children assessed as insecure at eighteen months. Considering this and other data, Vaughn et al. concluded that there is "compelling evidence that out-of-home care during the period when primary attachments are forming and becoming consolidated is associated with deviations in the expected course of emotional development."

In sum, those field studies which were more faithful to the psychometric properties of the Strange Situation, which looked for specific patterns of attachment, and which investigated out-of-home care starting in the first year of life, generate some evidence of disturbed parent-child attachments as a result of early day care. Even the most pessimistic

results, however, indicate that more than half the infants starting substitute care in the first year were securely attached at twelve months
(Vaughn et al. 1980). A number of factors may cause out-of-home care
to have more powerful effects on some parent-child attachments than
others. These include personality characteristics of the child and/or the
primary caregiver and degree of family stress. Although little research
has addressed the issue of individual differences, stress has been impli-
cated in two ways: (1) it seems to affect whether or not out-of-home care
produces insecure attachments; and (2) it seems to be a major factor in
predicting whether insecure attachments will lead to negative social developmental outcomes.

EFFECTS OF STRESS ON PARENT-INFANT ATTACHMENT

The role of stress in the development of insecure attachments can be
understood by considering its effects on both infant and caregiver. The
attachment relationship is generally viewed as the end result of interactional patterns occurring over time between parent and infant (Ainsworth et al. 1978). Since these partners exist within a larger environmental context, many events can impinge on the behavior of either
parent or infant, thus altering interactional patterns and, ultimately, the
attachment relationship itself.

An illustration of how stress can affect the quality of attachment
can be gleaned by examining more closely the study by Vaughn et al.
described earlier (1980). A high proportion of insecure attachments
(47%) was found among infants whose mothers had returned to work
or school before the infants were twelve-months old. Of course, this
was a lower SES sample, and economic status is one indicator of
stress. Added to this was the fact that higher levels of stress were reported by mothers who worked than by mothers who stayed at home.
By eighteen months, insecure attachments were also associated with
nonintact families.

These stress-producing environmental circumstances are likely to affect the mother's physical availability, but they may also affect her emotional availability, which is perhaps more important to the quality of
attachment with her infant. This notion was substantiated by Rosenblum
and Paully in a study of primate interactions (1984). Mother-infant pairs
were randomly assigned to stressful (unpredictable) or unstressful (predictable) environmental demands, which were equated for actual amount
of resources available. They found that in stressful environments, mothers though physically present were relatively unavailable to respond to
infant needs. In unstable environments, altered maternal patterns, disturbed development of infant independence, regressive patterns of

clinging, and heightened fear or wariness were reported. They noted that such conduct would fit the description of an anxiously-attached infant.

Attachment classifications have been shown to fluctuate in response to changing degrees of environmental stress. Given a stable caretaking environment, individual differences in quality of attachment remain relatively stable (Waters 1978). In less stable environments, Vaughn et al. found that stability of attachment classification significantly dropped from around 85% to 62% (1979). In this study, changes in attachment were found to be a function of *stressful life event* scores. That is, a change from secure to insecure attachment across a six-month period was associated with higher stress scores than attachments assessed as secure at both twelve and eighteen months. Vaughn et al. proposed that "changes in circumstances can lead to changes in interaction and therefore to changes in relationships." Stress presumably taxes the mother's energies, leaving her less responsive to the infant. Thus, "high levels of stress would often have a negative effect on interaction and eventually on the quality of the attachment" (p. 974).

Attachment classifications are modifiable in the other direction, from insecure to secure, as a result of reduction in life stress. In a study by Egeland and Sroufe (1981), thirty-one cases of extreme neglect and abuse were compared with thirty-three cases with a history of excellent care (all children were drawn from a poverty sample of 267 high-risk mothers). As predicted, at twelve months, the maltreatment group was characterized by a low proportion of securely attached infants (38% as compared to 75% in the excellent care group). When assessed again at eighteen months, classifications in the excellent care group had remained stable, whereas over half of the infants in the maltreatment group had changed classifications. There was considerable movement from type *C* to type *A*, and some movement to type *B*. There was substantial evidence that mothers of infants changing from insecure to secure attachments had experienced a reduction in stressful life events. Further, changes in attachment classification correlated strongly with changes in the caretaking environment. The authors offered tentative findings that "secure attachment within the maltreatment group was associated with the presence of a supportive family member, less chaotic lifestyle and, in some instances, a more robust infant" (p. 44).

Individual Differences

Egeland and Sroufe speculated that some infants "may be more robust with respect to patterns of care, and some infants may inadequately elicit proper care" (1981, p. 45). Others might be better able to elicit support. Since each type of infant can have different types of parents in different circumstances, the whole spectrum of attachment relationships becomes possible.

A sense of the intricacies of parent-infant reciprocity can be seen in a study by Crockenberg (1981). She investigated a complex set of interactions involving infant irritability, maternal responsiveness, and social support. She found that high infant irritability interacted with lack of maternal responsiveness to produce an insecure attachment only when the mother perceived her life to be stressful and felt a lack of social support. Although Crockenberg stated that "high irritability was associated with anxious attachment only for the low social support group" (p. 861), it is important to note that low social support was assessed as such only when the mother perceived that the amount of stress in her life exceeded the degree of support she had. Thus, the mother's perceived stress was an important intermediary between the infant's own characteristics and the larger environmental context. Perhaps a mother under stress can still be responsive to a less irritable infant, or perhaps these infants were more able to use the mothering they did receive to reorganize more quickly. Crockenberg concluded that "whether a mother behaves unresponsively appears to be influenced by the infant's irritability and her own attitudes ... as well as by the social support available to her as a mother. Further, the impact of her unresponsiveness seems to depend similarly on the infant's irritability and on his access to someone who is responsive to his needs (for social support)" (p. 864).

The determinants of quality of attachment, then, appear to be multiple, and the impact of these various factors remains operative at least through eighteen months of age. Attachment relationships can change; they are affected both by stabilizing and by disruptive influences in the lives of both parent and infant. Thus, the effects of day care on parent-infant attachment cannot be simply stated, but must be considered in the broader contexts of individual and environmental differences. Given a relatively unstressed family situation in which the primary caregiver is emotionally available to the infant on a consistent basis, it seems likely that daily separations will not seriously affect quality of attachment. In the context of an already stressful home environment, on the other hand, such separation might in itself be added stress on the infant. If the parent is also under stress and so less emotionally available, and if the infant is less robust with regard to such patterns of care, then this constellation of factors may place the infant at greater risk for the development of an insecure attachment.

Developmental Outcomes

Much of the worry about infant day care ultimately concerns whether the absence of a secure attachment in infancy has implications for vulnerability to stress throughout childhood. Given a linear-additive model of socioemotional development, one would expect that the cumulative frequency of stressful life events would increase the chance of negative developmental outcomes. Two major studies substantiate this.

Werner and Smith reported on an eighteen-year longitudinal study of the entire population of children born on the Hawaiian island of Kauai in 1955 (1982). The attrition rate of the sample from birth through age eighteen was only 12%, so the final data remain substantive. Among the most salient findings from this massive research project is that the cumulative number of stressful life events discriminated significantly between positive and negative outcomes for children from middle-class as well as lower-class homes. As the number of stressful events increased, more protective factors in the children and their caregiving environments were needed to counterbalance the negative aspects of their lives and to insure a positive developmental outcome. Another intriguing finding was that, regardless of stress, chances of a positive outcome were greater if the child received plenty of attention from the primary caregiver during the first year of life.

That a secure attachment with a primary caregiver is beneficial in the long run (at least for boys) is indicated by another longitudinal study reported by Lewis et al. (1984). They found that less than 6% of the boys classified as securely attached at one year showed signs of psychopathology at six years, while 40% of the insecurely attached males showed such signs. The other 60% were presumably well adjusted. Lewis et al. suggested that encountering significant life stress is likely to be the deciding factor:

> Such findings lend support to an interactive process wherein poor early attachment predisposes a boy to psychopathology if he is also subject to environmental stress. Thus insecurely attached males are more vulnerable to environmental stress. (p. 133)

What one may tentatively conclude from this is: (1) in families facing significant life stresses, substitute care during the first year increases the likelihood of insecure parent-child attachments; (2) an insecure attachment makes the child more vulnerable to the effects of stressful events encountered later; and (3) the best predictor of later pathology is a cumulative frequency of stressful life events coupled with an insecure attachment in infancy. This description fits a linear continuum model, with the chances for less than optimal outcomes increasing as a function of the number and magnitude of stressful experiences encountered.

EFFECTS OF DAY CARE ON SOCIAL RELATIONS

Unlike the attachment literature, the field research on the development of social relations contains no extensively tested instrument. Investigators have looked primarily at the amount of peer-initiated interaction among children, or at children's interactions with unfamiliar adults, as a function of various rearing conditions. From the research carried out to date, a tentative consensus emerges that early group care may have some fairly reliable effects on interactions with others (Barton and Schwartz 1984; Belsky et al. 1982; Rutter 1981). These studies have found, for example, children who have experienced early group care tend toward assertiveness, aggression, and peer rather than adult orientation.

Studies Reporting No Differences

Braun and Caldwell studied thirty children who entered day care either just before or after their third birthday (1973). The groups were matched on age, sex, and IQ. These investigators found no differences on a global rating of socioemotional adjustment, but the absence of a home-reared control group and the late age of entry into day care make these results difficult to interpret. Caldwell et al. (1970) studied forty-one children, eighteen of whom had been in center care from about one year of age, and they reported no differences between the home- and day-care groups in frequency of social behavior. Preexisting differences between these groups were substantial, however. Of the eighteen children in day care, fourteen were females, and twice as many of them as compared to home-reared children came from one-parent families. Rubenstein and Howes, using a naturalistic observation method, also found no differences in social behavior between home- and group-reared eighteen-month-olds (1979).

The most convincing of the no-difference reports is the Kagan et al. study (1982) of one hundred day-care and home-reared infants, matched on sex, ethnicity, and parental education. The infants started day care at three-and-a-half months; social behavior was studied at thirteen, twenty, and twenty-nine months. Social behavior was measured through noting changes in vocalization, play, and proximity to mother, all in the presence of an unfamiliar child. They found that 80% of the infants inhibited play or vocalization or increased proximity to their mothers following the introduction of an unfamiliar child into the room. The developmental function for the behavior traced an inverted U. The day-care children were most inhibited at thirteen months and the home-reared at twenty-months, but all differences disappeared by twenty-nine months.

The picture from this study is one of a fairly robust developmental course for *peer apprehension*. Kagan et al. concluded that this course is a function of the maturation of cognitive competencies, which guarantees that peer apprehension will merge at about twelve months, grow through the second year, and start to wane in the third, thereby setting the stage for more complex social interactions. This sequence occurs regardless of variations in socialization instantiated by a high quality day-care experience.

Studies Reporting Differences

The trend in other findings is certainly in the direction of identifying potentially troublesome effects of group care on young infants (Martin 1981; Schwarz et al. 1973, 1974). Schwarz, Krolick, and Strickland studied forty infants, half in day care since between nine and ten months and half home-reared (1973). The assessments (behavioral observations and affective ratings) were completed when the children were about three-and-a-half years old. Results indicated more positive affect and more interaction with peers among the day-care group. These children, however, were familiar with each other before they entered day care. (In a sample where the children were presumably less familiar with each other, Doyle [1975] found that center-care children initiated fewer social interactions, both positive and negative, than home-reared children.) In a second study on the same sample, Schwarz et al. reported that the day-care children were less cooperative with adults, more aggressive physically and verbally, and less tolerant of frustration (1974). Similarly, Farber and Egeland (1982) found that lower SES males who started group care before their first birthday were less enthusiastic, less compliant, and had higher negative affect scores on a problem-solving task than did their peers who remained at home or who started day care after eighteen months.

At least three studies have looked more closely at the type of day care which children experience. Schwarz studied the effects of day care on 122 children in four settings (1983): home care, at-home sitter care, sitter outside home, and group day care. No differences were found among home and sitter care (whether in or out of home), but group-care infants were seen as more apathetic, less attentive, less socially responsive, less verbally expressive, and more deviant. Those children who spent the longest number of hours in care were the least well adjusted. Golden et al. assessed the psychological adjustment of over four hundred low-income children in family, group, and home care (1978). Children were tested when they entered care and again at eighteen and thirty-six months. In addition, two cross-sectional home-reared control groups were tested, again at eighteen and thirty-six months. Like Schwarz,

Golden et al. (1978) found that day-care children developed as well or better than home-reared children, but that there were differences between family- and group-care children. Family day-care children were more competent linguistically, emotionally, and socially with adults than children reared in group care. The length of time in day care did not affect performance, and there were quantitative but not qualitative differences in the cognitive, language, and social-emotional stimulation provided by caregivers in the two programs. Age on entrance also had no effect. Since participation in the study was necessarily voluntary, however, the samples were not randomly selected, and participants were not matched on many demographic variables, including ethnicity, intellectual development, physical health and growth, sources of income, and maternal age. Cochran also studied types of day care for twenty Swedish toddlers (1977). Those receiving day-home or center care had been placed there between six and twelve months of age. Their home-reared matches were selected from day-care waiting lists, decreasing the likelihood of pretreatment group differences. The children were assessed at twelve, fifteen, and eighteen months. Compared with the center-care children, the home-reared and day-home groups showed more exploratory behavior and interacted more with adults.

Overall, then, this group of findings is inconclusive. Some basic research on social development suggests that one can expect inconclusiveness for two reasons. First, reactions to social deprivation are often complex. For example, work by Zigler and his associates shows that social deprivation results in both a heightened tendency toward interaction with supportive adults and a reluctance or wariness about doing so (Zigler and Balla 1982; Zigler et al., 1968). Second, consonant with the view that the child's own features help determine development, individual characteristics may have bearing on the effects of group care.

GENDER AND THE EFFECTS OF EARLY SUBSTITUTE CARE

Moore followed 167 children from birth into adolescence (1975). he included a *diffusely mothered* group of forty-eight children who had experienced substitute care for at least a year before the age of five (the mean starting age was two years and six months). He found that by age fifteen, boys who were home-reared demonstrated more conformity to adult standards, more self-control, more timidity, and more academic interests, while the diffusely mothered boys were less conforming, more aggressive, and more social and sexual in orientation. Results for girls were much less consistent.

In a study of 121 children, Robertson found no main effect for care, but she did find interesting sex-to-type-of-care interactions (1982).

Among low SES children, day care increased imitation in females and decreased it in males. With regard to cooperativeness and obedience, day-care males were generally more troublesome than were home-reared males. The younger day-care boys were described by teachers as disrespectful of rights of others, quarrelsome, disobedient, and demanding. Similar differences were found in the Farber and Egeland (1982) study, with those boys who started group care before their first birthday showing poorer social behavior than those who remained at home or who started out-of-home care after eighteen months.

Brookhart and Hock (1976) studied younger children, eleven- to twelve- months old, eighteen of whom were home-reared and fifteen of whom had been in day care at least two months. The home-reared males exhibited both more contact maintenance with mother and proximity-seeking toward a stranger than did home-reared females or day-care males. The behavior of the day-care females was similar to that of the home-reared males. These findings suggest that, for boys, the tendency is toward more adult orientation among home-reared children.

Moskowitz et al. studied twenty-four children who averaged 5.6 months in care (1977). They also found that home-care males were more oriented toward an adult stranger than were day-care males. This time the home-care males were more exploratory, but it is not clear that the exploration involved excursions out of the mother's sight.

Gender-linked results are also noted in the literature on maternal employment. Bronfenbrenner and Crouter (1982) found that, among preschoolers, mother's employment was associated with a more positive attitude toward daughters, while unemployed mothers showed more positive attitude toward sons. Stevenson reported similar results for second graders (1982). Stuckey, McGhee, and Bell found that employment status related to differences in attention paid to children (1982). In employed-mother homes, more attention was paid to daughters than to sons, whereas the reverse was true in homes where mothers did not work.

Such attitudinal differences may be responsible for reports that maternal employment affects boys and girls differently. Hoffman (1982) cited recurring findings that middle-class sons of employed mothers show lower academic performance in grade school and sometimes lower IQs. In a longitudinal study of Hawaiian infants through adolescence, Werner and Smith reported similar gender differences, finding that boys were more vulnerable to maternal employment (and the father's absence) than were girls (1982). Bayley and Schaefer (1964) also reported that intellectual and academic achievement were related to maternal warmth, but again, only for boys.

Other research not specifically related to day care also sheds light on the issue of gender differences. Martin reported an impressive longitudinal study in which thirty-five mother-child dyads were observed and tested at ten, twenty-two, and forty-nine months (1981). The purpose was to examine the effects of the style of the mother-infant dyad at ten months on later functioning. The results most interesting for our purposes concern the effect of maternal responsiveness at ten months on child compliance, coerciveness, and exploration at forty-nine months. Martin found that, for boys only, maternal responsiveness led to future child compliance, to decreases in child coerciveness, to increases in the likelihood of exploration out of mother's sight, and to increases in initiating interactions with an unfamiliar adult. Girls, on the other hand, were more likely to explore and to approach the stranger if mothers were unresponsive.

Another line of relevant evidence comes from research on stress. In 1970, Rutter concluded that the available evidence pointed to a general tendency for boys to be more vulnerable to the ill effects of family stress. He later noted that family discord and *bond disruptions* were more strongly associated with antisocial disorders in boys (Rutter 1972, 1977). Further, the effects of marital discord and divorce are more pervasive and enduring for boys. The effect again is toward noncompliance and aggression (Hetherington 1979). One explanation comes from Hetherington's discovery that, during the period following a divorce, boys receive less positive support and nurturance and are viewed more negatively by mothers and teachers than are girls (Hetherington 1979).

There is also some possibility that the increased sensitivity of males is more general. Block (1982) argued that because of both differential socialization histories and biological make-up, boys may respond to environmental variation through accommodation, that is by altering or abandoning, perhaps unnecessarily, ongoing personality and cognitive structures. Females, on the other hand, will tend to assimilate, thus conserving existing structures and providing more continuity with the past. If Block is right and these two general strategies are differentially employed by males and females, this would explain why boys are more strongly affected by environmental variations.

Another possibility is that early substitute care may actually have a similar effect on males and females. The differences reported may merely reflect the fact that the two genders start at different points on some behavioral continuum. If boys are somewhat more aggressive, coercive, and exploratory than females to begin with, then any treatment which has an identical effect on both sexes will not affect the magnitude of the post-treatment differences, but merely shift the difference along the behavioral continuum. Such spurious differential effects are easy to identify with the use of pretests, but that is often impossible in research with very young infants.

It thus seems highly probable that males may be more sensitive than females to variations in rearing styles associated with substitute care in infancy. One possible explanation is that the subsystem subsuming peer relations and relations with unfamiliar adults is less resilient in males. This review makes it very clear, however, that the research conducted to date is unable to answer questions about the definitiveness of early experience. Studies are hampered by small group numbers, a paucity of appropriate measures, and the fact that so many dimensions are relevant (gender, family situation, type and length of day care, et cetera) that comparison of results is confounded, if not impossible. More longitudinal work is needed, especially that which allows researchers to tease apart effects of early versus concurrent environmental effects. Nonetheless, it is our view that the existing evidence is such that blanket statements about the benign effects of infant day care on social competence, especially in males, may be premature.

POLICY IMPLICATIONS

This review has led us to be less confident than many of our colleagues about the effects of infant day care and less sanguine about it being the major policy option available to working couples in the United States. Some of the reasons derive from the research reviewed above, but there are other reasons as well.

One concern has to do with difficulties in providing high-quality infant day care. The conditions that help determine quality include highly involved staff, low infant to caregiver ratios, small group size, stability among caregivers, and caregiver competence (Belsky et al. 1982; Ruopp and Travers 1982). These conditions can be extraordinarily expensive to provide, and could send the cost of infant day care upwards of $150 per week. (Many working mothers earn little more than that.) If state or federal governments were to insist on such standards, infant day care would be a luxury only wealthy families could afford. Still, government has a clear responsibility to insure the safety of infant day care, just as it has to insure the safety of products and services offered by pharmaceutical companies or airlines. Regulatory actions must therefore balance the need for more and better day care with the financial means of those families who need it most.

The evidence reviewed above forms a strong statement that alternatives to infant day care should be available to those working couples who would prefer to be with their babies during the first months of life.

Kagan et al. while finding few effects of infant day care, nonetheless recommend that it not start before three months of age (1978). They also reported that the Peoples Republic of China, a nation which is presumably more familiar with group child rearing than is the U.S., does not allow infants to be placed in group care during the first four months of life. In this country, however, it is not unheard of for mothers to return to work as early as two weeks after the birth of their babies.

The most attractive alternative to infant day care is a policy of paid infant care leave for working parents during the first few months of their baby's life. With the exception of the United States, every industrialized Western nation makes some such option available to its citizens (Kamerman and Kahn 1978). Such leaves are not to be confused with maternity leaves of absence, which are given on the basis of physical disability and are usually unpaid. Instead, they are granted specifically for infant care. Although many nations provide these benefits only to mothers, ideally such a policy should be available to either parent. Infant care leaves would be a favorable option for those working couples who remain convinced of the value and importance of extensive infant-parent contact during the first few months of life. The evidence we have reviewed clearly shows that such parental concerns should not be easily dismissed.

REFERENCES

Ainsworth, M. 1979. Attachment as related to mother-infant interaction. *Advances in the Study of Behavior*, vol. 9. J. Rosenblatt, et al., eds. New York: Academic Press.

Ainsworth, M. 1982. Attachment: retrospect and prospect. *The Place of Attachment in Human Behavior*. C. Parks and J. Stevenson-Hinde, eds. New York: Basic Books.

Ainsworth, M., et al. 1978. *Patterns of Attachment*. Hillsdale, New Jersey: Erlbaum.

Barton, N., and Schwartz, C. 1984. The Effects of Infant Day Care Experience on Personality Development: A Review of Research. Unpublished manuscript, University of Connecticut.

Bayley, N., and Schaefer, E. 1964. Correlations of maternal and child behaviors with the development of mental abilities: Data from the Berkeley Grown Study. *Monographs of the Society for Research in Child Development* 29(6): serial no. 97.

Belsky, J., and Steinberg, L. 1978. The effects of day care: a critical review. *Child Development* 49:929–49.

Belsky, J., Steinberg, L., and Walker, A. 1982. The ecology of day care. *Child-rearing in Nontraditional Families*. M. Lamb, ed. Hillsdale, New Jersey: Erlbaum.

Blanchard, M., and Main, M. 1979. Avoidance of the attachment figure and social-emotional adjustment in day care infants. *Developmental Psychology* 15:445–46.

Blehar, M. 1974. Anxious attachment and defensive reactions associated with day care. *Child Development* 45:683–92.

Block, J. 1982. Assimilation, accommodation, and the dynamics of personality development. *Child Development* 53:281–95.

Braun, S., and Caldwell, B. 1973. Emotional adjustment of children in day care who enrolled prior to or after the age of three. *Early Childhood Development and Care* 213–21.

Brazelton, T., Koslowski, B., and Main, M. 1974. The origins of reciprocity: the early mother-infant interaction. In *The Effects of the Infant on Its Caregiver.* M. Lewis and L. Rosenblum, eds. New York: John Wiley & Sons.

Bronfenbrenner, U., and Crouter, A. 1982. Work and family through time and space. *Families that Work: Children in a Changing World.* S. Kamerman and C. Hayes, eds. Washington, D.C.: National Academy Press.

Brookhart, J., and Hock, E. 1976. The effects of experimental contest and experiential background on infants' behavior toward their mothers and a stranger. *Child Development* 47:333–40.

Bruner, J. 1977. Early social interaction and language acquisition. *Studies in Mother-Infant Interaction.* H. R. Schaffer, ed. London: Academic Press.

Caldwell, B. 1970. The effects of psychosocial deprivation on human development in infancy. *Merrill-Palmer Quarterly* 16:260–77.

Caldwell, B., et al. 1970. Infant day care and attachment. *American Journal of Orthopsychiatry* 40:397–412.

Clarke, A. M. 1984. Early Experience and Cognitive Development. Unpublished manuscript, University of Hull, England.

Clarke, A. M., and Clarke, A. D. B. 1976. *Early Experience: Myth and Evidence.* New York: Free Press.

Cochran, M. 1977. A comparison of group day care and family child-rearing patterns in Sweden. *Child Development* 48:702–07.

Crockenberg, S. 1981. Infant irritability, mother responsiveness, and social support influences on the security of mother-infant attachment. *Child Development* 52:857–65.

Doyle, A. 1975. Infant development in day care. *Developmental Psychology* 11:655–56.

Egeland, B., and Sroufe, L. 1981. Attachment and early maltreatment. *Child Development* 52:44–52.

Farber, E., and Egeland, B. 1982. Developmental consequences of out-of-home care for infants in a low income population. *Day Care: Scientific and Social Policy Issues.* E. Zigler and E. Gordon, eds. Boston: Auburn House.

Fox, N. 1977. Attachment of kibbutz infants to mother and metapelet. *Child Development* 48:1228–39.

Fraiberg, S. 1977. *Every Child's Birthright: In Defense of Mothering.* New York: Basic Books.

Golden, M., et al. 1978. *The New York Infant Day Care Study.* New York: Medical and Health Research Associates of New York.

Hetherington, E. 1979. Family interaction. *Psychopathological Disorders of Childhood,* second ed. H. Quay and J. Werry, eds. New York: John Wiley & Sons.

Hoffman, L. 1982. *Maternal employment and the Young Child.* Minnesota Symposium on Child Psychology. Manuscript.

Jensen, A. 1978. The current status of the IQ controversy. *Austral. Psychol.* 13:7–27.

Jensen, A. 1983. Again, how much can we boost IQ? *Contemp. Psychol.* 28:756–58.

Jones, E., and Prescott, E. 1982. Day care: short or long-term solution? *Annals Amer. Acad. Polit. Soc. Sci.* 461:91–101.

Kagan, J. 1982. *Psychological Research on the Human Infant: An Evaluation Summary.* New York: A. W. T. Grant Foundation.

Kagan, J., Kearsley, R., and Zelazo, P. 1978. *Infancy: Its Place in Human Development.* Cambridge, Mass: Harvard University Press.

Kagan, J., and Klein, R. 1973. Cross-cultural perspectives on early development. *Amer. Psychol.* 28:947.

Kamerman, S., and Kahn, A. 1978. *Family Policy: Government and Families in 14 Countries.* New York: Columbia University Press.

Kessen, W., Haith, M., and Salapatek, P. 1970. Human infancy: a bibliography and guide. *Carmichael's Manual of Child Psychology*, vol. 1. W. Mussen, ed. New York: John Wiley & Sons.

Konner, M. 1982. Biological aspects of the mother-infant bond. *The Place of Attachment in Human Behavior.* C. Parks and J. Stevenson-Hinde, eds. New York: Basic Books.

Lamb, M., et al. (In press.) Security of infantile attachment as assessed in the Strange Situation: Its study and biological interpretation. *Behav. Brain Sci.*

Lewis, M, et al. 1984. Predicting psychopathology in six-year-olds from early social relations. *Child Development* 55:123–36.

Martin, J. 1981. *A Longitudinal Study of the Consequences of Early Mother-Infant Interaction: A Microanalytic Approach. Monographs of the Society for Research in Child Development* 46(3): serial 190.

Moore, T. 1975. Exclusive early mothering and its alternative: the outcome to adolescence. *Scand. J. Psychol.* 16:255–72.

Moskowitz, D., Schwarz, J., and Corsini, D. 1977. Initiating day care at three years of age: effects on attachment. *Child Development* 48:1271–76.

Portnoy, F., and Simmons, C. 1978. Day care and attachment. *Child Development* 49:239–42.

Ragozin, A. 1980. Attachment behavior of day care children: naturalistic and laboratory observations. *Child Development* 51:409–15.

Ricciuti, H. 1976. Effects of Infant Day Care Experience on Behavior and Development: Research and Implications for Social Policy. Prepared for the Office of the Assistant Secretary for Planning and Evaluation, Department of Health, Education, and Welfare.

Robertson, A. 1982. Day care and children's responsiveness to adults. *Day Care: Scientific and Social Policy Issues.* E. Zigler and E. Gordon, eds. Boston: Auburn House.

Roopnairene, J., and Lamb, M. 1979. The effects of day care on attachment and exploratory behavior in a strange situation. *Merrill-Palmer Quarterly* 24:85–89.

Rosenblum, L., and Paully, G. 1984. The effects of varying environment demands on maternal and infant behavior. *Child Development* 55:305–14.

Rubenstein, J., and Howes, C. 1979. Caregiving and infant behavior in day care and in homes. *Developmental Psychology* 15:1–24.

Ruopp, R., and Travers, J. 1982. Janus faces day care: perspectives on quality and cost. *Day Care: Scientific and Social Policy Issues*. E. Zigler and E. Gorden, eds. Boston: Auburn House.

Rutter, M. 1970. Sex differences in children's response to family stress. *The Child in the Family*, vol. 1. E. Anthony and C. Koupernik, eds. New York: John Wiley & Sons.

Rutter, J. 1972. *Maternal Deprivation Reassessed*. Hammondsworth: Penguin.

Rutter, M. 1977. Individual differences. *Child Psychiatry: Modern Approaches*. M. Rutter and L. Hersov, eds. Oxford: Basil Blackwell.

Rutter, M. 1981. Social-emotional consequences of day care for preschool children. *American Journal of Orthopsychiatry* 51(1):4–28.

Scarr, S., and Kidd, K. 1983. Developmental behavior genetics. *Mussen Handbook of Child Psychology*, 4th ed., vol. 2. M. Haith and J. Campos, eds. New York: John Wiley & Sons.

Scarr-Salapatek, S. 1976. An evolutionary perspective on infant intelligence: species patterns and individual variations. *Origins of Intelligence*. M. Lewis, ed. New York: Plenum Press.

Schwartz, P. 1983. Length of day care attendance and attachment behavior in eighteen-month-old infants. *Child Development* 54:1073–78.

Schwarz, J. Krolick, G., and Strickland, R. 1973. Effects of early day care experience on adjustment to a new environment. *American Journal of Orthopsychiatry* 43:340–46.

Schwarz, J., Strickland, R., and Krolick, G. 1974. Infant day care: behavioral effects at pre-school age. *Developmental Psychology* 10:502–06.

Schwarz, J. 1983. Infant day care: effects at 2, 4, and 8 years. Paper presented to Society for Research in Child Development, Detroit. (Abstract: Resources in Education, January 1984. ERIC Clearinghouse on Elementary and Early Education.

Stern, D. 1974. Mother and infant at play: the dyadic interaction involving facial, vocal, and gaze behavior. *The Effect of the Infant on the Caregiver*. M. Lewis and L. Rosenblum, eds. New York: John Wiley & Sons.

Stevenson, N. 1982. The role of maternal employment and satisfaction level in children's cognitive performance. Ph.D. dissertation, University of Michigan.

Stuckey, M., McGhee, P., and Bell, N. 1982. Parent-child interaction: the influence of maternal employment. *Developmental Psychology* 18:635–44.

Urban Institute. 1982. *The Subtle Revolution: Women at Work*. Washington, D.C.: Urban Institute.

Vaughn, B., Deane, K., and Waters, E. (In press.) The impact of out-of-home care on child-mother attachment quality: another look at some enduring questions. *Child Development*.

Vaughn, B., et al. 1979. Individual differences in infant-mother attachment at 12 and 18 months: stability and change in families under stress. *Child Development* 50:971–75.

Vaughn, B., Gove, F., and Egeland, B. 1980. The relationship between out-of-home care and the quality of infant-mother attachments in an economically deprived population. *Child Development* 51:1203–14.

Waddington, C. 1962. *New Patterns in Genetics and Development.* New York: Columbia University Press.

Waddington, C. 1971. Concepts of development. *The Biopsychology of Development.* E. Talback, L. Aronson, and E. Shaw, eds. New York: Academic Press.

Waters, E. 1978. The reliability of individual differences in infant-mother attachment. *Child Development* 49:483–94.

Werner, E., and Smith, R. 1982. *Vulnerable But Invincible.* New York: McGraw-Hill.

Zigler, E. 1968. Developing the intellect versus developing the whole child. *Proceedings*, 19th Annual Conference, Southern Association on Children under Six, Birmingham, Alabama, pp. 48–62.

Zigler, E., and Balla, D. 1982. Motivational and personality factors in the performance of the retarded. *Mental Retardation: The Developmental-Difference Controversy.* E. Zigler and D. Balla, eds. Hillsdale, N.J.: Erlbaum.

Zigler, E., Balla, D., and Butterfield, E. 1968. A longitudinal investigation of the relationship between preinstitutional social deprivation and social motivation in institutionalized retardates. *Journal of Personality and Social Psychology* 10:437–45.

Zigler, E., Balla, D., and Hodapp, R. 1984. On the definition of mental retardation. *American Journal of Mental Deficiency.* 89:215–30.

Zigler, E., and Butterfield, E. 1968. Motivational aspects of change in IQ test performance of culturally deprived nursery school children. *Child Development* 39:1–14.

Zigler, E., and Triclett, P. 1978. IQ, social competence, and evaluation of early childhood intervention programs. *American Psychologist* 33:789–98.

A Reassessment of Infant Day Care*

JAY BELSKY

Almost a decade ago the Department of Health, Education, and Welfare commissioned a series of reports concerning characteristics, consequences, and usage of child care services in the United States. As a member of one team charged with reviewing and summarizing the current state of knowledge regarding the effects of day care on child development, I helped produce a technical report and a subsequent publication critically evaluating what was then known about the effects of supplementary care arrangements. This report has been cited widely in both the scientific and popular press (Belsky and Steinberg 1978; Bronfenbrenner, Belsky, and Steinberg 1976). Careful scrutiny of published and unpublished research reports revealed that day-care rearing had neither salutary nor adverse consequences for the intellectual development of most children; that there was little support for the claim that day care disrupts the child's emotional development by disturbing his/her tie to mother; but that group rearing at early ages appeared to be associated with greater peer orientation and lessened responsiveness toward adults, including heightened aggression and noncompliance.

In the time since the publication of our initial review of the research evidence, I have twice taken the opportunity formally to update and extend our analysis of the effects of day care (Belsky 1984; Belsky, Steinberg, and Walker 1982). Our conclusions regarding cognitive development have remained substantially unchanged, as have those regarding social development. By 1982 and 1984, though, including a congressional testimony to the U.S. House of Representatives Select Committee on Children, Youth, and Families (Belsky 1985), notes of

*Work on this article was supported by a grant from the National Institute of Child Health and Human Development (R01HD15496) and by an NIMH Research Scientist Development Award (K02MH00486).

caution were interjected with respect to the effects of nonmaternal care on socioemotional development, particularly in the case of children who began nonmaternal care before their first birthday. In view of the fact that no comprehensive analysis of the research literature focusing exclusively upon such children has been reported, and that virtually one of every two women with infants under one year of age is employed (Kamerman 1986), my purpose here is to examine what is currently known about the socioemotional development of children who began day care in their first year of life.

This review is comprised of three sections. In the first I consider the emotional tie of infant to mother, as defined by the attachment relationship. In the second, attention is turned to the social development of preschool and school-age children who have been reared since infancy in day care. Unfortunately, most of the studies to be discussed in this second section do not involve the same samples as those considered in the earlier section, because few day-care children have been studied both in infancy and during subsequent developmental periods. In spite of this general absence of longitudinal evidence, I will draw what I believe to be theoretically meaningful connections between the two sets of studies in order to argue that the evidence reviewed pertaining to the assessment of attachment in infancy *and* later social development is strikingly consistent with basic theoretical propositions of attachment theory and that, as a result, both sets of data become particularly noteworthy. Indeed, it is the juxtaposition of these distinct, but apparently related sets of evidence, that leads me to raise concerns about infant day care and highlight some policy implications in a concluding section.

INFANT DAY CARE AND INFANT-MOTHER ATTACHMENT

The emotional tie between infant and mother, that is, the attachment relationship, figures prominently in most writings about infant socioemotional development. Certainly since the time of Freud, notions of the developmental significance of this first relationship have been prominent in the study of child development. Bowlby's (1969, 1973), Ainsworth's (1973, 1982), and Sroufe's (1979; Sroufe and Waters 1977) theoretical and empirical writings have done much to promulgate the position that the quality of this relationship, particularly in terms of the security it affords the developing child, is likely to be influenced by the nature and quality of care the child receives and to affect the child's future development. It is for this reason, as well as a result of classic studies of institutional rearing linking motherless care and disturbed development in the first years, that the attachment bond between infant and mother has been a central focus of research concerning infant day care.

Consideration of research bearing upon the association between non-maternal care in the first year of life and infant-mother attachment reveals a need to distinguish between studies initiated prior to and following the establishment of a valid methodology for assessing individual differences in attachment security. The first set of studies, conducted before 1980, and consisting principally of samples enrolled in high-quality, university-based, research-oriented facilities, revealed few consistent differences between infants cared for at home and in day-care centers (Cochran 1977; Cummings 1980; Doyle and Somers 1978; Hock 1980; Kagan, Kearsley, and Zelazo 1976, 1978; Ricciuti 1974; Saunders 1972). Important to note, however, is the fact that most of these investigations focused upon the degree to which infants became distressed following a brief separation from mother and/or by the presence and approach of an unfamiliar adult—this in spite of the fact that it was never clear whether it was considered developmentally advantageous or problematical for the child to display greater or lesser stranger wariness and/or separation distress.

Measuring Attachment

This issue of the meaning of behavior is one that eventually became central to scientists interested in understanding the characteristics, consequences, and determinants of individual differences in the infant-mother attachment relationship (Masters and Wellman 1974; Waters 1978). In fact, frustration with the meaning of any number of potential indexes of attachment resulted in a great deal of basic research being carried out, all of which was not in the least bit concerned with day care, but which nevertheless produced a means of discriminating secure from insecure relationships and, thereby, of enhancing day care research. In the years which *followed* the publication of most of the initial day-care attachment studies, basic research on infant development revealed that it was not so much crying upon separation or even willingness to approach an unfamiliar person which reliably indicated the security of the attachment relationship, but rather the behavior that the infant/toddler directed, or failed to direct, *to the mother upon reunion following separation.* Studies by Waters (1978) and others at the University of Minnesota (Matas, Arend, and Sroufe 1978; Waters and Sroufe 1983) convincingly demonstrated that the behavior of secure infants was characterized by their tendency to greet their mothers positively following separation and approach (especially if they were distressed) and to be comforted by her (when they were upset by separation). Babies whose relationships were insecure tended to engage in one of two quite different behavior patterns. Those whose relationships were labeled *insecure-avoidant* actively avoided psychological contact with mother, moved away from her, aborted approaches to her, or averted their gaze so as not to make eye contact with her. Those whose relationships were labeled *insecure-avoidant* actively avoided psychological contact with mother, moved away from her, aborted approaches to her, or averted their gaze so as not to make eye contact with her. Those whose relationships were labeled *insecure-resistant* actively resist contact with mother (by pushing away), even after seeking such contact, and are likely to cry in an angry, petulant manner, or angrily to push away a toy that is offered by mother.

Evidence of the validity of these distinctions comes from a large number of follow-up studies, which indicate that infants who avoid and/or resist their mothers to such an extent that they can be classified as anxiously attached generally seem less competent as they grow older. Not only have such infants been found, as toddlers and preschoolers, to be less empathic, less compliant, less cooperative, and to exhibit more negative affect and less self-control (Egeland 1983; Joffee 1981; LaFreniere and Sroufe 1985; Londerville and Main 1981; Main 1973; Main and Weston 1981; Maslin and Bates 1982), but they have also been found, as five- and six-year olds, to be more at risk for developing behavior problems (Erickson et al. 1985; Lewis, Feiring, McGuttog, and Jaskir 1984; these findings were for boys only, but see Bates, Maslin, and Frankel 1985, for failure to replicate).

The point to be made here is not that each and every study indicates that reunion behaviors in the Strange Situation and the attachment classifications derived from them discriminate children's subsequent functioning in other settings, but rather that incontestable trends are evident in the literature regarding the future functioning of children with secure versus insecure attachment relationships. The implication which derives from this observation is that the initial day care research concerned with infant-mother attachment was misguided given its focus upon infant behaviors, which ultimately proved to be insensitive indicators of the affective quality of the attachment bond.

Since 1980 and the emergence of evidence validating the focus upon infant reunion behavior as a *window* on individual differences in the security of the infant-mother attachment bond, a number of studies, mostly of community as opposed to university-based nonmaternal care for infants in the first year, have been reported. Of special interest is the fact that five separate studies have documented an association between nonmaternal care in the first year and heightened avoidance of mother upon reunion following separation. These have involved studies of impoverished infants cared for in unstable, low-quality family day care (Vaughn et al. 1980); of middle-class infants (boys only) cared for in centers and family day-care homes (Hock and Clinger 1980); of middle- and upper-middle-class infants reared in full-time, family day-care arrangements (Schwartz, 1983); of middle-class infants reared by babysitters in their own homes (Barglow 1985; Barglow et al. in press); and of working- and middle-class infants cared for on a full-time basis in a variety of caregiving arrangements (Jacobsen and Wille 1984; Wille and Jacobsen 1984).

Before it is concluded that the experience of nonmaternal care in the first year is routinely associated with avoidance of mother and, possibly, insecure-avoidant attachment, several points must be made. First, even in those studies which document a reliable association between infant day care and avoidance, it is clear that not all day-care-reared infants display heightened avoidance and, conversely, that some home-reared children do; nevertheless, these studies do indicate that, on average, more avoidance is displayed by infants reared in supplementary care during the first years than by those reared at home. A second important point that needs to be made is that the evidence clearly indicates that day-care-reared infants are emotionally attached to their mothers and prefer them to caregivers as sources of support and comfort (Farran and Ramey 1977; Kagan et al. 1978); thus, to the extent that early supplementary care affects the attachment relationship, it should be apparent that what is being influenced is the *quality* of the bond. Finally, it must be recognized that even among day-care studies which assess reunion behavior, and particularly avoidance, several discern no rearing group differences.

Of special significance with respect to these latter investigations is the fact that, with the exception of one, all are marred by methodological limitations that seriously undermine their ability to illuminate the developmental correlates of infant day care. In this case of two studies by Hock, which documented no differences between groups as a function of rearing experience, for example, the reunion behavior of infants was not videotaped but merely described verbally for subsequent transcription and coding (Brookhart and Hock 1976; Hock 1980). Given the often subtle but significant forms in which avoidance can be displayed, and given the fact that no investigators today would rely upon any data-collection procedure other than those which would permit repeated viewing of the child's greeting behavior (videotape), it remains possible that these two investigations of middle-class infants in a variety of day-care arrangements may well have been insensitive to differences between rearing groups as a result of the procedures employed.

Insensitivity to group differences also seems possible in the case of two studies conducted by Doyle of middle-class Canadian children enrolled in centers (Doyle 1975) and in a variety of arrangements (Doyle and Somers 1978). In these cases, the virtual failure of the investigators to discern any avoidance *or* resistance upon reunion in some 130 home-

and day-care-reared infants through the use of a time-sampling method raises questions as to whether Doyle and her colleagues were alert to the forms in which avoidance and resistance can be displayed. No other studies, be they concerned with day-care infants or not, have reported such an inability to observe any behaviors indicative of insecurity. Also to be noted is the fact that infants in these studies ranged in age from five to thirty months, and that the validity of procedures for assessing reunion behavior have only been established for children ranging from eleven to twenty months of age.

Regardless of the limitations of these studies, there remains good evidence that avoidance or insecurity is not universally associated with nonmaternal child care in the first year of life. In what may be the most careful investigation done to date, Chase-Lansdale and Owen (1986; Owen 1986, personal communication) compared the attachment relationships of some ninety-five middle-class, twelve-month olds who had been reared exclusively by the mother, with agemates who had been cared for in family day-care homes or by sitters (but not in centers). No differences were discerned in the rate of secure or anxious-avoidant attachments to the mother, a finding that was replicated when a subsample of these infants was studied again at the age of twenty months (Easterbrooks and Goldberg 1985). Of special significance, however, is the finding that, at twelve months of age, boys whose mothers worked (and who were therefore in some type of childcare arrangement) experienced significantly higher rates of insecurity in their relationships with their *fathers* in comparison to boys whose mothers stayed at home to care for them. As a result, when the constellation of attachment relationships was considered—that is, security to mother plus security to father—sons in supplementary child care were found to have fewer secure attachments (Chase-Lansdale and Owen 1981). Since it has been observed on more than one occasion that infants securely attached to both parents look more competent than those securely attached to only one parent—or to neither—(Belsky, Garduque, and Hrncir 1984; Main and Weston 1981), this finding of greater insecurity to the father of sons in supplementary care in the only study ever to consider fathers takes on added significance.

Preliminary Conclusions

It should be evident from the preceding analysis that not every study of attachment has discerned differences between infants reared at home or in some kind of childcare arrangement sometime during their first twelve or so months of life. At the same time, however, it would appear to be incontestable and unavoidable that some degree of association between avoidance and infant day care exists. This finding is actually consistent with trends in the more general day-care literature concerning preschoolers. As Clarke-Stewart and Fein (1983) observed in their comprehensive review of the evidence appearing in the most recent edition of the *Handbook of Child Psychology,*

> children in day care are more likely than children at home to position themselves further away from mother, to spend less time close to or in physical contact with mother, and to ignore or avoid mother after a brief separation. The difference is not observed in every child or every study, but the consistent direction of the differences is observed (p. 948).

The point to be made, then, is that there is an emerging pattern, particularly in studies of infant care reported since 1980, in which non-maternal child care, especially that initiated in the first year, whether in homes or in centers, is associated with the tendency of the infant to avoid or maintain a distance from the mother following a series of brief separations. Some contend that such behavior reflects an underlying doubt or mistrust about the availability of the mother to meet the baby's needs and, thus, an insecure relationship. Moreover, since it is known that this behavior pattern is related to a set of developmental outcomes which most developmentalists would regard as less than desirable, some are inclined to conclude that the quality of the mother-child bond and, thereby, the child's future development may be in jeopardy (Fraiberg 1977).

Yet, other scientists read *the very same evidence* in a *very different way.* Even though the same pattern of avoidance is noted, it is interpreted not as deficit or disturbance but rather as adaptive and possibly even precocious behavior. After all, day-care infants experience many separations; thus it seems sensible for them not to orient toward mother: "Perhaps day care children have simply had more experience in the type of situation used to assess attachment, so they find it less stressful and therefore exhibit less overt and intense attachment behavior (i.e., proximity)" (Clarke-Stewart and Fein 1983, p. 956). In addition, because the behavioral tendency of children as they get older is to remain more distant from their parents, the behavior of day-care-reared twelve to eighteen month-olds may be evidence of maturity:

> In children receiving care exclusively from mother, avoidance may be a pathological response reflecting an interactive history with a rejecting mother, while for children in day care greater distance from, or ignoring of, mother at reunion may be an adaptive response reflecting a habitual reaction to repeated daily separations and reunions. In these latter children, greater physical distance from mother and apparent avoidance may, in fact, signal a precocious independence (Clarke-Stewart and Fein 1983, p. 949).

Which interpretation is correct—insecurity or precocity? Here I concur with Clarke-Stewart and Fein that "there is no way to determine at this point if the apparent avoidance of mother observed in day care children in *some* studies is a disturbed or adaptive pattern" (1983, p. 949, emphasis original). But this very uncertainty leads me to reexamine other evidence in the day-care literature linking nonmaternal child care in the first year with subsequent social development in hopes of gaining some insight. In this regard it is useful to keep in mind that several investigations concerned not at all with infant day care have reported associations between anxious-avoidant attachment in infancy and subsequent noncompliance, aggressiveness, social withdrawal, and behavior problems more generally (Erickson et al. 1985; Main and Weston 1982; Maslin and Bates 1982; Sroufe 1983). Many of these very same outcomes are also associated with infant day care experience.

THE SOCIAL DEVELOPMENT OF DAY-CARE-REARED INFANTS

The results of the very first study of the social behavior of preschoolers reared since infancy in day care alerted scientists and policymakers alike to the possibility that problematical developmental outcomes might be associated with the infant day-care experience. In following up a sample of children at three and four years of age who entered infant day care during their first year of life, Schwarz and his colleagues (1974) discovered that these children were more aggressive (both physically and verbally) with adults and peers, less cooperative with grown-ups, less tolerant of frustration, and more motorically active than a comparison group for whom the preschool represented their first supplementary care experience. To be noted, too, is the fact that these same children with infant day-care histories were more social with agemates (Lay and Meyer 1973) and that the differences between groups of children with varying rearing histories diminished over time (Meyer 1979).

In a variety of respects these findings regarding children first enrolled in an experimental infant center at Syracuse University are much like those subsequently reported in the literature. Consider, for instance, Rubenstein and Howes' (1983) study of a small sample of middle-class children who had been enrolled in one of five community-based, infant-toddler centers toward the end of their first year, and who were found at three-and-one-half years, when compared to a group of children who had been continuously reared at home by their mothers, to have more fears, to be more active, to throw more frequent and intense temper tantrums, and to be less compliant with maternal directives. These data led Rubenstein and Howes to conclude that:

noncompliance in this study reflected a more anxious or angry child... It should be emphasized that noncompliance and temper tantrums are more characteristic of two-year-old rather than three-year-old behavior. Thus, we are considering the differences in the day care children to reflect a delay in the negotiation of an age-appropriate developmental issue. At this point it is unclear whether this delay has any significant long term implications (1983, p. 34).

That it *might* is suggested by an even more recent study, this one of the social behavior of lower-class kindergarten and first-graders who had been reared on a full-time basis at the Frank Porter Graham Child Development Center (affiliated with the University of North Carolina) throughout their first four years of life. Ratings made by school teachers at the end of each of these two school years indicated that children who received center-based care in the first year of life, in contrast to those receiving care any time thereafter, were

> more likely to use the aggressive acts hit, kick, and push than children in the control group. Second, they were more likely to threaten, swear, and argue. Third, they demonstrated those propensities in several school set-tings—the playground, the hallway, the lunchroom, and the classroom. Fourth, teachers were more likely to rate these children as having ag-gressiveness as a serious deficit in social behavior. Fifth, teachers viewed these children as less likely to use such strategies as walking away or dis-cussion to avoid or extract themselves from situations that could lead to aggression (Haskins 1985, p. 700).

But, like Meyer (1979) in his follow-up study of the more aggressive three- and four-year-olds from the Syracuse infant center, Haskins (1985), too, discerned a trend suggesting "that the excess aggressiveness of children in the experimental group appears to diminish" across time (p. 701), though even by the end of the third year of schooling (second grade) significant differences between childcare groups remained on several measures of aggression.

This pattern of differences between children with varying infant care experience, which are evident initially and generate clear cause for con-cern, yet appear to dissipate over time, is evident in other studies. In this regard, the results of the comprehensive testing of a large number of two-year-olds (twenty-four to thirty months) on the island of Ber-muda, which enabled Schwarz and his colleagues (1981; Schwarz 1983) to compare the functioning of children with varying child care histories, are notable. Those children

> who experienced predominantly center group care in the first two years of life, at two years of age were found to have poorer communication skills than children cared for at home, according to the mother's own report

and ratings by our testers. During the assessment, which occurred in the home, center group care infants were rated by teachers as more apathetic, less attentive, and less socially responsive. They were judged by testers to be more deviant than children cared for at home (Schwarz 1983, p. 2).

To be noted in this case are the facts that these group differences (1) held principally for black children; (2) emerged even after controlling for a host of important background variables (for example, mother's IQ or parents' educations and occupational prestige); (3) were related to variation in quality of care; and (4) diminished over time (Schwarz 1983). These longer-term findings mitigate to some extent the concern raised about center-rearing in the first years of life, at least as experienced by most Bermudan infants. However, another report by this same research group concerning a larger number of three- to five-year-olds rekindles concern: "Children who began group care in infancy were rated as more maladjusted than those who were cared for by sitters or in family day care homes for the early years and who began center care at later ages" (McCartney et al. 1982, p. 148). In effect, they were judged by caregivers to be more anxious, aggressive, and hyperactive—patterns of behavior remarkably consistent with those observed by Schwarz et al. (1974), Haskins (1985), and Rubenstein and Howes (1983).

Although it is not clear whether the differences associated with infant care disappeared over time, or even if they did, whether they should be regarded as unimportant, the case remains that not all studies point to their eventual disappearance. There is, for example, a retrospective investigation of some 191 middle-class, nine- and ten-year-olds using reports of behavior made by the children's agemates (Barton and Schwarz 1981). Even after controlling for both parents' education, it was found that children who entered day care before twelve months of age, or between twelve and eighteen months, were viewed as most misbehaving, with children who experienced substitute care in their first year "most likely to be labeled troublemakers" (p. 7). Similar results emerged when the variable of interest was *likelihood to cry*, with those entering day care on a full- or part-time basis prior to eighteen months rated most highly on this behavior. These early children also appeared susceptible to such internalizing behaviors as withdrawal, and they were most often characterized as loners.

As was the case with respect to the association between infant day care and attachment, not all studies of social development in the post-infancy years discern reliable differences between children with varying infant care experience; moreover, several studies indicate that those with a nonmaternal care experience in infancy seem more socially skilled or well adjusted. In this regard, Ramey and Campbell (1979) found that children from their high-quality, university-based center appeared more

socially confident during testing throughout the first and second year
of life than those without infant care experience (Ramey, McPhee, and
Yeates 1982). At the same time, Fowler and Khan discerned no group
differences in a similar study (1974/1975). Another investigation which
pointed toward positive effects of infant day care involved a comparison
of two-year-olds using the very same rating scales employed by Schwarz
et al. (1974) which had shown day-care infants to be more aggressive
and uncooperative at age four. In this study of sixteen children it was
observed that those who began care in the first year scored higher on
the ability to get along with others than children entering care at around
two years of age, and also that these two groups were equivalent with
respect to cooperation with adults, aggression, and tolerance of frustration (MaCrae and Herbert-Jackson 1975). Although MaCrae and Herbert-Jackson interpret their findings as a failure to replicate those of
Schwarz et al. (1974), the question can be raised as to whether the fact
that *all* of the children in their investigation were two years younger
than those participating in the Schwarz study might actually indicate that
the differences discerned by Schwarz et al. (1974) may take time to
emerge. Certainly, the findings of Haskins (1985) regarding heightened
aggression in the first two years of public schooling of children with
infant-care experience are consistent with this possibility, since Ramey
and Campbell (1979) actually found that these eventually more aggressive children looked more confident when tested at six, twelve, eighteen,
and twenty-four months of age. Could it be the case, then, that studying
the Schwarz et al. subjects at two years of age would have revealed few
differences (in fact, it did—see Caldwell et al., 1970), whereas studying
the MaCrae and Herbert-Jackson (1975) subjects at four would have
revealed more pronounced differences between groups? Might there be
a need to consider, then, manifest and latent effects?

This possibility is suggested by a follow-up study of the very sample
on which an association between insecure-avoidance and nonmaternal
care in the first year was first chronicled. Although, on the basis of their
analysis of the problem-solving behavior of these Minnesota children
when they were two years of age, Farber and Egeland (1982, p. 120)
were led to conclude that "the effects of out-of-home care were no longer
striking" and "that the cumulative adverse effects of out-of-home care
were minimal," careful scrutiny of the data leads to a different conclusion. Not only was it the case that toddlers whose mothers began working
prior to their infants' first birthdays displayed significantly less enthusiasm than children without early experience in day care, but it was also
the case that these day-care-reared infants tended to be less compliant
in following their mothers' instructions, less persistent in dealing with a
difficult problem, and they tended to display more negative affect. A

more thorough analysis of these same data by Vaughn, Deane, and Waters (1985) revealed, moreover, that while two-year-olds with insecure attachment histories seemed less competent, irrespective of their infant-care experiences, those with first-year experience in nonmaternal care who had been classified as securely attached at eighteen months "showed a deterioration in the quality of adaptation over the period from 18–24 months" (p. 133) and were indistinguishable from formerly insecure children. Thus, it was only formerly secure infants without early care experience who displayed the competencies that might be expected on the basis of their histories of secure attachment relationships. When considered in developmental perspective, these data raise the possibility that one consequence of early care may be heightened vulnerability to subsequent stress, irrespective of early attachment history.

CONCLUSION

What are we to make of all the evidence we have reviewed? On the one hand, the data are seemingly too inconsistent to draw any definitive conclusions. Yet, if one does not feel compelled to draw only irrefutable conclusions, a relatively persuasive circumstantial case can be made that early infant care may be associated with increased avoidance of mother, possibly to the point of greater insecurity in the attachment relationship, and that such care may also be associated with diminished compliance and cooperation with adults, increased aggressiveness, and possibly even greater social maladjustment in the preschool and early school-age years.

What is most noteworthy about these very possibilities is that they are strikingly consistent with basic theoretical contentions of attachment theory. Also striking is the fact that, for the most part, the total body of evidence on nonmaternal care *in the first year*, including the early attachment *and* later social development data, has not been organized in terms of such a theoretical framework (or any other for that matter—but see Gamble and Zigler 1986). It is certainly not inconsistent with attachment theory that repeated separations in the first year of life, as routinely associated with day-care usage, might affect the emerging attachment relationship, and even disturb it from the standpoint of security (or at least avoidance). Further, the theory clearly assumes that avoidance reflects some doubt on the part of the infant with respect to the availability and responsiveness of the mother and may well serve as a coping strategy to mask anger (Main and Weston 1982). Finally, the theory clearly assumes that an avoidant attachment places the child at risk (based on probability) for subsequent social difficulties, with lack of compliance and cooperation, increased aggressiveness, and even maladjustment being, to some extent, expectable outcomes.

The point of this essay, and my reason for writing it, have not been to argue that infant day care inevitably or necessarily results in an anxious-avoidant attachment and, thereby, increased risk for patterns of social development that most would regard as undesirable, but rather to raise this seemingly real possibility by organizing the available data in such terms. As I have stressed repeatedly, there is enough evidence to lead a judicious scientist to doubt this line of reasoning; by the same token, however, there is *more than enough* evidence to lead the same judicious individual to entertain it seriously and to restrain from explaining away and thus dismissing findings that may be ideologically disconcerting.

This would seem to be especially wise in view of the fact that the correlates of day care which have been chronicled (avoidance, aggression, noncompliance, withdrawal) have been found across a host of ecological niches and caregiving milieus. Thus, these developmental correlates of early supplementary care have been found in samples of impoverished (Haskins 1985; Vaughn et al. 1980), middle-class (Rubenstein, Howes, and Boyle 1981), and upper-class families (Barglow et al., in press), and with children cared for in unstable family day care (Vaughn et al. 1980), high-quality centers (Haskins 1985; Schwarz, Strickland, and Krolick 1974), poor quality centers (McCartney et al. 1982) and even in-home, babysitter care (Barglow et al., in press). In spite of the variation in the samples studied, the similarity in the developmental outcomes associated with nonmaternal care in the first year leads me to conclude that entry into care in the first year of life is a risk factor for the development of insecure-avoidant attachments in infancy and heightened aggressiveness, noncompliance, and withdrawal in the preschool and early school years. Under a variety of imaginable conditions pertaining to the care arrangement, the child, and the family, it seems likely that risk associated with early care would increase.

In this regard, the quality and stability of care experienced by the infant are of first importance. A great deal of evidence indicates that small groups, with well-trained staff, are in the child's best interest (see Belsky 1984, for review), and recent research also reveals that frequent changes in care arrangements or the absence of a stable caregiver are more stressful for the child (Cummings 1980, 1986; Suwalsky et al. 1986). Thus, when groups are large, staff are poorly trained, and/or arrangements are unstable, the risk to the child certainly increases.

Next in order are the characteristics of the child. It is well recognized that males are more vulnerable to stress across the lifespan, and there is some indication that boys may be affected more adversely by early nonmaternal care than are girls (Chase-Lansdale and Owen 1981; Cochran and Robinson 1983; Gamble and Zigler 1986; Hock and Clinger

1980; Rutter 1981). It is also likely that some infants, simply because of their constitutional make-up, may find the experience of daily separation associated with day care and the coping it necessitates to be especially difficult.

Finally, the characteristics of the family also need to be considered. Infants whose families are experiencing economic stress would seem to be at special risk, not only because of the cost of quality care, but also because such stress can undermine the parents' capacity to be emotionally available to and supportive of their offspring. Even when economic stress is not severe, parental care may be affected by a host of processes operating within the family (for example, marital conflict) and beyond (for example, job stress) that may influence the quality of care provided in the home and thereby the child's development (Belsky 1984). Evidence that variation in care received in the home is of consequence for understanding variation in outcomes associated with infant care comes from a recent study of employed mothers. Consistent with research and theory from the attachment literature (Ainsworth 1973; Sroufe 1979), Benn (1985) found that those women who provided sensitive and responsive care had infants who developed secure attachments, whereas those providing less sensitive care developed insecure attachment relationships.

Several sets of data in the literature lead me to speculate that it may be overstimulation in particular that may be responsible for the anxious-avoidant attachment we have seen to be associated with infant day care. First, several studies not concerned with day care indicate that mothers of infants who develop anxious-avoidant attachments are excessively stimulating, possibly to the point of intrusiveness (Belsky, Rovine, and Taylor 1984; Isabella 1986; Lewis et al. 1984). Second, observational studies conducted by Pedersen and his colleagues (1984) indicate that mothers who are employed interact with their infants so much at the end of the day that their husbands actually have even less time to interact with their infants than do fathers whose wives do not work outside the home. And finally, Schwartz (1983) observed that not only was infant day care associated with heightened avoidance of the mother but also with elevated levels of maternal kissing and hugging of the infant at the end of the day. What all this suggests to me is that some mothers may overstimulate and thereby overwhelm their infants' information processing capabilities in their desire to establish contact with them after a long day of separation and, in so doing, promote the very avoidance we have found to be associated with nonmaternal care in the first year of life. Although such behavior may be understandable, especially as it seems so consistent with the ethic of "quality time," it may well serve the needs of the mother far more than those of her infant.

POLICY IMPLICATIONS

In view of the fact that risk associated with infant care is likely to be increased depending upon characteristics of the care arrangement, the child, and the family, the task for policymakers in this day and age when even infant day care appears to be the norm is to help establish buffers to the host of stresses that may be associated with infant care. One direct strategy for doing this is to enable parents to stay at home with their infants during the first months of life. A parental leave policy which guaranteed the right of one parent to provide care for the infant without losing his/her job and, preferably, with some continuation of salary and/or fringe benefits might help to alleviate a great deal of stress (Young and Zigler 1986).

The government can also assist parents through regulatory mechanisms to influence the quality of care provided and the continuing education of care providers. Federal Interagency Day Care Requirements (FIDCR), which were designed to set standards for group sizes, staff-child ratios, and caregiver training, have been withdrawn. One consequence of this is that 16% of the states have no ratio requirements for the care of children under two, with only three states meeting the 1980 FIDCR standards of 1:3. Similarly, 62% of the states have no group size regulations for day-care centers, and group size is not specified in any state regulations for family and group homes; only three states comply with the withdrawn FIDCR standards of six for infant group size. Finally, with regard to caregiver training, 80% of the states permit infants and toddlers to be cared for by persons who have no specific training to work with children under three years of age. It would appear, then, that the existing state day-care regulations are clearly deficient in mandating a safe and healthy environment for infants and toddlers (Young and Zigler 1986). When this reality is considered alongside the fact that most parents are relatively uninformed consumers of day care (Fuqua and Labensohn 1986) and that high-quality infant care is prohibitively expensive, it should really come as little surprise that infant day care may place a child at developmental risk.

REFERENCES

Ainsworth, M. D. S. 1973. The development of infant-mother attachment. B. M. Caldwell and H. N. Ricciuti (eds.). *Review of child development research* (Vol. 3, pp. 1–94). Chicago: University of Chicago Press.

Ainsworth, M. D. S. 1982. Attachment: Retrospect and prospect. In C. M. Parkes and J. Stevenson-Hinde (eds.). *The place of attachment in human behavior* (pp. 3–30). New York: Basic Books.

Barglow, P. 1985. *Other-than-mother, in-home care, and the quality of the mother-child relationship.* Paper presented at the biennial meetings of the Society for Research in Child Development, Toronto.

Barglow, P., Vaughn, B., and Molitor, N. In press. Effects of maternal absence due to employment on the quality of infant-mother attachment in a low-risk sample. *Child Development.*

Barton, M., and Schwarz, J. 1981. *Day care in the middle class: Effects in elementary school.* Paper presented at the American Psychological Association's Annual Convention, Los Angeles.

Bates, J., Maslin, C., and Frankel, K. 1985. Attachment security, mother-child interaction, and temperament as predictors of behavior problem ratings at age three years. I. Bretherton and E. Waters (eds.). *Growing points in attachment theory and research.* Monographs of the Society for Research in Child Development, vol. 50.

Belsky, J. 1984. The determinants of parenting: A process model. *Child Development,* 55:83–96.

Belsky, J. 1984. Two waves of day care research: Developmental effects and conditions of quality. R. Ainslie (ed.). *The child and the day care setting* (pp. 1–34). New York: Praeger.

Belsky, J. 1985. Prepared statement on the effects of day care. In Select Committee on Children, Youth, and Families, House of Representatives, 98th Congress, Second Session, *Improving child care services: What can be done?* Washington, DC: U.S. Government Printing Office.

Belsky, J., Garduque, L., and Hrncir, E. 1984. Assessing performance, competence, and executive capacity in infant play: Relations to home environment and security of attachment. *Developmental Psychology,* 20:406–17.

Belsky, J., Rovine, M., and Taylor, D. 1984. The Pennsylvania infant and family development project. III: The origins of individual differences in infant-mother attachment: Maternal and infant contributions. *Child Development* 55:706–17.

Belsky, J., and Steinberg, L. D. 1978. The effects of day care: A critical review. *Child Development,* 49:929–49.

Belsky, J., Steinberg, L. D., and Walker, A. 1982. The ecology of day care. M. Lamb (ed.). *Childrearing in nontraditional families* (pp. 71–116). Hillsdale, N.J.: Erlbaum.

Benn, R. 1985. *Factors associated with security of attachment in dual-career families.* Paper presented at the biennial meeting of the Society for Research in Child Development, Toronto.

Bowlby, J. 1969. *Attachment and loss: Vol. 1. Attachment.* New York: Basic Books.

Bowlby, J. 1973. *Attachment and loss: Vol. 2. Separation.* New York: Basic Books.

Bronfenbrenner, U., Belsky, J., and Steinberg, L. 1976. Day care in context: An ecological perspective on research and public policy. A report to the Department of Health, Education, and Welfare, Federal Interagency Day Care Requirements Policy Committee, Washington, D.C.

Brookhart, J., and Hock, E. 1976. The effects of experimental context and experiential background on infants' behavior toward their mothers and a stranger. *Child Development* 47:333–40.

Caldwell, B. M., Wright, C. M., Honig, A. S., and Tannenbaum, J. 1970. Infant care and attachment. *American Journal of Orthopsychiatry* 40:397–412.

Chase-Lansdale, L., and Owen, M. T. April 1981. *Maternal employment in a family context: Effects on infant-mother and infant-father attachment.* Paper presented at the biennial meetings of the Society for Research in Child Development, Boston.

Chase-Lansdale, L., and Owen, M. T. 1986. *Maternal employment in a family context: Effects of infant-mother and infant-father attachments.* Manuscript in preparation.

Clarke-Stewart, K. A., and Fein, G. 1983. Early childhood programs. M. M. Maith and J. J. Campos, eds. P. H. Mussen (series ed.) *Handbook of Child Psychology: Vol. 2. Infancy and Developmental Psychobiology.* New York: John Wiley & Sons.

Cochran, M. 1977. A comparison of group day and family childrearing patterns in Sweden. *Child Development* 48:702–07.

Cochran, M., and Robinson, J. 1983. Day care, family circumstances, and sex differences. S. Kilmer, ed. *Advances in Early Education and Day Care*, vol. 3. Greenwich, Conn.: JAI Press.

Cummings, E. M. 1980. Caregiver stability and day care. *Developmental Psychology* 16:31–37.

Cummings, E. M. April 1986. *Caregiver Stability and Day Care: Continuity vs. Daily Association.* Paper presented at the International Conference on Infant Studies.

Doyle, A. 1975. Infant development in day care. *Developmental Psychology*, 4:655–56.

Doyle, A., and Somers, K. 1978. The effects of group and family day care on infant attachment behaviors. *Canadian Journal of Behavioral Science*, 10:38–45.

Easterbrooks, M., and Goldberg, W. 1985. Effects of early maternal employment on toddlers, mothers, and fathers. *Developmental Psychology*, 21:774–83.

Egeland, B. 1983. Comments on Kopp, Krakow, and Vaughn's chapter. M. Perlmutter (ed.). *Minnesota Symposium in Child Psychology* vol. 16. Hillsdale, New Jersey: Erlbaum.

Erickson, M., Sroufe, A., and Egeland, B. 1985. The relationship between quality of attachment and behavior problems in preschool in a high-risk sample. I. Bretherton and E. Waters (eds.). *Growing points in attachment theory and research* (pp. 147–66). *Monograph for the Society for Research in Child Development*, Serial No. 209, Vol. 50, No. 1–2.

Farber, E. A., and Egeland, B. 1982. Developmental consequences of out-of-home care for infants in a low income population. E. Zigler and E. Gordon (eds.), *Day Care* (pp. 102–25). Boston: Auburn.

Farran, D., and Ramey, C. 1977. Infant day care and attachment behaviors toward mothers and teachers. *Child Development*, 48:1112–16.

Fowler, W., and Khan, N. 1974/1975. *The development of a prototype infant and child day care center in metropolitan Toronto.* Ontario Institute for Studies in

Education, Year III Progress Report, December 1974; Year IV Progress Report.

Fraiberg, S. 1977. *Every child's birthright: In defense of mothering.* New York: Basic Books.

Fuqua, R., and Labensohn, D. 1986. Parents as consumers of child care. *Family Relations*, 35:295–303.

Gamble, T., and Zigler, E. 1986. Effects of infant day care: Another look at the evidence. *American Journal of Orthopsychiatry*, 56:26–41.

Haskins, R. 1985. Public school aggression among children with varying day-care experience. *Child Development*, 56:689–703.

Hock, E. 1980. Working and nonworking mothers and their infants: A comparative study of maternal caregiving characteristics and infant social behavior. *Merrill-Palmer Quarterly*, 26:79–101.

Hock, E., and Clinger, J. 1980. Behavior toward mother and stranger of infants who have experienced group day care, individual care, or exclusive maternal care. *Journal of Genetic Psychology*, 134:49–61.

Isabella, R. 1986. The origins of infant-mother attachment: An examination of interactional synchrony during the infant's first year. Ph.D. diss. The Pennsylvania State University.

Jacobsen, J., and Wille, D. 1984. Influence of attachment and separation experience on separation distress at 18 months. *Developmental Psychology*, 20:477–84.

Joffee, L. 1981. The quality of mother-infant attachment and its relationship to compliance with maternal commands and prohibitions. Paper presented to the Society for Research in Child Development, Boston.

Kagan, J., Kearsley, R., and Zelazo, P. 1976. The effects of infant day care on psychological development. Paper presented at the meeting of the American Association for the Advancement of Science, Boston.

Kagan, J., Kearsley, R., and Zelazo, P. 1978. *Infancy: Its place in human development.* Cambridge, Mass.: Harvard University Press.

Kamerman, S. 1986. Infant care usage in the United States. Report presented to National Academy of Sciences Ad Hoc Committee on Policy Issues in Child Care for Infants and Toddlers, Washington, D.C.

Kamerman, S., and Kahn, A. 1978. *Family policy: Government and families in 14 countries.* New York: Columbia University Press.

LaFreniere, P., and Sroufe, L. A. 1985. Profiles of peer competence in the preschool: Interrelations between measures, influence of social ecology, and relation to attachment history. *Developmental Psychology*, 21:56–68.

Lay, M., and Meyer, W. 1973. *Teacher/child behaviors in an open environment day care program.* Syracuse University Children's Center.

Lewis, M., Feiring, C., McGuffog, C., and Jaskir, J. 1984. Predicting psychopathology in six-year-olds from early social relations. *Child Development*, 55:123–36.

Londerville, S., and Main, M. 1981. Security, compliance, and maternal training methods in the second year of life. *Developmental Psychology*, 17:289–99.

MaCrae, J. W., and Herbert-Jackson, E. 1975. Are behavioral effects of infant day care programs specific? *Developmental Psychology*, 12:269–70.

Main, M. 1973. Play, exploration, and competence as related to child-adult attachment. Ph.D. diss., Johns Hopkins University.

Main, M., and Weston, D. R. 1981. The quality of the toddler's relationship to mother and to father: Related to conflict behavior and the readiness to establish new relationships. *Child Development*, 52:932–40.

Main, M., and Weston, D. R. 1982. Avoidance of the attachment figure in infancy: Description and interpretation. C. Parkes and J. Stevenson-Hinde (eds.). *The place of attachment in human behavior* (pp. 31–59). New York: Basic Books.

Maslin, L., and Bates, J. 1982. *Anxious attachment as a predictor of disharmony in the mother-toddler relationship*. Paper presented at the International Conference on Infant Studies, Austin, Texas.

Masters, J., and Wellman, H. 1974. Human infant attachment: A procedural critique. *Psychological Bulletin*, 81:218–37.

Matas, L., Arend, R. A., and Sroufe, L. A. 1978. Continuity of adaptation in the second year: The relationship between quality of attachment and later competence. *Child Development*, 49:547–56.

McCartney, K., Scarr, S., Phillips, D., Grajek, S., and Schwarz, J. C. 1982. Environmental differences among day care centers and their effects on children's development. E. Zigler and E. Gardon (eds.). *Day care: Scientific and social policy issues* (pp. 126–51). Boston: Auburn House.

Meyer, W. 1979. Developmental effects of infant day care: An empirical study. Paper presented at the annual meeting of the American Educational Research Association, San Francisco.

Pedersen F., Cain, R., Zaslow, M., and Anderson, B. 1984. Variation in infant experience associated with alternative family roles. L.Laosa and I. Sigel, eds. *The Child and Its Family*. New York: Plenum.

Ramey, C., and Campbell, F. A. 1979. Contemporary education for disadvantaged children. *School Review*, 87:171–89.

Ramey, C., MacPhee, D., and Yeates, K. 1982. Preventing developmental retardation: A general systems model. L. Bond and J. Joffee (eds.). *Facilitating Infant and Early Childhood Development* (vol. 6, Primary Prevention of Psychopathology). Hanover, New Hampshire: University Press of New England.

Ricciuti, H. N. 1974. Fear and the development of social attachments in the first year of life. M. Lewis and L. A. Rosenblum (eds.). *The origins of fear*. New York: JohnWiley & Sons.

Rubenstein, J., and Howes, C. 1983. Adaptation to toddler day care. In S. Kilmer (ed.), *Advances in early education and day care*. Greenwich, Conn.: JAI Press.

Rubenstein, J., Howes, C., and Boyle, P. 1981. A two year follow-up of infants in community-based day care. *Journal of Child Psychology and Psychiatry*, 22:209–18.

Rutter, M. 1981. Socioemotional consequences of day care for preschool children. *American Journal of Orthopsychiatry*, 51:4–28.

Saunders, M. 1972. Some aspects of the effects of day care on infants' emotional and personality development. Ph.D. diss., University of North Carolina.

Schwartz, P. 1983. Length of day-care attendance and attachment behavior in eighteen-month-old infants. *Child Development,* 54:1073–78.

Schwarz, J. C. 1983. Effects of group day care in the first two years. Paper presented at the biennial meeting of the Society for Research in Child Development, Detroit, Michigan.

Schwarz, J. C., Scarr, S., Caparulo, B., Furrow, D., McCartney, K., Billington, R., Phillips, D., and Hindy, C. 1981. Center, sitter, and home day care before age two: A report on the First Bermuda Infant Care Study. Paper presented at the American Psychological Association Annual Convention, Los Angeles.

Schwarz, J. C., Strickland, R. G., and Krolick, G. 1974. Infant day care: Behavioral effects at preschool age. *Developmental Psychology,* 10:502–06.

Sroufe, L. A. 1979. The coherence of individual development. *American Psychologist,* 34:834–41.

Sroufe, L. A. 1983. Infant-caregiver attachment and patterns of adaptation in preschool: The roots of maladaptation and competence. M. Perlmutter, ed. *Minnesota symposium in child psychology,* vol. 16. Hillsdale, New Jersey: Erlbaum.

Sroufe, L. A., and Waters, E. 1977. Attachment as an organizational construct. *Child Development,* 48:1184–99.

Suwalsky, J., Zaslow, M., Klein, R., and Rabinovitch, B. 1986. Continuity of substitute care in relation to infant-mother attachment. Paper presented at the annual meetings of the American Psychological Association, Washington, D.C.

Vaughn, B., Deane, K., and Waters, E. 1985. The impact of out-of-home care on child-mother attachment quality: Another look at some enduring questions. I. Bretherton and E. Waters, eds. *Growing points in attachment theory and research. Monographs for the Society for Research in Child Development.* Serial No. 209, Vol. 50, Nos. 1–2.

Vaughn, B., Gove, F. L., and Egeland, B. 1980. The relationship between out-of-home care and the quality of infant-mother attachment in an economically disadvantaged population. *Child Development* 51:971–75.

Waters, E. 1978. The reliability and stability of individual differences in infant-mother attachment. *Child Development* 49:483–94.

Waters, E., and Sroufe, L. A. 1983. Social competence as a developmental construct. *Developmental Review,* 3:79–87.

Wille, D., and Jacobsen, J. 1984. The influence of maternal employment, attachment pattern, extrafamilial child care, and previous experience with peers on early peer interaction. Paper presented at the meetings of the International Conference on Infant Studies, New York.

Young, K., and Zigler, E. 1986. Infant and toddler day care: Regulations and policy implications. *American Journal of Orthopsychiatry* 56:43–55.

SEVEN

Infant and Toddler Day Care: Regulation and Policy Implications

KATHRYN T. YOUNG
AND EDWARD ZIGLER

With the increasing number of mothers who by choice or necessity work out of the home, there have been dramatic changes in the way many of the nation's children are being raised. In 1982 the Census Bureau reported that 41% of women with children under one year of age, and 38% of women with children under three were employed outside the home. Just a year later the Bureau of Labor (1983) reported comparable statistics of 45% and 44% respectively. And although after-school care has long been a common practice, today much younger children are routinely placed in day care. Perhaps this explains why day care for infants and toddlers is currently the fastest growing type of out-of-home care (Jones and Prescott 1982).

The environments in which children of working mothers are being cared for include both licensed facilities (day-care centers, family day-care homes, and group day-care homes) and unlicensed family and group homes. It would not be surprising if the unlicensed facilities far outnumber those which are licensed. Undoubtedly the most common arrangement is for a relative or friend to babysit while the parents work, because such settings are usually closer to home and less costly than more formal types of care.

This rapid shift in childrearing environments for very young children raises many important questions. The most crucial concerns the effects of day-care environments on the psychological development of infants and toddlers. The effects of day care on children's development have been the focus of research and lively debate for fifteen years (Gamble and Zigler 1985), but in this chapter we examine existing federal and state standards for the group care of infants and toddlers in order to suggest a realistic and constructive childcare policy for children and families in the 1980s.

RESEARCH INFORMING DAY CARE STANDARDS

One of the first studies to describe the character of group day-care facilities in America was *Windows on Day Care* (Keyserling 1972). The picture the investigators painted was fairly grim. Only 9% of nonprofit day-care centers were described as providing superior care. Half of the centers were "fair or custodial in nature providing no educational services beyond the meeting of physical needs" (p. 5). A shocking 11% were rated as poor, with vivid descriptions of "double-decker cardboard cribs in a room with open gas heaters" and "babies in a dark room strapped into an infant seat inside a crib and crying" (p. 64). Although the methods of evaluation were subjective and very global, the study alerted social scientists and policymakers to the need for more rigorous assessment of day-care environments.

Clearly, being tied in a crib all day is not in the child's best interest. But exactly what *is* in the child's best interest? This question might seem unanswerable, since theorists cannot agree on what parents themselves do to optimize their children's development or on what practices are best suited to different children. Nonetheless, there are some tentative but common-sensical ideas.

Beginning with the children themselves, a number of studies and reviews have failed to identify negative consequences of early entry into day care (Belsky and Steinberg 1978; Caldwell et al. 1970; Clarke-Stewart 1982; Kagan et al. 1978; Ramey et al. 1981; Ricciuti 1974; Rutter 1982). Clarke-Stewart (1982) not only found no risk, but even suggested that day-care children are more mature intellectually and socially than home-reared children when they begin school.

In another frequently noted study, Kagan and his colleagues (1978) offered similar positive findings that infants who entered day care as early as three-and-one-half months were no different in measures of attachment, cognition, and social play than infants reared at home. In spite of their conclusion that a young child's social, emotional, and cognitive development can proceed normally in a day-care facility, these investigators recommended that infants not begin group day care before three months of age, and that one caregiver be responsible for no more than three infants. Rutter (1982) also stressed the importance of an adult not caring for more than three infants. Many of the studies failing to find any negative consequences of early group day care appear to be open to two major criticisms. First. the centers investigated in most of these studies are not representative of those typically available to most parents, and second, the longitudinal aspects of the studies were not of a long enough duration to support any final conclusions.

Other workers have noted the potentially damaging effects on the psychological development of children as a result of early group day care (Ainsworth 1973; Brazelton 1984; Fraiberg 1977; Gamble and Zigler 1985; Zigler and Muenchow 1983). This concern stems in part from findings that in the early months of life an interactive phenomenon is developing between mother and infant which requires close proximity and considerable time together (Brazelton et al. 1974; Stern 1974). This work demonstrates that the mother and the infant are repeatedly learning how to respond to rhythmic changes in each other, a process characterized by reciprocal influence. These early interactions not only reflect depth of attachment but also provide opportunities for the infant to learn about the environment and how to function within it.

Several investigators have expressed concern about the effects of early group care on attachment behavior (see Gamble and Zigler 1985). For example, Farber and Egeland (1982) followed a low income population who used community based day care. Infants who had begun day care before their first birthday had an increased likelihood of exhibiting anxious-avoidant attachments toward their mothers. At 24 months these same infants displayed less enthusiasm and were less compliant in problem-solving tasks than those children who had begun day care at a later age. These findings have been replicated by other investigators. It should be emphasized that these studies involved poor quality community day care and unstable child care arrangements with frequent changes in caregiving.

In terms of eventual consequences, these types of anxious attachment relationships have been found to predict problems in adjusting to peers during the preschool years (Arend et al. 1979; Baron and Schwartz 1981; McCartney et al. 1982). Gamble and Zigler (1985) suggested that such problems may be more evident in males, who appear to be more sensitive to variations in caregiving environments than females. These reviewers also concluded that early group care may be particularly detrimental to the development of young children who reside in families who are already experiencing stress.

However these conflicting findings on the effects of early group care are reconciled, workers appear to agree that poor quality care in general and unstable caregivers in particular can be detrimental to infant development. Belsky (1984) analyzed how the findings concerning quality of day care are consistent with those on family influences in child development. The same qualities of parental care which promote healthy psychological development in infancy and toddlerhood are also necessary for caregivers in day-care settings. That is, caregivers need to be involved and sensitive to the child's developmental needs, to be able to control behavior without being restrictive, and to facilitate linguistic communication.

This brings us to the issue of caregivers and the qualities they must possess to be suitable parental substitutes. Like day-care settings, caregivers can be licensed or unlicensed, good or bad. The National Day Care Study (NDCS) systematically investigated the effects that variations in day-care staff (staff-to-child ratio, group size, staff qualifications) had on the development of young children (Ruopp et al. 1974). They reported that for infants and toddlers, "high staff:child ratios (fewer children per caregiver) as well as small group size were associated with less overt distress and apathy on the part of the children, less exposure to potential physical harm, and less management activities on the part of caregivers (Ruopp and Travers 1982, p. 82). The NDCS also indicated that for staff, specialized training in areas such as child development, day care, or early childhood education, rather than general level of formal education, was a more significant variable in promoting a high degree of social interaction with the children. Caregivers' training also positively influenced gains on the children's scores on standardized tests (Ruopp and Travers 1982). A further study of family day-care environments supported the NDCS findings that both group size and caregiver training influence the quality of a child's experience and subsequent development.

CURRENT DAY CARE REGULATIONS

Federal Level

Since 1968, the federal government has vascillated in its involvement with day-care regulations (Cohen and Zigler 1977; Nelson 1982). During this period experts who represent the best wisdom in the field have proposed, revised, and reproposed federal regulations for day care. Because of the cost implications (Ruopp and Travers 1982), the suggested regulations have not been optimal but rather minimal standards for day care—a standard below which the child's development could be impaired. To date the federal role is still unclear, and the Federal Interagency Day Care Requirements (FIDCR) have been withdrawn. In spite of this, the withdrawn FIDCR have repeatedly served as guidelines for minimum standards when day-care quality is being discussed. Therefore, in this paper the 1980 FIDCR will serve as a basis of comparison in examining the existing state regulations for day-care centers, family day-care homes, and group day-care homes.

The FIDCR propose separate guidelines in several areas for each type of setting. The staff-to-child ratio for day-care centers is 1:3 for infants (birth to twenty-four months) and 1:4 for toddlers (twenty-four to thirty-six months). The ratio for family day care is 1:5, provided that no more than two of these children are under two years of age. In a day-care home in which all children are under two years of age, the staff-to-child ratio is 1:3. The ratio is 1:6 only if all children are over two years of age. The proposed group size for all types of day care is six for infants and twelve for toddlers. The FIDCR also recommends that state agencies establish and implement specialized training programs in child care so that caregivers must be knowledgeable in child care in order to be employed in a day-care facility. In terms of a program of care for the children, there is a general proposal for developmentally appropriate activities that promote social, intellectual, emotional, and physical development.

State Level

Information for the analysis of the current state regulations was obtained from the *Comparative Licensing Study, Profiles of State Day Care Licensing Requirements for Day Care Centers, Family Day Care Homes and Group Day Care Homes* (Administration for Children, Youth, and Families, Office of Human Development Services 1982). This five-volume work is a secondary source; it does not print each state's complete regulations as written, but rather has reorganized the information so that the format is the same for each state. We have examined regulations for each of the fifty states in regard to staff-to-child ratio, group size, staff training in child development, specific program objectives for infants and toddlers, entry age for infants, and staff qualifications. The distinction between the three types of day care (center, family, or group) was based on two factors: the number of children enrolled and the location of the facility. Day-care centers which generally provide care for no fewer than twelve children are located in nonresidential buildings. Both family and group day-care operate in private homes, where the caregiver may be related or unrelated to the children. The number of children served ranges from more than one to twelve.

All fifty states have regulations to guide the operation and licensing of day-care centers (table 1). Forty-four states regulate family day-care homes (table 2) but only fourteen states have specific regulations for group day-care homes. However, based on the number of children served, in all but six states group day-care licensing is covered by either day-care-center or family day-care-home regulations. A summary of the state regulations is presented in table 3.

Table 7.1: Day-Care Center Characteristics

	Staff:Child Ratio		Group Size		Specialized Staff Training in Child Care		Developmentally Appropriate Program of Care for Infants/Toddlers (Meets FIDCR)
	Infant	Toddler	Infant	Toddler	Director	Caregiver	
FIDCR	1:3	1:4	6	12			
Alabama	1:6	1:6	6	6	No	No	Yes
Alaska	1:5	1:10	*	*	No	No	Yes
Arizona	1:8	1:10	*	*	No	No	Yes
Arkansas	1:6	1:9	*	*	No	No	No
California	1:4	1:12	*	*	Yes	No	No
Colorado	1:5	1:5	*	*	Yes	Yes	Yes
Connecticut	1:4	1:4	8	8	No	No	No
Delaware	1:5	1:8	8	8	No	No	No
Florida	1:6	1:8–12	*	*	No	No	No
Georgia	1:7	1:10	*	*	No	No	No
Hawaii	*	1:10	*	*	Yes	No	*
Idaho	1:6	1:8	*	*	No	No	Yes
Illinois	1:4	1:5	12	15	Yes	No	Yes
Indiana	1:4	1:5	8	10	Yes	No	Yes
Iowa	1:4	1:6	*	*	No	No	Yes

Table 7.1: (*continued*)

	Staff:Child Ratio		Group Size		Specialized Staff Training in Child Care		Developmentally Appropriate Program of Care for Infants/Toddlers (Meets FIDCR)
	Infant	Toddler	Infant	Toddler	Director	Caregiver	
Kansas	1:3	1:5	9	12	Yes	No	Yes
Kentucky	1:6	1:8	*	*	No	No	Yes
Louisiana	1:6	1:12	*	*	No	No	No
Maine	*	1:8	*	*	Yes	No	*
Maryland	*	1:6	12	20	Yes	Yes	*
Massachusetts	1:3	1:4	7	9	Yes	Yes	Yes
Michigan	1:4	1:10	*	*	Yes	No	No
Minnesota	1:4	1:7	*	*	Yes	Yes	Yes
Mississippi	*	*	*	*	No	No	No
Missouri	1:4	1:8	8	8	Yes	No	Yes
Montana	*	1:10	*	15	No	No	*
Nebraska	1:4	1:5	*	*	Yes	No	No
Nevada	1:4	1:8	*	*	Yes	Yes	Yes
New Hampshire	*	*	*	*	No	No	*
New Jersey	*	1:10	*	*	Yes	Yes	No

State							
New Mexico	1:7	1:15	*	*	No	No	No
New York	1:4	1:5	8	10	Yes	No	No
N. Carolina	1:8	1:12	7	9	No	No	Yes
N. Dakota	1:4	1:4	*	*	No	No	No
Ohio	1:8	1:10	16	16	Yes	No	No
Oklahoma	1:4–1:6	1:8	*	*	No	No	Yes
Oregon	1:4	1:4	8	8	Yes	No	Yes
Pennsylvania	1:4	1:5	*	*	Yes	No	No
Rhode Island	*	*	*	*	Yes	Yes	*
S. Carolina	1:8	1:12	*	*	Yes	No	Yes
S. Dakota	1:5	1:5	20	20	No	No	*
Tennessee	1:5	1:8	16	16	No	No	*
Texas	1:5–7	1:9–13	*	35	No	No	Yes
Utah	1:4	1:7	8	25	No	No	*
Vermont	1:5	1:5	*	*	No	No	No
Virginia	1:4	1:10	*	*	No	No	No
Washington	1:5	1:7	10	14	Yes	No	*
W. Virginia	1:4	1:8	*	*	Yes	No	Yes
Wisconsin	1:3	1:6	8	16	Yes	Yes	Yes
Wyoming	1:5	1:8	*	*	No	No	No

Source: Information from *Comparative Licensing Study*, 1982.
*Not specified.

Table 7.2: Family Day-Care Characteristics

	Group Composition	Specialized Staff Training in Child Care		Developmentally Appropriate Program of Care for Infants/Toddlers (Meets FIDCR)
		Director	Caregiver	
FIDCR	1:5 staff child ratio with no more than 2 children under 2 yrs. old			
	1:3 if all children under 2 yrs. old			
	1:6 if all children 2–3 yrs. old			
Alabama	1:6	Yes	No	*
Alaska	1:8; 2 under 2 yrs. old	No	No	Yes
Arizona	No Regulations			
Arkansas	1:6; 3 under 2½ yrs. old	No	No	Yes
California	1:6; 2 under 2 yrs. old	No	No	*
Colorado	1:4 for 0–2½ yrs. old	Yes	Yes	No
	1:3 if under 1 yr. old			
Connecticut	1:5; 1 under 2 yrs. old	No	No	No
Delaware	1:3 infants	No	No	*
Florida	1:5 pre-schoolers	No	No	No
Georgia	1:3; 3 or more under 2½ yrs. old	No	No	No
Hawaii	1:5; 2 under 2 yrs. old	No	No	*
Idaho	1:6	No	No	No
Illinois	1:8; 2 under 2 yrs. old	No	No	Yes
Indiana	1:6	No	No	*
Iowa	1:6; 4 under 2 yrs. old	No	No	*
Kansas	1:6 with 1 infant	No	No	*
	1:5 with 2 infants			

	Group Composition	Specialized Staff Training in Child Care		Developmentally Appropriate Program of Care for Infants/Toddlers (Meets FIDCR)
		Director	Caregiver	
Kentucky	1:6	No	No	Yes
Louisiana	No Regulations			
Maine	No Regulations			*
Maryland	1:4	No	No	*
Massachusetts	1:3 with 3 or more under 2 yrs. old	Yes	Yes	*
Michigan	1:6; 2 under 1 yr.	No	No	
Minnesota	1:5 1:4 infants	No	No	Yes
Mississippi	*	No	No	No
Missouri	1:6	No	No	*
Montana	1:6; 2 under 2 yrs. old	No	No	*
Nebraska	1:8; 2 under 18 mos. 1:4 infants	No	No	No
Nevada	1:6	No	Yes	Yes
New Hampshire	1:6; 2 under 2½ yrs. old 1:4 infants	No	No	No
New Jersey	No Regulations			
New Mexico	No Regulations			
New York	1:6; 2 under 2 yrs. old	No	No	*
N. Carolina	1:6	No	No	*

Table 7.2: (continued)

State				
N. Dakota	1:6; 3 under 2 yrs. old	No	No	*
	1:4 infants			
Ohio	No Regulations			
Oklahoma	1:5	No	No	Yes
Oregon	1:5; 2 under 2 yrs. old	No	No	*
Pennsylvania	1:6; 4 under 3 yrs. old	No	No	No
Rhode Island	*	No	No	No
S. Carolina	1:3	No	No	Yes
S. Dakota	1:4; 0–3 yrs. old	No	No	*
Tennessee	1:7	No	No	No
Texas	1:4; 0–2 yrs. old	No	No	*
	1:4 infants			
	1:6 2 infants			
Utah	1:6; 2 under 2 yrs. old	No	No	No
	1:2 infants			
Vermont	1:6; 2 under 2 yrs. old	No	No	Yes
Virginia	1:4 infants	No	No	*
	1:6; 2 under 2 yrs. old			
Washington	*	Yes	No	No
West Virginia	1:6; 2 under 2 yrs. old	No	No	No
Wisconsin	1:3 infants	Yes	Yes	Yes
	1:4 all under 2½ yrs. old			
	1:5 3 under 2½ yrs. old			
Wyoming	1:6; 3 under 2 yrs. old	Yes	Yes	*

Source: Information from *Comparative Licensing Study*, 1982.
*Not specified.

Table 7.3. Summary of State Regulations for Infant and Toddler Day Care

| | Meets FIDCR | |
Facility	Yes	No
Day-Care Centers		
Ratio		
Infant	3	47
Toddler .	4	46
Group Size		
Infant	3	47
Toddler	11	39
Staff Training in Child Care		
Director	24	26
Caregiver	8	42
Program of Care	21	29
Family Day-Care Homes		
Group Composition	11	39
Staff Training in Child Care		
Director	6	44
Caregiver	5	45
Program of Care	10	40

Staff-to-Child Ratio. State ratio regulations for infants in day-care centers range from 1:3 to 1:8. Sixteen percent of the states have no ratio requirements for children under two. Only three states meet the withdrawn FIDCR, while eighteen allow a 1:4 ratio for infant care. The regulations for staff-to-child ratio for toddler care range from 1:4 to 1:15, with only four states complying with the proposed FIDCR. Forty percent of the states allow eight or ten toddlers to be cared for by a single adult. Only one state, Massachusetts, meets the FIDCR staff-to-child ratio for both infants and toddlers.

Although many states do not have specific regulations for staff-to-child ratios in family day-care homes, the regulation for maximum number of children allowed serves as a comparable measure. Eleven states comply with FIDCR for group composition. Twenty-two states allow one adult to care for six children without a limitation on the number of infants or toddlers allowed. The staff-to-child ratio for group day-care homes ranges from 1:3 to 1:12, with eight out of the fourteen states that have regulations allowing a 1:6 ratio. None of these states comply with the 1980 FIDCR in specifying a maximum number of infants or toddlers within an established childcare ratio.

Group Size. The NDCS indicated that group size is an important characteristic in the quality of day-care environments. However, by statute or regulation, 62% of the states find it quite acceptable not to have group size regulations for day-care centers. For the states which do, the range is from six to twenty for infants, with eight being the most commonly cited number. Only three states comply with the withdrawn FIDCR of six for infant group size. The range for group size for toddlers is from six to thirty-five. Eleven states comply with the FIDCR of twelve. Only one state, Alabama, meets the proposed FIDCR for group size for both infants and toddlers.

Group size is not specified in any of the state regulations for family and group homes. Rather, the concept of maximum number of children allowed is specified and will be used here in place of group size. In family day-care home regulations, the maximum number of children includes the day-care provider's children who are under school age. The range is from four to sixteen with half of the states allowing a maximum of six children. Only thirteen states limit the number of infants or toddlers allowed in the facility. For group day-care homes, the maximum number of children allowed ranges from six to thirteen but the states vary as to whether the day-care provider's children are included in this number.

Staff Training. In view of the NCDS findings and the withdrawn FIDCR, it is disappointing that 52% of the states allow a person with no previous training in child care or development to be a director of a day-care center. For family and group day-care homes only a minimal number of states (six and five, respectively) require the operators of homes to have had a course in child development or child care. The picture is even more bleak in regard to training for caregivers. Only eight states require caregivers in day-care centers and group day-care homes to have had training in child care. Five states require caregivers in family day-care homes to have had specific training. Although many states recommended the Child Development Associate (CDA) credential as one option for training in child development, only one state specified it as a minimum requirement to work in a group day-care facility. A majority of states, however, do make some attempt to recommend training in child care as part of an inservice or postemployment program.

Program of Care. The withdrawn FIDCR specify that the program of care for children in all types of day-care facilities should include developmentally appropriate activities which promote social, intellectual, emotional, and physical development. In our analysis, each state's regulations were rated on a scale of 1 to 3, reflecting the degrees to which they met the withdrawn 1980 FIDCR. The criteria for each category were as follows:

1 = No program regulations for infant and toddler care.
2 = Regulations exist pertaining to factors such as nutrition, health, and safety, but they do not specify a developmentally oriented program of care.
3 = Regulations meet the FIDCR.

Interrater reliability was 95% for ten randomly selected states' program-of-care regulations for both day-care centers and family day-care homes.

For day-care centers, 58% of the states do not mandate developmental programs of care for infants and toddlers. The regulations were so minimal in some states that items such as toilet training or formula refrigeration were all that were included. In one state the "regulations" specified only that "infants and toddlers should be offered water at intervals. Infants shall not remain in cribs, baby beds or playpens all day" (1982, vol. 2, p. 25). It must be noted that the 1980 FIDCR for program of activities are so ambiguous that compliance is simply the matter of the right rhetoric. Many of the twenty-one states which did comply showed no way to put the developmental program they mandated into operation. Five states, however, had regulations which far exceeded the withdrawn FIDCR and included the concepts of individualized care, continuity, rest, stimulation, parent participation, and readiness.

For family day-care homes, twenty states do not specify any program of care for infants or toddlers. Fourteen states do have minimal standards which fail to meet the FIDCR. Ten states, however, specify developmentally oriented programs of activities which meet the FIDCR. In relation to the fourteen states which have group day-care regulations, two states have no program regulations, five have regulations which do not meet the FIDCR, and seven meet the FIDCR.

Day-Care Components Not Addressed by FIDCR. The FIDCR omit several areas particularly relevant to the care of very young children. First, there is no recommendation for the minimum age an infant can enter group day care. With this increased demand for day care for infants and toddlers and the disagreement among experts about its effects, prudence dictates that some guidelines be considered. Second, the withdrawn FIDCR have very general recommendations for staff qualifications. Not only are there no age, education, or experience requirements, but there is no differentiation according to position (aide, caregiver, director). Although training in child care is specified, there is no mention of specialized training in the care of very young children. The developmental tasks of infancy and toddlerhood are unique, and we believe that caregivers for this age range need to be knowledgeable in order to provide appropriate care. In spite of this lack of federal attention, individual states have taken varying degrees of responsibility in establishing licensing requirements for minimum entry age for infants and more specific staff qualifications.

Entry Age. The majority of states (32) either do not specify a minimum entry age, or else they allow infants to be cared for anytime after birth in day-care centers. Only one state, Virginia, requires that an infant be three months old before entering a day-care center. For family day care, a vast majority of states (41) do not specify a minimum age. Two states, Alaska and Tennessee, do require an infant to be six weeks old, and New York requires that the infant be eight weeks old. Almost all of the fourteen states which regulate group day-care homes do not limit the minimum entry age. Connecticut requires the infant to be four weeks old, and Tennessee specifies six weeks for group home care.

Staff Qualifications. Many states have a range for age, education, and experience qualifications for directors and caregivers, so the minimum requirement was used in our analysis. In thirteen states, day-care-center directors do not have to be a certain age. The majority of states require the director to be at least eighteen or twenty-one years old. The minimum educational level varies from twelve states with no specifications to one state requiring a bachelor's degree with course work in child development. A majority (31) of states require the director to have at least one year's previous experience in a day-care facility.

For the director or operator of a family day-care home, eleven states have no minimum age requirement, and twenty-seven states require the operator to be at least eighteen years old. A minimum educational level is not specified in a majority of the states (28). Only two states demand a high school diploma, and forty-one states allow a person to be the director of a family day-care home without any previous day-care experience. Most of the fourteen states with regulations for group daycare homes require the director to be at least eighteen years old. The educational requirements range from six states with no requirement to five that require a high school diploma. Five states do require the director of a group day-care home to have at least one year's experience in a day-care facility.

Qualifications for employment as a child caregiver are somewhat less restrictive. In day-care centers, 50% of the states require caregivers to be at least eighteen years of age. However, eleven states have no age requirement, and nine states allow individuals as young as sixteen to be primary caregivers, not aides who work under supervision. The educational levels for child caregivers is minimal, with thirty-one states not even requiring a high school diploma. Only fourteen states require previous experience in a childcare facility. The qualifications for child caregivers in family day care are similar to those for director or operator. The minimum age ranges from fourteen to twenty-one years old, but thirteen states have no age requirement. Thirty-one states have no minimum educational requirement; thirteen states did demand some some education but none of these exceeds a high school diploma. Virtually all of the states (43) require no previous experience. The qualifications for child caregivers in group day-care homes are similar to those for family day care. However, five of the fourteen states that have regulations require some sort of previous training or experience with children in order to work in a group day-care home.

To date, 80% of the states allow infants and toddlers to be cared for by persons who have not had any specific training or course work with children under three years of age. The situation for family and group day-care homes is even worse. Colorado (family day care) and Delaware (group day care) are the only states that stipulate that at least one caregiver have training or experience with children under two years of age.

Interpretation

This analysis of existing regulations presents a very bleak picture with great variation among the states in standards for infant and toddler day care. Only one state meets the 1980 FIDCR for staff:child ratio for both infants and toddlers in day-care centers. Further, a large majority of states do not even address the issue of group size for any type of day-care facility. In this context, it is worth mentioning again that the National Day Care Study emphasized the importance of small group size for the healthy development of young children. Without group size specifications, day-care facilities could easily comply with regulations for staff:child ratio while having warehouse operations in which large numbers of infants and toddlers are cared for in one space where noise, chaos, and assembly-line care prevail.

The overall regulations for staff qualifications for all three types of day care are so minimal that the possibility of having a "qualified" staff is virtually nonexistent. In 80% of the states, directors and caregivers are allowed to take care of infants and toddlers without any course work or training specific to children under three years of age. In a majority of states, the existing regulations allow these very young children to be cared for by a staff that would have a mean age of 18, has not graduated from high school, and has no previous group day-care experience. This situation exists despite the fact that twenty-one states specify some type of developmentally appropriate program of care for infants and toddlers in day-care centers and ten in family day care. How these programs are to be carried out by untrained personnel is puzzling. Further, the majority of states allow infants to enter group day care anytime after birth.

The thought of placing a newborn infant in the care of a novice is shocking. (Even new mothers receive some guidance during their hospital stay.) Perhaps the implicit assumption is that little knowledge or experience is necessary in order to care for them. Although an informal network of learning about child care can work well within the family structure, the personal relationships and provision of care are different when one is caring for someone else's children in a group setting (Provence 1982).

We must mention briefly the issue of enforcement of day-care regulations. We noted earlier that perhaps the majority of day-care facilities (most likely family day care) are unlicensed. These operate outside of regulation, but it seems reasonable to expect the standards of care to range from horrendous to superior. Licensed facilities must comply with state regulations in order to open their doors, but whether the standards are maintained is an open question. States vary in their policies of periodic inspections, unannounced visits, and procedures for license renewal. One would not predict 100% compliance with state regulations in any case, and where these are weak to begin with and not enforced in the end, this leaves the possibility of the legal licensing of facilities where children are subjected to custodial care or neglected.

CHILDCARE POLICY IMPLICATIONS

The existing state day-care regulations clearly are deficient in mandating a safe and healthy day-care environment for infants and toddlers. The response to this day-care dilemma by those concerned with the well-being of children and families has been to continue to push for enactment of federal standards for day care. Given the present political and social climate in America, the orientation is away from federal regulation towards one of state and personal responsibility (Nelson 1982; Ruopp and Travers 1982; Zigler 1984). The withdrawal of federal leadership since 1980 has been tragic. However, the lowering of state standards, the reductions in funding, and the incidents of child abuse have been evidence to many that federal guidance in day care is still needed. In addition to the 1984 Department of Health and Human Services Recommendations for model day care, Congress has recently proposed several initiatives in the area of child care (U.S. Senate 1985). Congress has proposed improvements in staff:child ratio, staff training, licensing and monitoring, health and safety, and parent involvement.

The current zeitgeist generates three policy initiatives. First, steps need to be taken to allow states to benefit from research findings on day care. There is an abundance of information on day care that needs to be available to providers and consumers. A national conference on day care would provide the forum for state policymakers, care providers, and parents to become more knowledgeable about the characteristics of day care particularly important to infant and toddler development. In preparation for such a conference, the federal government should fund a cost analysis of quality day care for the consumer (Ruopp et al. 1974). Gamble and Zigler have noted that infant and toddler day care is very expensive (1985). Specifically, they estimated the weekly cost of care which includes high staff:child ratio, small group size, stability among caregivers, and trained personnel as at least $150 per child. If states are to insist on these standards, which insure safety and quality, then mechanisms need to be established so that care is not limited to the small number of families that can afford it. There is little value in establishing standards which make day care too costly for the majority of parents. In addition, quality child care can only occur in an environment that has trained caregivers. Therefore, resources necessary for staff training programs need to be part of the overall cost analysis.

A natural outgrowth of such a conference would be the establishment of a national day-care clearinghouse (Ruopp and Travers 1982). Although there are many local efforts to provide information about day care, there is also considerable duplication of effort. A national clearinghouse would serve the function of gathering, evaluating, and providing the most current information to legislators, providers, parents, and policymakers at all levels.

The second policy initiative relates directly to the value our society places on the care of infants and toddlers. When parents choose day care, they are not merely buying a service that permits both of them to work, but rather they are purchasing an environment which influences the development of their child. As consumers of day care, parents have the potential to be a powerful force in influencing aspects of their infants' and toddlers' day-care experiences. In the tradition of Head Start, model day-care programs that have a formal parent-provider partnership need to be established in order to educate both parents and providers. Necessary components of these model programs would include the parents' right to unlimited access to their child's program, and the provider's responsibility in providing parents with periodic progress reports. In the long term, this type of parent-provider partnership may be more effective than the perfunctory yearly state licensing visits. Yet, up to this time, parents' involvement in their child's day care appears to have been minimal (Zigler and Turner 1982).

As a third policy initiative, our nation should examine the possibility of paid infant care leaves. Given the concern about early entry into group day-care settings, many workers have recommended that infants remain in the care of the parents for the first three to six months of life (Brazelton

1984; Kagan et al. 1978; Zigler and Muenchow 1983). For health reasons alone, an argument could be made for keeping very young children out of group settings. A recent study found that for infants under one year old, the chance of getting a bacterial disease that is the leading cause of meningitis and epiglottitis in a child is 12.3 times greater if the children are in day care rather than cared for at home (Redmund and Pichichero 1985). Furthermore, a longer period at home also allows the continuation of breast-feeding, which strengthens the infant's defenses against disease.

In addition to physical health considerations, we must recognize that parents do not become skillful in parenting overnight. It takes time and effort on the part of parents and the infant to develop a satisfying relationship. A period of three- to six-months at home allows them time to get to know each other and to form a solid attachment. Once this relationship has been established parents are better able to make appropriate childcare choices for their infant and themselves (Committee on Public Policy and Public Education 1984). It should be emphasized that the United States is the only Western nation that does not have some form of uniform paid infant care leave available to all new parents. Given the high cost of quality infant day care, more information is needed to determine if paid infant care leaves would be more cost effective in the long run.

Although government licensing and monitoring alone cannot guarantee the safety and security of these very young children, they can contribute significantly to ensuring that these goals are met. As a society we are at a crossroads. We can continue to treat children and families as we have since World War II or we can take account of the changing demographic trends. It is clear that the growing number of infants and toddlers in group day-care environments necessitates constructive thought and action in order to insure the healthy development of the next generation.

REFERENCES

Administration for Children, Youth and Families, Office of Human Development Services. 1982. *Comparative Licensing Study, Profiles of State Day Care Licensing Requirements for Day Care Centers.* U.S. Department of Health and Human Services, Washington, D.C.

Ainsworth, M. 1973. The development of infant-mother attachment. *Review of Child Development Research*, vol. 3. B. Caldwell and H. Ricciuti, eds. Chicago, Illinois: University of Chicago Press.

Arend, R., Gove, F., and Sroufe, L. A. 1979. Continuity of individual adaptation from infancy to kindergarten: a predictive study of ego-resiliency and curiosity in preschoolers. *Child Development* 50:950–59.

Baron, M., and Schwartz, C. 1981. Day care in the middle class: effects in elementary school. Paper presented at the American Psychological Association Annual Convention, Los Angeles, Calif.

Belsky, J. 1984. Two waves of day care research: developmental effects and conditions of quality. *The Child and the Day Care Setting*. R. Ainslie, ed. New York: Praeger Publishers.

Belsky, J., and Steinberg, L. D. 1978. The effects of day care: a critical review. *Child Development* 49:929–49.

Brazelton, T. B. 1984. Stress and supports for families in the 1980s. Presentation at a conference at Harvard Medical School, Boston, Mass.

Brazelton, T. B., Koslowski, B., and Main, M. 1974. The orgins of reciprocity: the early mother-infant interaction. *The Effect of the Infant on Its Caregiver*. M. Lewis and L. Rosenblum, eds. New York: John Wiley.

Caldwell, B., Wright, C., Honig, A., and Tannebaum, J. 1970. Infant care and attachment. *American Journal of Orthopsychiatry* 40:397–412.

Clarke-Stewart, A. 1982. *Daycare*. Cambridge, Mass.: Harvard University Press.

Cohen, D., and Zigler, E. 1977. Federal day care standards: rationale and recommendations. *American Journal of Orthopsychiatry*. 47:456–65.

Committee on Public Policy and Public Education. 1984. *Who Will Mind the Babies?* National Center for Clinical Infant Programs, Washington, D.C.

Farber, E., and Egeland, B. 1982. Developmental consequences of out-of-home care for infants in a low income population. *Day Care: Scientific and Social Policy Issue*. E. Zigler and E. Gordon, eds. Boston, Mass.: Auburn House.

Federal Register, 1980. *Federal Interagency Day Care Requirements*. Department of Health, Education, and Welfare, Washington, D.C.

Fosburg, S., and Hawkins, P. 1981. *Final Report of the National Day Care Home Study*, vol. 1. Cambridge, Mass.: Abt Associates.

Fraiberg, S. 1977. *Every Child's Birthright: In Defense of Mothering*. New York: Basic Books.

Gamble, T., and Zigler, E. 1986. Effects of infant day care: another look at the evidence. *American Journal of Orthopsychiatry* 56:26–42.

Jones, E., and Prescott, E. 1982. Day care: short and long term solution? *Annals of the American Academy of Political and Social Science* 461:91–101.

Kagan, J., Kearsley, R., and Zelazo, P. 1978. The effects of infant day care on psychological development. *The Growth of the Child*. J. Kagan, ed. New York: W. W. Norton.

Kamerman, S. B., and Kahn, A. J. 1981. *Child Care, Family Benefits and Working Parents: A Study in Comparative Policy*. New York: Columbia University Press.

Keyserling, M. 1972. *Windows on Day Care*. New York: National Council of Jewish Women.

McCartney, K., Scarr, S., Phillips, D., Grajek, S., and Schwartz, J. C. 1982. Environmental differences among day care centers and their effects on children's development. *Day Care: Scientific and Social Policy Issues*. E. Zigler and E. Gordon, eds. Boston, Mass.: Auburn House.

Nelson, J. 1982. The politics of federal day care regulation. *Day Care: Scientific and Social Policy Issues*. E. Zigler and E. Gordon, eds. Boston, Mass.: Auburn House.

Provence, S. 1982. Infant day care: Relationships between theory and practice.

Day Care: Scientific and Social Policy Issues. E. Zigler and E. Gordon, eds. Boston, Mass.: Auburn House.

Ramey, C., Dorval, B., and Baker-Ward, L. 1981. Group day care and socially disadvantaged families: effects on the child and family. *Advances in Early Education and Day Care.* S. Kilmer, ed. Greenwich, Conn.: JAI Press.

Redmond, S., and Pichichero, M. 1985. Hemophilus influences type B disease: an epidemiologic study with special references to day care centers. *Journal of the American Medical Association* 252:2581–84.

Ricciuti, H. 1974. Fear and development of social attachments in the first years of life. *The Origins of Human Behavior: Fear.* M. Lewis and L. A. Rosenblum, eds. New York: John Wiley & Sons.

Ruopp, R., and Travers. J. 1982. Janus faces day care: perspectives on quality and cost. *Day Care: Scientific and Social Policy Issues.* E. Zigler and E. Gordon, eds. Boston, Mass.: Auburn House.

Ruopp, R., Travers, J., Glantz, F., and Coelen, C. 1974. *Children at the Center.* Cambridge, Mass.: Abt Associates.

Rutter, M. 1982. Social-emotional consequences of day care for preschool children. *Day Care: Scientific and Social Policy Issues.* E. Zigler and E. Gordon, eds. Boston, Mass.: Auburn House.

Stern, D. 1974. Mother and infant at play: the dyadic interaction involving facial, vocal and gaze behaviors. *The Effect of the Infant on Its Caregivers.* M. Lewis and L. A. Rosenblum, eds. New York: John Wiley & Sons.

United States Senate. 1985. *Congressional Record* (Mar. 28). Washington, D.C.: GPO.

Zigler, E. 1984. Child care: beginning a national initiative. Testimony, House Select Committee on Children, Youth, and Families. Washington, D.C.

Zigler, E., and Muenchow, S. 1983. Infant day care and infant-care leaves. *American Psychologist* 38:91–94.

Zigler, E., and Turner, P. 1982. Parents and day care mothers: a failed partnership? *Day Care: Scientific and Social Policy Issues.* E. Zigler and E. Gordon, eds. Boston, Mass.: Auburn House.

PART III

Supporting the Family with Parental Leaves

EIGHT

Strengthening Family Systems

URIE BRONFENBRENNER

Today we acknowledge that the massive alteration of the natural environment made possible by modern technology and industrialization can destroy the physical ecosystem essential to life itself. We have yet to recognize that this same awesome process now also has an analogue in the social realm as well: the unthinking exercise of massive technological power, and an unquestioning acquiescence to the demands of industrialization, can unleash forces which, if left unbridled, can destroy the human ecosystem. Based in the family unit, but extending far beyond, this ecosystem comprises the social fabric that sustains our capacity to live and work together effectively, and to raise our children and youth to become competent and compassionate members of our society.

The heart of our social system is the family. If we are to maintain the health of our society, we must discover the best means of nurturing that heart. What does a family system need to grow and succeed? What do children, our society's future, need within that system to thrive? These questions point to an ecological approach to the study of human development. Forming the foundation for scholarly research over the past decade, this approach seeks to clarify and define what conditions are best suited to our development as individuals and as members of society. In this regard, the ecology of human development has been defined as "the progressive, mutual accommodation between the developing person and the changing properties of the immediate and broader contexts in which the person lives" (Bronfenbrenner 1979a).

Like a set of Russian dolls, the contexts of human development work in a nested fashion, each one expanding beyond but containing the smaller one. Each one also simultaneously influences and is influenced by the other. Thus the context of the family fits into that of the neighborhood; the context of the neighborhood into the larger contexts of city, work, and government; and all contexts into the largest context of culture. Whatever factors affect any larger level will filter down to affect the innermost unit, the family (Bronfenbrenner 1979).

The two contexts of work and family represent central activities necessary for human survival. Work serves as a means for transforming our environment. From an evolutionary viewpoint, human beings are remarkable in their capacity to make such transformations. It is primarily parents who show us how environments can be changed, and thus prepare us for the world of work. To a greater extent than for any other living creature, the capacity of human offspring to survive and develop depends on care and close association in activity with older members of the species. Without extended parenting, we are unable to perform in the world we have created.

Yet today, particularly in the United States, these two principal contexts for human development, family and work, are often pitted against each other. Given the growing disarray in the lives of families and children, our society needs to move rapidly to reunify these two key spheres of activity. The testimony of this book reveals a dilemma that many working parents feel: all too often a person cannot do a good job in one sphere without making sacrifices in the other. Nowadays, with work frequently an economic necessity for both parents, less by decision than by default, we allow our families and our children to absorb the stress and suffer the consequences.

In this chapter I attempt to delineate the nature of the family ecosystem and its scope; the processes taking place within it; how and why the work-parenting conflict is affecting that structure; and what can be done to retard or even to reverse prevailing trends of the work-family conflict.

ENVIRONMENTAL PRINCIPLES OF DEVELOPMENT

Because this volume specifically addresses the issue of children's development in regard to the parenting relationship, my focus is on children's needs: What are the implications of mass societal changes for the development of children? To examine this issue, it is necessary to determine which environmental and social conditions are most crucial for the development of human beings from early childhood on. In an analysis of the available knowledge on this topic, I have found it sobering to discover that the principal conclusions from these data could be summarized in two tentative propositions. Shorn of their technical terminology, the two propositions do not sound very earthshaking; but when applied to our present world, they may shake us up nevertheless.

Proposition 1. In order to develop normally, a child needs the enduring, irrational involvement of one or more adults in care of and in joint activity with that child.

In short, somebody has to be crazy about that kid. But that is not all the proposition stipulates. Someone also has to be there, and to be doing something—not alone, but *together* with the child. This brings us to the next proposition, which defines a second environmental condition equally essential if development is to occur.

Proposition 2. The involvement of one or more adults in joint activity with the child requires public policies and practices that provide opportunity, status, resources, encouragement, stability, example, and, above all, time for parenthood, primarily by parents, but also by other adults in the child's environment, both within and outside the home.

The two propositions epitomize much of what we know about human development, for they identify the two environmental conditions both necessary and desirable for human learning and human development, for enabling us to become human.

The family is at the heart of proposition 1. Of all the settings that help make us human, the family provides the most important developmental conditions: the love and care that a child needs to thrive, the "someone crazy about that kid." A healthy child and future adult is one who has such crazy people actively engaged in her life—those who love her, spend time with her, challenge her, and are interested in what she does and wants to do, in what she accomplishes from day to day. Other settings, such as school, church, or day care, are important to a child's development, but none can replace this basic unit of our social system: the family is the most humane, most powerful, and by far the most economical system known for making and keeping human beings human.

Further, it is the family that determines our capacity to function effectively and to profit from experience in the other contexts in which human beings live and grow—the school, peer group, higher education, business, community, and our society as a whole. In all those settings, what we learn, as well as what we can contribute, depends on the families we come from and the families in which we now live. This is true from early childhood on, until the day we die.

But the family is not without its vulnerabilities, and thus we have proposition 2. To a far greater extent than we have previously imagined, the capacity of the family to function effectively, to create and sustain competent and compassionate human beings, depends on the support of other, larger contexts. Either social support (such as a business providing family benefits for its workers), or lack of support (such as parents' not having job security if they take off too long to attend to a new infant), filters down to the innermost social unit, the family, and determines the confidence or stress that parents bring to their relations with their child. Even the decreased interaction resulting from the stresses and demands of work can impair the quality and effectiveness of the parent-child bond.

I shall now use these propositions as a basis for evaluating the implications for human development of the revolution that has been taking place in American family life.

FAMILY CHANGES AND THEIR EFFECTS

That the family is changing and that the family is in danger seem to be common knowledge—if we are willing to admit it. Today the topic is, once again, in vogue. The mass magazines from *Newsweek* and *Time* to *Woman's Day*, *Ms.*, and *Esquire*, carry feature stories on the subject, every national organization wants an address on this topic at its annual convention, and the major television networks produce documentaries on the family breakup, complete with statistics and case studies. Nowadays, we all know about the rocket rise in single-parent homes (today more than a fifth of the nation's children reside within them), the decline of extended family households (they are almost gone now, save among blacks and ethnic minorities), and the falling birthrate (except among unwed teenage girls). In short, American families—adults and children sharing a household—are getting smaller.

So far as the development of the young is concerned, one of the most consequential change is the rise in maternal employment. In this respect, 1978 was a landmark year; for the first time, the majority of American mothers were in the labor force. Since 1970, the increase has been greatest among mothers of children under three, but regardless of the ages of their children, the majority of working mothers are employed full time. Given current economic pressure and aspirations, few have any other choice.

THE PHENOMENON OF WORKING MOTHERS

As many more mothers go to work, and fathers do not go back into the home, there are fewer adults left in the household to look after the child (Bronfenbrenner and Crouter 1982). In increasing numbers of families, there is only one parent, usually the breadwinner, who works full-time and lives in an independent household. What is the significance of the conditions for the requirement stipulated in proposition 2 of "opportunity, status, resources, encouragement, stability, example, and above all time for parenthood"? What does this complex of circumstances imply, in turn, for proposition 1? To be sure, when parents are working full-time, their irrational involvement with the child may not diminish, it may even increase. But what happens to joint activity?

Evidence shows that, in contrast to other modern nations, American society has given little recognition to the demands of parenting, and thus has left parents with little time to meet those demands. Frighteningly, in many families, joint activity never begins—the time needed to build foundations is denied them from the start. An overwhelming number of new mothers, both single and married, are expected to return to work within three or four weeks of an infant's birth. Parenting by fathers is given even less time and encouragement. A four-week, or two-week leave treats childbirth as a purely physical experience, and the developing parent-infant relationship is ignored. In a recent provocative book, *Working and Caring*, T. Berry Brazelton delineates four stages necessary to build a relationship of joining interaction and mutual trust (1985, especially chapter 4). At the end of four weeks, stage one is barely completed. Mothers report that they deal with this loss through denial: denial of the infant's and their own emotional and interactive needs, lest they perform badly at work and lose jobs they cannot afford to lose. The question is not just what happens to time for parenting, but what happens to the development of the infant.

With such demands on a parent's time, the infant is in danger of becoming an object, another duty to be taken care of. A typical day for working parents might be as follows: get up, dress for work, change baby, help the children dress, fix breakfast, feed the children, drop off children at day care, go to work, leave work, pick up children, go home, feed the baby, prepare dinner, eat dinner, play if there is time, clean up, put children to bed. To be sure there is a lot of activity, but not much that can be joint or interactive. Nor are parents given much time for themselves. Furthermore, this schedule may not be one the family is permitted to grow into, establishing interactive patterns first, and then adapting them to outside demands. One of the great changes in child care over the last few years is the increasing number of three- and four-week-old infants—even two-week-old infants—in day-care centers. Clearly, such conditions imposed by the work-parenting conflict can make it difficult to establish the good foundation of joint activity so necessary to the growth and maturation of the young child.

Although the issue of an infant care leave focuses on the first year of life, the conflict between the demands of work and parenting can continue throughout much of a child's life. In *Parenting in An Unresponsive Society*, S. Kamerman analyzes the principal findings of a survey of 200 working mothers in both single- and two-parent families (1980).Two themes emerge from this study that have special relevance to a family-leave plan. The first is the severe stress reported both by single parents and two-worker families around the issue of obtaining satisfactory child care. In contemporary American society, providing for such care often requires a delicately orchestrated schedule combining the use of day-care centers, babysitters, and shifting parental responsibilities. The strains generated by the task of establishing and maintaining these complex arrangements are documented both in statistical data and case study vignettes. The second theme emerging from the survey relates to the heightened stress experienced by the mother in single-parent households, where all the burdens of work, child rearing, and coordinating child-care arrangements fall on her shoulders. In such situations, the desire for parenting and caring may be there, but the "time for parenthood" may be rapidly diminished.

There is a further aspect to this stress that parents may feel. Currently, parents are provided leave time for their own needs—but not for their children's needs. As a result, putting first things first, parents often use their own leave time not to care for their own health or personal needs, but to attend to their children's illnesses or crises. Such a confounding of leave time to meet too many demands or to cover too many contingencies allow parents little time for their own needs, and stress begins to build.

THE CHANGING AMERICAN CHILD

Regrettably, as yet too few investigators have taken the next step of examining the impact of familial stress on the behavior and development of children. One review of the research (Bronfenbrenner and Crouter 1982) gave some evidence that conflict between work and family roles reduces both the quantity and quality of parent-child interaction and is associated with lower achievement in school, particularly among boys. The studies in this area are weakened, however, by the failure to establish the successive causal links between the objective conditions at work and at home, the degree and nature of stress generated by these conditions, their effect on family functioning, and the resultant impact on the behavior and development of the child. This causal chain is now being delineated in relation to single-parent families (Hetherington, Cox, and Cox 1978, 1979; Dornbusch, et al., 1985; Steinberg 1987). For example, Hetherington and her colleagues traced the progressive deterioration in mother-child interaction following divorce and its disruptive carryover effects on the social behavior and academic performance of children in school.

While some working parents may thrive on multiple demands on their time and energy, the opposite also often occurs. In addition, parents who work are often overwhelmed by having too much asked of them by too many people. As we have seen, parents are caught up by social and economic forces over which they have little control. They do not choose work over parenting, but rather they struggle to survive the conflicts of the two. And circumstantial evidence at least suggests that children are the ones who pay the price.

For these reasons, it is instructive to examine trends in data on children that parallel those that have taken place for families. The most salient statistics are time series data reflecting the impaired well-being and development of children as manifested in declining levels of academic performance and rising rates of child homicide, suicide, teenage pregnancy, drug use, and juvenile delinquency (Bronfenbrenner 1986; Bronfenbrenner 1986a; National Academy of Sciences 1976).

The title of a Senate report published a decade ago still applies to the present scene: *The Nation's Schools: A Report Card: "A" in School Violence and Vandalism.* Then, as now, the pattern was not restricted to larger cities, slum areas, or particular ethnic groups. As the title implies, school violence is a national phenomenon. Every school now has its security budget and often a security force. As Wynne (1980) has documented, the American school has become a major breeding ground of alienation, vandalism, and violence.

These trends constitute danger signs for American society. Three additional features are especially disquieting. First, all of the demographic changes are occurring more rapidly among younger families with small children and are increasing in direct proportion to economic deprivation and urbanization, reaching their maximum in low-income families living in the central core of our large cities (Bronfenbrenner 1986; Bronfenbrenner 1986a; National Academy of Sciences 1976). Second, the rate of change has not been constant, but has accelerated markedly since the mid–1960s. It was precisely during this same period that the scope and budgets of federally-sponsored programs directed at low-income families were expanded. Yet it is clear that this expansion was not adequate to arrest, let alone reverse, the demographic trends reflecting disarray in the lives of families and children. The third and perhaps most telling fact revealed in the data is that the general trend is not limited to the urban poor; it applies to all strata of society. Indeed, in terms of the proportion of working mothers, number of adults in the home, single-parent families, teenage pregnancy, falling achievement scores, or exposure to vandalism and violence in the schools, the experiences of middle-class families of the 1980s increasingly resemble those of low-income families of the 1960s. It is this expanding pattern of change that makes the search for new strategies an imperative for those concerned with the well-being and development of children in the 1980s. As a society, America—especially industrial America—needs to recognize that the family represents the most critical unit of society. Without time for and recognition of parenting as the key nurturant force in all of society, we are faced with the potential disintegration of our social fabric.

THE NEED FOR A NATIONAL INFANT-CARE-LEAVE POLICY

The Deficit Model

Until recently, the concept of the family has received attention in America in direct relation to the degree of its demise. Repairing a faltering family has been at the base of many public policies and practices, both past and present. I call this approach the *Deficit Model*: in order to get help, a family has to prove that it has become inadequate. Yet this very inadequacy is indirectly a product of public attitudes. We in America believe that family integration and growth come naturally, and that family responsibility is a private matter—even as we put its members in a position that leaves little support or time for family life. The belief that our families need no national recognition or protection paradoxically leads to more families than ever needing that support. There is no recognition of the kind of support healthy families need to keep them healthy, or that new families need to help them become healthy.

When a family is finally inadequate enough, it can then get some support. The deficit model pervades all arenas, but its distinctive properties are revealed in highest relief in our welfare system. To qualify for help, potential recipients must first prove over and over, with corroborating documentation, that they and their children are in fact the inadequate persons they claim to be. Moreover, our mode of service is categorical: to obtain needed help, potential recipients must first be classified into the types of problems they represent. The only way in which they become whole human beings again is to have enough things wrong. Then they can be defined, and dealt with, as "problem children," or better still for bureaucratic purposes, as "multiproblem families."

Business and the Infant Care Leave Policy

Alternatives to the deficit model are beginning to emerge in several spheres. The first arises from a dawning national recognition of the need for support for parenting. Currently before Congress, the proposed Family and Medical Act would require that businesses provide time for new parents to spend with their infants before returning to work, and that parents who must attend to time-consuming, family problems—such as a child's illness—be given the time and support to do so. The act is seriously deficient in one area—financial provision during the leave time—but it does recognize the need for both time to parent and job protection during that time.

Businesses are also beginning to address independently the conflict between work and parenting. As documented in a recent review by Kamerman and Kingston (1982), an increasing number of public and private employers are offering their employees fringe benefits designed to be responsive to family needs. Among them are such provisions as maternity leaves, family health plans, on-site day care, part-time jobs, job sharing, sick leave for parents when children are ill, and flextime. The last involves a schedule whereby employees work full-time, but have some freedom in determining hours of arrival and departure. Nollen and Martin (1978) estimated that 2.5 to 3.5 million workers (6% of the total labor force) are in some variation of flextime. These businesses and corporations recognize that employee contribution and family satisfaction have a direct relationship to each other.

The idea of an infant-care-leave policy is still at a very early stage of development in the United States. In comparison with programs provided in other industrialized countries, our existing supports are limited, and our planned policy does not include pay while the parent is on leave. This contrast is reflected in the following statement of findings from an ongoing project directed by Sheila Kamerman and Alfred J. Kahn:

> Mothers of very young children are working outside the home in growing numbers in all industrialized countries. Two-parent two-wage earner families (and single-parent, sole-wage-earner families) are increasingly the norm.... Some countries are expanding child care services as well as cash benefits to protect child and family life. However, the United States lags far behind such European countries as France, Sweden, and the Federal Republic of Germany in the West, and the German Democratic Republic and Hungary in the East in providing either (Kamerman and Kahn, 1978).

Two problems arise as businesses address the parenting-work conflict without a coherent national policy. The provision of family benefits associated with work has been concentrated primarily in large corporations, whose employees are already in a more favored economic position. By contrast, those most in need of such benefits, such as heads of single-parent households or of large families, are likely to have low-paying jobs or no jobs at all. This circumstance therefore serves to widen the already existing gap between the rich and the poor.

Further, many small and midsize businesses, and even large ones, choose not to address the parent-work conflict because they believe they cannot afford to provide family leaves. Employers may not recognize the increased benefits to themselves and society in general that can accrue if they accept and provide for the duality of work and parenting. What is needed now, however, is not numerous, small, disparate leave policies, but an overall, societal awareness of and commitment to the importance of family integrity to society at large. A national policy for an infant care and parenting leave represents a first step in achieving that awareness and needed change in direction.

A FORWARD LOOK: FIVE "PREPOSTEROUS PROPOSALS"

There is evidence that, in the United States, work-associated family benefits may not, by themselves, have much impact on the capacity of families to function effectively in their child-rearing role. For example, Bohen and Viveros-Long (1981) obtained measures of family strain and of participation in home activities from employees working in two federal agencies, one of which operated with flexible hours. Ironically, significant differences favoring flextime were found for only one group of families—those without children. Two explanations are proposed for the absence of effects on families with children: first, that the arrangement did not go far enough to meet the complex scheduling problems experienced by today's parents; second, that childrearing values were not sufficiently salient to ensure that the flexible time would be used for parental activities. Unfortunately, no data were available to permit further investigation of these possibilities.

Thought needs to be given to policies through which families can be supported by all of society—policies fostering attitudes and actions that recognize, maintain, and strengthen families. We need to create social forms that encourage and allow us to help one another; an infant care leave is but one of those forms. The following hypothetical cases address three crucial contexts affecting the well-being and development of children in contemporary society: the school, the family's social networks, and the parents' world of work. These three domains are the principal sources both of Americans' gravest problems and of their most promising and powerful counteractive strategies. Nevertheless, the strategies have a serious and perhaps fatal shortcoming; given the present state of American society, they can only be implemented gradually, if at all. For this reason, I refer to them as *preposterous proposals*.

Preposterous Proposal I

It is now possible for a young person to graduate from an American high school without every having had to do a piece of work on which someone else depended. It is also possible for a young person, female as well as male, to graduate from high school, college, or university without every having held a baby for longer than a few seconds; without every having had to care for someone who was old, ill, or lonely; without every having had to comfort or assist another human being who needed help. Yet all of us, sooner or later, will desperately require such comfort and care, and no society can sustain itself unless its members have learned the motivations, sensitivities, and skills that such caring demands.

One way to counteract these gaps is to introduce a *curriculum of caring* in the schools, from the earliest grades onward. The purpose of this curriculum would be not to learn about caring, but to engage in it; that is, all children would be asked to take responsibility for spending time with and caring for others—the elderly, the young, the sick, and the lonely. The curriculum for caring has special significance for the increasing numbers of older children who are in fact caring for their younger brothers and sisters in the absence of adequate and affordable day-care services in our country. Obviously, such caring activities cannot be restricted to the school; they have to be carried out in the community itself. It would be desirable to locate caring institutions, such as day-care centers, adjacent to or even within schools; it would be even better for the young caregivers to come to know the environments and the other people in the lives of their charges. For example, older children taking responsibility for younger ones should become acquainted with the latter's parents and with the places where their charges live by escorting them home from school. In this way, children would come to know firsthand the living conditions of the families in their community. This is surely an essential aspect of public education in a free society; yet it is one that Americans have neglected almost completely.

Preposterous Proposal II

This proposal extends the curriculum for caring into the adult world. It builds on a distinctively American institution for its implementation. That institution is the Cooperative Extension Service, which is supported by federal, state, and local funds in every section of the nation, urban as well as rural. This program represents an already-existing alternative to the deficit model, since it operates on the principle of mobilizing and relying on local initiatives and resources. The role of Extension personnel would be to facilitate informal support networks and to supply needed technical information. The experience of the Extension Service in working with families and youth groups at a community level makes it well suited to the task of creating and strengthening informal support systems built around neighborhood school and workplace.

A pilot experiment along this line, under the direction of Moncrieff Cochran, is currently being conducted in a medium-sized city in upstate New York. Known as Family Matters, it involves a total of one hundred and fifty families with school children distributed over twelve neighborhoods. In each neighborhood, a team of two field workers employs both home visits and group meetings to involve families in common activities in behalf of themselves and their children. The aim of the experiment is to enhance parent empowerment through the creation of supportive social networks that not only link family members to each other but also provide access to needed resources and to centers of power within the community (Cochran and Woolever 1980).

Field observations continue to indicate that informal social networks can be developed and that families who participate in them do experience a sense of enhanced support and self-sufficiency. But the creation and maintenance of these informal systems encounters a serious obstacle in contemporary American society. To function effectively, they require the participation of relatives, friends, and neighbors who are available on an enduring, reliable basis. How can such time and dependability be assured in a highly mobile society in which most able-bodied people are working in full-time jobs?

Preposterous Proposal III

One solution to the time for parenting, and the support for a more caring society in general, is the proposed Family and Medical Leave Act. Another approach, however, to the resolution of the parenting-work conflict involves a radical change in the American way of work life: altering the prevailing pattern of employment so that both men and women would work on *three-quarters* time. The remaining quarter would be free for family activities, visiting friends and relatives, participating in the life of one's neighborhood and community, and looking at the sunset—in short, a quarter of one's life for living. The introduction of such a pattern would have the additional fringe benefit of reducing unemployment, since cadres would be needed to maintain national levels of production. Under what circumstances could such a revolutionary proposal be adopted in American society? This query brings us to the next and even more outlandish proposal.

Preposterous Proposal IV

In order for families to meet the needs created by the rapid and profound social changes that have taken place in recent years, it will be necessary to introduce significant changes in public policy and practice in domains outside the family itself. Such innovations will require broad vision and hard-headed decisions by those persons who occupy positions of power and responsibility both in the public and the private sectors. In spite of the impressive achievements of the women's movement, the fact remains that the overwhelming majority of persons in such influential positions today are men.

Given the prevailing pattern in the upbringing of children and youth in American society, males are particularly likely, from earliest childhood on, to have been isolated from experiences of caring or from close association with those needing care (Gilligan 1977). As a result, men are less able to understand the needs of such persons, the circumstances in which they live, their human potential, the necessity and nature of the support systems required to realize this potential, and the very practical social and economic gains that would be achieved as a result. In contrast, those in our society who possess such experience and knowledge are predominantly women, primarily because women confront these situations more often than do men in the course of their lives. Women, however, typically do not occupy the positions of power that would permit their experience and knowledge to be translated into public policy and practice. This state of affairs calls for a substantial increase in the number of women in positions of decision making and power, both in the public and private sector.

Preposterous Proposal V

The basis for this final and most pressing recommendation is found in a research trajectory reaching back half a century. Beginning in the mid-1930s, a series of investigators analyzed the impact on the family of the father's loss of a job during the Great Depression (Angell 1936; Cavan and Ranck 1938; Komarovsky 1940; Morgan 1939). The principal effects documented in these investigations were loss of status by the father, marked increase in family tensions and disagreements, and withdrawal from social life outside the family. Children appeared in these early studies only as participants in the father's drama rather than as persons themselves affected by the experience. Four decades later, however, Elder et al. used archival data from two longitudinal studies in order to focus on the impact of the Great Depression on the subsequent development of children whose families had been subjected to severe economic stress (1974, Elder, et al., 1985; Elder, et al., 1986).

Elder took advantage of this natural experiment to divide each of the two samples into two otherwise comparable groups, differentiated on the basis of whether the loss of income as a result of the Depression exceeded or fell short of 35%. The fact that the children in one sample were eight years older than those in the other permitted a comparison of the effects of the Depression on children who were adolescents when their families became economically deprived versus those who were still young children.

The results for the two groups presented a dramatic contrast. Paradoxically, for youngsters who had been teenagers during the Depression years, the family's economic deprivation appeared to have a salutary effect on their subsequent development. They did better in school, were more likely to go to college, had happier marriages, exhibited more successful work careers, and in general achieved greater satisfaction in life, both by their own and by societal standards, than did nondeprived children of the same socioeconomic status. These favorable outcomes were more pronounced for adolescents from middle-class backgrounds, but were evident among their lower-class counterparts as well. Elder hypothesized that the loss of economic security forced the family to mobilize its own human resources, including those of its teenagers. The youths had to take on new responsibilities in order to help get and keep the family on its feet. This experience provided them with effective training in initiative, responsibility, and cooperation. In the words of Shakespeare's banished duke, "Sweet are the uses of adversity."

Adversity was not so sweet for children who were still preschoolers when their families suffered economic loss. Compared to controls from nondeprived families, these youngsters subsequently did less well in school, showed less stable and successful work histories, and exhibited more emotional and social difficulties, some still apparent in middle adulthood. Presumably, the struggle for existence created the same conditions which work demands create today: little time for parent-child interaction, at a time when the child most needs that interaction to lay a foundation for growth.

FACING THE FUTURE

The last problem in the establishment of a national infant care and family leave policy is perhaps the most important one we face as a nation: it concerns the millions of families who would be unaffected by such a policy because the parents are not employed, come from a background not conducive to employment, and have no future in employment. Until these families are rewoven into the fabric of society, the parenting and family crisis can never truly be resolved. Work and parenting are but two halves of a social whole: parenting is that process of creating mature and productive adults, who in turn through their work and service, contribute to society.

The implications of the foregoing evidence and argument are underscored by recent census figures and research findings. The official U.S. Census report on family income for 1980 documented what it described as "the largest decline in family income in the post World War II period," resulting in the addition of 29.3 million persons below the poverty level, for a total of 13% of the U.S. population (U.S. Bureau of Census, 1981, p. 1). By 1981, this figure had risen to 31.8 million (U.S. Bureau of the Census, 1982, p. 1). As revealed in the tables accompanying the report, the poverty rates for children were even higher, especially for the very young. Specifically, as of March 1984, more than one-fourth (22%) of all children in America up to the age of six were living in families below the *poverty line*, compared to 13% for the population as a whole, and 16% for those under 65. The poverty line is based on the minimum income sufficient to meet the cost of the Department of Agriculture's economy food plan. The index is adjusted to reflect the different consumption requirements of families based on size, composition, and other relevant demographic factors.

The effects of this most recent economic downturn are already being reflected in research findings. In a longitudinal design, Steinberg, Catalano, and Dooley (1981) studied the effects of inflation on 8,000 families in California. Correlational analyses of data over a thirty-month period revealed that increases in child abuse were preceded by periods of high job loss, thus confirming the authors' hypothesis that "undesirable economic change leads to increased child maltreatment" (p. 975). An Associated Press report on this research begins with the lead sentence: "The toll of children battered, maimed, and slain by parents and other relatives is climbing, and experts say the economy—especially unemployment—appears to be a key factor." Alas, for once the media did not exaggerate the facts.

Such findings give added significance to the growing number of children being cast into poverty in our own time. They also raise questions about the severe cuts that have been put in force affecting programs and resources made available to low-income families and their children in the United States. Even more destructive than these cuts is the implicit philosophy that we hold as a nation toward the resource of our families. The United States fails to recognize the importance of jobs for the survival of families, not only economically, but—what is even more important—psychologically. By tolerating growing unemployment now, the United States risks creating new generations of unemployable Americans.

There are those who say that that is exactly what we are doing, that Americans have ceased to care about each other. Such critics claim to see the rise of a new separatism across the land, a turning away from a concern with the problems of others to a preoccupation with maintaining and maximizing the status and power of particular groups. To be sure, such phenomena are occurring in some segments of American society, but I do not believe that they constitute the broader and deeper streams and strengths of contemporary America. They are merely filling a vacuum during a period of temporary inertia in the historical movement of the United States in pursuit of its ideals. At this moment, the best of America is conscience-stricken and confused. The country is momentarily immobilized by the conflict between the distinctive values derived from its past and the dissonant realities created by the economic and social changes taking place not only in the United States, but around the world. The vacuum created by this temporary inertia leaves the field open to destructive forces that can divide the nation. Once again the Union is threatened, not the political union of the states, but the spiritual union of the basic parts of our pluralistic society—the diverse families, communities, generations, and religious and cultural groups that make the magic of America. The nation was founded, and has thus far been sustained, on the principle of *e pluribus unum*. What has happened to the *unum*? What is the state of the union?

These questions would seem to take us far beyond the domain of child and family policy, yet this fact points to the heart of the problem. One telling criterion of the worth of a society—criterion that stands the test of history—is the concern of one generation for the next. A nation's child and family policy is the measure of that concern. Under these circumstances, what is the responsibility of the development researcher concerned with policy issues at a time of national crisis? The answer to that question leads in two directions. Social scientists are subject to an ethical code that prohibits them from exposing children to situations that are injurious to their welfare. Unfortunately, there is no such re-striction on the nation as a whole or on its duly empowered leaders and policymakers. The latter are free to run their economic and social ex-periments without such niceties as prior parental consent or review by qualified professionals. It remains the responsibility of researchers, how-ever, to monitor these experiments and give early warning of any un-intended effects. What will be the consequences of cutting back funds for prenatal care, child nutrition and health, day care, and recreational and vocational programs for school-age children? What will the conse-quences be of refusing to create a national mandate providing time for essential parenting? In assessing these effects, researchers must use the best scientific methods at their command. There may be difficulties in finding matched control groups, but there should be no problem with sample size. It is the irony and limitation of our science that the greater the harm done to children, the more we stand to learn about the envi-ronmental conditions that are essential for the human condition. It there-fore becomes our professional obligation to employ the most advanced research designs at our disposal in order to forestall the tragic oppor-tunity of significantly expanding our knowledge about the limits of the human conditions for developing healthy human beings.

The responsibilities of the researcher extend beyond pure investi-gation, especially in a time of national crisis. Scientists in our field must be willing to draw on their knowledge and imagination in order to con-tribute to the design of social inventions: policies and strategies that can help to sustain and enhance our most precious human resources—the nation's children.

REFERENCES

Angell, R. C., 1936. *The Family Encounters the Depression.* New York: Scribner.

Bohen, H. H., & Viveros-Long, A. 1981. *Balancing Jobs and Family Life.* Philadelphia: Temple University Press.

Brazelton, T. B. 1985. *Working and Caring.* Boston: Addison-Wesley.

Bronfenbrenner, U., 1979. *The Ecology of Human Development.* Cambridge: Harvard University Press.

Bronfenbrenner, U. 1979(a). Beyond the deficit model in child and family policy. *Teachers College Record.* 81(1):95–104.

Bronfenbrenner, U. February 1986. Alienation and the four worlds of childhood. *Phi Delta Kappan* 67:430–36.

Bronfenbrenner, U. 1986a. The war on poverty: won or lost? America's children in poverty: 1959–1985. *Newsletter of the Division of Child, Youth, and Family Services* 9:2–3. Washington, D.C.: American Psychological Association.

Bronfenbrenner, U., and Crouter. Work and family through time and space. 1982. *Families that Work: Children in a Changing World.* Washington, D.C.: National Academy Press.

Cavan, R. S., and Ranck, K. H. 1938. *The Family and the Depression: A Study of 100 Chicago Families.* Chicago: University of Chicago Press.

Cochran, M., and Woolever, F. 1980. *Family Support Strategy: Fusing Family and Neighborhood Components.* Ithaca, New York: Cornell University Press.

Dornbusch, S. M., Carlsmith, J. M., Bushwall, S. J., Ritter, P. L., Leiderman, H., Hastorf, A. H., and Gross, R. T. 1985. Single parents, extended households, and the control of adolescence. *Child Development* 56:326–41.

Elder, G. H., Jr. 1974. *Children of the Great Depression.* Chicago: University of Chicago Press.

Elder, G. H., Jr., van Nguyen, T., Caspi, A. 1985. Linking family hardship to children's lives. *Child Development* 56:361–75.

Elder, G. H., Jr., Caspi, A., and van Nguyen, T. 1986. Resourceful and vulnerable children: family influence in stressful times. R. H. Silbereisen, ed. *Development as Action in Context.* Heidelberg: Springer.

Gilligan, C. 1977. In a different voice: Women's conception of self and morality. *Harvard Educational Review.* 47(4):196–204.

Hetherington, E. M., Cox, M., and Cox, R. 1978. *Mother-Child, Father-Child Relations.* Washington, D.C.: National Association of the Education of Young Children.

Hetherington, E. M., Cox. M., and Cox, R. 1979. Play and social interaction in children following divorce. *Journal of Social Issues* 35(4):26–49.

Kamerman, S. B., and Kahn, A. J. 1978. *Personal Correspondence.*

Kamerman, S. B., and Kahn, A. J. 1978. *Family Policy: Government and Families in Fourteen Countries.* New York: Columbia University Press.

Kamerman, S. B. 1980. *Parenting in an Unresponsive Society.* New York: Free Press.

Kamerman, S. B., and Kingston, P. 1982. *Families That Work: Children in a Changing World.* Washington, D.C.: National Academy Press.

Komarovsky, M. 1940. *The Unemployed Man and His Family.* New York: Dryden Press.

Morgan, W. L. 1939. *The Family Meets the Depression.* Minneapolis: University of Minnesota Press.

National Academy of Sciences. 1976. *Toward a National Policy for Children and Families.* Washington, D.C.

Nollen, S., and Martin, V. 1978. *Alternative Work Schedules. Part I: Flexitime. Part II: Compressed Work Weeks and Permanent Part Time Employment.* New York: AMICOM.

Steinberg, L. D. 1987. Single parents, step parents, and the susceptibility of adolescents to antisocial peer pressure. *Child Development* 58:269–75.

Steinberg, L. D., Catalano, R., and Dooley, D. 1981. Economic antecedents for child abuse and neglect. *Child Development* 52:975–85.

U.S. Bureau of the Census, 1981. *Money Income and Poverty Status of Families and Persons in the United States. Current Population Reports* (Series P–60, No. 127). Washington, D.C.: Government Printing Office.

U.S. Bureau of the Census. 1982. *Money Income and Poverty Status of Families and Persons in the United States. Current Population Reports* (Series P–60, No. 134). Washington, D.C.: Government Printing Office.

U.S. Senate Committee on the Judiciary. 1975. *Our Nation's Schools-A Report Card: "A" in School Violence and Vandalism.* Washington, D.C.: Government Printing Office.

Wynne, E. 1980. *Looking at Schools: Good, Bad, and Indifferent.* Lexington, Mass: Heath Lexington.

NINE

Managing Work and Family:
Hopes and Realities

ELLEN A. FARBER,
MARGUERITE ALEJANDRO-WRIGHT,
AND SUSAN MUENCHOW

Does the United States need an infant-care-leave policy? The question needs to be addressed from a variety of perspectives, among them the number of families who would be affected and how families are currently managing without such a policy. Based upon the demographic data already presented in this book, it is evident that a significant and growing number of families would be affected by the creation of a uniform national infant-care-leave policy, yet little is known about how families are currently managing. We need to know what leave benefits families have for childbirth and early child care, when women who take leaves return to work, and the childcare arrangements used for infants. In addition to factual information, we need to know the attitudes of women toward a national leave policy. In order to address just these issues, we conducted interviews of employed and nonemployed mothers of one year olds. In this chapter, we present the results of those interviews and draw conclusions about ways in which infant care leave and other benefits might mutually help families and employers.

Studies which address some of these issues have focused either on analyzing company policies or on the experiences of select groups of women. In a 1981 mail survey of one-thousand midsize to large employers (with a 20% response rate) followed by a telephone survey of fifty employers (with a 100% response rate), Kamerman, Kahn, and Kingston found that the majority of employers surveyed did not offer any paid leave under private insurance or company benefits (1983). In spite of the passage of the Pregnancy Discrimination Act in 1978, which requires that companies provide the same disability

benefits to women who must take time off because of childbirth as
they do to employees temporarily disabled for other reasons, only
48% of the employers surveyed provided short-term disability insurance as a form of parental leave, with a typical duration of these
leaves being six weeks. Sixty-six percent of the companies provided a
paid sick leave, but women with brief service usually received less
than two weeks of pay and those with longer service less than a
month. In sum, among relatively large employers, paid leaves were
the exception. As the authors noted, the survey covered fewer small
firms, which are apt to have less generous policies.

Catalyst, an organization for professional women, found that most
corporate professional women returned to work within three months of
delivery. Many women did not take as much time as they were entitled
to because they felt that staying out longer was professionally unwise
(Catalyst 1981). This study did not discuss the actual benefits for the
sample, such as reimbursement and type of leave, or the care arrangements that they were able to make. Furthermore this sample of highly
educated, well-paid professional and managerial women is not typical
of the vast majority of working women in this country. Eighty percent
of women in the work force are in clerical, sales, and service jobs, and
approximately 40% of working women come from households whose
income would be over 15,000 dollars per year exclusive of their contribution (Congressional Caucus for Women's Issues 1985). Therefore,
we need to focus our investigation more broadly to determine what is
typical of working women.

The one study that addressed many of the issues that interest us—
benefits, length of leaves, and childcare arrangements—was conducted
by Sheila Kamerman (1980), who interviewed working mothers with
children under compulsory school age. The study was not designed to
be a precisely representative sample of working women, but rather a
look at different types of working women: black and white; single and
married; professional, clerical, and unskilled; and women who returned
to work within six months of delivery or after an eighteen-month hiatus.
The women were volunteers recruited through community agencies.
Only 13% of the women who returned to work within six months of
delivery had any paid leave. Six weeks was the modal and median amount
of time taken. Another 15% of women were able to use a combination
of personal sick leave and vacation benefits to cover one to six months
of paid leave. In total, less than one-third of the women employed at
the time of childbirth had any kind of protection related to a maternity
leave (Kamerman 1980).

Another important finding in the Kamerman (1980) study relates
to childcare arrangements. Seventy-five percent of the sample used

one or more types of care that the investigator referred to as *child care packages*. In addition to their preschoolers, many of the mothers also had school-age children for whom care had to be arranged to cover the parts of the day before and after school while the parent was at work. Fewer of the preschool children required more than one type of care.

In spite of the growing interest in the childcare arrangements made by working mothers, however, most surveys place all children under the age of two or three in the same category. Indeed, the Kamerman data were not analyzed separately for infants. Yet, clearly, the care of infants elicits different considerations than the care of toddlers and preschoolers, for reasons that include limited availability (many centers have a minimum age), high costs, risk of infection to developing immune systems, and a recommended ratio of one adult to no more than three infants.

Two recent reports provide us with data on childcare arrangements used in the first year of life. According to the United States Census Bureau (1983) 47% of families have relatives care for their infants, and 10% use day-care centers. In addition, a recent national survey listed similar patterns of infant-care arrangements for 778 women with a child under the age of one (Klein 1985).

When we began our survey, then, we knew that the majority of companies did not offer infant care leaves, but that approximately one-third of working women were able to take some type of paid leave. We had, however, no information on women's attitudes toward a leave policy. Our goals were to interview a randomly-selected group of women in one community in order to gather factual and attitudinal data on infant care leaves, childcare arrangements, and conflicts associated with fulfilling the dual role of new parent and employee. In essence, this was an exploratory study, and therefore a relatively small sample was used. Although we knew we might not be able to generalize to the entire population of working women, we felt this study could provide some important insights into the dilemmas and desires of working mothers that might be followed up in future studies.

WHO ARE THE RESPONDENTS

In interviews which ranged from twenty-five minutes to one hour, we spoke with women about their employment history, infant care leaves and benefits, childcare arrangements, attitudes toward a paid leave policy, and health and employment concerns. Female interviewers followed a structured interview with primarily open-ended and some forced-choice questions.

The respondents were 181 women who had given birth within approximately twelve months before our phone call. These women were divided into three categories: 108 women were working in the year before their child was born and returned to work within one year after delivery (group one); 40 women worked in the year before but not after their child was born (group two); and 33 women did not work in the year before or after their child's birth (group three).

Names of participants were randomly selected from the maternity records of a teaching hospital which draws patients from urban, suburban, and rural areas. Since it is estimated that only 41% of women with a child under age one work, we were not surprised that we reached many women who were not currently working. In order to focus on working women, after interviewing a number of nonworking women we chose to call women whose maternity records indicted that they were employed.

Even though our sample was random, because it was limited to those women we could reach by tracing a one-year-old address and phone number, we probably eliminated some low-income and/or single parents who moved frequently, thus slightly biasing the sample in favor of stable two-parent families. Only two women were single at the time of the interviews. The women who were interviewed ranged in age from nineteen to forty-six, with a median of thirty. Almost all of them had completed high school, but more of the working than nonworking women had completed college (51% versus 27%). Ninety-five percent of the women in the two working groups had earned or were earning less than twenty-five thousand dollars per year. The husbands of the women who did not return to work (group two) earned on average more than the husbands of women who returned to work or did not work at all during the time of the pregnancy (groups one and three). Our respondents were in all lines of work ranging from professional to laborer. For both working groups, the median Hollingshead classification for job status was six (the scale ranges from one to nine, with nine indicating the most prestigious jobs). Category six includes skilled work such as clerical and secretarial jobs.

A frequent difficulty with interview studies is that those who are called can be reluctant to participate, and this limits the representativeness of the sample. Considering how busy parents of infants are, we had an excellent response rate. Only a few women declined to be interviewed; others were just never reached. Of those we did manage to contact by telephone, most often in the evening, the overwhelming majority were willing to discuss their child and their current work situation. They were eager to participate in a study on the issues and conflicts of working and nonworking mothers.

INFANT CARE LEAVES: DO THEY EXIST?

In reviewing infant care leave benefits, we were interested in three components (see Kamerman et al. 1983). First, was the women entitled to a job-protected leave? In other words, could the woman take time off for childbirth and child care and return to the same or a similar job? Second, what were the lengths of leave that various women took? Third, how many of the leaves were reimbursed, and what was the degree of reimbursement?

Of the 108 women to whom we spoke who worked before and after their child's birth, 53% were working a full-time schedule of thirty hours or more per week. With the remaining 47%, who worked part-time (less than thirty hours a week), we expected to find that many of the women were not eligible for infant care leave. Most of the part-time employees were not eligible for any benefits.

Sixty-three women (58%) reported that they were eligible for infant care leave and could return to their original job or a similar position. A 1981 survey found that 72% of employers provided an unpaid leave that guaranteed the woman's job and seniority status (Kamerman et al. 1983). Considering that many of the women in our survey worked for smaller companies than those represented in the Kamerman survey, our figures are relatively comparable.

The second component of interest is the length of leave before and after delivery. A number of factors enter into the consideration of granting leave time, including the physical and emotional health of the mother and baby, financial costs to the family and employer, type of job and ease of replacement, and availability of infant care. Overall we found that women took more time than official company policy dictated, but less time than they would have preferred.

The typical pre-delivery leave ranged from two to four weeks, with some women working right up until they went into labor. Many of the women worked into their eighth month of pregnancy before taking a leave. Unlike the expectations of several decades ago when as soon as a woman was visibly pregnant she had to leave the workplace, only one woman, a flight attendant named Beth, was expected to stop working after the first trimester of pregnancy. None of the other women were expected to stop working sooner than they wished, although a few who had jobs involving hard physical labor were able to switch to less strenuous work.

The length of post-delivery leaves that women were permitted to take ranged from zero to fifty-two weeks. The longest leave, fifty-two weeks of unpaid time, was available for Beth, the flight attendant, whose regular schedule required her to be away from home several days in a row. In spite of the wide range of time used for leaves, where there was a company policy the average policy dictated six weeks of official leave time. Many women, then, took an additional six weeks in order to create a three-month post-delivery leave.

Although the median length of leave that was taken was three months, when the women were asked how long a leave they would have preferred, the median response was six months. There were many reasons for this preference, including having time to get to know the baby, adjusting to the baby's schedule, and waiting until the baby was sleeping through the night. Some women mentioned that they would be willing to return to work sooner if they did not have to return immediately to a full-time schedule but could gradually increase their working hours. Most employers were unwilling to allow their employees to phase in their return to work. This dilemma was solved for one woman through job sharing. Pat had decided to resign rather than return to work full-time two months after delivery. One week after leaving, Pat's employer called and offered her the opportunity to share her administrative job with another woman who also preferred a part-time schedule. At the time of our interview almost ten months later, Pat and her new colleague were still each working two-and-a half days per week, a schedule they enjoyed.

The third component of interest is the degree of wage replacement. Although sixty-three women, 58% of group one, reported that they were given job protection while on leave, less than half were given paid leaves. Of the twenty-nine women who had some paid leave, over half of them (sixteen) were paid their full salary. Thirteen women received between one-half and three-fourths of their salary.

Since so few women were offered paid leave, many had to develop other means of financing the time they took off. Of those women entitled to job-protected leave, thirty-five were paid only for the sick leave and/ or vacation time they had accumulated. Fifteen women used sick leave and vacation time to increase the length of their paid leave after disability benefits had ended. For most of these thirty-five women, this meant that they no longer had sick or vacation time available for future needs. Twenty women took time off without any form of reimbursement. For nine women a leave was not relevant; either they were self-employed or in a job where the birth coincided with time regularly taken off, such as teachers whose babies were born in the summer. Fifteen women had resigned from their jobs and were not included in any of the above categories.

For the women in group two, 47% were eligible for leaves, 58% of which were paid. In total, 28% of the women in group two were eligible for a paid leave. Eleven of the forty women took a leave and then resigned. Most of the women who took leaves had intended to return but for numerous reasons, such as changes in the workplace, they did not.

What is more interesting is that many women were either unclear about their benefits, or else the idea of a paid leave was so foreign to them that they misunderstood our question. We asked all of the women, "Does your employer offer a maternity leave as part of company policy for pregnant women?" Many women responded affirmatively, but further questioning revealed that they were actually allowed not a maternity (or disability) leave, but a leave based on the sick and vacation time they had earned.

We began this section by discussing the three critical components of a leave—its length, job protection, and wage replacement. We found that the majority of women had a job-protected leave but only one-fourth were paid leaves through disability. Half the women were able to finance part of a leave through their sick time and vacation benefits. Reimbursement usually lasted less than six weeks. Since the average length of leave taken was three months many women were off for several weeks without pay.

This fact brings up an equally important factor in considering the need for paid leave: the financial hardship that unpaid leave places on families. Women did not take off as much time as they would have liked because their families depended on their income for survival.

Another consideration in determining an appropriate length of leave is the health of the mother and child. When we asked mothers how soon after delivery they felt physically and emotionally able to return to work, most of the women reported that they were physically able to return to work within three months but emotionally they were not ready to return for six months. Although the majority of the babies were healthy (12% were either premature or had serious health problems), one-fourth of the mothers reported they had delivery complications which delayed their return. For example, caesarean deliveries were not uncommon, and even though many women did not view them as a complication, having one usually extended the amount of time required for physical recovery.

WHERE ARE THE INFANTS?

When mothers return to work within three months of childbirth, they often find few options for child care, so in our investigation we were curious about where the child was placed, the cost of the care, and whether obtaining child care was a stress on the family. In our sample, fifty-two, or almost half of the children were cared for by their immediate family or other relatives. Four of the women cared for their own children while they worked. For example, a preschool teacher brought her baby to school with her. Twenty-one of the infants were cared for by their fathers; usually this involved the mother arranging to work evenings or on weekends so that the family did not have to use outside care. Twenty-seven of the infants were cared for by a relative outside the immediate family, usually the maternal grandmother.

Having a relative provide care was very comforting for most of the families that chose this solution. It was not uncommon to hear remarks such as, "I trust my mother and I don't have to worry about my child competing for love with other children—my child loves it," or "he's with family, he's raised the way I would want." At the same time, working mothers reported feeling guilty about accepting their relative's generosity. A nurse reported, "My mother-in-law refuses to accept any type of compensation. She says her payment is being with her grandson. She's gone overboard in outfitting her home for him. I feel guilty in having such a perfect arrangement..." Jean, a secretary, expressed similar sentiments, "...my mother is young and likes to do things. Even though she loves the baby and offered to do this, this is really not the best arrangement for her."

The other care arrangements used were family day-care (twenty-one children), non-relative sitter (sixteen children), and day-care center (ten children). Eight of the children were not listed in any of the above categories because their families used a combination of two or more care categories, and none was the primary arrangement. Other children had complex care packages where one arrangement was primary but another one was needed to fill in specified hours. For example, some women who worked shifts beginning in the late afternoon left the child with a babysitter for an hour until the husband or older children came home. The majority of children, whether cared for by relatives or others, spent their days outside of their own home.

The cost of infant care ranged from zero to 550 dollars per month. For those who did pay, the average cost was about two hundred dollars per month. The majority of women using relatives did not pay for infant care, while others paid a nominal amount. Many women could not have worked without using relatives because their entire salary would have gone to the care provider.

One of the common assumptions about infant day care is that it is an additional stress for the already stressed family. We asked the mothers to rate a number of potential problems on a four point scale ranging from no problem to a large problem. Only one-third of working mothers reported problems, from minor to moderate in degree, in finding a care arrangement, of the reliability of the care provider, of transportation to and from care, or of cost.

In spite of reporting minimal problems with infant care, one-fourth of the families changed their care arrangement at least once in the first year of their child's life. Seventeen families changed their care arrangements once, and twelve families changed their caregivers two or more times in that first year. The problems associated with discontinuity of setting and caretakers have been discussed elsewhere (Farber and Egeland 1982). Research has shown that children thrive best when they have stable, responsive caretakers.

In addition to asking the mothers about specific problems that we had identified, we also wondered if they might identify other problems. We asked two open-ended questions, "What do you like best, and what do you like least about your current childcare arrangement?" When we asked each woman what she liked least, rather than finding fault with the care itself, mothers complained about having to separate from the child to go to work. We heard many comments such as, "I hate having to leave him, he cries when I go," or "I don't like being away from him all day." Other negative and stressful elements of infant care included having to take the child out of the house—"getting ready in the mornings is a zoo . . . I feel guilty about waking him and taking him out on cold mornings." Some mothers were also concerned about their child not having contact with other children, while others were concerned about their child having too much contact with other children and always being sick.

One concern we heard from many women was the difficulty in finding someone appropriate to provide individual care in the child's home. One woman reported interviewing thirty women before she found one that she felt was qualified to stay with her baby. Pat had a college degree and her husband was a well-paid professional. She felt that because child care is one job which has traditionally not required specific training, many women who could not find other employment responded to her advertisement. Pat mentioned that the problems of inadequate and abusive care have come to light in the 1980s with national media attention and several well-publicized trials. She further emphasized her concerns when she asked, "Who are the people who watch the people watching our kids?"

When asked about the feature of their childcare situation they liked best, most women spoke about the caregiver's personal qualities. Those women who had their children with relatives noted that they felt very secure with their child in this kind of care. Those who had other arrangements made comments such as "she loves children" or "she's wonderful with him." Other positive aspects of child care that were mentioned were the stability of the arrangement and the caregiver's ability to be flexible about the schedule.

MOTHERHOOD AND WORK: HASSLES AND HAPPINESS

Another aspect of our survey dealt with the advantages and disadvantages of combining motherhood and work or of being primarily a homemaker. The most common disadvantage cited of pursuing both motherhood and out-of-home work was the fact that there are only twenty-four hours in each day. As a result, working women become acrobats juggling tight schedules. Sue, a secretary, told us that "having to have a rigid schedule means you have to impose a rigid schedule on the baby . . . " A social worker expressed similar sentiments: "Children are not predictable and jobs expect you to be predictable, like be on time when the child is sick." The time pressures and inflexible job schedule led Donna, a physician's assistant, to conclude, "I didn't feel like I was doing anything real well. I'd arrive at work late, leave in a whirlwind and come home in a whirlwind." Donna was one of the few women that we interviewed who quit their jobs after working several months following childbirth. These women conceded defeat to the overwhelming time pressures of both roles.

Another frequently mentioned drawback of being both a mother and an employee was persistent fatigue. Several women replied that they were simply "tired, tired, tired." Many working mothers felt that working outside of the home, caring for child(ren) and spouse, and maintaining a household was physically and emotionally draining, and as a result they were not performing any of their roles to their own satisfaction. However, when we asked mothers who were not working out of the home what they felt were the disadvantages of full-time motherhood, we heard the same response—exhaustion. Not surprisingly, motherhood is a full-time and tiring job for the majority of women, most of whom have little outside help in running their household. So, a job outside the home in addition to that can either be perceived as relief from the unrelenting demands of caring for an infant or as an additional stress.

A third common stress that working mothers report is the guilt and frustration of having to separate from their children on a regular basis and coping with feelings of jealousy toward the alternative caregiver. Jennifer, a businesswoman, related feelings of jealousy "when my child leaped out of my arms into the babysitter's." Ann, a teacher, whose mother cared for her daughter while she worked reported similar feelings: "My mother comes first for Amy in my head . . . it's jealousy I guess."

For some mothers, separating from their child was an additional burden because they were trying to nurse; leaving was emotionally as well as physically difficult. Women who worked part-time reported that if they adhered to a strict schedule they could often continue nursing while working. Women working full-time often stopped nursing at three months, when they returned to work. It is interesting to note that a slightly greater percentage of working mothers than nonworking mothers (73% versus 62%) breastfed their infants. It may be that working mothers feel that they can enhance the infant-mother relationship prior to returning to work. Both the mother's jealousy and inability to continue breastfeeding are probably much more problematic for the mother than for the child.

The numerous stresses that working mothers report revolve around the need to develop a relationship with their infant, to feel secure in that relationship, and to establish a regular schedule. It seems that the sooner women rush back to work the more difficult it is for them to feel comfortable about who their child is or about their relationship with the child.

At the same time, there were two major advantages to combining work and motherhood. Sixty-two percent of the women felt that having a job gave them a sense of emotional well-being, self-worth, and an identity "beyond being just a mother." For example, Lia, a nurse, said "It's good to have an out-of-house interest. I'm the type that would go crazy if I were in the house all day." Similarly, Paula stated that working made her feel very competent: "It makes me feel better about myself. I feel more whole." The second most frequent advantage of combining work and motherhood was the financial reward. For most families, the income was important for maintaining their style of living. Furthermore, some women felt that working enabled them to provide more than just basic necessities for their child.

Other advantages of combining motherhood and work included the belief that the time spent away from the child while working enriched the quality of the time mother and child spent together. Joan, a guidance counselor, said that having to "budget my time makes me more attuned to the baby's needs and makes our time together real quality time." For women in professional jobs, combining both roles was a necessity in order to keep pace with their chosen fields. These women had invested years in their education and training, and working during their children's infancy ensured that they did not "waste" their education. Another group of women thought that it was advantageous for their child to be exposed to multiple caregivers. For example, Joan felt that outside caregivers were "beneficial to the baby because he gets stimulation from others and learns to trust more people." Last, an interesting point cited by several working mothers was that their husbands became more involved in child care as a result of the mother's multiple responsibilities. Consequently, the father and child had a close relationship, and the mother was not depended upon as the exclusive caregiver.

When we asked women in groups two and three about the advantages and disadvantages of staying home to care for an infant, their responses were fairly consistent across groups, regardless of whether the women had stopped working just before this baby was born or several years before. There were three major advantages to staying home with an infant and not returning to work. They included being the primary caretaker for one's own infant, being able to observe the baby's developmental milestones, and having the energy to devote to motherhood.

Most of the mothers felt that staying home full-time allowed for a stronger emotional bond between mother and child and for enjoying each phase of the child's development. At age thirty-three, Sarah resigned her management position before her second child was born. Out of financial necessity Sarah had worked while her older child was an infant and she still regretted it. "When he was hurt he didn't run to me but to the careprovider—that was painful for me. Part of the reason one has children is to have people who belong to them. I missed a lot with the first child and didn't want to again. It left an empty spot."

The disadvantages of staying home that were cited most often were fatigue, isolation, and loss of income. Again, mothers who were not working outside of the home felt that having to be constantly available to meet a child's demands left them fatigued. The feelings of isolation and boredom after spending all day with a child were expressed in such comments as "my brain turns to mush," "no adult conversation . . . sometimes I feel that I'm just a mother not a person," and "I begin to lose my self-respect as a person." One mother who was at home all day in an area with few nonworking mothers said she would drive her husband crazy when he got home. Another difficulty some women had with not working was having to adjust to living on one income and to having no personal income. It should be noted that mothers in group three were reluctant to discuss the disadvantages of staying home. They had made a choice and at first did not want to talk about the negative aspects of that choice.

A PAID LEAVE POLICY

All of the respondents were asked whether they thought women who work should be given a paid leave to take care of their infant. The majority of employed and nonemployed mothers agreed that there should be a paid infant care leave policy. Although very few women were opposed to a paid leave, it was not surprising to find that more of the nonemployed mothers than the employed mothers were opposed to a leave policy. Eleven percent of the women in group one, fifteen percent of group two, and twenty-five percent of group three were opposed to a paid leave policy. The most common response was that there should be a paid leave of three months, with an additional three months unpaid leave allowed.

Those women opposed to a paid leave policy believed that working was a woman's choice and that it was her responsibility, not the employer's, to provide for her leave. Several women thought that having a paid leave policy would result in employees agreeing to return, and then quitting, thus leaving their employer with a vacancy after limited advance notice. Others were concerned about the cost of such a program to the taxpayer.

All of the women were asked whether they would take leaves with and without a job guarantee, and with and without pay. The overwhelming majority of women (94%) would have taken a paid, guaranteed leave if it was available, and 72% would have taken additional unpaid time if their job had been guaranteed. Above all, job protection was very important; only one-third of the respondents would have taken off additional time knowing that their specific position was not guaranteed.

CONCLUSION

What do women want and need in order to be effective parents and employees? We felt that finding out what parents wanted and what difficulties they faced with currently existing policies would help in making realistic policy decisions. We found that the women in our sample were working primarily for financial reasons, yet only 15% were eligible for a paid leave at full salary. The leaves were usually for six weeks and based on the concept of physical disability following pregnancy and delivery; that is these were maternity leaves, not infant care leaves based on the principle that employees and their families should have time to adjust to the birth of a child. Although there were few formal paid leaves, a significant number of women found that their accrued sick and vacation time enabled them to take several weeks paid leave without incurring significant financial hardship. Few of the women, however, found that the time technically allotted them was enough to adjust to the demands and pleasures of caring for a new infant. The average length of leave taken was three months, but the average preferred length of leave was six months. Women returned to work sooner than they preferred because they needed the money and they feared losing their jobs. In considering the need for paid leave, financial hardship is an important factor. National statistics indicate that 41% of married working women have husbands who earn less than $15,000 per year (Congressional Caucus for Women's Issues 1985).

Of interest is the fact that the majority of women interviewed, regardless of whether or not they were working, supported the idea of a paid infant care leave. One of the concerns expressed by both working and nonworking women was that employees might take advantage of employers by taking leaves, stating an intention to return and then quitting after receiving their leave pay. Although this can create a problem for employers who need to plan their personnel needs, it is not a problem associated exclusively with maternity or infant care leave. It is, in fact, common for employees who intend to leave a position to use their sick or vacation time prior to announcing their resignation. It is a benefit they have earned that they feel is rightfully theirs. As infant care leaves become more common, employers will become more realistic about the fact that not all women will know in advance whether they want to return following childbirth. One large company gave women six weeks of paid leave, and an additional four months unpaid leave during which time they could decide if they were going to return to work.

The data on infant care arrangements in this sample are consistent with those reported by the United States Census Bureau (1983) and by Klein (1985). Those studies found that almost half of the families in this country use relatives to care for infants, and only 10% of families use center care, with the remainder using group day care or babysitters. Our sample was representative of working women in this country with respect to their infant care arrangements.

Infant care arrangements were of great concern for all mothers. They were extremely concerned about the personal qualities of the care providers. Even though many of the mothers felt fortunate to have a relative caring for their child, they were still upset by daily separations from their children. Most of the mothers found it difficult to leave their child with someone else for the entire day despite trusting that the child would be cared for well. Some women found that thinking about their child in a house or center far from their place of employment distracted them from concentrating fully on their jobs. These findings suggest that childcare centers on or near employment sites might make it easier for parents to devote themselves more fully to their jobs while in the office. For some parents, knowing that the child is physically close and that the parent will be able to visit during breaks and lunch hours would alleviate the guilt and sense of loss incurred by eight-to ten-hour daily separations.

In recent years several communities have benefited from local companies joining together to support affordable high-quality day-care centers within close proximity to the work place. If centers which are subsidized by employers are available, and if women have the opportunity to witness high-quality care, they may change their negative attitudes about day-care centers. Both employer and employee could benefit from this type of arrangement.

A goal of this study was not to state that there are more advantages to staying home or to working. Clearly, women who work, out of either necessity or personal desire, will continue to do so, and those women who prefer to be full-time mothers will continue to do that. Research has shown that children do best when their mothers are satisfied with their decision (Hoffman 1984). By asking questions about the advantages and disadvantages of employment and nonemployment, we hoped to find out whether certain difficulties that are unique to working mothers could be considered in formulating recommendations for infant care leave and other family-related policies. Flexible job schedules, childcare referral services, subsidized high-quality day care, and day-care centers conveniently located to places of employment are all factors which women are telling us that they need.

Clearly, this is not just a woman's issue, but at the present time leaves, when they are available, are primarily for women. Thus we interviewed only women. Infant care leave implies, however, that either parent may take time off for early child care. It is equally important to gather attitudinal data from men, who still tend to exert greater influence on the creation of business and national policies. But statistics can not tell the whole story. Percentages and frequencies can not tell us what parents want; nor can surveys of company policies tell us about the discrepancies between leaves available and leaves actually taken. The opinions of the women in our sample, who were in all types of jobs and professions, can help guide future research and inform us of issues obscured by statistics. When creating a national policy affecting families, it is critical to know how parents in a variety of professions and life situations are managing.

REFERENCES

Calvert, G. 1982. Employee benefits: Adjusting to future change. D. Salisbury ed. *America in Transition: Implications for Employee Benefits.* Washington, D.C.: EBRI.

Catalyst Career and Family Center. 1981. *Corporations and Two-Career Families: Directions for the future.* New York: Catalyst.

Congressional Caucus for Women's Issues. 1985. *Background on the Parental and Disability Leave Act of 1985.*

Farber, E., and Egeland, B. 1982. Developmental consequences of out-of-home care for infants in a low-income population. E. Zigler and E. Gordon, Eds. *Day Care: Scientific and Social Policy Issues.* Boston: Auburn House.

Hoffman, L. 1984. Work, family and the socialization of the child. R. Parke, ed. *Review of Child Development Research,* vol. 7. Chicago: University of Chicago Press.

Kamerman, S. 1980. *Parenting in an Unresponsive Society: Managing Work and Family.* New York: Free Press.

Kamerman, S., Kahn, A., and Kingston, P. 1983. *Maternity Policies and Working Women*. New York: Columbia University Press.

Klein, R. 1985. Caregiving arrangements by employed women with children under one year of age. *Developmental Psychology* 21: 403–06.

United States Bureau of the Census. 1983. *Current Population Reports*. Washington, D.C.: Government Printing Office.

TEN

Fathers and Infant Care Leave

JOSEPH H. PLECK

This chapter considers infant care (or parental) leave for fathers—the topic generally known as paternity leave. It first considers the background of parental leave policies as they apply to fathers in the United States. Next, data on the availability, utilization, and effects of parental leave by fathers in the United States and Sweden are examined. Finally, the chapter takes an overview of paternity leave's future prospects.

BACKGROUND

Kamerman et al. (1983) have argued that policies concerning parental leave in the United States have largely focused on the disability (as opposed to the childcare[1]) aspect of leave, and that these policies have been primarily rooted in laws regarding sex discrimination in employment. These two themes in U.S. policies have potentially contradictory implications for fathers. The disability conception, by itself, allows no place for paternity leave. Indeed, to many who hold only the disability perspective, paternity leave is simply incomprehensible. An employer who rejected a male employee's request for an unpaid parental leave (always approved for female employees) was quoted in the press: "I didn't know Tim was pregnant. Gynecology is not my field. I don't know if this man has had a sex change operation or what" (Scioli 1983).

Nondiscrimination by sex in employment, the other theme in U.S. policy, has the opposite implication. New mothers in many organizations are, in reality, able to take various categories of leave without having to

1. In this paper, parental leave and infant care leave are used as terms for the broader construct; disability leave and child care leave are used as the terms for the two major subcategories of parental leave.

document medical disability. In many of these situations, a new father's claim to take the same leave would not be accepted. The nondiscrimination principle in U.S. law has enabled fathers with such employers to win leave benefits equal to those for mothers in at least five recent cases or settlements.

Under a June 1985 consent decree between Commonwealth Edison (Chicago) and the EEOC, male employees have the same rights as female workers to take unpaid leave to take care of infant children (*EEOC v. Commonwealth Edison*, U.S.D.C. N.Ill., No. 85–C–5637). Prior to the settlement, Commonwealth Edison routinely gave women six months of unpaid leave to care for their newborns (and in at least one case, an adopted infant), under a contract clause with the IBEW providing for leave of absence without pay "for justifiable reasons." The company denied it to Stephen Ondera, a male employee, who subsequently sued (Bureau of National Affairs 1986; Catalyst 1986). A February 1986 mediated settlement between the Hartford city police and the IBPO established that policemen whose wives give birth are entitled to the same amount of leave granted to female officers who give birth (Bureau of National Affairs 1986). Leeds (1983a) cites three additional New York cases in which discrimination was found in granting medical leave or sick days to mothers with no proof of disability, but denying it to fathers.

Most United States policy analysts now recommend, first, providing for the needs of mothers recovering from childbirth through a broader leave policy for temporary medical disability. Second, they recommend that, distinct from leave for temporary medical disability, leave for purposes of providing child care should also be available. The reformist view, reflected in the parental and disability leave legislation introduced in Congress in 1985 and 1986 (see also Coalition of Labor Union Women 1983; Zigler and Muenchow 1984), is that employers should be mandated to offer both kinds of parental leave with a job guarantee, at least on an unpaid basis.

Under this plan, the two thrusts in U.S. policy noted by Kamerman et al. (1983) are elegantly integrated, and in a way that supports paternity leave. Only women are eligible for that part of parental leave intended for the temporary medical disability following pregnancy (although men will have claims for other kinds of temporary disabilities). But both sexes are eligible for the childcare component of parental leave. This formulation seems to make possible an accommodation of women's special needs related to maternity with the disability component, without violating the principle of gender-neutrality through a benefit explicitly restricted to mothers. It also makes leave available to both parents in a gender-neutral way in the childcare component. In addition, since maternity-related medical disability is typically certifiable for the relatively short period of eight weeks, mandating childcare leave increases the total amount of leave mothers can take (eighteen additional weeks in the 1986 federal bill), as well as makes leave possible in cases of adoption.

However, this joint strategy integrates the policy themes at the cost of mandating two different leave benefits, either of which of itself faces considerable obstacles. The coalition campaigning for parental leave may be unable to obtain both. The leading alternative strategy appears to be the advocacy of disability leave only, thus providing leave only to mothers and for the relatively short period medically certifiable under disability. Five states currently mandate state-supervised, paid, temporary disability insurance. Other states are reviewing this approach, or, like Massachusetts, are considering mandated unpaid disability leave.

Another, even narrower reform strategy is to advocate maternity leave not under the rubric of temporary disability, but as a *special protection* needed by working mothers, as it is conceptualized in many European countries. This approach has been upheld in the "Garland" case (*California Federal Savings v. Guerra*, 307 F.E.P. 849, No. 85–494). The statute at issue establishes an unpaid but job-protected leave for maternity which does not exist in California law for any other medical or other condition. Montana and Massachusetts,[2] among other states, have similar laws. Though most feminist groups have come out against such maternity leave statutes, other feminist, women's, and family organizations have supported them. Hewlett (1985), for example, explicitly argues for special protection, criticizing what she sees as a narrow *equal rights* focus in American feminism that has failed to provide women the kind of maternity leave they really need.

In effect, the United States is at a crossroads about whether to broaden the availability of parental leave at all, and if so, in what form. To the extent that the campaign for better parental leave includes childcare leave as an objective, paternity leave will become more available. But to the extent that leave reform focuses only on disability leave (or on maternity leave as a special protection for employed women), fathers will be left out. Thus, whether paternity leave becomes more available depends on which of several reform strategies, if any, proves successful.

2. As noted above, Massachusetts is now considering mandating unpaid disability leave. Currently, it mandates employers to offer eight weeks of unpaid maternity leave "for purposes of child care." Largely at the instigation of a local paternity leave activist, bills were introduced in 1984, 1985, and 1986 to both lengthen the leave period and offer it to fathers as well. In response to these bills, Massachusetts established a state Study Commission to recommend new legislation. Its consideration of dropping childcare leave entirely in favor of temporary disability is somewhat ironic in light of the proposed bills which led to the creation of the commission.

AVAILABILITY, UTILIZATION, AND EFFECTS OF PATERNITY LEAVES

United States

Three different forms of parental leave for fathers need to be distinguished: (1) long-term, paid; (2) short-term, paid; and (3) unpaid. These three types differ in their availability, utilization, and other respects.

Long-Term, Paid Paternity Leave. A tiny handful of U.S. organizations (such as the Ford Foundation and the Bank Street College of Education) offer a paid parental leave of a substantial duration for which fathers are eligible. In 1980 the Bank Street College of Education began offering three months of paid coverage to both parents. Initially, it was available only to the professional staff, but it was extended in 1986 to the college's service employees, represented by AFSCME. Although no systematic data are available, the number of fathers who take such leaves, in the few places they are available, is reported to be quite low (Bureau of National Affairs 1986:115–118).

Short-Term, Paid Paternity Leave. Of the 384 large companies responding to a 1983 survey (Catalyst 1986), only four provide one or two weeks of paid leave other than vacation to new fathers. Likewise, only two of the 250 firms in Kamerman et al.'s survey of Dunn and Bradstreet companies (1983) provide several paid-leave days explicitly designated for fathers for purposes of parenting. About a quarter of the firms in the latter study, however, report that they permit fathers to take a few days off with pay at the time of the birth of a child by using other paid leave, often sick leave. Three or four days appear to be the upper limit for this kind of leave.

In 253 firms surveyed in 1983 by the Bureau of National Affairs (1986), two-fifths have one or more leave provisions allowing male employees to take time off from work for the birth of their children. In these firms, nearly half permit employees to use paid vacation or annual leave in this way. This report also showed that larger companies are somewhat more likely to permit the use of annual leave for this purpose, and somewhat less likely to offer sick leave. Almost no data are available on the extent to which fathers take advantage of the policies documented in these two studies.

If one assumes that most workers have relative freedom to take sick days and to schedule vacation days at their convenience, the ability to use sick or vacation days for parental leave may seem a trivial matter. However, many workers are required to provide medical certification when they claim paid sick leave. Some unions report that companies discourage workers from using their full entitlement of paid sick days.

Many workers do not choose when they take vacation. Thus, policies formally allowing fathers to use these other paid leave accruals for child care may be more significant than they first appear. However, it must be noted that taking sick or vacation days for paternity deprives the father of that leave when he actually needs it for illness or vacation.

Unpaid Paternity Leave. This form of leave is becoming relatively common in union contracts for state and municipal employees, including teachers. In the Catalyst (1986) survey of 384 companies, 119, or 37% of those responding to the question, said that they offered unpaid leaves to fathers, with the lengths of time offered comparable to those provided mothers. These leaves were not usually called paternity or parental leave, but instead were covered under the company's personal leave or leave-of-absence policy. In some cases, companies had extended unpaid parental leave to both parents (rather than mothers) only to avoid the appearance of sex discrimination. On the crucial question of utilization, only nine companies in the Catalyst survey reported that a father had actually taken such unpaid leave under these policies.

Although utilization is low, the right to take unpaid childcare or personal leave is the issue in many of the legal settlements and decisions noted above, as well as in many of the cases reported in the media of fathers fighting for paternity leave. Accounts of what these fathers go through to obtain unpaid leave suggest that among the small minority of fathers who want one, the desire for it is very strong. In some cases, the father's motivation is not just a wish to be actively involved with the newborn, but occurs because the mother is unable to take a leave from her job or she or the child is experiencing postnatal medical complications.

Sweden

Sweden is not the only European country formally providing at least some paternity leave. Norway, Denmark, Finland, Iceland, West Germany, France, and Portugal do so as well (Bureau of National Affairs 1986:181–90; Kamerman, chapter 14, below; see also Schirmer 1982:117–19, on Denmark). The Swedish policy is of particular interest, however, because it is by far the most generous, the oldest, and the most consciously intended to promote paternal involvement. Since 1974, Sweden's social insurance scheme has offered several different categories of parental leave to fathers. The exact provisions of the program have gradually been modified, and they are still changing.

The program provides two major types of *parent's benefits* (FP/SFP), as well as a *temporary care* benefit (VAB). The basic FP is for 180 days during the child's first nine months, at 90% of the parent's salary, and can be used by either parent. The *special parents' benefit* (SFP), initiated in 1978, is for 180 days to be used during the child's first four (earlier, eight) years; the last ninety days are paid at a subsistence rate, however.

Previous reviews of the data between 1974–80 indicated that the proportion of eligible fathers using the FP benefit rose to and then plateaued at about 10% during this period (Lamb 1982; Lamb and Levine 1983; Pleck 1986; Hwang 1987). Almost 28% used at least some of the SFP benefit in 1980 (Hwang 1987, citing SOU 1982 as the most recent official data).

Starting in 1986, government reports tabulate the utilization of the regular FP leave and the special SFP leave together. In effect, Swedish policymakers now consider use of the SFP during the child's first year to be equivalent to use of the FP. In 1983, the most recent year for which information is available, the percentage of fathers taking leave (either the FP *or* the SFP during the child's first 12 months) was 22.0%, with an average of forty-four days taken by users (National Social Insurance Board 1986). (By comparison, 99.3% of mothers took leave, for an average of 258 days.) In addition, this report also retabulated the data going back to 1978 (when the special leave was introduced) to aggregate the use of the FP and SFP. Fathers' use of paternity leave during 1978–80 was now reported to average 22%, rather than the 10% for usage of the FP alone emphasized in earlier reports (Kamerman 1985).

The introduction of the special benefit in 1978, then, helped to increase the proportion of Swedish fathers taking paid paternity leave. In fact, as many or more Swedish fathers now take paternity leave in the child's first year through the provisions of the special SFP leave as through the explicitly postnatal FP leave. In my view, these data suggest that one factor depressing fathers' FP utilization in the 1974–80 statistics was that if the father took any FP leave, the mother necessarily had to take less FP leave herself. That is, in some families, fathers took no leave not because they did not want to, but because the wife or couple decided the mother would take all the leave. Whether Swedish policymakers introduced the SFP leave in 1978 in part to overcome this possible barrier to paternal utilization, it appears that the introduction of the SFP benefit, a new category of leave which fathers could take without reducing mothers' usage of the FP leave, doubled the overall rate of paternal leave-taking in a single year.

Several ancillary statistics are also useful. If one extends the time period during which fathers' use of the special leave is counted from the child's first year to the first two years, fathers' overall utilization rate rises to 29.1% (for 1981, the most recent available year), with payment for an average of forty-seven days (National Social Insurance Board 1986). Thus, Swedish fathers' utilization of these benefits appears even higher by this index than the 22% given above. On the other hand, Lamb points out that fathers who take as little as one day of leave are counted as users in the official statistics (Lamb 1982; Lamb and Levine 1983). In data for earlier years, only half the fathers taking any leave did so for thirty days or more. Applying this ratio to the most recent data, only about 11% of eligible Swedish fathers take paternity leaves of one month or more during the child's first year. By this criterion, fathers' utilization of leave appears more modest. Interestingly, at least one study (Lamb, et al. 1982) finds that the majority of a sample of fathers who took FP leave did so not at birth, but when the mother finished her leave when the child was five or six months old.

As an entirely separate temporary-care-leave benefit (VAB), Sweden also provides sixty days per child per year of paid leave to take care of a sick child, or to take care of a child when the regular caretaker is unable to do so, for children under twelve (*parent's benefit for temporary child care*). About 30.3% of married fathers drew some of this benefit in 1984, for an average of 5.3 days, compared to 40.2% and 6.5 days for married mothers (SOU 1986). As a special provision of this leave, fathers are entitled to a special leave of ten days in connection with a mother's childbirth (the *ten-day benefit*). In 1976, 64% of eligible fathers used this benefit for an average of 7.5 days: 40% of those eligible took all ten days (Kamerman 1980:44; Lamb and Levine 1983). A 1981 report cited by Hwang (1987) shows that 85% of new fathers use at least some of this benefit (see also Trost 1983).

The reality of Swedish fathers' use of paternity leave is both higher and more complex than has sometimes been thought. It is interesting that the high degree of utilization of the ten-day benefit has received so little attention, perhaps because that benefit is intended to allow fathers to help with child and home care in order to help the mother recover from birth, rather than for the father to provide child care *per se* (Lamb 1986). Likewise, fathers' relatively frequent use of the temporary care benefit (and, when it was tabulated separately, the SFP benefit) is far less known than their lower use of the FP benefit.

Integrating the data for all leave categories together produces the following composite portrait: At the birth of a child, about 85% of Swedish fathers take an average of 7.5 days off from work through the ten-day benefit. Roughly one-quarter of this 85% spend an additional month or more on leave in the child's first year through the FP/SFP (assuming that most users of the FP/SFP also used the ten-day benefit), although not necessarily immediately after they take the ten-day benefit. Some fathers of children aged one to three use additional SFP days as well. Further, in any given year, 30% of married fathers of children under age twelve take an average of five temporary care (VAB) leave days. When the data are summarized in this way, Swedish fathers' utilization of paternity leave seems far from trivial.

Another way of characterizing Swedish fathers' participation is in comparison to that of mothers. Fathers' and mothers' use of parental leave for sick, older children differ relatively little. Both fathers and mothers take paid leave at high rates in the period following birth. But mothers do so for an average of eight and-one-half months, while most fathers do so for ten or fewer days, with a smaller subgroup taking up to a month or more in addition, often in the later months of infancy. Thus, the difference between fathers and mothers is primarily in the length and timing of the leaves taken during the child's first year, and not in the use of later leaves.

In my view, the Swedish data demonstrate that fathers' use of paternity leave is limited, but in a particular sense. It is not that very few Swedish fathers take leaves, but that among the rather substantial proportion of fathers who do, the leaves are short and are not taken just at the child's birth. Flexibility in how long and when to take paternity leave seems essential for significant numbers to make use of them.

Effects of Paternity Leave

Several Swedish studies provide information on the consequences of fathers' taking parental leave. Lamb et al. (1982; Hwang 1987) compared seventeen fathers in Goteborg, Sweden, who took leaves of one month or more with thirty-five fathers who did not. The average amount of time away from work for the seventeen on leave was about three months, usually starting when the infant was five or six months old. This study examined the hypothesis that fathers who are primary caretakers by virtue of being on leave would show more of certain behaviors thought to be typical of mothers (smiling, talking, kissing, hugging, touching). The study found that significant differences remained between mothers' and fathers' behaviors in the on-leave group, and that there were few differences between the two groups of fathers. The study also found no differences associated with the father's leave status in the children's tendency to prefer the mother for comfort or interaction, or the security of the infant's attachments to mother and father.

A second study (Hwang 1987) examined the behaviors of *home fathers* and working fathers when mothers were present and when they were absent. No average differences were evident when mothers were present. When mothers were absent, however, leave-taking fathers showed more caretaking behaviors than other fathers, but spent less time playing (a more traditional paternal behavior). If replicated, this finding suggests that paternity leave may be associated with limited changes in paternal behavioral style under certain conditions.

A third, longitudinal study of 145 Swedish fathers investigated the correlates of paternity leave in fathers' later behavior with their children. Lamb, et al. (1986) found modest but consistent relationships in these data between amount of paternity leave taken and the father's later involvement in and responsibility for child care. These analyses conclude not that taking a paternity leave causes later involvement, but that usage of a leave is one aspect of a larger, moderately stable pattern of higher than average involvement among some fathers.

A final category of research relevant to the question of effects is a group of studies concerning fathers' and mothers' satisfaction with and evaluation of paternity leave (see Hwang 1987; Trost 1983). These studies find that fathers' and mothers' reactions are generally positive, and that fathers are surprised to discover how difficult infant care is. Hwang 1987 quotes one Swedish father as saying: "At work, at least I knew when the coffee break was!" A small minority of users report that the leave was not a good experience for them. In many of these cases, the father had not wanted to take a leave, and had done so only because his wife chose not to use part or all of the FP entitlement for some reason (Hwang 1982).

Factors Affecting Utilization of Paternity Leave

The factors influencing fathers' utilization of paternity leave can be discussed at two levels: narrowly, in terms of the demographic and other correlates of leave usage noted in several Swedish cross-sectional studies; and more broadly at an analytical level. To consider the empirical correlates first, Swedish research indicates that use of the FP leave is higher among fathers employed in the public sector (Lamb and Levine 1983; Kamerman 1980; Trost 1983; Hwang 1987). This may occur because fathers employed in the private sector receive 90% of their regular salary when they are on leave (up to a fixed maximum level), while fathers in public-sector jobs receive 100% of their salary, with no maximum (Lamb and Levine 1983) and thus give up less when taking a leave than private-sector fathers. Public sector utilization may also be higher because the official government encouragement of paternal leave has more impact there. Further, the higher the mother's earnings, the more likely it is that the father will take at least some leave (Kamerman 1980). Families have more to lose economically if the high-earning parent of either sex, in the private sector, takes a leave.

Trost (1983) examined the correlates of the use of parental leave (FP, SFP, and ten-day benefit combined) and the temporary-care benefit in a survey of several thousand Swedish men aged twenty-one to sixty. Trost found parental leave to be higher if the father was employed in the public sector, the wife had higher education, or the father was unmarried. Use of temporary care leave was higher among fathers who were younger, whose youngest child was younger, and whose wives were employed in the public sector.

At a broader level, it is often assumed that if paternity leave is available, whether a father uses it is a direct reflection of his desire to to be involved as a father. Actually, fathers' utilization of paternity leave is influenced by several factors in addition to their own motivation and attitudes: the length and timing of the leave, whether and how the leave is paid, and employer attitudes toward male employees who take these leaves. First, the length and timing of the leave make a difference. Short leaves will be utilized far more often than long-term ones because they are less disruptive to the father's job or career, a disincentive to taking a leave even when loss of income is not an issue. Some fathers are more likely to take leave time when the infant is older rather than immediately after birth, because they feel more comfortable and competent with older infants and children.

In the United States, there is also some indication that fathers more often take leave when it is called something other than paternity or parental leave (which is probably facilitated if it is short-term and not only at the time of birth). Catalyst (1986) found that few fathers had used unpaid parenting leave (reported by only nine of 114 companies saying they formally offered this benefit). Human resource policymakers in the firms surveyed indicated, however, that it was nonetheless "fairly common" for fathers to take a few days off at the time of birth. They used vacation or sick days, or took time off informally as paid or unpaid personal days.

Second, whether and how the leave is paid also has an effect, but this appears to be the decisive factor relatively infrequently. The Swedish data noted earlier concerning the influence of sector of employment (public/private) and of wives' earnings suggest that economic variables do explain some variance in utilization. Since the use of paid leave for long durations is low both in the U.S. and Sweden, it is clear that the presence of compensation alone will not lead most fathers to take a long leave. At the same time, probably even fewer fathers take long-term leaves that are unpaid, showing that compensation does have an impact. To understand further the role of compensation, it would be especially valuable to know the effect of its presence or absence on the utilization of short-term leave in the U.S. Needed particularly are data on fathers' utilization of short-term paid leave in the approximately one-quarter of large firms where this benefit is available, and on their utilization of unpaid short-term leave.

Employers' attitudes toward fathers who take paternity leave are a third factor affecting utilization. Many corporations directly state they consider it inappropriate for a father to use paternity leave. In the Catalyst (1986) study, 62.8% of all companies indicated that they believed *no* amount of paternity leave was reasonable for fathers to take. Even within the subgroup of companies officially offering unpaid paternity leave (37% of the sample), 41% reported that they considered no paternity leave time to be reasonable. Thus, the proportion of companies both officially providing leave to fathers *and* reporting that they thought it was appropriate for fathers actually to use it was only 22% (59% of 37%). Catalyst also observed that companies do not notify men that they have an entitlement to parental leave. As noted earlier, many companies had apparently extended unpaid parental leave to both parents only to avoid the appearance of sex discrimination, not because they wanted or expected fathers to use paternity leave.

Negative employer attitudes toward paternity leave have also been documented in Sweden. Hwang (1987) surveyed fifty fathers who took one month or more of parental leave in 1980, and a small sample of employers, both in Goteborg, Sweden. A substantial proportion of both fathers and employers reported that employers do in fact view leave-taking fathers negatively and may penalize them in various ways. This result occurred in spite of explicit legal prohibitions against employers penalizing fathers who take leaves.

In summary, a variety of factors influence fathers' decisions to use parental leave. While the father's own degree of motivation to be directly involved in the care of his child is probably the strongest determinant, it is clearly not the only one. Social attitudes and structural variables inhibit the development of the motivation to take paternity leave. Institutional factors such as the duration and timing of the leave being offered, economic variables, and employer attitudes will influence utilization among men who have the motivation.

FUTURE PROSPECTS

Paternity leave is an issue that strikes people in a variety of ways. To some, it is a key to future change in sex roles, and therefore highly desirable. To others, it is frivolous and irrelevant. To still others, the idea seems personally threatening. In particular, some males fear that if employers are mandated to offer paternity leaves, fathers will then be expected or required to take them, and that fathers who do not will be thought the less for it. In the October 1985, House hearings on parental and disability leave, Rep. Austin Murphy (Pennsylvania) told Rep. Patricia Schroeder (Colorado): "I say to be careful. You know some of us guys really don't want this protection. We might have to stay home and take care of the kids. [Laughter.]" Schroeder replied: "There is an honest man" (*Parental and Disability Leave* 1985:16). I have also observed that men often mistakenly think the occasionally-used technical term *mandated parental leave* (that is, employers are mandated to offer it) actually means that fathers would be required to take it!

The perception that paternity leave is either frivolous or threatening can have effects that should not be underestimated. One Northeastern industrial union local negotiated for a single day off with pay for fathers on the day of the birth. After prolonged struggle, the company finally agreed, but only with the stipulation that the birth had to occur during the worker's actual shift on that day; a birth before or after working hours would not count (Dudzic 1983). In another example, the Department of Labor, the AFL-CIO, and the National Association of Manufacturers cosponsored a 1986 national conference on work and family issues at which I was scheduled to speak about paternity leave. At just this time, a contract dispute arose between the prestigious private organization administering the conference and one of its unions, in part over the issue of paid paternity leave; the union threatened to picket the event. At the last minute, the organization canceled the conference at considerable expense and embarrassment, rather than give in on paternity leave (*Wall Street Journal* 1986).

As noted at the outset, the United States is at decision point about parental leave. The need for better parental leave is being increasingly recognized, but actual policies are changing only slowly, and many groups remain entirely unprotected. The campaign for parental leave can follow one or more of three routes: disability leave, explicitly-designated maternity leave, and gender-neutral childcare leave. The first two benefit only women, while the third provides parental leave to men as well. If U.S. policy *does* elect to include fathers in parental leave reform, current experience suggests several considerations. First, for whatever reasons, it is clear that fathers will take advantage of infant care leave to a far lesser extent than mothers. Infant-care-leave policies may be gender-neutral in principle but they will not work in a gender-neutral way in practice. Although the term *parental leave* (as opposed to maternity leave) is intended explicitly to include fathers, it must do so with the awareness that fathers will not necessarily use it to an equal degree or in the same way. This should not be viewed as a failure of the policies or of fathers.

Second, the popular conception of paternity leave is at variance with what fathers actually use, both in Sweden and the U.S. There is a tendency in the U.S. to assume that paternity leave is a six-month leave taken by the father when a child is born, and that anything else is not really paternity leave. This model is probably largely derived from the six-month paid leave (FP) available to fathers in Sweden. However, the actual duration and timing of Swedish paternity leave in practice (relatively short-term leaves, not only at birth) would be a better model for the United States than the six-month theoretical entitlement. The few organizations in the U.S. offering long-term paid paternity leave are to be applauded for broadening the field of debate. At the same time, it must be recognized that the real frontier of parental leave for fathers in the U.S. is not increasing the availability of six-month paid leave, but rather of other forms that are considerably less generous: short-term paid leave and unpaid leave (the majority of which will also be short term).

Swedish research to date indicates that leave-taking does not lead to a transformation of fathers' behavioral styles with infants, or to children being less attached to their mothers. At the same time, it also suggests that leave-taking *is* related to the father's later degree of involvement and responsibility. Taking a paternity leave is not a random behavior of no particular significance; it is part of a broader dimension of paternal involvement.

One of the major questions which paternity leave raises for consideration is the meaning and value of short term leaves—those of a few days or weeks. Some might object that such short leaves are too brief to make much difference. Whatever a paternity leave provides for father, child, or family, more leave obviously provides more of it. But this does not mean that even relatively short leaves should be viewed as insignificant, either in promoting later involvement or in reducing family stress during a critical period.

Much about paternity leave can be summed up in the following apparent paradox: A substantial minority of large companies formally offer unpaid leave, but few fathers use it. (Instead, they put together a leave of a few days from other paid- and unpaid-leave categories, at a rate which is unfortunately undocumented, but which probably is fairly substantial.) At the same time, other organizations have formal policies permitting only women to have unpaid parental leave, or to use sick or disability days (without documentation of disability) for child care. Fathers in these organizations can and will fight strenuously for the same right. Thus, while only few fathers may use a paternity leave benefit when formally available, they are willing to sue for it when it is not.

This coexistence of low use of formal paternal-leave benefits where they exist, and a small activist minority fighting for them where they do not, may contribute to uncertainty and confusion among employers about the effect of making paternity leave more available. The policy option supporting paternity leave that receives the most consideration today is unpaid childcare leave, either mandated by federal or state legislation or established by collective bargaining. The effect of such legislation and labor agreements would in all likelihood be small as far as fathers are concerned. A significant proportion of fathers appear able to take short leaves under current arrangements, both formal and informal. Among those to whom the benefit would be newly extended, the most reasonable projection is that mandated childcare leave will result in a very small proportion of fathers who will take a leave of longer duration (weeks or months), and a somewhat larger proportion, but still a minority, who will take a leave of quite short duration (a few days).

Thus, the needs of the very small group of fathers likely to take a longer-duration leave, and of the somewhat larger group of fathers likely to take shorter-duration leaves, can be met at relatively low cost and inconvenience to employers. The combination of increasing the options for those fathers who want to be more involved in the care of their children, and at relatively low cost to employers, makes this policy option worthy of support.

REFERENCES

Bureau of National Affairs. 1986. *Work and Family: A Changing Dynamic.* Washington D.C.: Bureau of National Affairs.

Catalyst 1983. *Maternity and Parental Leaves of Absence.* New York: Catalyst.

Catalyst. 1986. *Report on a National Study of Parental Leave.* New York: Catalyst.

Coalition of Labor Union Women. 1983. *Bargaining for Child Care: Contract Language for Union Parents.* New York: Coalition of Labor Union Women.

Dudzic, M. 1983. Remarks to the "Changing the Workplace" Workshop at the Fatherhood Forum, New York, June.

Erler, G. 1982. Maternity and parental leaves in Europe. *Work Times* 1:1–5.

Erler, G., Jaeckel, M., and Sass, J. (1982). *Results of the European Study Concerning Maternity Leave/Parental Leave/Home Care Support Measures in Finland, Sweden, Hungary, Austria, and German Federal Republic—Summary.* Munich: Deutsches Jugendinstitut.

Hewlett, S. A. 1985. *A Lesser Life: The Myth of Women's Liberation in America.* New York: Morrow.

Hwang, C.-P. 1982. Unpublished presentation to the Bank Street College Research Colloquium, New York.

Hwang, C.-P. 1987. The changing role of Swedish fathers. M. E. Lamb, ed. *The Father's Role: Cross Cultural Perspectives,* 115–138. Hillsdale, N.J.: Erlbaum.

Hwang, C.-P., Lamb, M. E., Broberg, A., Frodi, M., and Hulth, G. 1985. Effects of early father participation on later paternal involvement and responsibility. Paper presented at the Society for Research in Child Development, Toronto, April.

Kamerman, S. B. 1980. *Maternity and Parental Benefits and Leaves: An International Review.* New York: Center for the Social Sciences, Columbia University.

Kamerman, S. B. 1985. Address to the Association of Junior Leagues. Conference on Parental Leave, Arden House, New York, March 7.

Kamerman, S. B., Kahn, A. J., and Kingston, P. W. 1983. *Maternity Policies and Working Women*. New York: Columbia University Press.

Lamb, M. E. 1982. Why Swedish fathers aren't liberated. *Psychology Today*. October: 75–77.

Lamb, M. E. 1986. Personal communication, August 5.

Lamb, M. E., and Levine, J. A. 1983. The Swedish Parental Insurance Policy: An experiment in social engineering. M. E. Lamb and A. Sagi, eds. *Fatherhood and Family Policy*, 39–51. Hillsdale, N.J: Erlbaum.

Lamb, M. E., Frodi, A. M., Hwang, C., and Frodi, M. 1982. Varying degrees of paternal involvement in infant care: Attitudinal and behavioral correlates. M. E. Lamb and A. Sagi, eds. *Nontraditional Families: Parenting and Child Development*, 117–38. Hillsdale, N.J.: Erlbaum.

Lamb, M. E., Hwang, P., Broberg, A., Bookstein, F., Hult, G., and Frodi, M. 1986. The determinants of paternal involvement in a representative sample of primiparous Swedish families. Unpublished paper.

Leeds, M. H. 1983a. Maternity leave for fathers: Part I. *New York State Bar Journal* February: 32ff.

Leeds, M. H. 1983b. Maternity leave for fathers: Part II. *New York State Bar Journal* April: 15–17.

National Social Insurance Board. 1986. *Social Insurance Statistics—Facts 1985*. Stockholm: National Social Insurance Board.

Parental and Disability Leave. 1985. Joint Hearing Before Subcommittees of the Committee on Post Office and Civil Service and of the Committee on Education and Labor, House of Representatives, October 17.

Parental and Medical Leave Act of 1986. 1986. Joint Hearing Before the Subcommittee on Civil Service and the Subcommittee on Compensation and Benefits of the Committee on Post Office and Civil Service on H.R. 4300, House of Representatives, April 10.

Pleck, J. H. 1986. Employment and fatherhood: Issues and innovative policies. M. E. Lamb, *The Father's Role: Applied Perspectives*, 385–412. New York: John Wiley & Sons.

Ritter, K. 1986. Unpublished tabulations, Social-Departmentet, Sweden.

Schirmer, J. G. 1982. *The Limits of Reform: Women, Capital, and Welfare*. Cambridge, Mass.: Schenkman.

Scioli, T. 1983. Telephone interview, January 29.

Statens Offentliga Utredninger (sou). 1982. *Enklare Foraldraforsakring*. Stockholm: Betanhande au Familjestodsutredningnen.

Trost, J. 1983. Parental benefits—A study of men's behavior and views. New York: Swedish Information Service (Social Change in Sweden, no. 28).

Wall Street Journal. 1986. News item, p. 1, April 22.

Zigler, E., and Muenchow, S. 1984. Infant day care and infant-care leaves: A policy vacuum. *American Psychologist* 38:91–94.

PART IV

Existing Leave Practices
in the United States

ELEVEN

Public Servants, Private Parents: Parental Leave Policies in the Public Sector

KATHLEEN MAKUEN

In this volume, much has been made about the absence of a federal policy for a parental leave and the provision of a national requirement to provide for such leave. Nowhere is this absence more apparent than in the United States public sector itself. Employees of the federal government and the armed forces have no official protection or recognition of their parenting needs, except through the Pregnancy Discrimination Act of 1978. This act does not protect the needs of the family nor the needs of an individual as parent; rather, it simply permits an employee to be away from work for the time to give birth and recover from delivery. Such a provision recognizes the needs of mothers only in a most limited sense, that of biological function.

Because federal and state governments are employers, they are subject to the same legal guidelines as are all employers. Yet, these guidelines are open to interpretation. Furthermore, existing legal guidelines provide for pregnancy only as a disability, and only require that pregnant workers be given disability leave. Specific requirements are few; the employer can, and often does, define the term of disability for the employee. Finally, leave for pregnancy need only be provided if the employer carries disability insurance.

In the absence of a national policy or any legal requirement other than disability, each federal agency has come up with its own guidelines for maternity leave. In spite of the widely varying practices of numerous federal agencies, a dictum exists which unifies these practices, and thus a kind of de facto leave policy has arisen. The one consistent feature of federally-approved leaves, no matter what the length of leave or what type of leave is used, is that such leave is always up to the discretion of the supervisor. The supervisor is always the one to decide whether to honor an employee's request for leave, what the length of the leave will be, and what kind of economic support it will have. This situation exists in almost all agencies of the federal government.

Leave practices in the armed forces show more consistency because clearer, more specific guidelines are provided, but these leaves are also subject to the discretion of the supervisor. Further, supposedly consistent policies differ radically between one locale and another (between Fort Bragg and Fort Worth, for example). Thus, consistency exists only within a single military installation. In fact, the differences between installations are so marked that military leave practices can be called arbitrary.

For most employees of state governments, the leave situation is limited to the time needed for delivery and recovery. In most states, a new mother can be required to return to work within four weeks, after her "disability" has ended. Only five states have legislation that provides more than a minimal amount of time for returning to work.

In order to expand the picture of the varying leave practices in the public sector, the Bush Center first instituted a survey of the state governments. Thirty-three, or 66%, of the states have responded thus far (in his *Survey Research Methods*, Earl R. Babbie considers a response rate of 60% good, and a rate of 70% or more very good). Some of the information provided by the questionnaires may reflect the attitudes or perceptions of the individual administrators who responded to the survey. The data discussed here for the federal government and its agencies, and for the armed forces, are available from a number of different printed sources. The recently compiled report on federal government leave practices by the Subcommittee on Civil Service is especially valuable in its data and discussion. This report is derived from a questionnaire sent to fifty-eight executive agencies of the federal government, of which fifty-three responded. It is revealing in its coverage of the widely differing practices that are routine in the federal government, all of which are dependent on the discretion of the supervisor.

A DEFINITION OF MATERNITY LEAVE

The first state policy was issued in Wisconsin over one hundred years ago with the passage of protective legislation that restricted women's hours of paid employment (Kamerman, Kahn, and Kingston). From that time, in both the private and public sectors, women could be dismissed from many jobs for being pregnant. During World War II the situation began to change with the creation of the Women's Bureau of the Department of Labor. In 1942 it published "Standards for Maternity Care and Employment of Mothers in Industry," which recommended six-week prenatal and two-month postnatal leave rights, as well as the right to reinstatement and seniority.

On January 1, 1974, the Supreme Court rendered its decision in the case of *Cleveland Board of Education v. LaFleur* (No. 72–777). The case involved the school board of Cleveland, Ohio, which required every pregnant school teacher to take unpaid maternity leave beginning five months before the expected birth of her child. She was not allowed to return to work until the next regular semester after her child was three months old. The Court found that the arbitrary cutoff dates, which failed to take into account the individual woman's physical condition, were unconstitutional. While pregnancy results in temporary disability, any actual disability affecting employment must be considered on an individual basis.

In April 1979 the Equal Employment Opportunity Commission issued Amendments to Guidelines on Discrimination Because of Sex (amending its 1972 guidelines published at 39 Federal Register [April 5, 1972]) and Questions and Answers Concerning the Pregnancy Discrimination Act (both at 29 C.F.R.§ 1604). The Pregnancy Discrimination Act reaffirmed the 1972 Guidelines and clarified that Title VII forbids discrimination on the basis of pregnancy, childbirth, and related medical conditions. Congress passed the Act, following the Supreme Court ruling in *General Electric Co. v. Gilbert*, (429 U.S. 125 [1976]) that the company's exclusion of pregnancy-related disabilities from its comprehensive disability plan did not violate Title VII. The Court held that exclusion of pregnancy was discrimination between pregnant and nonpregnant persons, not between men and women. In a related case, *Nashville Gas v. Satty* (434 U.S. 137 [1977]), the Court ruled that employers may refuse sick pay to women employees who are unable to work due to pregnancy and childbirth, but that they may not divest those women of their accumulated seniority merely because they take maternity leave.

Currently, the term *maternity leave* refers to a period of leave granted before and after childbirth during which a woman is physically unable to work outside the home and for which benefits are available similar to those granted to any other temporarily disabled employee, as required by the 1978 Pregnancy Discrimination Act [Pub. L. 95–555, 92 Stat. 2076, 42 U.S.C.§ 2000e (k)], an amendment to Title VII of the Civil Rights Act of 1964. Maternity leave may also refer to an additional period of leave for which benefits frequently are not available; these benefits may be denied on the grounds that childrearing is not related to an inability to work.

FEDERAL GOVERNMENT

For most employees of the U.S. government, infant care leave consists of using existing leave in the following order: sick leave, annual leave, and leave without pay. Thus, in the absence of a discrete policy, employees must fashion a package that meets the needs of their families and employers. During the paid-leave periods, benefits are continued; during the leave-without-pay time, they are continued only at the employee's expense. In the language of the Office of Personnel Management's *Manager's Handbook,* "absence for maternity purposes must be treated as any other medically certified disability ... the length of absence must be decided on individually by the employee and the leave-approving office...". There is an element of contingency, in that, "if [the supervisor is] reasonably certain she intends to return to duty, [he or she] may advance annual or sick leave."

The handbook of Office of Personnel Management serves only as policy guideline, without the full force of law. The common thread connecting the inter- and intra-agency variation around a nonspecified norm is the arbitrariness with which leave is granted. When an employee requests a package of substitution policies, the supervisor decides if, when, and how that parent takes a leave. Idiosyncratic issues like personality conflicts, petty grievances, and bureaucratic rotation of key personnel can interfere with even the most uniform of personnel policies. This kind of arbitrary decision-making is susceptible to irrational influences. An additional factor is that most of those who take leaves are female, and most managing supervisors are males who are less likely to be familiar with the demands on a primary caregiver.

Of the fifty-three federal executive agencies surveyed by the Congress, only a minority had generous, clearly-defined policies. The best agencies included Education, Health and Human Services (which had Absence for Family Care Leave), Housing and Urban Development, Justice, Labor, the Equal Employment Opportunity Commission, the Federal Trade Commission, the General Accounting Office, and the National Labor Relations Board. The worst, with unspecified policies, are too numerous to list here, but they include such huge agencies as the Environmental Protection Agency, the General Services Administration, and the Postal Service. The Postal Service is, in fact, the defendant in several pending lawsuits in which women plaintiffs claim they were unjustly terminated from duty because they were pregnant and had requested maternity leave. In the public sector, as in the private sector, horror stories abound: women who were fired outright, women who were emotionally and/or sexually harassed to the point where they quit their jobs "voluntarily," women losing years of seniority and pension benefits.

Some agencies have collective bargaining agreements. The U.S. Department of Labor and AFL-CIO Local No. 12 have negotiated a more liberal leave policy which provides that an employee may be granted any combination of annual leave or leave without pay for as much as two years, "for the purpose of pregnancy, or for assisting or caring for minor child while the mother is incapacitated for maternity reasons." There is no standard federal leave policy for the two million federal employees (excluding the Postal Service), of whom about 41% are women. Although it is mandatory to approve a request for accrued sick leave for a period of incapacitation, subject to the presentation of such acceptable medical documentation as the agency may require, agencies differ in the conditions under which annual leave and leave without pay are granted.

Sick leave may be used only for the period of the mother's incapacitation, including physical examinations. Sick leave is earned at the rate of thirteen days per year with unlimited accrual. Annual leave may be used at the discretion of the agency. It is accrued at the ratio of:

Thirteen days per year with less than three years service;
Twenty days per year with three to fifteen years service;
Twenty-six days per year after fifteen years service.

Young and/or new employees, who are the ones most likely to become new parents, are at a disadvantage under this system.

The benefits are offered as part of a fixed package provided to civilian employees of executive agencies. All benefits—health, life insurance, pension plan—are continued for both employees and their dependents during the leave period. While an employee is on sick leave or annual leave, benefit coverages continue for the duration of the leave. With leave without pay, the health and life insurance coverage continues for up to twelve months, and retirement coverage continues indefinitely. Payment is achieved through a combination of employee and employer contributions. The exception to this is health insurance, which the employee pays for while on leave without pay is as follows:

	Health	Life	Retirement
Employee	40%	66.7%	7%
Employer	60%	33.3%	7%

In terms of job protection, employees of both sexes are guaranteed the same or a comparable job upon their return, unless termination is required for reasons unrelated to the absence (for example, if termination is part of a reduction in the number of employees). Promotional status (the opportunity to take examinations, for example) is guaranteed. Staff adjustments during employee leave periods and work schedule changes to facilitate the employee's return to duty are matters of administrative discretion on the part of each agency. Day care is not offered. Precisely because maternity and paternity leave policy is considered part of fringe benefits, there is no reliable data on financing, percentage of employees taking leave, percentage of leave takers returning, or the average length of leave time, although such data is available at the state level.

To cite one respondent: "The major strength of the federal policy on infant care is that requests for sick leave, annual leave, and leave without pay for maternity and infant care leave purposes must be evaluated and acted upon on the same basis as leave requests for any other purpose. Federal agencies are not permitted to discriminate against employees who make leave requests for maternity and infant care leave purposes. The major weakness of the federal policy is the fact that the discretionary nature of leave approval for annual leave and leave without pay results in some inconsistencies among federal agencies."

Not only do these established guidelines overlook the real issue, that parenting needs a separate leave category, but they do not necessarily require or standardize anything but the minimum. This is the real crisis of the existing leave situation in the federal government: that whatever leave an individual takes is determined by his/her supervisor, and thus personal factors and relationships that are not part of the parenting situation may enter into the decision to grant a leave. In recent testimony before the United States House of Representatives (Spring 1986) by the Joint Committee on Civil Service, cases were cited such as that as the woman who committed suicide because her supervisor was overly stringent, even punitive, in his leave decisions.

THE FIFTY STATES

Of the state governments participating in the survey (table 11.1), twenty-seven had benefit protection with paid leave, and twenty-three had some form of job protection explicitly stated in their personnel policies, of which copies were returned along with the questionnaires. In nearly all cases, extended leave was granted at the discretion of the supervisor. In some instances, part of the leave policy is spelled out explicitly in state statutes, civil service rules, or labor-management contracts. In other cases, part of the leave policy (for example, that which promises a comparable job upon return) may be an implicit understanding. Such a provision, in other words, may *not* be a contractually defined entitlement but, rather, a privilege, the expectation of which constitutes a set of norms upheld by both labor and management. On the question of employee retention, most states reported that approximately 90% of leave takers returned to work full time within the year, with 5% returning part-time and 5% not at all. Louisiana reported a low of 70% returning. The average length of time taken ranged from a low of six weeks (Utah) to a high of twenty-six (Vermont and Hawaii). The state of Washington estimated that a six-month leave without pay cost the state $1,002.

New Jersey is the only state in which public-sector workers are covered by a system of temporary disability insurance that also covers workers in the private sector. The most rigorously defined policies concerning public sector employees exist in New York and Illinois. In Illinois, parents have the right to take up to fifty-two weeks of Family Responsibility Leave. For new parents, this leave begins after disability has been exhausted. Yet there is a catch in the provision for job protection. If an employee returns from a leave of absence of six months or less, "the agency shall return the employee to the same or a similar job in the same class in which the employee was incumbent prior to commencement of such leave . . . if leave exceeds six months and there is no vacant position available to him/her in the same class in which the employee was incumbent to such leave or leaves commencing, the employee may be laid off in accordance with the rules." This provision was negotiated by AFSCME with the state.

In New York, it is formally incorporated into the labor-management contract that employees are entitled to (unpaid) infant care leave as an absolute right for parents of either gender—seven months on a mandatory basis and two years on a discretionary basis. The weaknesses of the policy as defined by the respondent related to the fact that pay for leave depends upon the availability of accrued leave credits, and that sick leave accruals were only available for the period of disability—four weeks prior to and six weeks after birth. Although state day-care centers accept children as young as two months, their supply fulfills only a fraction of the demand for their services.

Particularly liberal policies, from the point of view of parents, seem to be correlated with a high degree of unionization in the public-sector work force. Such states include New York, Vermont, Illinois, and Montana. The exception to this pattern was Maryland, where a liberal policy, and concern on the part of the state for the issues involved in its implementation, exists in the absence of unions. A liberal Democratic governor and/or a well-organized women's movement may account for Maryland's progressive policy. Nationally, it appears that maternity leaves are included in approximately 36% of all (public and private sector) collective bargaining arrangements. Although unionization does

Table 11.1. Results of the 1985 Survey of Parental Leave Policies for State Employees

| State | Type of Leave Package | | | Job Guarantee for Some or All Leave Period (B, C) | Benefits Continued for Some or All Leave Period (B, C) |
	A Paid Sick/ Annual Leave	B Paid Pregnancy/ Maternity Disability Leave	C Leave without Pay for Parenting		
Arizona	x		Mother only	no	yes
Arkansas	x		Mother only	no	no
California	x	x	Either parent	yes	yes
Colorado	x		Either parent	yes	yes
Delaware		x		yes	yes
Florida	x	x	Either parent	yes	yes
Hawaii		x		yes	yes
Illinois		x	Either parent	yes	yes
Indiana	x	x	Mother only	yes	yes
Iowa	x			yes	yes
Kansas	x		Mother only	no	yes
Kentucky	x		Mother only	yes	yes
Louisiana	x		Mother only	yes	yes
Maine	x		Either parent	yes	yes
Maryland	x	x	Either parent	yes	yes

State					
Massachusetts	x	x	Either parent	yes	yes
Minnesota		x	Either parent	yes	yes
Missouri	x		Mother only	no	yes
Montana	x		Mother only	yes	yes
Nevada	x		Mother only	yes	yes
New Hampshire	x		Mother only	yes	yes
New Mexico	x		Either parent	yes	yes
New York	x	x	Either parent	yes	yes
N. Carolina	x		Either parent	yes	yes
N. Dakota	x		Mother only	no	yes
Ohio	x		Mother only	yes	yes
Oregon	x		Either parent	yes	yes
S. Carolina	x		Mother only	no	yes
S. Dakota	x		Mother only	yes	yes
Utah	x		Mother only	yes	yes
Vermont	x	x	Either parent	yes	yes
Virginia	x		Mother only	yes	yes
Washington	x		Either parent	yes	yes
W. Virginia	x		Mother only	yes	yes
Wisconsin	x	x	Mother only	yes	yes
Wyoming	x	x	Mother only	no	yes

Note: Only states that responded to the survey are included in this table.

have a significant impact on many types of fringe benefits, the impact of unionization on maternity leave benefits has been slight. Unionization only increases chances that a worker will receive maternity leave with full reemployment rights by 8%, whereas unionization seems to decrease the probability that a worker will receive maternity leave with pay by 3%. Unions have increased the probability that day care will be offered by 8%. At the same time, different interpretations exist regarding the influence of unions, among them the idea that the threat of unionization has influenced nonunion employers to implement certain policies (Freeman and Medoff 1984).

From the perspective of employers, leave policies may act as incentives to promote employee retention, thereby maximizing continuity and minimizing costs by avoiding the necessity of training new employees. The question then becomes whence did the policies come? In some instances, they were designed to build a bulwark against various kinds of putative lawsuits. In the case of Vermont, the respondent wrote that "the State has deliberately stayed away from presumptive period of disability determinations in maternity cases ... It is some times difficult to ascertain the point in time when paid sick leave (disability) should cease and unpaid (childrearing) leave should start." By contrast, the respondent for North Dakota said that "by considering pregnancy like any other disability, and by using sick leave, I believe we have avoided legal action against the state ... using sick leave for maternity and considering it a disability complies with Federal regulations concerning pregnancy." The respondent stated that the main weakness of the policy is that annual leave must be taken. In its personnel policies, at least one state, Wyoming, officially declared its suspicion that new parents might abuse leave policies: "Agency heads shall ensure that such employees do not take parental leave for reasons not reasonably and approximately associated with or necessitated by, the birth of the child."

Another perception by employers that affects the creation of an infant care leave is that employees already have available to them large blocks of leave time. Not only may this perception be incorrect, but it also requires that an employee use leave meant for individual needs (sick, personal, and annual days) to fulfill a need—parenting—for which this leave was *not* designed. Married parents with more than one child or a married parent whose spouse works a different schedule (for example, at night) may need more time. Depending on the job level, lower income parents may suffer substantially from income loss. Furthermore, the general trend is that while benefits, and the shared cost thereof, continue during paid leave status, benefits are continued only at the employee's expense during any kind of leave without pay. However, no breakdown of data by job level exists. As little statistical evidence is available, the leave-takers who are dissatisfied with the current policy—or who are forced to take second jobs to compensate for income loss—may get "lost", as they are unaccounted for.

THE ARMED SERVICES

In the aggregate, the military does have a specific program for maternity leave, in contrast to its civilian counterpart, where pregnancy is treated like any other disability. Prior to 1976, when the military's policy was implemented, pregnant women were required to request a waiver to remain on active duty. Typically, they were discharged. Now, women in the services are eligible for some prenatal leave and convalescent leave following the birth of the child; both of these are at the determination of a physician.

The Army

Since service members are considered to be on duty twenty-four hours a day and ready for worldwide assignment, if the attending physician determines that complications preclude any type of duty responsibility, the member is assigned a duty status of *sick-in-quarters*. This is the status any service member would hold if he or she were unable to perform twenty-four hours a day. The soldier remains in this status until admitted to the hospital due to complications, or the onset of labor, or until her medical condition permits her to return to duty.

It is important to remember that pregnant women are ineligible for enlistment, but may be commissioned if they happen to become pregnant after entry. The United States Military Academy has policies similar to the rest of the Army. Pregnancy is treated like any other temporarily disabling condition. If a cadet becomes pregnant and discloses her condition prior to becoming disqualified to perform her duties as a cadet she may opt to take leave, resign, or stay. If the pregnancy is confirmed at the point at which she becomes disqualified to perform her duties as a cadet (normally at the end of the first trimester of pregnancy), determination is made by the superintendent whether the cadet should be placed on leave with pay, leave without pay, discharged, or retained for a brief time to complete a semester. The cadet may be readmitted following pregnancy if she does not have legal custody of a child and meets all other entry requirements.

Apart from sick-in-quarters status, leave time is authorized for pregnant soldiers. Commanders are authorized to grant ordinary, advance, and excess leave to members who desire to take leave to return home, or to another appropriate place, for the birth of the child or to receive other maternity care. The woman's rank can often affect the ease with which her condition is accommodated, because pregnant soldiers in grades E–7 and above are authorized to reside off post, while soldiers in grades E–6 and below *may* be authorized to move off post and receive housing allowances, but only on a case-by-case basis.

The Navy

The Navy has the most extensive set of practices and policies related to pregnancy. There are approximately 2,600 active-duty Navy women who give birth at medical treatment facilities each year. Pregnant service-women must be retained unless they request separation on the basis of pregnancy or childbirth. Few requests are disapproved; approximately 1,100 annual discharges are due to pregnancy. Pregnant women on overseas assignment may not be transferred during the advanced stages of pregnancy (seven to ninth month), or to areas where there are not adequate medical or housing facilities (either military or civilian). Ship-board assignment restrictions currently require servicewomen to be transferred to shore duty upon confirmation of pregnancy. Current Navy policy includes the following points. Light duty is usually pre-scribed at around the thirty-eighth week of pregnancy. Convalescent leave is limited to a maximum of thirty days following uncomplicated vaginal delivery or uncomplicated Cesarean section. Duty restrictions are permitted in the case of medical indication, questionable harmful effects of technology, or the physical configuration of the job. Women who are *nuclear qualified* are immediately removed from the Nuclear Power Program. The reason given for this is that prototype- and ra-diological-controls-facility personnel must be able to perform strenuous tasks, including responding to drills and being prepared to handle casualties.

In spite of the fact that most requests for separation due to pregnancy are granted, those requests that are made in order to care for an infant may be disapproved for the following reasons: obligated service exists as a result of initial and advanced skill training which requires obligation beyond initial enlistment contract; obligated service exists due to full or partially funded education; if, while pregnant, the person has executed orders or entered a program requiring obligated service; or, if the in-dividual is in a rating with a significant personnel shortage. The last criterion implies that a person whose position is highly valued because of scarcity of replacement personnel is less likely to obtain separation than a person who is easily replaceable. Reserve officers on active duty who have not completed their total military service obligation, or who desire to retain their commission on inactive duty must request release from active duty (RAD).

The Marine Corps

The Marine Corps requires that an enlisted Marine who is pregnant and who intends to remain on active duty will notify her commanding officer in writing within forty-five days of the medical certification of her pregnancy. This notification must include a statement of arrangements that have been made for the care of the child—but only for women who will be single parents and/or who have not completed their first enlistment. The Marine must state that she understands that she may request separation and still remain eligible for maternity care until the birth of the child. As negative incentives to continued service, she is warned that she is available for worldwide assignment, and that there is no guarantee of special consideration in duty assignments or duty stations based solely on her pregnancy or the fact that she will have a dependent, and that there are limitations as to eligibility for dependent housing and shipment of household goods. These warnings apply only to corporals and below with two years of service or less.

A related issue would be the makeup of military personnel by race: the percentage of minority women in lower positions as opposed to higher positions. We know that 73% of all women who work for the federal government are in the lowest paid classifications grades (1–8); we can assume that women in the armed services are similarly situated. Thus, a legal analysis of such a rule could find it resulting in de facto discrimination by race.

The Marine Corps has a specific transfer policy: that pregnant Marines will not be ordered to an overseas tour; that pregnant Marines stationed in the continental United States and Hawaii will not be detached after their sixth month of pregnancy; and that if serving overseas in a dependents-restricted tour, pregnant Marines may be detached at their normal Rotation Tour Date (RTD) when that date occurs after the sixth month of pregnancy, provided that medical certification authorizing travel can be obtained. Pregnant Marines will not be deployed in contingency operations.

The Air Force

The Air Force requires, for the "management of pregnant active duty members," a cooperative effort among the patient, attending practitioners, line supervisors, and profile officers. This service specifically mentions that it is important for service members whose jobs involve potential exposure to chemical or physical agents which may be harmful to the developing fetus to confirm pregnancy at the earliest possible time. This potential exposure, however, does not warrant exclusion of pregnant women, as duty restriction determination is based on *objective medical reasons* related to the work environment. Flight crew members are temporarily removed from flying status once pregnancy is confirmed. Pregnant members are not normally reassigned to another duty location unless they are in an isolated or remote area without the availability of adequate obstetrical care. If prenatal complications arise, women may be placed in excused-from-duty status. The attending physician may grant up to four weeks of convalescent leave. Postpartum women must comply with physical fitness and weight control regulations by three months following delivery, whether or not they are breastfeeding their infants.

The Coast Guard

The Coast Guard actually acknowledges that the purpose of service policies regarding pregnancy may be for infant care leave. "In order to afford the female member who gives birth to a child the opportunity to make suitable childcare arrangements while continuing to fulfill professional responsibilities" is a provision of the preface to their maternity policy. Pregnant women assigned to shore duty in the continental United States who are otherwise eligible for shipboard or overseas assignment will be deferred from such assignment during pregnancy. The deferral continues for six months following childbirth. Pregnant women will not be required or permitted to perform physical duties that could threaten the pregnancy or cause them to be located beyond the availability of medical attention. Such duties could include aircraft and boat crews or vessel inspection teams. Women who become pregnant while assigned to shipboard duty will be reassigned by permanent change of station (PCS) to duty ashore. When a member who is pregnant elects (after an early discharge) to re-enlist, the following documentation is required: (1) a statement from the member recognizing that the rearing of a child is a personal resonsibility that cannot interfere with the performance of her duties and affirming her eligibility for worldwide assignment; (2) evidence of an established childcare plan that demonstrates the care of the child will not interfere with the member's performance of duty; (3) data on the member's performance. Area and district commanders and commanding officers may, upon recommendation of a physician, place a pregnant member in a limited duty area. District commanders and commanding officers may grant a cumulative total of thirty days sick leave for prenatal and postnatal periods. Only a commandant may approve requests for sick leave beyond thirty days. Last, the wearing of the U.S. Air Force maternity uniform, information about which can be found in Coast Guard Uniform Regulations, is required when pregnancy becomes apparent.

The Pentagon

For the more than one million civilian (nonuniformed) employees of the Department of Defense, no official infant care policy exists, although the Pentagon's Civilian Personnel Office does have guidelines for installation commanders on how to administer sick or annual leave, as well as leave without pay in relation to pregnancy. Benefits are continued for up to twelve months of total leave (paid plus unpaid). Both sexes enjoy job protection, can expect the same job upon return, and have uninterrupted promotional status. The average number of weeks taken for a leave is 10.5. The leave is financed as a fringe benefit, and the cost is split evenly between the employee and the government. Approximately half of the employees covered by this policy are represented by unions. The respondent to our survey noted that the strength of existing options for infant care leave is that it is fair, equitable, and tailored to individual and family needs. The weakness of these options is that the guidance for their use in not sufficiently articulated at the grassroots level.

PUBLIC AND PRIVATE SECTORS: A COMPARISON

Private-sector and federal workers seem to have almost equivalent leave privileges. Although federal workers may have greater access to some types of leave, the amount of time that can be taken is limited. Private-sector workers seem to have more generous benefits, and they do not have to use annual leave as often. Protection of seniority and pensions during maternity leave is nearly comparable, although before passage of the Retirement Pension Equity Act in 1984 (Pub. L. 98–397) federal workers on extended maternity leave or prenatal leave often lost pension benefits due to a *break-in-service* (CRS, 1985). Federal workers also enjoy protected seniority and pension protection up to the first six months of leave without pay.

Survey data are lacking on the perceptions of civilian public servants or military personnel about the adequacy or the equity of the implementation of existing policy, although there are case studies and personal testimony on this issue. For some, the time spent with the newborn or newly-adopted infant may be more important; for others, the income, benefits, and job protection may be more crucial. In either case, it is clear that the unmet need for infant care leave is a concern for many families in which at least one parent works in the public sector.

Conclusions

Perceptions on the part of respondents, who represent government-as-employer, of the importance of infant care leave for their staff ranged from "we are proud of our policies to accommodate working parents in our state" and "we have recently surveyed our state employees to see what their perceptions are on this very issue" to "this is an issue whose consequences are overestimated." The net financial cost did not seem to be an issue, as costs of leaves were simply absorbed into existing leave packages. Some respondents mentioned the problem of replacing the leave-taker temporarily; but most indicated that work was accomplished in the absence of the employee. And, while a private firm's accountability is to its stockholders and customers, the public sector's responsibility is to provide efficient, effective government to its citizens—some of whom are also, of course, its employees. The importance of the public sector taking the leading role on this issue cannot, therefore, be under-estimated.

REFERENCES

Congressional Research Service. 1985. *Maternity and Parental Leave Policies: A Comparative Analysis.* Congressional Research Service Report No. 85–148GOV. Washington, D.C.: The Library of Congress.

Freeman, R. B., and Medoff, J. L. 1984. *What Do Unions Do?* New York: Basic Books.

Kamerman, S. B., Kahn, A. J., and Kingston, P. 1983. *Maternity Policies and Working Women.* New York: Columbia University Press.

U. S. Office of Personnel Management. 1976. *Federal Personnel Manual: Absence for Maternity Reasons.* FPM Supplement 976 972. Washington, D.C.: Government Printing Office.

TWELVE

Parental Leave Policies
of Large Firms

RANDY SHEINBERG

WHY LOOK AT THE LEAVE POLICIES OF LARGE CORPORATIONS?

The first question that anybody examining the infant-care-leave policies of large corporations might ask is, "Aren't the policies of the giant companies idiosyncratic enough to have no bearing on the average American workers experience?" The answer is yes—and no. It is generally true that large companies have more resources and are therefore more generous in providing employee benefits. A Columbia University study on parental leave indicates that this trend is as true for job-protected maternity leaves as it is for other benefits. This means that any researcher assuming that what holds true for large companies also holds true for the working population as a whole would arrive at an inaccurate view of the benefits picture. Provided that this trap is avoided, however, looking at the leave policies of large corporations can illuminate current business trends and possibly point the way to changes in both corporate and social responsibility toward parenting. Because of their unique characteristics, parental leave policies in large corporations have larger implications for the country as a whole.

One unique feature of corporate parental leave policies is their universal applicability. Leave policies, like other corporate policies, are structured and formal. They are often available in writing to employees, and they may be part of the hiring contract. By creating such a publicized policy, a company commits itself to a standard for all its employees, executive or blue collar, across all departments and divisions (Kamerman et al. 1983). This situation may not exist in smaller firms that lack a formal policy, or in government agencies, where leaves are frequently granted at the discretion of the supervisor.

211

Large companies are also trendsetters and are often looking for ways to gain a competitive edge over others in their industry. Some are beginning to realize that a well-formulated parental policy may be a competitive tool. Whether the policy is offered out of a sense of responsibility, or out of job enhancement, or both, an employee-oriented policy serves as a model for the industry as a whole in attracting highly qualified personnel (Kamerman et al. 1983; Catalyst 1986b). Where one well-known company is seen offering an extended childcare leave, or providing some form of childcare assistance, others are likely to follow close behind.

Although only a minority of America's work force is employed by large corporations (14%, according to Catalyst 1986a), the policies of large corporations can and have precipitated change across industries and in national policy. Looking at this fraction of the industrial picture can provide insights into what some working parents have available to them today, and what others could have in the future. The fact that some businesses have already implemented such parental leave policies, without a government mandate, suggests the feasibility of such policies on a wider scale.

Indeed, the problems that businesses face in implementing a parental leave policy are the problems that the entire country faces. Key among these is the issue of pay. The trend everywhere is to give parents more time off than ever before—but not to pay them during that time. Without some form of reimbursement, many parents are unable to take advantage of the leaves they are offered. Although granting an unpaid leave demonstrates some commitment to an employee's family needs and responsibilities, it requires that individual to carry the financial burden of those responsibilities alone.

RESEARCH TO DATE ON CORPORATE INFANT CARE LEAVES

With close to 50% of the work force comprised of women, most of whom are of childbearing age, parental leave is a timely issue. Recently there has been a flurry of interest in the media about what kinds of leaves companies are offering to their employees. Widely-distributed magazines such as *Vogue, Fortune, Money,* and *U.S. News and World Report* have all included articles on working parents within the last few years. The academic community is beginning to explore the issue as well. The two most comprehensive studies of private-sector infant care leave to date are the Columbia University study of 1982, "Maternity Policies and Working Women," and the Catalyst study of 1984, which resulted in two publications, "A Report on a National Study of Parental Leaves," and "The Corporate Guide to Parental Leaves."

The Catalyst study was conducted as a follow-up to a preliminary study conducted in 1981. The 1984 study focused exclusively upon the nation's top fifteen-hundred companies by level of annual sales. Three-hundred-eighty-four companies responded to a written survey questionnaire, for a total participation rate of 26%. In addition, Catalyst conducted interviews with employees who had recently taken infant care leaves and with personnel executives. Annual sales of the sample companies ranged from $500 million or less to more than $2 billion (Catalyst 1986b). Unlike the Catalyst study, the Columbia study presented a broader view of the private sector. Two-hundred-fifty companies of varying sizes and wealth, but with a minimum net worth of $500 thousand, responded to this written survey. Companies ranged in size from 500 to 80,000 employees, of whom between one-third and two-thirds were women (Kamerman, et al. 1983).

Because both the Columbia and the Catalyst studies are based on relatively small sample sizes, their results cannot be considered conclusive for the populations they represent; however trends in these two studies are supported in part by the findings of other smaller scale studies. The Bureau of National Affairs included parental leaves in its survey of general leave policies in 1983 (Catalyst 1986b); the Conference Board conducted a study of corporate policies relating to maternity in 1978 (Kamerman, et al. 1983); and the 1977 Quality of Employment Survey included a discussion of maternity leave among its study of the availability of benefits (Kamerman, et al. 1983). Taken together, these studies yield considerable data about corporate leave policies.

LEAVE POLICIES: THE FACTS

Leave policies can be judged on three primary criteria: how long a leave they offer; what kind of compensation, in the form of salary replacement or benefits payments, an employee receives while on leave; and what kind of impact a leave has on an employee's work once she or he does return to the job.

Eligibility Requirements

Although most companies do offer an infant care leave to their employees, some require that the prospective leave-taker be employed by the company for a minimum length of time before she or he is eligible to take it. The Columbia study found that most employees of medium and large companies need at least six-months service in order to receive sickness or vacation benefits, and that 84% have some minimum service requirement to qualify for a maternity leave (Kamerman, et al. 1983). The Catalyst study, which focused exclusively on large companies, cited a significantly lower percentage. Fully 50% of all Catalyst respondents had no service requirements whatsoever for a leave, and another 20% had a service requirement of only three months (Catalyst 1986b). These figures suggest that larger companies are willing to grant their parent employees the benefit of the doubt that their commitment to the company is a long-term one, and thus larger companies have less stringent eligibility requirements.

The Leave Itself

An infant care leave consists of two major components: disability and unpaid leave of absence. The disability portion of the leave applies only to pregnancy, while the unpaid leave may be used for child care beyond the physical disability period. Although an unpaid childcare leave may often be used by new mothers and fathers alike, women are the ones who most often take parental leaves in companies today.

Unlike those in small businesses and public sector organizations, women in large companies do not need to assert their right to take a parental leave. In the vast majority of large corporations once an employee meets the length of service requirements her eligibility for maternity leave is assumed. As the Conference Board study indicated, women are no longer told when they must stop working or when in their pregnancy a maternity leave must begin (Kamerman, et al. 1983). By and large, a career-minded executive will not tarnish her professional reputation if she chooses to have a child and to take a leave from work to do so.

Although an employee's right to take a parental leave is not usually questioned, the length of leave allowed varies from company to company. For example, the Columbia study contrasted the case of a large utility company that guaranteed its employees a job if they return to work within six months of the date that their leave began with that of a company that offered no leave whatsoever beyond the physical disability period. Statistics from various studies on the length of leave offered tell somewhat different stories on this count. The Columbia study found that a two- to three-month leave, offered by 61% of respondents, was most common (Kamerman, et al.). In the Conference Board study, slightly less than half of respondents had a maximum leave of between four and six months (Kamerman, et al.). And the Catalyst study indicated that the average unpaid leave offered to women is generally three months or less (Catalyst, 1986b).

Whichever study is consulted, the typical leave offered ranges from a minimum disability period of a few weeks to an extended leave of several months or even a year. This finding holds true for large and small companies alike. Even in the public sector, leaves depend on various factors and range from a few weeks to a full year. Although large businesses may be more able to afford longer leaves in order to retain a valued employee, they are not necessarily more likely to grant them.

Reimbursement During Leave

During an extended leave, the employee often receives payment for only a portion of the time she is away. In nearly all cases, paid leave for parents is confined to a disability leave. In general, disability policies provide some form of salary reimbursement during the period that an employee is deemed physically unable to continue working (Catalyst 1986a). The Pregnancy Discrimination Act of 1978 stipulated that if a company has a disability policy, pregnancy must be included among the disabilities which that policy covers. Women working in such companies are entitled to some form of salary reimbursement for the time they are physically unable to work—generally up to two weeks prior to birth and six weeks following birth for a normal pregnancy, and up to eight weeks or more following delivery for a cesarean birth. If the job demands excessive strenuous activity, these lengths may be extended. Fully 95% of the respondents to the Catalyst survey have disability policies (Catalyst 1986b).

While a disability leave is customary in the nation's largest corporations, it is not as widespread in the population of smaller companies. The Columbia study found that 47% of its respondents with more than 500 employees had some form of paid maternity leave, but only 37% of those with between 50 and 500 employees, and 10% of those with fewer than 10 employees, had such a policy (Kamerman, et al. 1983).

In spite of their acknowledgment of a need for some form of extended leave, large companies often fall short of fully recognizing parenting needs. Paid leave is clearly one of the distinguishing marks of a large company's policy, but paid leave does not necessarily mean fully paid. Only 39% of large companies in the Catalyst study fully reimbursed disabled employees during their absence; the remaining 57% paid only a portion of their salary during this time.

Parental leaves are generally not fully paid primarily because of their funding mechanism. In virtually all cases, the money provided for these leaves does not come from a parental leave fund, but instead is provided by a disability or sick leave policy. These funding mechanisms for parental leaves limit the amount of money available, the duration of time it can be paid, and the employees who are eligible to take it. While corporations perhaps should not be solely responsible for financing the time that parents need away from the work place, some balance must be found between corporate and parenting needs. Requiring both employers and employees to contribute to the cost of infant care leaves, in whatever proportion, may alleviate heavy financial burdens for the family at the same time that it would encourage responsible parenting.

Another caveat in instituting a fully-paid, mandated parenting leave is that it may exacerbate current discrepancies in employment opportunities for men and women. Even in cases where both men and women are entitled to a parental leave, women are overwhelmingly the ones who take it (Catalyst 1986b). Knowing that this is true, and that they are required to offer paid parenting leaves to all employees, potential employers may be discouraged from hiring women. Such potentially adverse effects should be fully investigated before a fully-paid parental leave becomes nationally mandated.

Other Benefits

In addition to salary reimbursement, a company can also provide financial support to an employee on infant care leave through the continuation of medical benefits. A typical health insurance policy covers hospitalization and physical-care costs for both mother and infant before, during, and after the birth (Kamerman et al. 1983). With the current high costs of having a baby (the Columbia study cites a 1983 estimate of the cost at between $2300 and $3500), to say nothing of the expense of health care, benefits coverage is a significant factor in an employee's financial picture (Kamerman et al. 1983). Over 90% of Catalyst's respondents continue an employee's full benefits coverage during her disability leave (Catalyst 1986b). Beyond the disability period, the story changes dramatically. In just over half the companies, an employee's benefits continue unchanged if she chooses to take an unpaid leave beyond disability for childcare purposes. But one-third of companies require the employee to pay the full amount of the premium in order to continue coverage, and in 6% of the cases, coverage stops altogether (Catalyst 1986b).

UNPAID LEAVES

In addition to the paid disability portion of a leave, many large companies offer an unpaid leave to new parents. These leaves are a way that companies can extend the amount of job-protected time a new parent may spend away from the office, with little or no cost to the company. Although an unpaid leave can be a viable option for a two-salary family, it is often problematic for a single parent or a single-salary household (Catalyst 1986a). Nonetheless, many companies and many working parents rely heavily upon unpaid leaves.

Although some companies refer to these unpaid infant care leaves in written policy, as childcare leaves or parenting leaves, others view this time off as a form of personal leave, or as a leave of absence. Thus the provision of the leave may not represent an acknowledgement of the special needs of working parents, and it may instead be simply an extension of the policies offered to all employees. Indeed, the equity of offering different policies to parent employees than to non-parents is still an open question for many employers (Catalyst, 1986a).

According to Catalyst, 52% of large companies offer unpaid leave to women for parenting purposes. Reinstatement from an unpaid leave comes with a guaranteed return to a comparable job in half the cases and to the same job in 40% of the cases. The longer that an employee is away, the harder it becomes for a company to hold her job open for her. Thus a company will often do anything it possibly can to keep a woman from extending her leave. Indeed, offering a guaranteed return to the same job with a limited-length absence, as opposed to a comparable job guarantee for an extended absence, is one incentive companies use to encourage shorter leaves.

It should be noted that the policies discussed thus far refer only to leaves taken by new natural mothers. This is by no means an all-inclusive group of working parents. It is, however, the group for which most leave policies are written. Large companies, like smaller organizations and like the law, still do not acknowledge fathers and adopting parents as equally deserving of infant-care-leave rights.

FATHERS

The attention that paternity leave has received in the press recently demonstrates the country's increasing interest in the role that men play in child rearing. But what the few men interviewed in the press say they want for a paternity leave and what they actually get are often two different things.

According to the Catalyst study, 37% of large companies offer an unpaid parenting leave with a job guarantee to men. This leave ranges in length from one to six months and is roughly comparable to that offered to women in the same companies, if the disability period is excluded (Catalyst 1986b). What is formally available in company policy, however, is rarely the same as what is actually used. In spite of the large number of companies that report a paternity leave as part of their formal policy, only a handful cite cases of fathers actually taking leaves under the policy. Catalyst suggests a variety of reasons for this phenomenon. Paternity leave is rarely described as a separate part of leave policy; instead it is usually found within a personal-leave or leave-of-absence section of the employee handbook. A father-to-be must sometimes play detective to find his company's policy and to ascertain that he is eligible to use it. By not listing paternity leave as a separate policy option, a company often gives an implicit message that such leaves are not actually sanctioned. When asked how long a leave was considered acceptable for a father to take, 41% of Catalyst respondents said no time at all, and another 23% said two weeks or less (Catalyst 1986b). Even though companies have paternity leave policies on the books, they do not necessarily provide the climate to encourage their use. More often, men choose to take only a few days or a week off from work at the time of their child's birth. They can do this informally, or by using some of their vacation days (Catalyst 1986b). This practice saves them from publicizing their reason for taking the time off, if they perceive the workplace culture as unfriendly toward paternity leaves. Unfortunately, it also obscures men's interest in taking paternity leaves, and it does little to challenge and thereby change the corporate norms.

ADOPTIVE PARENTS

Even companies with fairly comprehensive parental leave policies too often ignore their parent-employees who adopt children. Adoption benefits are on the rise, but they are still available in only a limited number of larger companies. The Columbia study cites a 1980 report in which fourteen companies were found to provide adoption benefits (Kamerman et al. 1983). The Catalyst study shows a significant increase in that number, up from 10.3% in 1980 to 27.5% by 1984 (Catalyst 1986b). Although this change is dramatic, it belies some crucial missing pieces in adoption policy. Of those companies granting adoption benefits, only a little more than half (64%), or 17.5% of the total number of respondents, do so as part of formal written policy. In the 10.5% of cases where benefits are offered informally, employees may well be expected to initiate discussion about and pursue such benefits on their own (Catalyst 1986b). And even when they are provided, adoption benefits rarely, if ever, provide the same coverage as natural parents receive.

Adoption policies come in two forms. The most common type is an unpaid leave, made available to new parents as part of a general, unpaid leave policy. In this case, adoptive parents receive absolutely no remuneration during their absence from work. Less often, companies reimburse adoptive parents for all or some fraction of their adoption expenses. A reimbursement policy usually provides a ceiling of up to $1,000, or covers only the medical expenses incurred with the adoption (Catalyst 1986b). Unlike a biological mother, who receives wage replacement for the first six weeks of her leave under a disability policy, an adoptive parent receives no salary during his or her leave. The expenses covered by an adoption reimbursement plan are analogous to those covered by a biological mother's health insurance, nothing more.

OTHER SUPPORTS FOR WORKING PARENTS

The length and type of leave made available to parents is only one piece of the picture of a corporation's support for infant care. As important to many new parents as how much time they can get off from work is how adaptable the workplace is to their new needs once they return to work, and how helpful the company is in facilitating that return. Large companies assist their employees in this regard through a variety of policies (Catalyst 1986b).

Limited Part-Time Returns

Time, a crucial and scarce commodity to a working parent, is one gift that several companies have found to be valuable in allowing parents to remain effective workers. A popular option among leave-takers is a limited part-time work schedule. Such a schedule smooths the transition from home back to work, and it enables the employee to gain confidence in her support systems before returning to work full time (Catalyst 1986a).

Fully 60% of large companies make a limited part-time return option available to some employees, both in management and nonmanagement positions (Catalyst 1986a). Most of the time, a part-time return is arranged on an individual-by-individual basis. Because of the informal nature of part-time arrangements, not all employees who want such schedules are able to get them. It requires initiative, persistence, and a favorable work climate in order to work out an arrangement. Although both levels of employees can be eligible for part-time return, the terms of their arrangements differ. A manager can frequently rearrange her job responsibilities so that she can do approximately the same work in fewer hours. By agreeing to be in contact with the office during her time off, or by delegating a small part of her work to others in the department, a manager can often retain her job and not lose any career ground during a part-time schedule. Most likely, she receives a prorated salary, and she continues to receive her same benefits, or a portion of them. The biggest danger with a manager's part-time schedule is that because she is indispensible to the office, she ends up working so many hours beyond the part-time schedule that it becomes virtually indistinguishable from a full-time job (Catalyst 1986a).

Nonmanagers, on the other hand, are usually able to keep their part-time status once it has been arranged. But they are much more likely to be placed in a different job once they return part-time, and this change can affect their careers (Catalyst 1986a). Many companies will circulate part-time, clerical staff through an in-house temporary pool or other temporary arrangement (Catalyst 1986a). Thus a returning nonmanagerial employee is much more likely to be placed in a new job, perhaps one she is less happy with, and she may also lose out on benefits or be forced to take a salary cut.

Most companies offer part-time schedules on an informal basis, but some forward-thinking companies provide part-time returns as part of their formal policy. For Home Box Office, Inc., for example, providing a part-time option encourages employees to return to work earlier than they might otherwise (Catalyst 1986a). This arrangement benefits the company, since it enables them to get valuable workers back more quickly, and it also benefits the parent, who may prefer to trade a given amount of full-time time away from work for an extended part-time period at home. The Kellog Company, Corning Glass Works, and General Foods Corporation all view offering a part-time return option as one way of accommodating the needs of working parents, and thereby assuring their long-term tenure with the company (Catalyst 1986a). The General Foods policy, as quoted in Catalyst's *Corporate Guide to Parental Leaves*, illustrates this attitude;

> If, after completing a maternity or child care leave, you feel that your family situation requires you to consider working a flexible time schedule, part-time, or in a job-sharing arrangement, you're encouraged to explore possibilities with your supervisor. Such arrangements can be made for a year following the birth or adoption of your child. General Foods' policy is to be as accommodating as the demands of the business will allow with the ultimate test being the unit's ability to achieve its business goals (Catalyst 1986a).

Permanent Part-Time

Some parents desire a part-time schedule on a more long-term basis. Such a schedule enables them to participate more fully in child rearing while still maintaining a career. Although part-time professionals have been increasing in numbers recently, this trend is not evident in larger companies. A company may choose to create a part-time managerial position rather than lose a valued employee; however, most companies do not make a practice of hiring part-time professionals. Where part-time managerial positions do exist, they are most often in service and financial industries, such as the Zale Corporation, Ameritrust, and Safeguard Business Systems (Catalyst, 1986a).

Even when they are offered, permanent part-time positions have some serious drawbacks. Part-time employees sacrifice a great deal in terms of their career growth. They are often pushed into less challenging jobs or ones with less visibility and fewer opportunities for promotion. Nearly half of part-time employees in large companies (47%) receive no parental leave benefits, and those who do often receive fewer than their full-time counterparts (Catalyst 1986b). In addition, of the less than 20% of the United States work force that is currently part-time, fully 67% are women (U.S. Dept of Labor 1987). Currently, most organizations consider their part-time positions to be *second-class* ones. If women continue to dominate these positions, and move away from full-time ones, they may well continue to be considered secondary members of the work force. Unless our nation's attitude toward part-time work changes, relying on these positions to solve the parenting crisis will only perpetuate gender discrimination in the workplace.

Childcare Assistance

Whether parents work a part-time or a full-time schedule, they still face the problem of what to do with their children while they are at the office. For these parents, finding reliable, quality child care is not a luxury; it is a necessity to enable them to continue working and maintain their peace of mind (Catalyst 1986a). Deciding upon a type of child care and selecting a particular provider are personal matters, but helping employees find their options and finance them are becoming corporate ones. Although the number of companies actually providing childcare services is relatively small, it appears to be growing (Catalyst 1986b). Rather than provide an on-site or near-site childcare facility, many companies opt for a less costly, less involved means for childcare support. For example, IBM is in the process of developing a network of childcare information and referral services in cities where its offices are located. These services help employees (and the community at large) to locate available child care and determine whether it suits their needs (Catalyst 1983). Thirty percent of Catalyst's survey respondents had some form of childcare information service available to employees (Catalyst 1986b). Still other companies provide a flexible benefits plan or salary reduction plan that includes a childcare option to help defray the employee's childcare costs. Although less than 10% of Catalyst respondents actually had such policies in place, nearly 70% favored them, suggesting that more of these initiatives will be seen in the near future (Catalyst 1986b).

Flexible Work

When a company does not participate in an employee's childcare arrangements, it may focus instead on making the workplace as accommodating to parents as possible. Forty-six percent of large corporations have instituted flexible work hours so that employees can have some freedom in choosing when they will work (Catalyst 1986b). In other cases, employees are allowed to complete some of their work at home, using telecommunications systems or computer networks to keep in contact with the office (Catalyst 1986a).

Concluding Thoughts

Although parental leave policies in the larger companies are quite generous compared with those of other organizations, they are far from optimal. Both from the employee's and the company's perspective, there is more that could be done to foster successful work and family lives. By confining the paid portion of a leave to the length of disability, companies effectively focus their attention solely upon the new mother's physical condition. Such a policy implies that it is only the mother's physical health that is important and not her relationship with the newborn. Six weeks has become the standard length of paid leave because that is what most physicians agree is the time needed for the body to recover from birth. Although much research of late has focused on the optimal amount of time needed for an adequate bond to be formed between parent and child, few corporations consider this aspect of parenting—or translate that consideration into time off, benefits, and pay. Payment based solely on disability also minimizes the role that men can play in child rearing and, arguably, discriminates against adoptive parents. Our country as a whole, and the large companies that are a part of it, have as yet failed to recognize parenting itself as a right worthy of paid leave.

REFERENCES

Catalyst. 1983. *Child Care Information Service: An Option for Employer Support for Child Care*. New York: Catalyst.
Catalyst, 1986a. *The Corporate Guide to Parental Leaves*. New York: Catalyst.
Catalyst. 1986b. *Report on a National Study of Parental Leaves*. New York: Catalyst.
Kamerman, S. B., Kahn, A. J., and Kingston P. 1983. *Maternity Leaves and Working Women*. New York: Columbia University Press.
U.S. Department of Labor, Bureau of Statistics. 1987. *Employment and Earnings January 1987*. Washington, D.C.: Government Printing Office.

THIRTEEN

Parental Leave:
Attitudes and Practices
in Small Businesses

BARBARA BUTLER AND JANIS WASSERMAN

This study of small businesses is an attempt to identify existing attitudes and policies with regard to infant care leave, and to anticipate the problems that a mandated leave policy would create for small businesses. The experience of small businesses is especially vital to the discussion of infant care leave because of the large percentage of the American work force employed by these firms.

In 1983, for example, the Small Business Administration (SBA) estimated that employers of less than five hundred persons provided jobs for the majority (58%) of the work force in this country, whereas firms employing more than one hundred but less than five hundred workers provided jobs for 13.9% of all workers. Almost one-half (44%, or 26.2 million) of all American workers were employed by small businesses of less than 100 employees, and employers of fewer than twenty-five persons provided jobs for 17.9 million workers, a sizeable 30.3% of the work force. Of the almost one-half of the work force employed by small businesses with less than 100 employees, 44% were women. According to the SBA, the 7.9 million women employed by firms with fewer than twenty-five employees make up approximately 30.9% of the total female work force.

According to available statistics, there are more than 14 million small businesses in the U.S., which in 1985 accounted for $1.4 trillion or 40% of the GNP. These firms employ 50% of the civilian work force and have generated almost all of the 10.5 million jobs created since 1980 (*New York Times*, August 23, 1986). During this same period, according to David Birch of the Massachusetts Institute of Technology, the 500 largest industrial corporations have laid off 2.2 million people. "It's clear most of the new jobs are coming from firms of 20 or fewer employees," he says (*Nation's Business*, October 1986). According to the SBA, women today are the fastest growing segment in the labor market: between 1950 and 1985 the number of women in the labor force increased by 178%, while for men the number rose only 47%. When these statistics are combined with the fact that women hold 80% of the new jobs created in the economy since 1980 (*New York Review*, August 1986), it is apparent that a great many women are employed by small businesses.

In 1983, 67.2% of all firms offered employees health coverage, but only 38.7% of business with fewer than twenty-five employees offered employees a health plan. By comparison, 85.4% of companies with over 500 employees provided a health plan. This is a problem, since in its May 1985 publication, *The State of Small Business: Report of the President*, the SBA clearly states that "A small business' ability to attract and maintain a quality work force is directly related to the benefits it offers. An employer's compensation package includes wages and expenses for employee retirement, health, life, disability benefits, and other fringe benefits... Firms offering equal wages but greater benefits are better able to attract more productive workers and, as a consequence, increase their competitiveness in the marketplace."

SMALL BUSINESS REACTION TO INFANT CARE LEAVE LEGISLATION

Because small firms employ such a large proportion of the work force, there is a legitimate concern over the type, character, and scope of benefits that they are obliged to offer their employees. This concern was expressed most recently in 1986, when the White House Conference on Small Business voted to reject government-mandated employee benefits, such as employer-paid health benefits, parental leave, and disability leave. In spite of the fact that approximately one-third (608) of the 1,823 delegates at the conference were women, 1,360 out of 1,715 delegates who cast ballots on the conference recommendations opposed parental and disability leave. A recent article suggested that women who are business owners believe they would be disproportionately hurt by a government-mandated parental leave option because they own small businesses and the majority of their employees are women of childbearing age (*Wall Street Journal*, September 24, 1986). Women now own about 25% of small businesses, up from 5% in 1976, and they are expected to control 50% by the year 2000, according to the SBA.

The growth of self-employed women is increasing at a rate greater than the rate at which women are entering the labor force, indicating that women who are already employed are opting to start their own businesses. In 1985, 2.8 million women were self-employed, a 75% increase since 1975, compared to a 12.1% increase in the number of self-employed men (*New York Times*, August 18, 1986). According to 1982 Census Bureau figures, women own 2.9 million businesses with receipts of $98.3 billion. Of those firms 312,000 had employees numbering 1.4 million and, according to the IRS, nearly 75% are in services and retail trades.

These statistics, however, do not explain why women are entering small businesses in such record numbers, rather than pursuing careers in the more structured and traditionally less flexible corporate world. John Naisbitt and Patricia Aburdene, in *Re-inventing the Corporation*, suggest that the difficulty of coping with two full-time jobs, one inside and one outside the home, has encouraged women entrepreneurs to start businesses sensitive to the needs of other working women. And, an article in the July 1986 issue of *Inc.* magazine ("Why There Aren't More Women In This Magazine . . . Maybe it's because women are creating a business world all their own") suggests that there is powerful evidence that women go into business for different reasons than men. The article quotes Paula Mannillo of the Women's Economic Development Corporation in St. Paul, Minnesota: "Mostly, these women are just trying to support themselves, to bring balance and flexibility to their lives in ways that the corporate world can't. And won't. They are out to redefine work, not to restructure the economy."

EMPLOYER ATTITUDES TOWARD PARENTAL LEAVE

In the course of our study we interviewed thirty small organizations in Connecticut, New York, and New Jersey, in order to provide some information on the attitudes that small business owners have toward leaves and on the real problems that leaves cause in their work force. The companies interviewed included professional firms, private nonprofit agencies, service companies, retail and manufacturing organizations. They ranged in size from five to five-hundred employees.

Some interesting themes emerged from the interviews. First of all, no two firms were alike, confirming our hypothesis that small businesses had many variables and each experience was somewhat unique. Yet, if the small sample we used is any indication, many small businesses function now with policies, both formal and informal, that parallel the legislation so adamantly opposed by delegates to the 1986 White House Conference on Small Business. More important, these organizations are guided by these policies because they believe it is in their best interests to do so. As one partner in a Connecticut law firm told us, "I'm not a benefactor. This is a businessman's decision. Key personnel are hard to get and keep. It would cost me more to replace them with the same caliber employee than it does to replace them temporarily, and if it's a good year, I may be able to pay them something too."

This example indicates a principle that held throughout the sample: if an employee is very good, the employer will put energy into making it possible for the employee to have the needed infant care leave and to return to his/her (guaranteed) job afterward. Barbara Haas, the president of Pension Parameters, spoke on the problems of small employers at a conference on parental leave sponsored by the Association of Junior Leagues in March 1985. She suggested that while companies sometimes have to do what is best for the company, not simply what is best for the employee, many will do practically anything to accommodate and retain a valued employee.

It was interesting to observe that while the policies which existed varied with each individual firm, employers wanted a policy that was fair and equitable, as well as economically sound. There was a very strong sense that conditions had changed more quickly and more extensively than anyone had anticipated, and employers and employees both were unsure about what was reasonable. Employers needed a policy that made good financial as well as moral and organizational sense, and they felt that employees needed to concern themselves with balancing child nurturing with career momentum and ambition.

Another consistent theme had to do with the influence of the founder on the organization's attitude: if the founder placed a high value on family life, then the policy, in some cases informal and handled on a case-by-case basis, tended to be generous. One small production company of about twenty-five employees located in Connecticut is a good example of this. The three-year-old firm has a mostly young unmarried staff, and it has no official *maternity* leave policy because it hasn't yet needed one. Since almost 50% of its staff is composed of females between the ages of fifteen and forty-five, and since in four out of the six "company" weddings in the past year the bride was the employee, the vice president to whom we spoke anticipates that they will write an infant-care-leave policy before long.

This company does, however, have an informal *paternity* leave policy, because the three babies that have been born since the company was founded have been the offspring of male employees, one of whom is the vice president of finance. The paternity leave policy consists of a *mandated* two-week paid leave: "Whatever you may be in the middle of when the baby is born, leave on your desk... someone else will figure it out and we'll see you in two weeks." The company spokesperson acknowledged that the policy places increased demands on staff members who have to take on an additional work load temporarily, but no one seems to object to the principle at stake. The vice president concluded,

"The three fathers involved and their families have been enormously grateful for the opportunity to begin the process of becoming a family with this gift of time."

The explanation for the informal and as yet unchallenged mandate is two-fold. First, theirs is a hectic, deadline business, with great importance placed on client relationships. It would rarely, if ever, seem possible to drop whatever the worker is involved in at any given moment unless it was absolutely necessary. Second, the two (male) partners place high value on "health, family and career," in that order. The paid aspect of the policy is essential to the philosophy of giving the family the opportunity to share two unpressured weeks together. Removing the pressure of time and introducing the stress of reduced income would be self-defeating. This instance was one of the stronger examples of the influence of the founders' values on the organizational culture and norms.

Edgar Schein, in his article "The Role of the Founder in Creating Organizational Culture," identifies the "unique functions" that founder/owners, "by virtue of their position and personality . . . tend to fulfill in the early history of their organizations." The function pertinent to this discussion is that of "embedding non-economic assumptions and values." Schein observes that " . . . founder/owners are in a position to insist on doing things which may not be optimally efficient from a short-run point of view, but which reflect their own values and biases on how to build an effective organization . . . [they] often start with humanistic and social concerns that become reflected in organizational structure and process."

In the example given above, the benefit to the company of an appreciative, loyal, productive employee far outweighs the inconvenience of the two-week absence. Interestingly, the person whom we interviewed commented that for some positions, such as a producer, it would actually be easier if the person were to take a three- to six-month leave, allowing the company to make a short-term contractual arrangement with someone outside the firm. This company also encourages flextime or job-sharing arrangements as a way to give the company a more flexible situation, and to have trained staff available to pick up the extra workload temporarily when another employee is on leave.

Another organization that seems to have addressed these issues in a way that satisfies its concerns is a public health nursing association, also located in Connecticut. This nonprofit agency employs forty-five people, all women at the time of our interview, although they have had male employees in the past and may again. At least 50% of their employees are of childbearing age, and most of them have families. The agency has an unpaid maternity leave policy of up to three months before birth and up to three months after delivery. Although there is no parental leave per se, there is a general leave policy allowing up to one year with job guaranteed, and sick time is available for personal and/or family illness.

It is also interesting to note that in this instance, even with such comparatively generous (in terms of time) leave policies in place, most employees return to work approximately six weeks after the birth of their babies. This decision is probably strongly influenced by the availability of day care on the premises (provided by another agency), and the fact that the leave is unpaid. While on leave an employee is replaced by per diem substitutes who have prior experience with the organization, or by temporarily increasing the caseload of a part-time employee.

The fact is that small businesses choose their people carefully, have little overlap of personnel, and value good workers highly, so highly that they are generally more than willing to negotiate an arrangement that will satisfy a valued employee's need to spend some reasonable amount of time parenting, as well as the employer's need to have that person back as soon as possible. As more than one company said to us, "It would be inconvenient if one of our key people took a three-month leave, but the fact is that they are so good that it would be worse to lose any one of them permanently. . . . so we'd do what we needed to do to make it possible to hang on to them."

One company announced that they had solved the problem by declaring facetiously that "no one's allowed to get pregnant." They acknowledged the tension that they felt between what they personally and organizationally believed was morally right, and what problems (financially, operationally, and with regard to client relationships) they anticipated for their business. This company, a New York consulting firm, was one of the few which actually had a policy in place, allowing for a six-week maternity/disability leave followed by an optional three-month infant care leave, and a paternity leave of one month. The latter two were dependent upon "the individual's situation and the current workload" and would be negotiated individually. It may help put some of small business's fears in perspective to note that in this firm, in which 100% of the work force is of childbearing age, one employee has taken paternity leave in ten years, and no one has taken maternity leave.

It is an awareness of the uniqueness of individual situations that makes small employers so wary of legislation. The difficulty is that right now they fear the full burden of the proposed legislation, rather than seeing it as a response to social change, the burden of which must be shared by all of us. There is a great concern that temporary leaves, which may hold a cost to employers due to replacement salaries, training, work absorption, and the contributions to the leave itself, if it is a paid leave. This concern, while not unfounded, does not seem to be in proportion to the fact that most parents working today will spend thirty to forty years in the work force, and if they have two children during those years, there will only be two six-month periods when a mother and/or father may be away from the job.

There is another issue raised by one of the small business people interviewed, and that is whether a mother should be at home with her baby. It is important not to overlook the fact that traditional values are in some ways challenged by an infant care leave policy, and there are people who do not accept it as supporting the family, but see it instead as undermining the traditional family structure. Whether or not it is realistic to think that women can and should stay home with their babies, that feeling is there and must be addressed. And there is a legitimate concern regarding the current social change and whether or not the needs of our nation's children have been well considered in the midst of the upheaval. Indeed, it is concern about the needs of children and families that prompted the development of an infant-care-leave policy, but there are those who see child care as a family responsibility rather than a social one. As one (self-described) otherwise social and political liberal told us, "You don't have children unless *you* can care and provide for them. It's the parents' responsibility and no one else's."

PROBLEMS SMALL BUSINESSES FACE WITH INFANT CARE LEAVE

The areas of concern raised by most of the small organizations we interviewed fell into three distinct groups: financial, operational, and client relationships. Because the re-entry of large numbers of mothers of infants into the work force is a relatively new phenomenon, many of the problems associated with granting leaves are perceptual, the products of fear rather than experience.

Financial Problems

One of the most pressing problems that small businesses perceive is the cost of such a policy. They are fearful that they will have to carry the double burden of paying for the salary of an employee on leave as well as that of a replacement. As the representative of one small Connecticut advertising agency told us, "Unpaid leave is less of a problem, but paid leave presents real problems for us. A service business depends on production, and if we have to pay an unproductive employee, we lose money."

The problem may not be as insurmountable as these employers anticipate. First, many of the proposed leave policies are unpaid. In this case the only costs to the employer are continuing to contribute toward the employee's benefits and the financial loss from the presumed lower productivity of the replacement labor. The cost of a replacement worker's salary is offset by the probability that an employee not granted a leave might elect to withdraw from the work force, thereby forcing the employer bear the greater cost of recruiting and training a new employee. Second, in the case of paid leaves, all proposals to date call for employer-employee contributions toward an insurance scheme to finance leaves. Thus, employers would not be burdened with the cost of the salary of the employee on leave.

There are also important economic benefits which must be calculated into the equation when considering the cost of granting a leave, especially that associated with keeping a trained, competent employee. As one firm stated, "There's no dead weight here, and all our employees are carefully chosen. It takes us two to six months to train our staff. We can't afford the disruption, time, and expense involved in recruiting and training new people."

Operational Problems

Another important concern of small businesses in particular is the difficulty of shifting work from one worker to another. Often in small firms each employee is responsible for a discrete set of tasks, and they are not familiar with those of the other employees. There were important distinctions made in most of the firms we interviewed regarding different positions in the organization. Some positions are simply easier to replace on a temporary basis than others. Replacing a comptroller for three months poses serious problems, for example, whereas replacing support staff with temporaries is much less disruptive. Knowing the office routine and requirements appeared more critical in some businesses (for example, in a medical group) than in others. And certain industries are able to fill certain positions with freelance help, such as writers, editors, and designers, or through short-term contractual arrangements. One nonprofit agency addresses the problem by making a concerted effort to promote from within whenever possible, thereby indirectly cross-training its employees.

Client Relationships

In all businesses maintaining the relationship with the client is vital to the firm's success, but it seems safe to say that certain positions are more responsible for managing those relationships than others. The lawyer working on a case, the producer in the middle of a film, the account manager in a design firm or advertising agency, are all positions where the problems created by infant care leave are more complex.

A mandated infant-care-leave option would not be impossible for firms such as these to observe, but it would require more anticipation, coordination, and teamwork. In fact, parental leave as well as other types of temporary medical leave, can be anticipated and often planned for within existing company resources. And workers' and business needs can often be accommodated through phasing the worker back into work and flextime arrangements. As several such firms suggested, there may well be ways that employees on leave can manage to maintain that relationship by some minimal involvement from home, without compromising the leave and without losing the client. In any event, the problem is a legitimate concern, and careful consideration must be given to solving it.

Conclusion

In the course of this study the need for a comprehensive national policy has become clearer than ever. It must be one that provides for job sharing with prorated benefits, flexible hours, on-site day care, and other innovative approaches to complement the infant-care-leave option, because not every employee can afford unpaid leave, not everyone will want to exercise the three-month option, and some parents will want to work part-time and share the parenting.

Leave, whether paid or unpaid, is just one part of the solution to the problems faced by organizations and individuals, as we all try to deal with the realities of work and family obligations. Although small businesses may lack the extensive resources of some larger organizations, they may be able to be more flexible, and thus they may be more in a position to experiment with a variety of options as we seek to develop a policy that will meet the needs of the various interest groups involved.

We are dealing with two new phenomena: increasing numbers of women in the work force and the growing proportion of people employed by small businesses. These phenomena present real problems that must be addressed, and there is little evidence that firms in states with legislation mandating disability leave or those in the majority of nations of the world with paid infant-care-leave policies have suffered financially.

A society cannot consider one group's needs above those of all others. Society cannot consider the needs of business to the exclusion of employees and their families, anymore than it can consider the needs of employees and ignore the implications of recommended programs and policies for the employers: The needs of both must be balanced. Small businesses will gain from the increased stability and positive attitude of their work force, as the experience of the firms in this study has illustrated.

REFERENCES

New York Times. August 23, 1986.

Nation's Business. October, 1986.

New York Review. August 14, 1986.

The State of Small Business: Report of the President. Small Business Administration. May, 1985.

Wall Street Journal. September 24, 1986.

New York Times. August 18, 1986.

Naisbitt, John, and Aburdene, Patricia. 1985. *Reinventing the Corporation.* New York: Warner Books.

Wojahn, Ellen. 1986. "Why There Aren't More Women in This Magazine." *Inc.* July, pp. 45–48.

Schein, Edgar. 1983. "The Role of the Founder in Creating Organizational Culture." *Organizational Dynamics* 12(1): 13–28.

PART V

Parental Leave Policies in Other Nations

FOURTEEN

Maternity and
Parenting Benefits:
An International Overview

SHEILA B. KAMERMAN

Maternal and child health, economic security, and the psychological well-being of parents and children are the three major goals that shaped the development of maternity and parenting policies internationally. These goals emerged sequentially and over time in the various countries; by now, however, there is a remarkable degree of convergence on policy throughout the advanced industrialized world. Nonetheless, in spite of high and growing labor-force participation rates for women during the prime childbearing years, and for women throughout pregnancy and soon after childbirth, the United States remains out-of-step with and a laggard among the advanced industrialized countries in the development of maternity and parenting benefits. The U.S. is among the few countries still providing no national cash sickness benefits, no national health insurance benefits, no national maternity or parenting benefits, and no national policy mandating job-protected leaves at the time of childbirth.[1] In this chapter my purpose is to provide an overview of international developments concerning maternity and parenting benefits, in order to offer some perspective on the inadequacy of American policies as compared with those of the other advanced industrialized countries, including those of eastern and western Europe, Canada, Israel, and Australia.

1. Five states mandate temporary disability insurance, which covers the post-childbirth period as well as others short-term disabilities, and congress is considering legislation that would provide a job-protected maternity disability leave and a parenting leave. To date, nevertheless, there are no such national social policies.

THE HISTORY OF MATERNITY AND PARENTING BENEFITS

The history of maternity and parental benefits and leaves is a history of legislation designed primarily to protect the health of pregnant women, new mothers, and their infants.[2] The first paid maternity leave was provided in Germany in 1884, as part of the *invention* of social insurance (social security, in U.S. terms) by Bismark in 1883. Under this system, men and women who could not work because of illness, being injured on the job (workmen's compensation), or pregnancy or childbirth were paid cash benefits. A few years later, old age was added to the list of "social risks" that warranted protection under public policy. By 1940, twenty-four countries provided maternity benefits for working women. By 1960 the number was fifty-nine, and by the end of the 1970s seventy-two countries provided such benefits.

Since the 1960s, with the growth in social policies generally and the increase in female labor-force participation rates in particular, the maternity policy rationale has been broadened from maternal and child health protection to include concern with protecting the economic contribution women make to family income and with making it possible for workers, especially women workers, to meet their family responsibilities without undue stress or penalty. Implicit in the way that policies have developed in recent years is a redefinition of childbearing and childrearing as a contribution to the survival and well-being of society, not merely as a source of personal and individual pleasure.

A third theme, the concern with parenting and providing nurturance and care for the newborn or newly-adopted baby, has emerged still more recently. Consequently, it is only now, in the 1980s, that the focus is on turning maternity into *parenting* benefits, or supplementing existing maternity policies with additional, special parenting benefits.

THE BENEFITS PROVIDED

Three benefits are paramount in any discussion of maternity-related policies:

1. The right of an employed woman to a leave from work for a specified period at the time of pregnancy and childbirth with assurance of job

2. The best general reference to these benefits is U.S. Department of Health and Human Services, Social Security Administration, *Social Security Programs Throughout the World, 1985* (Washington, D.C.: Government Printing Office, 1986). A second excellent resource is International Labour Office, *Conditions of Working Life* published annually in Geneva. Still a third resource is International Labour Office, *Women At Work*, no. 2, 1986, special issue on "Protection of Working Mothers: An ILO Global Survey 1961–1984."

protection as well as protection of seniority, pensions, and other fringe benefits.

2. A cash benefit given the woman at the time of this leave, provided through the social insurance or social security system (or required to be paid by the employer), equal to all or some portion of the insured wage, for a similarly specified period.

3. Health insurance or medical care to cover prenatal care, physician and hospital care, and postnatal care for mother and baby.

In recent years, still a fourth benefit has emerged in many countries, and that is a supplementary unpaid or low-paid job-protected leave, either a maternity or parental leave, in addition to the basic paid leave, for those interested in, and able to take a longer period away from work to spend with their new child.

The guaranteed job-protected leave and the cash benefit to replace wages constitute what is usually described as the *statutory maternity benefit and leave*. In some countries, all or part of this benefit may be shared by fathers. When the sharing is for a small portion of the overall entitlement, the benefit still tends to be called a maternity leave. When fathers and mothers can share equally—that is, when either parent is eligible—the benefit is termed *parental leave*.

Eighty-five countries around the world provide paid sick leaves for workers that include both income protection and health care at the time of pregnancy and maternity as well as any other illness. In addition, at least sixteen countries provide maternity benefits through other policy devices such as unemployment insurance (Canada and Austria), parent insurance (Sweden), a special maternity benefit (Israel), an employment benefit (United Kingdom), a benefit combining health insurance with a mandated employer provision (Federal Republic of Germany), and family allowances (France). Thus, at least 101 countries, by the definition of the International Social Security Association (or 117 countries, if the definition of the International Labour Office is used), provide maternity benefits, whether through the sickness benefit system or other legislative measures.

BENEFIT DURATION

The minimum paid maternity leave ranges from six weeks in England to eight weeks in Singapore and several of the newly industrialized and developing countries, to twelve weeks in Israel and the Netherlands. The basic International Labour Office (ILO) standard is fourteen weeks, six before expected birth and eight after; this is the most prevalent standard around the world. Canada and the other European countries all provide at least sixteen weeks paid leave; the maximum is one year in Sweden. The modal benefit in Europe is six months. No country is currently discussing more than one year for fully paid maternity or parental leaves, although in several countries supplementary leaves, unpaid or paid at a low level, are now being established or discussed. Where these exist they are primarily for mothers, but increasingly they are covering fathers, too.

Most countries permit some portion of the leave to be taken before expected parturition, usually six weeks; but sometimes, as in the United Kingdom and Canada, as much as eleven weeks is permitted. Several countries mandate two to six weeks before expected birth and/or six to eight weeks after. Where prenatal leave is mandated, extensions are provided when the birth occurs later than anticipated. Some countries provide additional leave under special circumstances: for second and subsequent children (Czechoslovakia, the German Democratic Republic), for multiple births (France, in addition to the benefits already mentioned), for third and subsequent children (France), for single mothers (Austria). All countries provide extensions in cases of difficult pregnancies or deliveries. Many countries provide additional job-protected time off, beyond the paid leave, either as part of the basic leave (as, for example, in England where this leave covers forty weeks, with the paid portion limited to six weeks), or as a separate supplementary unpaid leave (as in France, where either parent can take up to two years of unpaid leave at the end of the paid maternity leave). Regardless of what is provided, most countries leave the decision to use the benefit, and of how much to use, to the individual woman (or parent).

BENEFIT LEVEL

In most countries, the benefit level is either 100% of insured wages (the maximum wage covered under social insurance) or 90% (that wage less social insurance contributions). In Canada and Israel, the benefit is equal to only a portion of the insured wage (60% and 75%, respectively). In the Federal Republic of Germany the maximum grant is equal to about 75% of average female wages for fourteen weeks; in addition, employers are mandated to supplement this benefit to equal full replacement of wages (if wages are higher than the grant) for this period, and the government provides a lower level benefit for the remainder of a 10-month parental leave (to be increased to 1 year in 1988).

In several countries employees of certain industries or specific companies may have supplementary coverage (full wage replacement over and above the insured wage, or a longer leave) as a consequence of collective bargaining agreements or voluntarily provided employer benefits. Similarly, several countries provide additional benefits or extended coverage to public employees. The cash benefit is tax free in all countries except Sweden and Canada.

ELIGIBILITY OR QUALIFYING CRITERIA

The basic maternity/parenting benefit is universal; that is, it is available to all women regardless of income, in all countries. In some countries, a supplementary benefit may be provided to low-income women or parents, or to women who are single parents. Except for Sweden, where a small minimum benefit is provided to any woman covered under health insurance (and housewives can be covered), eligibility for these benefits is restricted to women who have been employed for at least some minimum time before childbirth.[3] Many countries now define adoptive mothers as eligible for the benefit as well as natural mothers.

Sweden is the only country that provides this benefit to both parents equally, with fathers having approximately the same entitlement as mothers. All the other Nordic countries (Norway, Denmark, Finland, and Iceland) include fathers for at least some portion of the paid post-childbirth leave. And several European countries, including almost all those in the European Economic Community, are now providing supplementary parental leaves for working parents following childbirth.

COVERAGE

In many countries virtually all employed women who give birth are covered. Although the pattern of growth and development has slowed for this benefit along with all other social benefits, it remains popular everywhere that it exists. Among the industrialized countries, only the United Kingdom appears to be continuing to debate its merit or its use. In contrast, there is pressure in most other countries to extend the duration of the leave, to extend coverage to fathers as well as mothers, to include adoptive as well as natural parents, and to extend the duration of the paid leave for some parents, if not all.

ADMINISTRATION AND FINANCING

Although the specific benefit programs may vary from country to country, cash benefits are always considered one part of the social insurance or social security system. All are financed through social insurance fund-

3. Australia provides a benefit, on an income-tested basis, for twelve weeks prior to childbirth and six weeks after to women regardless of labor-force attachment.

ing (however that is determined), as either a contributory or noncontributory benefit. Where it is contributory, it is usually the employer and the government who bear the burden, although in several countries, including Canada, the employee contributes directly. Health insurance is the system most likely to carry administrative responsibility for maternity benefits. Israel, however, views it as an independent social insurance benefit, Britain handles it as an employment benefit, and Canada and Austria approach it either wholly or partly as an unemployment insurance benefit.

POLICIES OF INDIVIDUAL COUNTRIES

What follows are several brief descriptions of the maternity and parenting policies in selected countries.

Sweden

For the first twelve months following childbirth, working parents have a right to a paid, job-protected leave from work. The *Parent Insurance Benefit*, is a cash benefit that replaces 90% of the wage of the parent who is on leave, up to the maximum wage covered under social security, for nine months. A fixed minimum benefit is available for the remaining three months. (A nonworking mother would be entitled to a minimum cash benefit during the year also, but there are very few such women.) Parent Insurance can be used to cover a complete leave, or can be prorated to permit part-time work by either parent, for full pay, until the nine months of pay is used up. Thus a working mother might take off a full three months; she and her husband might then each work half-time for six months, sharing child care between them; or they might each work three-quarters time for nine months, without significant pay loss.

In addition, Swedish parents have the right to take an unpaid, but fully job-protected leave until their child is eighteen months old, and to work a six-hour day (without additional financial compensation) from the end of the parental leave until their child is eight years old. All working parents in Sweden are also given the right to a paid sick leave to care for an ill child at home for up to sixty days a year, if it is medically necessary.

France

Employed women in France are guaranteed the right to a sixteen-week, job-protected maternity leave, paid for under sickness benefits and replacing about 90% of wages up to a specified maximum. Up to six weeks can be taken before the anticipated birth, and ten weeks after; more time off is permitted and paid for if the child is a third or subsequent child, or if the birth is complicated, or if there are multiple births. In addition, a supplementary two-year job-protected unpaid leave is available to working parents to remain home to care for a baby after the end of the paid maternity leave, or to work part-time, if they prefer. This benefit is limited to those who are employed in a firm with one hundred or more employees; parents with three or more children who qualify for this leave are entitled to a cash benefit while on leave.

Federal Republic of Germany

Parents are entitled to a ten-month leave, with the same or a comparable job guaranteed upon return to work. The first fourteen weeks (six before birth and eight after) are limited to mothers. A *sickness insurance* benefit is paid by the social security system at a flat rate equal to about the average wage for women workers for the first fourteen weeks, and employers are required to supplement this benefit to cover the woman's full wage. In addition, job-protected parental leave paid for at a modest level is available for ten months (rising to one year in 1988) following the end of the paid maternity leave. West German working parents are also entitled to a minimum of five days of paid sick leave to care for an ill child at home. (Collective bargaining agreements tend to include this benefit also, and as a consequence most German workers are entitled to about ten or more days for this purpose.)

Italy

There is a mandatory maternity leave for working women for two months before childbirth and three months after. The cash benefit is provided as a social insurance benefit and replaces 80% of prior wage. A supplementary leave is available to either parent for six months, with full job protection, but paid at the rate of 30% of wages.

Greece, Portugal, and Spain

In Greece, employees with one year of prior service, working in companies with more than one hundred workers, are entitled to three-months parental leave per year for each child under two-and-one-half. The leave is unpaid, and each parent has a separate right to a leave. In Portugal, working parents are entitled to six-months unpaid, job-protected parental leave, while in Spain a three-year leave is guaranteed.

NEW DIRECTIONS: SUPPLEMENTARY MATERNITY, PARENTING, OR CHILDCARE LEAVES

In a number of countries over the last two decades several new benefits have emerged, adding a new and significant dimension to the economic security provided working mothers and fathers. The new benefits include several variations on the right to an extended, job-protected leave from work with provision of a cash benefit, but in these cases there is a flat grant rather than a wage-related grant. The period of leave varies between three months and about two-and-one-half years. The benefit name varies also, translated sometimes to mean a supplementary maternity leave (German Democratic Republic); a mother's wage (Czechoslovakia); a childcare grant or allowance (Hungary); an educational or childrearing grant (Federal Republic of Germany) or leave (France); or a parental leave (Sweden). The leader in this type of policy is Hungary, whose childcare allowance, initiated in 1967 and amended several times since then, has become an increasingly influential social innovation internationally.[4] Available to all women, regardless of income, who have had a specified period of prior labor-force attachment, this benefit supplements the twenty-week paid maternity leave by providing women the right to withdraw from the labor force until their child is three years old, have their job, seniority, and pension rights fully protected, and receive a flat-rate cash benefit equal now to about 35% of an average female wage. This benefit is extremely popular in Hungary, and over 80% of the eligible women take advantage of it for at least some portion of the permitted time. Well-educated women with good jobs tend to use it for shorter periods, usually not beyond the time their children are about eighteen months of age. Unskilled women use it longer. Women on leave can work as family day-care providers and care for others' children, yet still collect their childcare grant. Czechoslovakia and Poland, among the eastern European countries, provide similar benefits, but lasting only for two instead of three years.

Some illustrations of other supplementary leaves include the following:

- The German Democratic Republic provides a supplementary maternity leave beyond its basic twenty-six weeks, and this is paid at the rate of 90% of wages. After the birth of second child, or subsequent children, an additional twenty-six-week leave can be taken. Full job-protection is guaranteed, but the benefit level is that of sickness insurance and therefore equal only to a portion of wage.
- Austria provides a benefit available to all women at the end of their sixteen-week maternity leave for up to one year after childbirth. Entitlement to this leave carries with it the right to a cash benefit equal to a partial wage through the unemployment insurance system.
- The Federal Republic of Germany now provides a supplementary

4. For an extensive discussion of this benefit, see Sheila B. Kamerman and Alfred J. Kahn, *Child Care, Family Benefits and Working Parents* (New York: Columbia University Press, 1981).

ten-month parental leave, (twelve months in 1988) paid at a low level and available to either parent or shared between them.
• The French supplementary, two-year, unpaid parenting leave has become a paid leave to parents with three or more children.

Finally, the European Economic Community has proposed a directive that would require all member countries to mandate a minimum parental leave of three months per worker per child, though individual member states may fix a longer period. This means that in a family where both parents are at work there would be a total entitlement of at least six-months full-time leave, to be divided equally between mother and father. Both parents could not be on leave at the same time, nor could the leave entitlement be transferred from one parent to another. The leave could be taken at any time before the child reaches age two, or five in the case of an adopted child. The leave would be longer for single parents or for parents of a handicapped child. A cash benefit is recommended, but the details are left to the individual member states; any payment, however, would come from general revenue, not from employers. An estimate of the costs to employers of introducing such a three-month parental leave, including disruption, recruitment of substitutes, and so forth, is that it would increase the total wages and salaries bill by less than 0.01%.[5]

CONCLUSION

Almost all industrialized countries provide maternity and/or parenting leaves and related cash benefits as statutory social insurance benefits, wherein pregnancy and maternity are defined as societal as well as individual risks that result in temporary loss of income and, therefore, are subject to protection by social insurance. Begun in most countries initially out of concern for maternal and child health, they are increasingly being viewed as employment-related. Thus, they can involve dual and parallel policies in both employment and health systems, employment policies alone, or independent social insurance benefits. The particular system employed is as much an artifact of the governmental structure of a country as it is of earlier history and ideology.

The most rapid periods of benefit expansion were the 1960s and 1970s, decades that experienced an extraordinary growth in the number and proportion of women, especially young married women, entering the labor force. If maternal and child health concerns underlay the initial

5. Equal Opportunities Commission, *Briefings*, "Parental Leave—The Proposed E. C. Directive and the EOC Study of the Costs," May 1986.

development of these benefits, the expansion in these two decades was more a reflection of a growing concern with fertility decline, inflation, and pressure on family income in the context of a continued need for women in the labor market and a continued desire on the part of women to gain access to the pecuniary and nonpecuniary satisfactions that paid labor-market activity provides.

In contrast, developments in the 1980s suggest an effort at adjusting to the constraints imposed by limited public resources and the continued concern with unemployment. This has only been a decade of modest growth in these or any other social benefits. In spite of economic problems, however, these benefits have been protected. Clearly, they have come to represent an important *family benefit*, in that income and employment are protected at the time of childbirth, as is the opportunity for mother, and increasingly father, and child to get to know each other and adapt to a new situation and a new relationship.

Most industrialized countries provide such benefits as a matter of national legislation, through their social insurance systems. Some countries supplement existing statutory provision by employer-provided fringe benefits, as part of company or industry-wide agreement or labor union contracts, just as the social security system provides the primary form of old-age and retirement insurance even though private occupational pensions may supplement these. The foundation, however, remains the social insurance system. Maternity and parenting benefits are modest social policies but they are an essential part of any country's family policy. No industrialized country can be without such provision today.

FIFTEEN

European Infant Care Leaves: Foreign Perspectives on the Integration of Work and Family Roles

JOSEPH P. ALLEN

The United States is currently undergoing a major transition in patterns of work and family life. Birth rates are declining (Masnick and Bane 1981); increasing numbers of children are being raised in single-parent families (Bronfenbrenner and Crouter 1982); and the number and percentage of women in the labor force is increasing rapidly (Smith 1980). An unfortunate effect of these changes is a dramatic increase in the number of parents of newborns and very young children who must now choose between leaving their jobs and placing their children in day care. How parents make this difficult choice is not yet known (Farber, et al., in chapter 9, above). What is known is that these choices are affecting the psychological and physical well-being of our next generation of children (Gamble and Zigler 1986).

The situation in the United States contrasts sharply with that in other industrialized nations. Without exception, these nations have chosen to provide paid leaves to parents of newborns to help these parents manage dual work and childrearing roles (Kamerman 1980). Such leaves, lasting as long as nine months with pay, have been available for decades in these countries, while the United States has offered no similar aid to parents (Kamerman 1980).

These differences raise a number of questions about the nature and rationales of other countries' infant care leave policies, and about why similar policies have not been adopted in the United States. To address these differences and to consider whether infant care leaves could be used to improve the lives of families in the United States, this study explored the actual functioning of infant care leaves in three European nations. Particular attention was paid to the impact of the leaves on the societal groups they affect most: children, women in the labor force, and employers. The study focused on three issues of central importance to U.S. policies toward an infant care leave:

- Do employers—who may bear the heaviest cost of leaves—accept them, and why or why not?
- How are the leaves perceived by those struggling for equal rights and employment opportunities for women?
- Do differences between European and American attitudes toward children and families render the benefits of leaves in Europe inapplicable to the United States?

In this chapter I consider the infant-care-leave policies of other nations as they reflect different approaches to meeting the sometimes competing needs of children, parents, and employers. Although I focus on specific questions about how the leaves function when implemented on a large scale, I also touch on the underlying assumptions in the leaves about how best to meet the needs of children, families, and employers under difficult demographic conditions. It is hoped that knowledge about the functioning of leaves and the cultural values that support them in other countries can be useful in developing leave policies that are responsive to current demographic and social trends in the United States.

RESEARCH METHOD

Infant-care-leave policies in Sweden, the Federal Republic of Germany, and France were selected for study because these countries employ a range of approaches to leaves and have sociopolitical systems similar enough to the United States to yield some bases for comparison. In each country, basic information about the leaves was first obtained from available documentation and from interviews with government officials who administer the leaves. A series of in-depth interviews was then conducted with representatives of some of the major societal groups interested in the leaves, including government officials, representatives of women's organizations, researchers, union representatives, employers, and parents.

In choosing interviewees, no attempt was made to select a scientifically representative sample of a narrowly defined population. Rather, as befits an exploratory inquiry, the selection process was designed to tap a wide range of experiences, perspectives, and knowledge within each of the countries. Policy makers, women's group representatives, and researchers were selected after consultation with scholars and other knowledgeable persons in each country. Union representatives and specific employers were selected either because they resembled a large number of other companies or unions in an area, or because they embodied some unique feature that was relevant to the leaves (for example, they employed large numbers of young women). Parents were selected for interviews from the groups mentioned above, as well as through contacts with developmental psychologists conducting survey research, and also through informal contacts developed during the study. In all, sixty persons were interviewed. The interviews were conducted in May and June of 1983, a period characterized by economic recession and high unemployment rates in the countries visited.

Interview questions were standardized and focused on the three major issues discussed above:

1. How do employers cope with and react to parental leaves?
2. How do the leaves affect the push toward women's equality?
3. How well do the leaves further these nations' goals and values concerning the provision of infant care?

Each interviewee was questioned about each issue, although interviews focused on an interviewee's area of direct knowledge. All interviewees were told that data was being collected to inform potential U.S. policies in this area. Special emphasis was placed on the importance of learning more about the benefits and problems of the leaves, as well as ways they might be improved.

AN OVERVIEW OF INFANT CARE LEAVES IN THE COUNTRIES STUDIED

Sweden, West Germany, and France differ significantly in their approaches to infant care leaves. These differences illustrate the tremendous variety of methods available for implementing an infant care leave. The European term for infant care leaves—parental leave—can refer to a range of policies serving diverse and sometimes opposing functions. It is most often used to refer to leaves which are offered to both parents, however, and to distinguish these from maternity leaves offered only to women. The following brief illustrations of the leave policies of these three countries should be read not only for specific information about ways of implementing a leave system, but also for the perspective provided on the variety of functions that can be taken on by an infant care leave system.

Sweden

The Swedish system of leaves for infant care was selected for study because of its explicit commitment to improving equality between the sexes and because of its reputation for generosity and tremendous flexibility. The Swedish system allows a comparatively long period of paid leave time to either parent and provides a huge variety of options for using this time.

Swedish parents are given twelve months of leave in connection with the birth or adoption of a child. In two-parent families, the parents decide how best to divide this time between themselves. Parents receive 90% of their prior net salary (up to a maximum rate of $20,000 per year)[1] for the first nine months of their leave. This amount is not taxed. During the final three months of leave parents receive a uniform allowance of $150.00 per month regardless of previous wages. In addition, all fathers of newborns are given ten days of leave in connection with the birth of their child, to coincide with the first ten days of a mother's postnatal leave.

In order to qualify for wage replacement during leaves, a parent must have worked long enough to qualify for the basic social insurance program in Sweden. Either 270 days of continuous work in the prior year, or twelve months of work in the prior two years would be sufficient to meet this requirement. For those who do not meet this requirement, a minimum payment of five dollars per day is given as long as one parent is out of work during the first twelve months of a child's life. This last payment is given whether or not a parent has prior work experience.

Parents have tremendous discretion in using the leaves to best meet the needs of their family. Parents in two-parent families can split the twelve months between them in whatever manner they choose. The first six months of this leave must be used at the time of the child's birth. However, the last six months of leave (three of which are at full pay and three at minimum payments), may be deferred and used as a block, or as full, half-, or quarter-days off until the child's eighth birthday. In addition to paid leaves, parents may take unpaid leaves with full job guarantees until the child is eighteen months old. Finally, parents can reduce their workday from eight to six hours (without pay) at any time during the child's first eight years of life.

Leaves are financed primarily through employer and employee payroll contributions to the general social insurance system, although general government revenues also support this fund. For the fiscal year 1983/1984 the leaves were projected to cost $600 million, out of a total government budget of $33 billion (Swedish Ministry of Finance 1983).

The first nine months of the leaves are more than 95% utilized (Swedish Social Ministry 1982). Ninety-six percent of the population earns less than the current maximum reimbursement for the leave (Swedish Min-

---

1. For convenience of comparisons across countries, all amounts are listed in terms of U.S. dollars, based on exchange rates for each currency as of December 7, 1983. The Swedish krona was worth $0.13 at this time.

istry of Statistics 1982) and is eligible to receive full salary reimbursement. Data on the final three months of the leave, although less complete, suggest that it too is almost fully utilized (Swedish Social Ministry 1982).

The Swedes began providing leaves to parents in 1900 when they established a four-week unpaid leave for mothers to use immediately after childbirth. The leaves have been expanded greatly since then to meet the changing needs and demands of Swedish society. Much of the expansion in infant care leaves occurred in the 1930s, 1940s and 1950s. The leaves were increased in length to include time before as well as after childbirth, and they also began to provide increasing amounts of compensation for time spent away from work. This expansion has coincided so directly with low fertility rates in Sweden during this period that one observer calls the birthrates the "official godmother" of Swedish family policy (Liljeström 1978). In 1974, a parental-leave law was passed which, among other things, permitted fathers to take the leaves. This law grew out of a decade of study of possible means of promoting equality between men and women in Swedish society, and it was heralded as a step toward this equality. Thus far, however, its effect has mainly been symbolic as men use only 2% of the total parental-leave days taken in Sweden (Fallenius 1981).

Parental leaves in Sweden exist now in the context of an intentionally mixed economy in which the government attempts to promote free enterprise while at the same time seeking to lessen the gap between the very rich and very poor. The 1974 law made the leaves more explicitly a part of this goal by providing a minimum payment in connection with childbirth or adoption to persons who had never worked. The leaves partially replaced the general family allowance system Sweden had used until 1974. Currently, parental leaves comprise less than 2% of the total government budget, although this budget comprises 60% of the Swedish gross national product.

The Federal Republic of Germany

In contrast to Sweden, the Federal Republic of Germany provides a much more modest leave system to parents of newborns. Paid leaves exclude fathers and adoptive mothers, and are shorter than leaves in most neighboring countries, although some recent expansion has occurred. One potential reason for the smaller scale of the West German leave program may be that women in West Germany have not yet entered the work force on as large a scale as women in most other industrialized European nations (Lueck, Orr, and O'Connell, 1982). A second reason for the relatively smaller scale of leave programs in West Germany may be that these programs exist within a context of general ambivalence toward government family policy. Leaves in West Germany were selected for study because the relatively limited scope of the leaves there suggests that West Germany may be somewhat comparable to the United States in its approach toward government-supported family policies.

Like the Swedish system, the German system is divided into two parts: a fourteen-week fully paid leave around the time of the birth of the child, followed by a four-month supplemental leave with relatively low payments. (Illustrations of the basic features of leaves in all three countries are provided in figure 15.1.)

Payments are available only to women and are based upon their prior incomes. The first fourteen weeks of leave are divided into six weeks before and eight weeks after the birth of the child. During this time, mothers receive their full prior net salaries. The first $285[2] per month is paid by the semipublic insurance companies that handle sickness and disability payments for workers. These companies are funded through employer and employee payroll taxes. The mother's employer is required to make up the difference between this amount and the mother's net salary. After the initial fourteen weeks, all mothers who have worked receive salary reimbursement up to $285 per month from the social insurance companies, but the supplement from the employer ends.

All women who have been in the work force for nine months receive the initial fourteen-week leave. Nearly 100% of these women use the the entire fourteen weeks. Approximately 90% of the eligible women also use most or all of the remaining four months of leave (German Ministry for Youth Families and Health 1982). Those women who work in the public sector have the additional option of taking several years of unpaid leave with the birth of each child while retaining full job guarantees. In all, 340,000 women were expected to use the basic leaves in 1983, at a total cost to the government of $358 million (German *Bundestag* 1981).

German maternity leaves have a long history that has become increasingly controversial as the leaves have expanded. Initial *unpaid* maternity leaves date back to 1878, although it was not until 1937 that women were first given an eight-week paid leave. The leaves were initially provided under the rationale of protecting the health of mothers. While the leaves have been expanded in scope since 1937, the legislation has retained its focus on maternal health. This focus has hampered efforts to extend eligibility for the leave to fathers and adoptive parents. For example, in 1979, political considerations required that a major extension of the leaves be appended to existing legislation. As a result, eligibility for benefits continued to be restricted to biological mothers. Women's groups and unions, which had worked for over a decade to

2. Based upon an exchange rate of $0.38 per Deutsche Mark on December 7, 1983.

Table 15.1. Duration and Other Major Features of Infant Care Leaves in Sweden, France, and the Federal Republic of Germany

	Sweden	France	Federal Republic of Germany
Paid Leave	90% salary reimbursement for first nine months; $150/month for next three months	90% salary reimbursement for first four months	100% salary reimbursement for first three months; $285/month for next four months
Unpaid Leave	Job guaranteed for six months after first year. May be deferred and used in increments until child's eighth birthday.	Job guaranteed up to two additional years.	None.
Eligibility	Either parent may take any part of the leave.	Paid leave is available only to women. Unpaid leave is available to men and women in companies with more than 100 employees (one-third of work force).	Only biological mothers.
Financing	85% from payroll tax contributions to social insurance system; 15% from general government revenues.	From general social security system.	Payroll tax into employee insurance fund; supplemented by direct employer payments.

get a major extension of the leave, were ultimately disappointed in the extension because of its continued narrow focus (G. Erler, personal communication, June 1983; R. Brand, personal communication, June 1983).

At the time of this study, cutbacks in the leave were under active consideration. Proposals to make the fourth month of the extended leave unpaid and to reduce the maximum pay from $285 per month to $228 per month were being considered as part of a general austerity program in Germany. Reactions to this proposal were quite mixed. The comments of one union representative captured well the ambivalence toward this proposal. She described the cutbacks as: (1) necessary because of high unemployment; (2) part of a plan to keep total employee benefits from becoming more than 50% of gross salaries; (3) an indirect way to bring women back into the home; and (4) ironic, coming from a Christian Democratic administration which claimed to be pro-family. (H. Metz, personal communication, June 1983). Yet, even in the midst of recession-induced cutbacks, no one questioned the importance of maintaining a leave system of some sort.

France

The French leave system has a strong pronatalist character. It can also be seen as one part of a family policy which attempts to remain neutral on the question of whether mothers with young children should work outside the home. It was selected for study to examine the function of parental leaves within a system which was both explicitly pronatalist and openly ambivalent about the role of women outside the home.

The basic leave is available to women and consists of up to six weeks of leave before and ten weeks after the birth of the child. During this period women receive 90% of their prior salary, up to $1,000[3] per month, from the social security system. In addition, at the birth of their third child, the leave for women is expanded to six months of total leave. Although the basic leave is reasonably generous, especially when it is supplemented by a variety of economic family supports, it has received little public attention. Rather, all of the discussion and interest in France has centered around a new extended parental leave. This *Parental Leave for the Education of Their Children* gives either parent the right to take up to two years away from their work following the birth of a child. The leave is unpaid, but gives parents the right to return to their prior jobs and even to receive training if necessary at the time of their return. The leave is available only to persons employed by companies with more than 100 workers (*Femme Pratique* 1983). Although this restriction eliminates many firms, the eligible corporations employ as much as one-third of the French work force (Kamerman 1980).

A major feature of the French system is that companies quite often supplement the statutory leaves through employee benefit packages. Many companies, for example, supplement the 90% wage replacement from the social security system to provide full wage replacement to moth-

---

3. Based upon an exchange rate of $0.13 per French Franc as of December 7, 1983.

ers on leave. In addition, a variety of more lengthy and generous leave plans are offered to employees in many industries, often as a result of collective bargaining agreements. Some plans provide for elaborate job seniority protection, or for money during the unpaid period of leave. IBM France, for example, pays employees $276 per month for two years while they are on leave. Other plans, such as that offered to employees of the city of Paris, pay mothers who leave work after having a third child up to $204 per month for two years following the child's birth.

The French system of infant care leaves has always been at least somewhat pronatalist in character. The basic leave has existed since 1928 and has been expanded gradually since that time. The extended unpaid leave legislation was passed in 1977 and has been expanded slightly in scope since then. Most recently, the law was amended to apply to persons in corporations with more than 100 employees (instead of 200 as in the previous legislation). The pronatalist character of the leaves is most evident in the bonuses given for the birth of a third child. These bonuses were implemented in part in response to demographic studies showing that the decline in the French birthrate was primarily due to decreases in the numbers of couples having three or more children. However, no evidence to suggest a pronatalist effect of infant care leaves has yet been found.

Another noteworthy feature in the history of French infant care leaves is the role of corporate leave policies in anticipating and providing models for the expansion of statutorily-provided leaves. For example, the parental leave, which was adopted in 1977, had been implemented widely within the insurance industry and refined and developed by different companies well prior to 1977. In this role, French corporations have provided both a significant supplement to existing leave policies and a testing ground for the development of new benefits.

Summary

These brief overviews indicate the enormous variety of approaches for providing parents with leaves for infant care. Yet, beneath this variety of approaches lies a fundamental similarity: all three countries have opted to develop extensive programs to provide leaves to parents. This raises the question: If leaves for infant care are resilient enough in their function to be useful in such different societies, then might they not be equally valuable in the United States? This question is made even more intriguing by the universality of leave programs in modern industrial societies. Yet, it can be answered only if detailed information is available about the actual impact of the leaves: What do they do for employers, women, and children in different societies? How do their functions relate to their popularity?

EMPLOYER REACTIONS

Infant care leaves are not simply a family support, but a support of families *in relation to* the work place. To function well, leaves must be compatible with the needs and rhythms of both the family and the workplace. Employers may not be the chief beneficiaries of infant care leaves, but they feel their effects and may determine how well the leaves function. Conceivably, leaves could be quite disruptive to the workplace and the employer. If potential problems with an infant-care-leave policy in the United States are to be appreciated and minimized, employer reactions must be addressed. Knowing how employers have reacted to and coped with infant care leaves in other countries can provide clues about the effects of leaves on employers in the United States.

Interviews with employers focused first on the extent to which they supported the existing system of infant care leaves in their country. Of all the groups interviewed, employers were expected to show the greatest resistance to the leaves because they appeared to shoulder some of the heaviest costs and receive few benefits in return. The first question put to all employers interviewed was: Are you in favor of the leave system currently in place? Follow-up questions pursued both the mechanisms used by employers to manage the leaves and the amount of difficulty they experienced in coping with the effects of the leaves.

Overall Employer Support

The surprising response from the vast majority of employers in all three countries was in favor of the leaves as they currently existed. As outlined below, this response held up not only across countries, but across large and small companies in a wide range of industries.

Sweden. In Sweden, four of five employers or persons able to represent employer positions[4] expressed strong approval of the law. Asa Rundkvist, representative for family policies of the Swedish Confederation of Employers, stated that, "Some people might think it's too costly, but there's no question we need it...there's no way to measure all of the benefits to the next generation" (personal communication, May 1983). A researcher/consultant noted that among the ten employers he interviewed, the most common response to the question: "How do you deal

---

4. Employers included the manager of a Stockholm hotel that is part of an international hotel chain, the owner of a small computer software firm employing eight workers, and a manager of a fifteen-worker section of a bank with fifty branches throughout Sweden. The two nonemployers included a representative from the largest single employers' confederation in Sweden and a researcher/organizational consultant who had just finished a qualitative study of ten firms' reactions to a variety of employee leaves.

with problems that arise as a result of parental leaves?" was "Problems, what problems?". The consultant labeled this response "a repression" because he later found that many employers had at least some problems implementing the leaves. Nevertheless, this response is instructive because it indicates the strong desire of employers to be supportive of parental leaves.

Swedish employers may have been so supportive of leaves in part because they could often see the direct and indirect benefits the leaves provide to their companies. Employer attitudes in Sweden do not imply a lack of concern with profit, but instead reflect a broad notion of what factors lead to corporate success. The Swedish position is well-captured by Rundkvist's summary of the philosophy of the Swedish Confederation of Employers:

> It's important for labor to realize labor market policy is influenced by profitability ... it's very hard to measure what it's worth to me, my children and the next generation and society at large to give me time to care for my children after they are born. In Sweden we see the benefits as increased harmony ... It is possible [to have the leaves]. (Personal communication, May 1983.)

A Swedish banker puts the same notion more succinctly: "[The leaves are] good for the fathers and mothers and that *must* be good for the bank."

The one Swedish employer who did not approve of the leaves was the owner of a small computer software firm, employing eight highly trained workers. He felt that all leaves in Sweden, including the generous parental leave, simply made it harder for Swedish products to compete on an international market. He said that leaves created a great disruption to his firm because employees on leave were difficult to replace. He also mentioned that his own wife had raised their children from birth without leaves because she had never worked outside of the home. He stated that he believed he spoke for many other small businessmen in Sweden. His attitudes may represent a limited but significant conservative backlash against the costs of the leaves.

The Federal Republic of Germany. All six employers interviewed, ranging from the manager of a small international school to the personnel director of the largest steel firm in West Germany, said that they felt the maternity leave law was either "necessary," or "one they could live with," or both.[5] Re-

---

5. Companies visited included an international school employing forty-two teachers and twelve administrative staff; a major department store with 650 employees, 80% of whom were women; the largest steel manufacturer in Germany, employing 500 women among 7500 employees; a small refractory and mining company with 800 employees; a

actions varied from employers who felt that "It's a very good thing but it's really a heavy cost to employers," thus expressing qualified approval of leave laws, to the sentiment, "In normal cases we have no problems with this law, and we think the law should apply to normal cases."

France. In France, employers must cope with two distinctly different infant care leaves. The first—sixteen weeks for mothers in connection with the birth of their child—has existed since 1928 and is considered a fixture in the labor market. The extent of its acceptance is perhaps best indicated by the fact that questions in the first four interviews about attitudes toward this basic leave were all dismissed by interviewees as indicative of the naïveté of the interviewers; the leaves simply are not a source of controversy. The real issue in France is not whether initial paid leaves are acceptable to employers, but whether employers will choose to offer *extensions* of leaves at the end of the statutory leaves. Of five firms contacted in a variety of segments of French industry,[6] three had offered additional *paid* leaves beyond those statutorily mandated, and the other two expressed no reservations in their support of the statutory leaves.

The additional leaves offered by employers ranged up to two years in length (the length of the unpaid parental leave). Pay for these leaves ranged up to several hundred dollars per month. This indicates support of parental leaves that is strong enough for many firms to see value in supplementing them voluntarily. Unfortunately, this study was not able to include any of the smaller firms, which seem to be both least likely to have offered additional leaves and most likely to suffer significant workplace disruption as a result of the leaves. Whether and to what extent the strong support of larger companies for leaves generalizes to smaller employers remains unclear.

In all three countries, leaves for infant care were widely supported by employers and were not generally problematic. Both in their stated attitudes and in their actions, employers in each country made their support for the leaves clear. The reasons for their support focused largely upon the perceived benefits of the leaves for employers and for society. However, the relative deemphasis of problems created by the leaves may be at least as significant in explaining employers' attitudes. Understanding why such problems do and do not occur for employers in a country may help us un-

---

tool manufacturer employing 220 persons; and, a major cosmetics firm (manufacturing and sales) employing 450 persons.

6. Firms included a multinational computer firm with more than 10,000 employees; a federation of insurance companies with a combined total of over 90,000 employees; a publishing house with 260 employees; a chemical manufacturing laboratory with 1,100 employees; and the municipal government of the city of Paris.

derstand employers' support for leaves and may also suggest methods of sensitively implementing infant-care-leave systems.

Specific Problems and Adaptations of Employers

Follow-up questions to employers focused on problems that leaves might create for them. The strong support for the leaves did not indicate that they were always easy for employers to administer. And, even though employers mentioned a number of potential problems in coping with infant care leaves, they generally agreed upon a range of viable options for dealing with these problems.

One problem that was expected to be significant but which was seldom mentioned was the financial cost of the leaves. Even in West Germany, where employers provide partial salary replacement to employees on leave, no employer mentioned this cost as a significant burden for the company. This may be because employers needed only to make up the difference between a $300-per-month government subsidy and an employee's former after-tax income. The fourteen week leave thus costs companies less than even a much shorter period of sick leave. A second reason why cost may not have been mentioned as a problem is that the initial maternity leave has long been accepted as necessary for the health of mothers. Cost may only be an issue when what is paid for is not considered essential. When one German employer was asked if there was any sentiment, in either his company or among colleagues in other companies, that the initial fourteen weeks of leave be cut back because of its cost, he replied: "No, we don't think about it, your question is like asking how we feel about workers receiving Sunday as a day off."

The problem with the leaves most frequently mentioned by employers was the inconvenience of having to replace absent employees. A clear pattern emerged suggesting which employers would have the most difficulty dealing with this problem. Companies with few employees and companies with small divisions of highly trained specialists appeared to have the most consistent difficulties in replacing employees on leave. The one Swedish employer who objected to the leave policy fell into both of these categories. In addition, a Swedish management consultant stated that parental leaves tended to be problematic mainly for companies with few employees or employees who would be difficult to replace. Of the companies in this study in which the leaves presented no significant problems, all employed fifty or more workers. In contrast, the two companies in the study which had substantial difficulties administering the leaves both had either few employees or employees whose training was specialized enough so that they were not easily replaced while on leaves.

Requirements that parents give timely notice to employers of their intent to use the leaves facilitated several types of employer actions to cope with absences. The three options that companies used most frequently were: 1) hiring new employees temporarily; 2) shifting employees around within the company to fill vacancies; or 3) asking coworkers to take on a larger role. Use of these options varied by companies and country. The first option, for example, was used rarely in Sweden, where it is difficult to hire temporary employees. Among companies in other countries that did hire temporary employees, the economic recession and resulting high rates of unemployment were cited as making this process easier for employers. Both the options of hiring temporary employees and of moving employees around in a company were used more frequently by the larger companies. Four of the six firms with more than one hundred employees that were visited used one of these latter two methods, whereas none of six smaller companies did.

Smaller firms were much more likely to state that they adapted to the leaves by using employees already in the firm and by asking for coworkers' assistance. The latter procedure raised a number of concerns in the Federal Republic of Germany, where two of the three union representatives interviewed spontaneously voiced strong objections to this practice. A representative of public employees in a large German city noted that employees who have children have statutorily specified rights, whereas their coworkers, who often suffer extra burdens at work as a result of leaves, have no special protection.

Another problem mentioned in connection with the work place was coworker resentment of parents on leaves. Two of five union representatives, two of twelve employers, and two of ten parents interviewed in the study mentioned this problem. Such resentment was not always in connection with extra work given to remaining employees. On one occasion it was directed toward an immigrant worker in Germany who combined two births with a long period of sickness leave for questionable ailments to extend a leave over a period of several years. In several cases in France, the resentment dealt with employees on leave being given preferences in job reassignment, so as to be nearer their homes, when they returned to work. While coworker resentment was occasionally a problem, it was also often balanced by coworker pride in the new parents. And, in the majority of interviews with employers and parents, coworker resentment was simply not mentioned as a significant issue or problem.

Summary

The highly positive overall reaction of employers to infant care leaves results from a number of factors. One is the employers' experience and sophistication in handling other employee absences, which are usually much less predictable than absences resulting from parental leaves. Another factor is the employers' willingness to make sacrifices for larger societal gains. A third factor is the sensitivity of infant-care-leave policies to the needs of employers. Certain key provisions of the leaves, such as requirements for timely notice of the intent to take a leave and government financing of most of the costs of leaves reflect a high degree of sensitivity to employer needs. Finally, a number of employers see the leaves as working in their interest by helping build a more satisfied, healthy, and stable labor force within a company. Stories about women who returned to work too quickly after childbirth suggest employers' beliefs that offering leaves may actually increase workforce productivity by eliminating problems which reduce it. Although the leaves were not without problems for employers, those that did arise were usually manageable with careful planning and use of knowledge gained through experience with leaves.

WOMEN'S EQUALITY

The second major question addressed in this study was: How are leaves for infant care perceived by those struggling to obtain equal rights and opportunities for women? Concerns about women's equality in the United States, although related to child-welfare issues, clearly extend well beyond them. Any proposal to improve the functioning of children and families will (and should) be scrutinized to determine whether it could hinder the movement toward women's equality. The impact of leaves on women's equality thus determines the political viability of a leave policy and, thus, also the social status of parents—male and female. This status in turn affects the quality of care that parents can provide for their children.

This part of the study addressed one central concern about parental leave policies—that they might rigidify women's roles as homemakers and keep women from entering and advancing in the labor force. The extensive leave policies of the countries in this study were each examined to determine whether or not they had this effect. Employers, women's group representatives, workers, and government officials were interviewed in each of the countries visited. Interviews focused on two major areas of concern. The first was the effect of leaves on women's efforts to achieve equality in the work force. The second focus was upon the effect of the leaves on the push toward female equality in social and family roles. Finally, those interviewees who had knowledge about experimental policies and local variants of leave policies were asked about the effects of these variants in each of the two areas mentioned above.

Labor Market Equality

Perhaps the most important fact to understand in considering the effects of leaves on discrimination against women in the labor force is the widespread existence of such discrimination in each of the countries studied. Even in Sweden, which is considered one of the world's most progressive countries in equalizing male and female roles, women were earning only 81% of men's salaries while working in similar jobs with similar qualifications (Gustaffson 1981). Interviews strongly supported the notion that widespread discrimination exists. Interviewees were asked whether they had any direct knowledge of whether women faced discrimination in the work force. All six of the German interviewees who felt they had direct experience relevant to this question said that women faced discrimination in the job market. In Sweden, all four persons who spoke on this subject said they had seen evidence that women faced discrimination in the labor force.[7] In France, the issue of discrimination was not posed in interviews, although one interviewee noted the pay and job discrimination faced by women in France. No person in any of the three countries suggested that such general discrimination against women in the labor force did not exist.

Given this context, the appropriate question to ask is not "Are women who take leaves discriminated against?", but "Do women suffer any *additional* discrimination as a result of infant care leave policies?" This general question was addressed by a number of interviewees who felt that they were in a position to venture an answer. The question was also approached through three more specific questions about the most serious effects of the leaves for women in the labor market:

1. Do the leaves increase labor-force discrimination against women of childbearing age?
2. Do the leaves increase the likelihood that women will quit their jobs at the birth of a child and remain at home to care for the child?
3. Do the leaves place women at a significant disadvantage in their attempts to gain job expertise by removing them from the workplace around the time of childbirth?

All interviewees who stated that they believed women experienced labor-force discrimination went on to state that they felt that the discrimination was largely independent of leaves. The leaves did not appear to promote any additional discrimination, but pregnancy and childbearing did. Three persons mentioned that the decision to have a child

7. A number of other Swedish interviewees stated that they had no *direct* knowledge of discrimination, but had no doubt that it took place.

and raise a family is seen as indicating lack of interest in a career. Notably, all three of these persons lived in West Germany—a country with increasing numbers of women in the labor force and the lowest birthrate in the world (Lueck, Orr, and O'Connell 1982). Three other persons (two in Germany, one in Sweden) stated that women of childbearing age are discriminated against because pregnancies hurt companies and reduce productivity. However, any additional discrimination against women as a result of the leaves was seen as slight.

In attempting to explore the issue of labor-force discrimination in more specific contexts, the question was asked: What overall effect do the leaves have on women's attempts to enter and remain in the work force? In each country visited, leaves for infant care were almost unanimously seen as cementing women's ties to the work force by providing a mechanism through which work and family life could be integrated. The existence of the leaves made it significantly more likely that women would enter and remain in the labor force through their childbearing years.

In Germany, thirteen of twenty persons interviewed felt that the leaves increased female labor-force participation. Several persons mentioned that the offer of a job guarantee made it possible for women to care for their newborn children without giving up the opportunity to return to their jobs. One researcher suggested that this was more important than the money paid to mothers on leave. A public employees' representative noted that prior to the extension of the leaves in Germany in 1979, mothers tended to either come back to work very quickly after childbirth or not at all. Few, it seems, were able to find ways of remaining home with their children for more than the first six weeks after the child's birth while still retaining their labor-force connection. A group of women at a German mothers' center were asked: If you had been offered *no* maternity leave at the time you had your children, how would you have managed? All eight of the women replied that they would have quit their jobs to care for their children rather than return immediately to work.

In Sweden, five interviewees stated that the leaves helped women enter or remain in the labor force. Three of these five attributed this effect partly to the availability of leaves to both sexes: the leaves lessened discrimination against women by allowing men to share the job of raising a family. One researcher who had interviewed several dozen fathers of newborns found that several had spouses who were searching quite eagerly for jobs so as to establish a workforce connection (and hence eligibility for leaves) prior to becoming pregnant again (P. Hwang, personal communication, May 1983). Of course, the eligibility requirement of at least nine months of work immediately prior to taking the leave means that such a connection would be more than trivial. A coauthor of a recent

Swedish national study on equality between the sexes notes that the leaves were originally instituted as a way to support the entry of women into the labor force. He also stated what he termed a commonly held belief that the existence of some leaves is really almost a *precondition* for women's participation in the labor force (L. Jalmert, personal communication, 1983).

Although the question of the effects of leaves on women's ties to the work force was not raised directly in France, five of fourteen interviewees spontaneously volunteered opinions that the leaves helped women to remain in the work force while managing their family lives. Each of these persons was referring specifically to the longer leaves often available through their companies or the longer unpaid leave recently made available to all employees. There was no suggestion in any of the interviews that the shorter leaves might in any way break the connection of women with the labor force. What was expressed was the belief that still longer leaves would help maintain this contact by allowing smoother integration of work and family life.

The final question about the interaction of leaves and womens' roles in the labor force is whether the time spent away from work hurts women's chances to advance in their careers by decreasing their levels of experience. The available evidence suggests that such an effect may exist, although it appears to be small in size. In Sweden, panel data from a nationally representative sample of Swedish women found that the loss in average future earnings for each full year spent out of the work force for any reason was approximately 2% (Gustaffson 1981). No data were collected for those women who spent less than a year out of the labor force, but the study did find that the effect on future earnings of time away from the work force was roughly linear. This suggests that women staying out nine months or less would have even smaller decreases in wages. Gustaffson also found that women who temporarily switched from full- to part-time work suffered almost identical losses in wages upon returning to full-time work as did women who left the work force completely. Part-time work was equivalent to no work in terms of future earning ability.

This evidence supports the hypothesis that women's careers are often hurt by the time required to raise a family—whether they take time away from their jobs or cut back their hours to manage both work and family roles. The data also suggest, however, that any additional effects of a parental leave are minimal. The effects of time away from the workplace thus paralleled the general effects of the leaves. In both cases, the effects of taking time out to give birth and be a parent to a young child were disadvantages in the labor market. Few additional effects of leaves could be discerned either from carefully-designed demographic studies or from less formal interviews with workers and employers.

In each country, parental leaves seemed to play a significant role in encouraging women to continue their ties with the work force after childbirth. They gave parents a mechanism by which to allot time to both work and family life without requiring them to pit the two sets of demands against each other. The interviews clearly supported the notion that leaves are used to allow women to enter and remain in the work force more easily. Leaves for infant care help accommodate increasing rates of participation of both parents in the work force. Data from cross-cultural studies of family policies have reached parallel conclusions, noting that the countries with the highest rates of female labor-force participation were almost invariably the countries with longer leaves (German Youth Institute Family Policies Work Group 1982).

The leaves appear to work well in relation to women's equality in the workplace in part because they constitute a pro-family policy which is not anti-work. In all countries, leaves were designed in ways which acknowledged the demands placed upon fathers and mothers but were also sensitive to the rhythms of the work place. In this way, leaves provided a formal mechanism for parents to use to cope with their dual roles. By reducing stress in both the family and the workplace, the leaves made it easier for women to become integrated into the work force while retaining their capacity to bear and raise children. In this way, they clearly promoted equal access to the labor force.

Social Roles of Men and Women

Leaves for infant care seem to help women attain equal access to the labor force, but there is an important related question: Do leaves or can leaves be used to promote equality of social roles between the sexes? Two specific questions were asked in this area:

1. Can parental leaves shift the balance in favor of more equal distribution of home and work roles between the sexes?
2. Do leaves used only by women (as a result of legislation or social trend) reinforce the traditional distribution of home and work roles between the sexes?

Of the three countries visited, Sweden provides the most relevant case study for answering these questions. Of all modern industrial nations, Sweden has probably been the most active in using leaves to promote equality of social roles between the sexes (Lamb and Levine 1983). Yet, explicitly gender-neutral leave policies in Sweden seem to have had symbolic value, but very few tangible effects on the sex-role distribution of childrearing functions in Swedish society. The symbolic impact is illustrated by the fact that 10% of all Swedish fathers took leaves from work in 1981 in order to be with their children while the child's mother worked. This represented a five-fold increase from the figures of the second full year of the program in 1976 (Swedish Social Ministry 1982). The willingness of even a small minority of Swedish men to take such a break from traditional roles suggests that the leaves may begin to have an impact on how parenting roles are perceived in Swedish culture. This may in turn have a long-term impact on how these roles are actually shared in families.

A different perspective on male usage of parental leaves is that of the total number of days of parental leave available to families, 98% are taken by women. Although 10% of Swedish men take some parental leave, they typically take only one or two months of the nine to twelve months available. Even those who only take one day are included in the Swedish statistics (Swedish Social Ministry 1982). Thus, even in a country selected for its active promotion of sexual equality, patterns of leave-use reflect a continuing reliance on women as the primary childcare agents for very young children.

A slightly more positive view is gained by looking at data on Swedish men who remain home to care for sick children. The most recent data shows men taking 44% of all days used to care for sick children—a figure suggesting that in some ways the traditional sex-role definitions are changing (Arvedson 1981). Whether and to what extent the availability of parental leaves has encouraged men to take more responsibilities in caring for sick children and in caring for their children in general remains an unanswered question. (For an excellent extended discussion of the extent and effects of Swedish leave policies on childrearing practices, see Lamb and Levine 1983.)

Germany, as mentioned earlier, came close to adopting a parental leave system in 1979, but did not do so. One observer has suggested that at $300 per month, the idea of men taking leaves to care for their children is "a joke". In an experiment in one of the German *Lande*, a longer leave was made available to either parent. During the two years of the study, only two of the 439 people taking the leave were men (Schramm 1980). This is consistent with data collected in Sweden which suggested that higher incomes of men provide a disincentive for them to use parental leaves (Lamb and Levine 1983).

In France, the basic leave is maternal, and only the unpaid extended leaves are available to either parent. No official statistics have been compiled on usage of the unpaid leave, but the differences in average incomes between men and women in France, as in all major industrialized countries, provide a strong incentive for men not to take the leave.

These results all suggest that while leaves may shift the distribution of home and work roles between the sexes, to date these effects appear to be weak. At best the leaves appear to have contributed somewhat to more equal distribution of childrearing tasks in Sweden. At worst, leaves seem simply to reflect existing cultural and economic emphases on traditional sex roles in France and West Germany. Nonetheless, in considering centuries-old societal norms, any change at all may be quite important. Interestingly, a multinational research team has found that making fathers more active in the home is the reason most often given for supporting a leave that is parental (that is, available to either parent), as opposed to maternal (German Youth Institute Family Policies Work Group 1982). This suggests that the leaves may have a symbolic impact in sanctioning men taking care of their children. This encouragement may have effects well beyond the direct short-term changes in numbers of men and women leaving work to care for very young children.

Variations of National Infant-Care-Leave Policies

The data reported on leaves thus far, while reflecting a variety of positive functions in helping women's careers and pursuit of equality, do not necessarily indicate that all infant care leaves will be beneficial to women. On the contrary, although the particular leaves in effect in France, West Germany, and Sweden have proved beneficial to women, substantially longer leaves or leaves not based on attachment to the labor force might actually discourage women from working. In order to examine the effects of different ways of implementing a leave policy, a number of proposals and experimental variants on existing leaves were considered in each country, using the questions outlined above.

One proposed leave consisted of financial payments given to women at home following childbirth regardless of their prior labor-force participation. This payment exists in Sweden, where mothers receive the minimum payment of $5 per day, whether or not they have worked in the past. In Sweden a proposal has also been discussed to pay parents $30 per month to remain home to care for their older children. This is seen as an alternative to the state daycare subsidies (P. Hwang, personal communication, May 1983). In both cases, women's organizations opposed these plans because they provided an incentive to leave work, but gave no credit for having worked in the past. These proposals give the most help to mothers who have never worked and will not work in the near future. They become part of a general income supplement for children which is a leave only in the sense of being contingent upon parents, generally mothers, *not* working.

Another option is to offer greatly extended periods of leave. A major West German experiment carried out in Lower Saxony extended payments for mothers on leave to include the first eighteen months after childbirth. The results, showing that 90% of the women who took the full leave did not return to work after its conclusion, suggest that such a long leave is associated with permanent separation from the labor force (Schramm 1980). The director of the section on "Working Women" of the French Confederation of Employers attributes a similar effect to longer leaves in France, which are generally offered by individual companies (M. Villebrun, personal communication, July 1983). Clearly, these leaves have the potential to discourage a woman's return to work after childbirth.

The results of some of these alternative leave policies suggest that the conclusion that leaves enhance women's status needs to be carefully qualified. The well-thought-out leaves which are implemented nationally in each country do seem to improve women's status. However, the effects of the programs described in this section suggest that not every program involving payments and time off from work under the heading *parental leave* will automatically have a positive effect on women. Some leave policies may even push women out of the labor force. Nevertheless, the effects of experimental policies should not be allowed to obscure the overwhelming evidence that existing leaves have usually had quite positive effects in promoting women's equality. Typically, the leaves provide a formal connection to the work force during and after pregnancy; they greatly reduce the stress of a too early return to work after childbirth; they occasionally encourage women to enter the work force prior to pregnancy; and, when present as a true parental leave, they may enhance efforts to promote sex-role equality.

SOCIETAL ATTITUDES TOWARD THE FAMILY AND INFANT CARE

In order to apply the experiences of other countries with leaves to the United States, significant differences in relevant cultural attitudes and norms must be recognized and taken into account. While conclusions drawn from a brief interview study about differences in societal attitudes must be made with great caution, two basic differences between attitudes in the United States and in the countries visited were so striking as to warrant mention. In contrast to the United States, a strong sense of *societal* responsibility for family life and childrearing was found in the countries visited. Parents also expressed very strong beliefs that they needed to be with their children in the first months after birth. These parents also saw the need for peer contact for their children, but felt this should come at later stages of development. Peer contact and group care were not ignored, but were seen as more appropriate for children beyond nine months of age. Although this study was not initially designed to tap broad societal attitudes, surprisingly strong evidence of these beliefs was repeatedly encountered in each country visited. The strength of these beliefs in France, West Germany, and Sweden suggests their possible role in explaining fundamental differences in approaches to parental leaves between the United States and these countries.

Responsibility for Families and Children

The most frequently given explanation for why leaves were offered to parents in each country was, "It's in the best interest of society to support families and parenthood in whatever way possible." Comments ranged from "it's impossible to measure the benefits to society at large of having children well cared for," to the often repeated reference in Germany to low birthrates which was accompanied by the statement, "You can see why we need parental leaves." One possible explanation for heightened societal interest in the well-being of its next generation may be the presence of low or sharply declining birthrates. In all three countries studied the leaves have at some point been explicitly justified by their pronatalist effect (Kamerman and Kahn 1981; Lamb and Levine 1983). This is most clearly seen in France, where special bonuses are given for the birth of third and subsequent children (French Committee on Female Work 1979). It is not clear to what extent these bonuses resulted from studies which primarily attributed low French birthrate to the very small number of parents having more than two children. In Germany, the one societal consideration most frequently mentioned was that West Germany currently has the lowest birthrate of any country in the world (Lueck, Orr, and O'Connell 1982). Having children was repeatedly cited as "for the good of the country."

Associated with this perspective on leaves is the notion that parenting and childrearing are difficult, arduous, and only sometimes rewarding tasks. Whether the rewards of parenting outweigh the demands obviously will vary depending upon the individual family. However, one piece of hard data provides an excellent overall view of the balance of the rewards and demands of parenting in a society: the fertility rate. Given the existing rewards and demands of parenting, do people choose to have children? The answer in Europe in the first sixty years of the twentieth century was clear: many parents chose to have at most one or two children, and the birthrates were quite low by both historical and cross-cultural standards (van de Walle and Knodel 1980). Spontaneous comments during interviews paralleled this data; many people mentioned the strains of childrearing, while virtually no mention was made of children as a "luxury" for those who can afford them. In contrast, the United States has, until recently, seemed to focus upon children more as a "blessing" for individual parents than as a societal necessity.

Closely related to a society's interest in its children is an interest in the stability of the family as the social unit with primary childrearing responsibility. This interrelationship appeared particularly salient in Sweden where sociologists have noted that the rapid increase in cohabitation in the 1960s led to positive steps to protect the role of the family (Liljeström, Mellström, and Svensson 1978). The attempt to increase the involvement of fathers in childrearing was certainly a factor in the switch from maternal to parental leaves in 1974. Taken together, concerns about low fertility rates and high divorce rates seem to have led to a societal emphasis upon supporting families as the childrearing agents of choice. Parental leaves support families in Sweden at least in part because Swedes recognize a need to aid the social unit that has direct responsibility for childrearing.

Swedish, German, and French societies all exhibited a degree of collective responsibility for childrearing that is unparalleled in the United States. Significantly, this responsibility was related to an awareness of the difficulties of being a parent and the many benefits of children for society. These attitudes at least partially reflected awareness of the threat to a society posed by low or sharply declining birthrates. These attitudes also seemed to lead to a sense of societal debt towards parents who bear and raise society's children. At least until recently, high U.S. birthrates and an emphasis on individualism appear to have held back the development of similar attitudes.

Care of Infants

A second major factor in understanding different cultural values in the countries studied is an appreciation of their attitudes and practices regarding various methods of care for newborns and very young infants. There was a strong sense, expressed by interviewees in each country, that a special bond develops between parents and their infants—and that the time together provided by leaves helps facilitate this bond. Parents saw time spent with their children early in life as critical to their childrens' healthy development. This strong belief in the benefits of leaves for children, more than any other single specific factor, explained the overwhelmingly positive response given to the leaves in each country. An abstract interest in future generations may underlie this concern, but it was the desire to see children develop in healthy ways that excited the people in each country who spoke of the importance of infant care leaves. Although the enormous benefit of parental time spent with newborns may be as much a cultural belief as an empirically documented fact, it clearly accounts for the overwhelming support parents give to leaves.

In Sweden, a developmental psychologist cited the "prevailing norm" that it is somewhat irresponsible for parents to leave their children in care for *any* length of time in the first three months after birth. Placing a child in a day-care center after the first six weeks of care by a mother was "almost enough to bring a visit from a social worker to the child," according to Swedish psychologist Philip Hwang (personal communication, May 1983). Another Swedish psychologist who had interviewed fifty parents of young children noted that most hesitated to leave their children with *any* other person, grandparents included, during the child's first three months of life (A. Broberg, personal communication, May 1983). Still another social scientist, with extensive exposure to childrearing practices in both the United States and Germany, noted that Germany has a much stronger cultural value against leaving young children in the care of strangers than does the United States (G. Erler, personal communication, June 1983).

The strongest indication of beliefs about the importance of parental care for young infants probably remains the decision to take available leaves. An overwhelming majority of parents in all three countries choose to use the leaves, often including even the unpaid or minimally paid sections. Usage figures are over 95% in France, Sweden, and the Federal Republic of Germany. Although much of the emphasis of this study has been on the absence of strong negative effects of the leaves, this absence may be best viewed as representing the strong positive support given the leaves in all three countries. This support was strong enough that almost all interviewees had difficulty imagining a situation in which the leaves were not offered to parents of newborns.

These policies do not, however, seem to reflect a general cultural preference in Europe for more extensive parent-child contact than in the U.S. In Sweden, a strong norm mentioned by three different interviewees was that children should be put into situations where they are exposed to other children from about their first year of life onward. An emphasis on early parent-child contact did not imply a rejection of group care—only a belief that each has its proper time and place. In France, the social system is consciously designed to permit parents (primarily women) to work either at home or in the labor force. This *freedom of choice* policy has the effect of making roles at both work and home possible for parents. Yet, the leaves provide a clear bias in favor of home roles for women in the child's first year of life. It is possible that these beliefs about infant care are mainly rationalizations for existing situations (in which parental leaves exist for the first six months and day care is the major alternative thereafter). Even in this case, however, these beliefs are part of an emphasis which provides room to integrate the demands that work and family life place upon new parents.

IMPLICATIONS FOR UNITED STATES POLICIES

Clearly, the sociocultural norms in Sweden, West Germany, and France differ from those in the United States in ways which would make it impossible to transfer those countries' leave policies directly to the United States. The somewhat surprising ease with which infant-care-leave policies are implemented in Germany, France, and Sweden partly reflects the general feasibility of such leaves, but it also reflects the underlying societal support for helping parents cope with the demands of work and family life. Employer willingness to support leave policies, for example, appears related to both the minimal demands that leaves place on them and their recognition of the contribution that working parents make to society. Yet, although social norms related to leaves differ sharply from those in the United States, there are striking parallels between some of the demographic factors which presaged support for leaves in European societies in the past seventy years and demographic conditions in the United States today.

Examination of trends in fertility rates in Europe and the United States provides a major source of parallels. As mentioned, the sense of collective societal responsibility for childrearing in the countries visited appears partly attributable to low fertility rates in those countries. Over the past forty years, European countries have experienced sometimes unprecedented lows in fertility rates in contrast to the United States, which experienced a "baby boom" in this period. This contrast is important both in explaining differences in infant-care-leave policies and in its implications for future U.S. policies under changing demographic conditions.

This contrast strongly suggests that the U.S. "failure" to develop extensive leave policies to support parents and children may simply reflect the presence of a different set of societal conditions—one in which many parents did find children to be an affordable luxuryeven without a great deal of additional societal support. A society may be able to afford to pay less collective attention to its children when sufficient numbers of individual parents find that the pleasures and rewards of childrearing outweigh the costs.[8] Eloquent arguments have been made in support of the collective societal interest in children, but these arguments may not be nearly as persuasive as the sense of urgency created when large numbers of parents in a society stop choosing to have children. When doubts are raised about whether the next generation will be large enough to

8. Obviously, not all Americans found childrearing equally easy, and children of the poor often have to live in terrible conditions. However, this seems to reflect less an attitude toward children than toward poverty; poor adults certainly appeared to fare no better than children.

carry out the tasks that are critical in a society, the collective interest in children forces its way onto the social agenda. These doubts have been a prominent part of debates in Germany, France, and Sweden but, until recently, they could be easily dismissed in the United States.

Sophisticated demographic and historical analyses have shown that in Germany, France, Sweden, and most of the rest of Western Europe, major declines in fertility began approximately a century ago, and low points were typically reached in the 1930s and 1940s (van de Walle and Knodel 1980). It was during this period that the foundations of current infant care leave policies were established in the countries in this study. These policies were established along with other more directly pronatalist policies. Since that time, the leave policies have come to be viewed as critical to supporting the next generation although they have never been shown to increase fertility rates directly. In the 1950s, low fertility rates (combined with the devastation of World War II) resulted in labor shortages in a number of European countries. Sweden and France began to use women to fill vacancies in the labor force, and their leave policies helped make this move possible without abandoning the society's youth. Germany consciously chose to use imported labor instead of women and now has a significantly less generous infant care leave than either Sweden or France (Kamerman and Kahn 1981).

All of this must be contrasted with situation in the United States. Here, quite different trends in fertility existed through the 1930s and early 1940s, culminating in the baby boom of the 1950s. If anything, concern about overpopulation following the baby boom suggested the need to discourage childbearing rather than provide additional supports. While the United States government provided little general support to children, the United States populace did a quite successful job of raising a more than adequately large new generation. Examination of these demographic trends in European and American cultures over the past thirty years strongly suggests that the U.S. "lack of support" for families is somewhat of a misnomer. The United States may not have *collectively* provided for its children, but that was in part because American parents were individually in a position to provide almost unprecedented levels of such support.

A major implication of the above analysis is that use of leaves may be a critical policy tool for the United States as it enters a generation that all evidence suggests is reversing previous trends in fertility. While the entry into childbearing years of an unusually large cohort of women (as a result of the baby boom) masks it, in the past ten years, the United States has had the lowest fertility rate it has ever experienced (Gupta 1985). The Census Bureau, using moderate assumptions based on cur-

Table 15.2.   Ratio of Persons Aged 18 to 64 to Those
over 65 in the United States, 1950–2030

Year	Ratio
1950	7.5 to 1
1960	6.0 to 1
1970	5.7 to 1
1980	5.4 to 1
1990	4.9 to 1
2000	4.7 to 1
2010	4.6 to 1
2020	3.5 to 1
2030	2.7 to 1

Source: Calculated from Spencer, 1984.

rent fertility data, is currently predicting that women in the United States will bear an average of only 1.9 children in their lifetimes (Spencer 1984). At this rate, the next generation would be 5% *smaller* than the current generation, excluding effects of immigration. For a society which has become accustomed to large growth rates in population, the effects of this change may be even more dramatic and unsettling than they were in Europe.

The recent social security and Medicare funding crises are two portents of this coming change. In table 15.1 data are presented on the past and projected composition of the United States population. Thirty-five years ago there were 7.5 persons of working age for every person over the age of sixty-five, making the task of producing enough goods to support an elderly population relatively bearable. Currently, this ratio is down to about five to 1, and effects have been felt in social security tax increases and revisions in benefit plans. By the time the current generation of new twenty-year-old workers reaches sixty-five in 2030, this ratio is expected to drop an *additional* 50%. There will then be only 2.7 adults of working age to provide the goods and services needed to support each person over sixty-five (Spencer 1984). The bulge of the baby boom has created a lull which is temporarily masking the fact that our society is undergoing long-term changes that may eventually lead to a shrinking population. The bases for long-term changes in the composition of the U.S. population are being formed now, even though the effects will not be visible until these changes are solidly entrenched. The rapid decrease in birthrates following the baby boom may make these changes even more disruptive than would a longer period of gradually declining fertility rates.

If recent European history provides any lessons, they are that this

decline in fertility may be expected to lead to increased collective awareness and urgency around the question of who will bear and raise the
next generation of Americans. Clearly, American society needs to find
ways of compensating for factors that have made children more difficult
to raise. Infant-care-leave policies appear to be a valuable tool in this
regard. Although they do not encourage people to have more children,
they do address an increasingly urgent collective interest in seeing that
the children we do have are raised well. As a shrinking population of
children will eventually be called upon to support a growing population
of elderly, helping families raise them to become productive adults
should take on an increasingly higher priority. Infant-care-leave policies
may be one powerful tool to use in alleviating strains felt by increasing
numbers of parents as they try to juggle work and family roles.

The recent trends of female movement into the labor force have
added complexity to an already difficult problem. We are increasingly
moving toward the *full employment society* described by a Swedish demog-
rapher and business consultant (Arvedson 1981). Ours is becoming a
society in which all adult members are expected to be in the labor force;
social isolation is a major risk for the non-employed. The issue in such
a society then becomes: Who will take care of the children? Currently,
only two real options exist in the United States. Either parents can leave
the labor force and lose their connection to a significant part of our
society, or they can pay others to care for their children. In the case of
very young infants, paying others to provide care may often cost more
and be less effective than a parent's quitting work and remaining home
to provide such care. The third option, added by parental leaves, is that
parents may both care for their children directly and retain a stable
connection to the workplace.

Low fertility rates and strained family environments are by no means
separate issues. The decline in American fertility rates may in part indicate the increasing strain felt by parents in handling dual work and
family roles. This strain, which appears to be quite substantial (Hoffman
1982), poses a significant threat to the future well-being of the smaller
numbers of children currently being born. Yet, the pressures of trying
to integrate work and family life appear increasingly inevitable; parents
know they must avoid the even greater strains of social isolation and
poverty experienced by the unemployed in a full employment society.

Leaves for infant care are certainly not a panacea, but they do provide
a powerful tool for alleviating the strain of managing work and family
life during one of the most difficult stages of a family's development.
Universally in the three countries studied, infant care leaves were seen
as significantly improving family life. All of the evidence about social
effects of infant care leaves—from employer acceptance to their positive

impact on women's equality—suggests that leaves *could* work in the United States. Evidence of the direct benefit to families and children of the leaves argues strongly that some type of infant care leave *should* be quite seriously considered in this country.

REFERENCES

Arvedson, L. 1981. *Mot öklat Flexliv*. Stockholm: SNS.

Bronfenbrenner, U., and Crouter, A. 1982. Work and family time and space. S. Kamerman and C. D. Hayes, eds. *Families That Work*. Washington, D.C.: National Academy Press.

Fallenius, A. 1981. *Fanvaron i arbetet amfattning utveckling och Kostnader utredningsyppdrag*. Ricksrevision sverket Berggen, G.P.

Femme Pratique. 1983. 234(July):13–15 (Paris, France).

French Committee on Female Work (Comité du Travail Feminin). 1979. *Actualités du Travail des Femmes*, no. 22. Paris, France: Ministere du Travail et de la Participation.

Gamble, T., and Zigler, E. 1986. Effects of infant day care: Another look at the evidence. *American Journal of Orthopsychiatry* 56(1):26–42.

German *Bundestag* (Deutscher Bundestag). 1981. 9. Wahlperiode *Unterrichtung durch die Bundesregierung, Berich Über den Mutterschaftsurlaub*. (Drucksache 9/1210). Bonn, West Germany: Deutscher Bundestag.

German Ministry for Youth, Families, and Health (Bundesministerium Für Jugend, Familie and Gesundheit). 1982. *Sozialpolitische Umschau*. Bonn, West Germany: German Ministry for Youth.

German Youth Institute Family Policies Work Group (Deutsches Jugendinstitut AG Familienpolitik). 1982. Results of the European Study concerning maternity leave/parental leave/home care support measures in Finland, Sweden, Hungary, Austria, and German Federal Republic. Munich, West Germany: Deutsches Jugendinstitut.

Gupta, P. D. 1985. Future fertility of women by present age and parity: Analysis of American historical data 1917–1980. *Current Population Reports: Special Studies*, series P–23 (no. 142). Washington, D.C.: U.S. Government Printing Office.

Gustafsson, S. 1981. Male-Female Lifetime Earnings Differentials and Labor Force History. *Studies in Labor Market Behavior: Sweden and the U.S.* Proceedings of a Symposium at the Industrial Institute for Economic and Social Research Studies, Stockholm, Sweden, July 10–11, 1979. Stockholm, Sweden: Arbetslivscentrum (Swedish Center for Working Life).

Hoffman, L. 1982. Maternal Employment and the Young Child. Paper presented at the 1982 Minnesota Symposium on Child Psychology, Minnesota.

Kamerman, S., and Kahn, A. 1981. *Child Care, Family Benefits, and Working Parents: A Study in Comparative Policy*. New York: Columbia University Press.

Kamerman, S. 1980. *Maternity and Parental Benefits and Leaves: An International Review*. New York: Center for the Social Sciences Impact on Policy Series, Columbia University.

Kindlund, S. 1983. Director, Parental Leave Division, Swedish Ministry of Health and Social Affairs. Personal communication, May 1983.

Lamb, M., and Levine, J. 1983. The Swedish Parental Insurance Policy: An Experiment in Social Engineering. M. Lamb and A. Sagi, eds. *Fatherhood and Family policy*. Hillsdale, N.J.: Erlbaum.

Liljeström, R. 1978. Sweden. S. Kamerman and A. Kahn, eds. *Family Policy: Government and Families in Fourteen Countries*. New York: Columbia University Press.

Liljeström, R., Mellström, G., and Svensson, G. 1978. *Roles in Transition: Report of an investigation made for the Advisory Council on Equality Between Men and Women*. Stockholm, Sweden: Schmidts Boktryckeii, A.B.

Lueck, M., Orr A., and O'Connell, M. 1982. Trends in child care arrangements of working mothers. *Current Population Reports Special Studies*, series P–23 (no. 117). Washington, D.C.: U.S. Government Printing Office.

Masnick, G., and Bane, M. 1981. *The Nation's Families: 1960–1990*. Boston, Mass.: Auburn House.

Schramm, W. 1980. Accompanying Research in Family Policy—The German Pilot Project "Erziehungsgeld in Niedersachsen." J. Kutz, W. Speil, and J. Degner, eds. *Family Research and Family Policy—Pilot Projects Under Discussion*. International Colloquium on Family Research, February 27–29, 1980. Hannover, Federal Republic of Germany: Institut für Regionale Bildungsplanung—Arbeitsgruppe Standortforschung.

Smith, R. E. 1980. *The Subtle Revolution: Women at Work*. Washington, D.C.: Urban Institute.

Spencer, G. 1984. Projections of the population of the United States by age, sex and race: 1983 to 2080. *Current Population Reports: Population Estimates and Projections*, series P–25 (no. 952). Washington, D.C.: U.S. Government Printing Office.

Swedish Ministry of Finance. 1983. *The Swedish Budget 1983/4*. Stockholm, Sweden: Ministry of Finance.

Swedish Ministry of Statistics (Sverige Officielle Statistika Centrallbyran). 1982. *Statistiska Meddelanden*, Stockholm, Sweden: Sverige Officielle Statistika Centrallbyran.

Swedish Social Ministry (SOU). 1982. *Enklare Föräldraförsäkring*. Stockholm, Sweden: Betänkande av föräldraförsäkringsutredningnen, 1982.

van de Walle, E., and Knodel, J. 1980. *Europe's Fertility Transition: New Evidence and Lessons for Today's Developing World*. Population Bulletin 6(34). Washington, D.C.: Population Reference Bureau.

SIXTEEN

Uncertain Harvest: Maternity Leave Policies in Developing Nations

PEGGY PIZZO

When comparing U.S. social policies that benefit children and their parents with those of other nations, most analysts are inclined to look toward Europe. As the twenty-first century nears, however, it is especially important in the study of social policy to look elsewhere as well, particularly toward the developing nations.[1] Fresh sources of ideas, ways of prioritizing some policies over others (amid sometimes massive demands for scarce economic resources), and a "bootstrap" hopeful orientation toward the future in developing nations with high economic growth—these argue in favor of close U.S. study of social policy in the developing world. Certain realities, however, obstruct such study: some Third World policies are almost impossible to assess accurately, given the erratic use of data collection instruments (for example, birth and/or death registration in some countries). Also impeding the usefulness of comparative policy analysis between the U.S. and the developing world are the large differences in both scale *and* type of health and social problems which beset our respective nations. A related impediment is the tendency for comfortable U.S. policy analysts to misperceive or ignore substantially different rationales for Third World social policies that spring in some countries more from the deep discomfort of widespread death, disability, and profound human want, than from, for example, Western discontent

1. I also recommend a more intensive look at Japan, with the caveat that, as a geographically small nation with a long prenineteenth-century history of closure to the outside world, an extraordinarily low poverty rate, and unique cultural origins, for its social policies toward families (for example, Japanese beliefs about filial piety), Japan may be a source of good approaches to policy, but that these may not "transplant" in American policy seedbeds.

with the failure of the workplace to adapt supportively to the needs of working women.

In this chapter, I examine developing nations' policies guaranteeing paid employment leave around the time of childbirth, and I then discuss the scope of such policies; their historical origins; their cultural origins in deeply respected and sometimes contradictory themes and cultural images; their different rationales, given the profound differences between the lives many women lead in the U.S. and the lives many women lead in the developing world. Finally, I suggest that while an *equity* or *equal rights* rationale is often put forward as the basis for guaranteed infant care leave, the risks to life experienced by so many women in the developing world push a *health* protection rationale ahead of the pursuit of equal rights in the workplace as the basis for (specifically) maternity leave. The implementation and impact of infant leave policies in the developing world are only briefly discussed due to the paucity of data. What we do know invites more in-depth exploration of how these laws actually do reach families in Third World nations. For example, about 40% of all women of reproductive age in Mexico are eligible for a complete package of maternity benefits through social insurance—including paid maternity leave. But survey figures like the example from Mexico are difficult to locate and even more difficult to analyze, given data collection problems in many countries. Thus the uncertain harvest of the numerous national Third World policies guaranteeing maternity leave is explicitly acknowledged by the author.

OVERVIEW

In contrast to the United States, national governments in eighty-one developing countries have mandated a minimum period of paid leave to be extended to employed women in the perinatal period (before and after childbirth). Paid leave ranging from thirty days in Tunisia to 126 days (eighteen weeks) in Cuba is legislated in developing nations in Africa, Asia, Latin America, and the Middle East. Typically, mandated maternity leave in the developing world is paid, either partially or wholly. Most of these laws have been adopted in the last thirty-five years. However, some were adopted as early as 1934 (for example, in Argentina and Cuba) [U.S. Department of Health and Human Services 1983]. This period of leave is widely termed maternity leave. Paternity leave is virtually unknown as a sociological phenomenon among employed parents in the developing world. Consequently, no Third World law or policy assures fathers a right to paid or unpaid leave in the perinatal period.

Legal protection for maternity leave in developing nations often includes language assuring *nursing breaks* during the new mother's workday to permit her to continue breastfeeding once she returns to work. These nursing breaks vary in time from fifteen minutes three times a day (for example, Dominican Republic) to two breaks of half an hour each during eighteen months following childbirth. In some countries, these nursing breaks are paid (for example, Algeria, Egypt, Costa Rica, Dominican Republic, Saudi Arabia).

Governments typically require the financing of paid maternity leave either (1) by employers; (2) through some form of social security; or (3) a combination of both. Each of these financing strategies has a different impact. In addition, nations with organized social security programs often have laws assuring health care during pregnancy and the perinatal period as part of insured maternity benefits.

When countries with desperately low-income economies finance paid infant leave it suggests either that there is extraordinary commitment to a widely-respected reason for such leave, or that such leave is officially promoted but unofficially ignored. Little is known about the actual implementation of infant-care-leave policies. It may be that the costs of such policies are prohibitive of vigorous implementation. On the other hand, in the Third World, four out of every ten women are economically active (compared to five out of ten in the United States). Precisely that same widespread economic desperation in some countries and consequent maternal participation in the labor force may mean that some paid leave before and after childbirth is considered a necessity.

The most remarkable aspect of legally-protected maternity leave in the developing world, from the perspective of analyzing such social policies in the United States, is that, in spite of staggering burdens caused by economic distress, laws assuring working women of the right to maternity leave have been adopted in so many of these nations. The average GNP per capita in the United States is more than seventeen-and-one-half times the average GNP per capita in the developing nations as a whole, and almost fifty-three times the average GNP per capita in the thirty-four low-income developing nations, principally Africa and Asia (World Development Report [Table 1] 1984). The external public debt of low-income economies as a whole is close to one-fifth of the GNP of these economies (World Development Report [Table 14] 1984).

HISTORICAL ORIGINS OF INFANT LEAVE POLICIES IN DEVELOPING NATIONS

The developing nations adopted mandated infant leave as policy after the International Labour Organization (ILO) took the public stance in 1919 that national policies assuring *maternity protection* in the workplace were requisite to social justice. The International Labour Organization was founded in 1919 in order to improve internationally the horrible working conditions that prevailed in industry during the nineteenth and early twentieth centuries. The labor standards set by ILO, once ratified by member states, are *intended* to create *binding obligations* to put these standards into effect. A tripartite organization, with worker and employer representatives involved on an equal basis with governments, the ILO is one of the first of the specialized agencies (agencies addressing specific human needs, as, for example, the World Health Organization) to be associated with the United Nations. In 1984, 150 countries belonged to the International Labour Organization.

One of the earliest ILO actions was the development of a Convention— or agreement for ratification by sovereign nations—on maternity protection. This convention, with its protection for working mothers, was first introduced as the International Labour Convention no. 32 of 1919, and ironically enough, it was adopted at a general conference of the ILO convened by the United States of America. The United States is the only industrialized nation which never ratified the resulting convention on maternity protection (Kamerman et al. 1983).

The 1919 Convention advocated that women be (1) *prohibited* from working during the six weeks after childbirth; (2) *entitled* to stop work six weeks prior to childbirth; and (3) *paid*, during these absences, "benefits sufficient for the full and healthy maintenance of herself and her child . . . and as an additional benefit [she] shall be entitled to free attendance by a doctor or certified midwife" (International Labour Organization, 1919). This convention also provided for two nursing breaks of half-an-hour each during working hours for breastfeeding mothers; and it specified prohibitions against the dismissal of women during maternity leave or during pregnancy-related illness, with such absences not to exceed a maximum period fixed by each country.

In 1952, this Convention was revised at a general conference of the ILO convened at Geneva by the Governing Body of the International Labour Office. The resulting Convention on Maternity Protection (no. 103) provides the framework for many of the national policies and laws developed since then. This is particularly true in Africa and Asia, since the post-World War II independence movements, which resulted in repudiation of colonial rule and the establishment of sovereign nations, required the development of new indigenous constitutions and laws. In Latin America, where independence occurred earlier, eight countries ratified the 1919 Convention on Maternity Protection before the 1952 revision.

The colonial laws imposed in the developing countries of Africa and Asia in their preindependence periods reflected the prevailing Western ideology that women belonged at home. In Ghana, for example, the colonial administration decided in 1921 that women employees who married should resign; in 1936 this policy was "liberalized" to permit married women to maintain their jobs, but resignation was mandatory if the married women became pregnant (Date-Bah).

In the area of maternity protection, at least, the developing nations seem to have looked to the ILO 1952 Convention in particular as a resource for acceptable policies. Ghana, for example, has adopted the twelve-week maternity leave (that is, six weeks before and six weeks after childbirth) that the ILO standards specify. Not all the provisions of this Convention were deemed feasible. Still, many nations adopted the basic protections and then exempted a variety of occupations from compliance.

The 1952 Convention on Maternity Protection still retains six weeks of compulsory leave after childbirth, but the remainder of the twelve weeks of leave was recommended for either the period prior to confinement or following the end of the compulsory, postnatal leave "as may be prescribed by national laws or regulations." This revision also stipulated that cash benefits during maternity leave should be at least two-thirds of the woman's previous earnings, but also that employers should not be *individually liable* for the cost of benefits. Employers could decide to provide such benefits; but they were not required to do so. This provision was emphasized in 1952 because experience had shown that individual *employer* liability for maternity benefits resulted in employment discrimination against women (ILO 1952). It was also provided that individual governments could exempt certain categories of occupations: agriculture, private domestic work, women wage earners working at home, ocean transportation, or "certain categories of non-industrial occupations" (Article 7).

These exceptions and the specific exemptions for individual employer liability had significant impact for developing nations in their formulations of maternity leave legislation after 1952. In many countries all these exceptions were adopted, making infant care leave a privilege for government and large industry employees—and particularly for those eligible for social insurance. The predominant financing mechanism in Latin America became either social security or a blend of employer and social insurance contributions. In Asia and Africa, however, employer-required financing is still found in many countries, thus raising many questions about the practicality of mandated maternity benefits.

Presumably, those countries that have achieved independence and formulated their own laws in the last decade have had available a deep degree of historical insight and could therefore adopt a narrower range of benefits, or a different financing mechanism when the provisions of the 1952 Convention proved entirely impractical, and, in fact, this appears to be the case. Angola, whose first labor code since independence was implemented in 1981, provides only ninety-days maternity leave. However, Angola's policy also entitles single and married women workers with family responsibilities to one day's leave with pay per month, for fulfillment of those responsibilities (United Nations Fund for Population Activity 1982; ILO 1983). The countries of Grenada and Dominica, on the other hand, have adopted leaves of twelve weeks; Saint Lucia, thirteen weeks (U.S. Dept. of Health and Human Services 1984). Undoubtedly, of course, the economic and political philosophy, as well as the geographic and/or population size of the country, influences policymakers' perceptions of feasibility in all social policy, including maternity benefits.

CULTURAL ORIGINS: THE PLIGHT OF THE WORKING MOTHER

The ILO standards for infant care leave and the concept of maternity protection derived from the progressive reform movements that swept Europe and the U.S. in the latter half of the nineteenth century and which inspired women in the U.S. during the Progressive Era to campaign both for the rights of women to gainful employment and for protection against the horrible conditions of factories and other industries. In nineteenth-century Europe and in the United States, impoverished, abandoned, or widowed women had to work twelve- to fourteen-hour days, sometimes at heavy labor, amid conditions injurious to any human being's health, and certainly not conducive to the high level of health needed to emerge unimpaired from the biological demands of pregnancy. Unable at first to remedy these oppressive working conditions for all employees (as was later accomplished in the U.S. for the majority of factory and other workers through collective bargaining and protective labor legislation), social reformers pioneered the concept that at least women—and particularly mothers—should be spared the assaults to health which prevailed in the urban workplace.

The advocates of social policy protecting working mothers were participants in the settlement house and other movements designed to alleviate the suffering of immigrant and other urban populations. In their advocacy for women, they shrewdly built on the Edwardian ideals of a "pure" womanhood, sanctified by a life-giving, nurturing identity. Acceptance of these ideals in turn emphasized the pervasive cultural image of the ethereal feminine woman who redeemed the more brutal male. Women deserved protection, both because female life-giving functions mattered to men who sought healthy children and because women's redemptive spiritual qualities deserved the respect of males who through love for pure women narrowly escaped their own more "animal-like" instincts.

The plight of the working mother during this period of Western history was widely viewed as a tragedy visited upon women whose husbands either died or gave in to their "animal" instincts by drunkenness or desertion in order to pursue a sexually promiscuous life. These women were depicted as among the most deserving of all the poor. In the United States a raft of social legislation was enacted, including protections against the abuses of the industrial workplace; mothers' pensions (providing financial support to widowed or abandoned mothers so they could avoid the workplace and stay at home to raise their children); foster-care reforms (making it more difficult for well-heeled child advocates, prejudiced against "dirty tenement dwellers," to take away children from their employed mothers on the grounds of alleged child neglect). These movements to protect the vulnerable impoverished mother, coupled with a cultural wave described by one historian as "the ideology of educated motherhood"—a belief in the enormous power of educated mothers to reform the world by raising their children in refined ways—inspired both a cultural aversion to the employment of working mothers and a desire to enact legislation and social policy to protect mothers who could not be kept out of the workplace. These historical streams ran parallel to the movement for female equality inspired by the suffragettes, who sought maternity leave as one way to assure women's rights to be precisely in that workplace the doors of which others strove to close to mothers (Rothman 1978).

Many of the same cultural themes appear today in the societies of Latin America, Asia, and Africa, where urban workplaces can resemble or surpass the worst of the dangerous sweatshops that inspired the reforms of the Progressive Era. In these cultures, there is also veneration for the life-giving role of women, coupled with some fear of that power. So, too, the "angel" wife/mother, pure in all respects, is viewed as deserving protection against brutalization because she in innocent, but also because she inspires men to reject their more brutal "macho" forces. She purifies male culture, a function which must be preserved. The emphasis on female purity, for example, in many societies in the developing world rivals or exceeds that of the Edwardian era in industrialized nations. Over the last several decades, however, in Mexico, Brazil, Kenya, Bangladesh, Sri Lanka, Egypt, and other African, Asian, and Middle Eastern nations, women's self-help or women's rights organizations have emerged, sometimes on a national scale, to challenge the particular injustices toward women that are most unacceptable to large numbers of women in those societies. Women undertake these self-help efforts for a variety of goals, ranging from demands for adequate health care for women and children; to repudiation of the mutilating practice of female circumcision; to accomplishment of changes in law and policy that guarantee them the right to prevent unwanted pregnancy; to realization of equal opportunities in schools at the primary, secondary, and higher education levels.

As these movements for greater quality grow, the contradiction between the cultural image of the self-reliant, income-generating woman and that of the vulnerable (and therefore dependent) frequently pregnant and/or lactating woman will also grow. But in the developing world, as long as life experiences surrounding pregnancy are fraught with so much risk, the tension between these contradictory cultural themes will tilt policies concerning working mothers toward protection rather than toward assurance of equal status with men.

BACKGROUND: LIVES OF WOMEN IN THE DEVELOPING WORLD

Generalizations about human beings living in the 165 "geopolitical entities" that comprise the developing world need to be restrained. Some facts, however, do form a backdrop for understanding the lives that many (certainly not all) women live in parts of the developing world. Consider the following:

- Most women in the United States choose when and how often they will undertake pregnancy and childbirth. Of the fifty-four million women of childbearing age in the U.S., fifty-four percent practice some form of contraception. The average woman bears one or two children (Bachrach, 1982).
- Almost all women in the United States survive childbirth and pregnancy-related risks. Only about one in ten-thousand women die from childbirth now (U.S. Department of Health and Human Services 1981). About 1.4 million females a year choose to terminate a pregnancy; assuming all abortion-related deaths are reported, out of the 1.4 million women who terminate pregnancy each year, only nine will die during or after the procedure.
- Most women in the United States can protect their infants from death. Between ten and eleven in one-thousand infants in this country die in the first year of life—about one in one hundred. Black and other non-white women, however, experience the death of their babies at a rate almost twice that of the national average.
- For most American women, breastfeeding is a desirable activity but is not one which safeguards the baby from death. Many women in our country believe that breastfeeding promotes a close mother-child bond and affords some immunities for a few months against both

infectious illness and allergies. More than 60% of all mothers in the United States breastfeed their young infants, but this prevalence rate falls considerably by the time the infant is five or six months old.

- Most American women can protect their young children from death or serious illness. About seven in ten-thousand children aged one to four die each year. Accidents are the most common cause of death (U.S. Department of Health and Human Services, 1981). Serious illnesses, with the risk of death or permanent impairment are relatively rare, particularly among middle-class American children.

- In the United States more than one of every two women work outside their homes, almost two-thirds of them in white-collar jobs not ordinarily considered dangerous to physical health. Most of the remaining one-third are working at either blue-collar or "pink-collar" (service) jobs (U.S. Dept. of Labor 1983).

In contrast, in the developing world, the lives of many women are dominated by risk. Even with the many commendable health improvements, women are haunted by the specter of death—either theirs (during pregnancy or childbirth) or the death of their babies. Their lives as young women are pervaded by frequent pregnancies whose occurrence seem unpreventable.

- In developing nations, for example, the average women has four or five children. In some countries (Kenya, Syria, Bolivia, or Honduras, for example), the average woman has as many as seven or eight children. The number of pregnancies per average woman is not accurately calculable, but frequently exceeds the number of live births (Population Reference Bureau 1984).

- Only 20% of women in the developing world now use contraception to time or prevent pregnancies. Termination of unwanted pregnancy is common—and fraught with risk. About 20 million abortions per year take place in the developing world, typically in defiance of laws which forbid abortion. Clandestine abortion is a leading cause of death in some developing nations; in some countries efforts to save the lives of these women require the use of between 50% and 60% of the maternity ward beds in typical hospitals.

- For those who carry their pregnancies to term, the risk of death during or after childbirth is thirty to fifty times greater than that experienced by women in the United States (Johns Hopkins University Population Information Program 1984). While only one North American woman in ten thousand will die during or after childbirth, that rate rises to between thirty and fifty in ten thousand in much of the developing world. In some African or Asian countries, as many as one hundred in ten thousand (or one in one hundred) women die. Excluding Latin

America, in Africa and Asia alone about half a million women each year die from "maternal causes," leaving behind an estimated one million motherless children.

- A Third World woman safely delivered of a child, however, knows there is a one in ten chance that her baby will die before its first birthday; in parts of Africa and Asia those odds narrow to one of every five babies born (Population Reference Bureau 1984). In contrast, U.S. women know there is about one chance in one hundred of an infant's death; for Black women, a one in fifty chance. This contrast is one reason why breastfeeding is almost universal in Africa and parts of Asia for a postnatal period ranging from three to thirty-three months. Breastfeeding helps Third World women safeguard their children from death; it helps ward off the diarrheal diseases which in 1980 claimed 4.6 million children under age five (Johns Hopkins University Population Information Program 1984). For millions of poor or rural women, breastfeeding during the infant's first vulnerable months of life is not simply desirable—it is a vital necessity. Complete, prolonged breastfeeding also *helps* prevent another pregnancy, protecting both mothers and infants from the high mortality that prevails when pregnancies are too closely spaced.
- In the developing world, those infants who survive the first year of life will continue to be at great risk during their preschool years. In some parts of Africa, one in twenty children aged one to four die (Johns Hopkins University Population Information Program 1984). Even in developing nations with less loss of life among young children, children aged one to four die at tragic rates, ranging between one in fifty and one in one hundred (Johns Hopkins University Population Information Program 1984). This widespread risk of child death contrasts starkly with the U.S. rate of seven in ten thousand children aged one to four.
- Millions of women struggling to get through pregnancies, childbirth, and early childrearing without loss of life do so with sparse knowledge. Folklore about ways to avoid maternal or infant illness or death is centuries old, transmitted through many generations, unchanged by knowledge of modern, life-saving, medical breakthroughs. Women who are not literate may never know any other ways than those practiced hundreds of years ago by their female kith and kin. More than half of the women in developing nations can neither read nor write. In some countries this rate rises to 80%—four out of every five women (Population Reference Bureau 1982). Less than half the girls of primary school age are actually enrolled in school (United Nations Childrens Fund 1982, 1983). In the United States, women empower themselves with knowledge that transcends limited personal experi-

ences. In the developing world many women live, work, marry, bear children, and care for their families knowing almost the same fund of information about life's most basic processes (gestation, birth, lactation) as their mothers, grandmothers, and greatgrandmothers.[2]

In spite of the many maternity-related risks, however, women in the developing nations work outside their homes in large numbers, typically in low-paying domestic services or in manufacturing. More than 40% of women aged fifteen to sixty-four work; the figure drops to 28% when China is excluded (Population Reference Bureau 1981; ILO 1979). Women workers are also heavily concentrated in agricultural jobs. In parts of Africa up to 90% of women are in agricultural work. This proportion declines in Latin America to a level of 15% or less of all working women. Overall, a remarkable aspect of female income-generating activities in developing nations is just how physically demanding those activities are. The high mortality risks to which women are exposed coupled with the physically arduous nature of their income-generating activities undoubtedly influence the rationales explicitly and implicitly stated in the adoption of formal support for infant leave policies.

RATIONALES FOR INFANT LEAVE IN THE DEVELOPING NATIONS

Two profoundly different life experiences of young womanhood, one experienced by many (not all) women in developing nations and one experienced by many (not all) women in the United States, result in different rationales for policies like maternity leave. In the U.S. private sector, guarantees for paid maternity leave have been attributed to action by women who pursue social equality in the workplace as well as opportunities for economic security for themselves and their families. Protection against life-threatening risks for mother and child—or even against biological health risks of lesser measure—are not often forwarded as policy rationales for parental leave in the United States. Perhaps the support of the populace which seeks to reverse the significantly increased health risks of low-income or medically fragile children (and their mothers) would be more strongly secured for the advancement of infant care leave policies if the health rationale for such policies were more fully developed and communicated.

Rationales for guaranteed infant leave in the developing world reflect a unifying theme of *basic income security*. Almost all developing nations recognize that some women absolutely must generate income for them-

2. "Almost the same fund of information" because the growing ubiquitousness of radio, and in urban centers of television, provides opportunities for acquiring large amounts of wholly new information—even if not a single pamphlet or book has ever been read.

selves and their families, and that this need should prevail over unfair disruptions of productive economic activity by employers indifferent to the demands of the perinatal period. But the principal rationales also reflect two sometimes contradictory themes: *equity* (all working mothers and fathers are entitled to infant leave as a fundamental right, in order to guarantee that working women in particular will not be penalized in bearing or adopting children) and *protection* (all nations should grant infant leave as a benefit, to help mothers and their babies at a particularly vulnerable moment in life).

The protective rationale for benefits like infant care leave emphasizes women's frailty and can result in the relegation of women generally to a secondary status in the labor force, consequent diminution of earning power, and thus entrapment in a perpetuated state of needing protection from men. When laws assuring women certain benefits (freedom from being obliged to take night work) are compulsory (no women *may* work night shifts, even if some women wish to) the rationale for those laws— no matter what rhetoric is used—is protective. In the case of maternity leave in developing nations, the ILO stance that women should be prohibited from work for six weeks after childbirth emphasizes the highly protective rationale for the standards promulgated by the ILO and, in turn, adopted by many developing nations.

Currently, the ILO emphasizes an equity rationale for mandated infant leave: 500-million women worldwide are in the labor force and should be assured equality of opportunity in the workplace. In gaining this equality, maternity "still represents a severe handicap" (ILO 1984). The ILO explains that its program for the advancement of women "has moved from the purely protective area to the much wider one of promoting equality."

So, too, in the last decade have developing nations articulated an equity rationale for maternity protection. In 1978, for example, three years after the International Year on Women, member states formally commented on the 1965 ILO Recommendation on Women with Family Responsibilities, which called for policies of nondiscrimination toward women trying to combine work and family. Nations as diverse as Bangladesh (one of the poorest developing nations, where very few women are in the labor force, and where in rural areas women are confined in their homes under the rule of purdah) and Mexico (one of the "middle-income" developing nations, where women comprise 30% of the work force) discussed maternity protection within the overall context of promoting equality and prohibiting discrimination in the workplace. The necessity of special safeguards for pregnant women and new mothers, however, asserts itself even in these statements about the equality of women. The report to the ILO from El Salvador describes the relevant provisions of its 1962 Constitution: "The family, as the fundamental unit of society, must be specifically protected by the state, which will make the laws and regulations necessary for its promotion and for the protection and assistance of mothers and children" (ILO 1967). While all workers should be afforded protection by law, "working mothers," comments the Ecuador report, "are to be especially protected." Ecuador's comments quote from the Constitution of the State: "The State shall protect the family, and the institutions of marriage and motherhood" (p. 8). Uruguay's comments are quite explicit. Extensive legislation in Uruguay on protection of the rights of women "was inspired not only by a desire to protect women as workers, but also to protect them in the fulfillment of other tasks imposed on them by society, especially those associated with family responsibilities" (p. 88). This tension between women as workers (nondiscrimination) and protecting women as mothers (special protection) is forthrightly articulated by Brazil's report: "There is no discrimination based on sex in Brazil, except for measures which afford special protection for working women" (p. 6). Therefore, legislation in Brazil "provides for genuine advantages for women with family responsibilities." These genuine advantages, the report notes, include paid maternity leave.

In the developing world, an equity rationale for infant leave is unlikely to become the single most powerful force. Change in male attitudes, more extensive participation in primary and secondary schools, wider opportunities for higher education and for employment in professional occupations and in nontraditional trades will promote changes that bring more women into economic self-reliance and enliven women's pursuit of equality in the Third World. But at the center of the paradoxical tension between rights of women workers and rights of mothers is the haunting statistic: one in ten babies born to Third World women will die before their first birthday. Many women will themselves die in childbirth or in trying to terminate an unwanted pregnancy.

In my judgment, a protective rationale for infant care leave can be associated with a less vigorous implementation of infant-care-leave policies than an equity rationale (unless organized political activity insists on such protections, which may occur as part of national campaigns to promote breastfeeding, for example). An equity rationale for infant care leave in the developing world is, however, unlikely to predominate while women are so vulnerable to loss of life—theirs or their infants'.

IMPLEMENTATION AND IMPACT

Data on implementation of infant leave in the developing world is scarce. It seems reasonable to assume that employer financing of such leave (for example, in Africa and parts of Asia) is not as vigorously implemented as financing through social insurance (in Latin America and parts of Asia) to which both employer and employee contribute, or to which only the employee contributes. Some employers set up a welfare fund to which all female employees contribute. Employer-only responsibility for financing is reported in almost every ILO publication as a cause of discrimination against women workers, though substantial evidence to support this statement is not furnished.

In situations where occupational exclusions have been adopted by developing nations, women have sometimes established self-employed women's associations, to which they contribute some sum, particularly after the pregnancy is well established and is likely to continue. This contribution entitles them to some benefits, including cash benefits in the perinatal period.

Some implementation (with beneficial impact) of infant care leave policies, however, is evidenced by documentation of women's campaigns to *expand* the period of leave in some countries. Yet, intensive analysis of implementation of infant-care-leave policies in the developing world is needed. Actual use of guaranteed leave in Latin America, where maternity benefit laws have a longer history, social insurance systems are well established, and maternity leave is financed partially or wholly by social insurance, would be particularly valuable to study.

Also needed is an intensive analysis of the impact of such policies on (1) activities related to reduced maternity and child mortality and morbidity risks (for example, the use of breastfeeding, immunizations and family planning, emerging patterns of family size and spacing between births); and (2) policies designed to advance the educational, economic, and social equality of women with men in the developing world. Thus will the harvest of these policies—actual rather than hoped-for consequences—become more certain knowledge to those of us who seek their implications for the formation of a sound policy for the United States.

REFERENCES

Bachrach, J. 1982. Use of contraceptives in the United States. *National Center for Health Statistics Advance Data No.* 102. Washington, D.C.: Government Printing Office.

Date-Bah, E. n.d. Sex inequality in an African urban labour market: The case of Accra-Tema. *Population and Labour Policies Programme Working Paper No. 122.* Geneva: ILO.

International Labour Organization. 1919. *Convention Concerning the Employment of Women Before and After Childbirth.* Geneva: ILO.

International Labour Organization. 1952. *Revision of the Maternity Protection Convention 1919.* Geneva: ILO.

International Labour Organization. 1965. *Recommendation of Women with Family Responsibilities.* Geneva: ILO.

International Labour Organization. 1967. *Employment of Women with Family Responsibilities. Summary of Reports on Recommendation No. 123.* Geneva: ILO.

International Labour Organization: 1970. *Conditions of Work, Vocational Training, and Employment of Women: Eleventh Conference of American States, 1970.* Geneva: ILO.

International Labour Organization. 1983. *Women at work 1982–83.* Geneva: ILO.

International Labour Organization. 1984. Protection of Working mothers: an ILO global survey 1964–1984. *Women at Work,* No. 2, pp. 55–59.

Johns Hopkins University Population Information Program. 1984. *Healthier Mothers and Children Through Family Planning.* Baltimore, Maryland: Johns Hopkins University Population Information Program.

Kamerman, S. B., Kahn, A. J., and Kingston, P. 1983. *Maternity Policies and Working Women.* New York: Columbia Univerity Press.

Population Reference Bureau. 1981. *Data Sheet: Fertility and the Status of Women.* Washington, D.C.: Population Reference Bureau.

Population Reference Bureau. 1982. *World's Children Data Sheet 1982.* Washington, D.C.: Population Reference Bureau 1982.

Population Reference Bureau. 1984. *World Population Data Sheet 1984.* Washington, D.C.: Population Reference Bureau.

Rothman, Sheila. 1978. *Woman's Proper Place: A History of Changing Ideals and Practices, 1870 to the Present.* New York: Basic Books.

United Nations Children's Fund. 1982. *State of the World's Children 1982.* New York: United Nations Children's Fund.

United Nations Children's Fund. 1983. *State of the World's Children 1983.* New York: United Nations Children's Fund.

United States Department of Health and Human Services. 1981. *Better Health for Our Children: A National Strategy.* The report of the select panel for the promotion of child health to the U.S. Congress and the Secretary of Health and Human Services, vol. 3. Washington, D.C.: Government Printing Office.

United States Department of Health and Human Services. 1984. *Social Security Programs Throughout the World—1983.* Washington, D.C.: Government Printing Office.

United States Department of Labor. 1983. *Handbook on Women Workers.* Washington, D.C.: Government Printing Office.

United Nations Fund for Population Activity. 1982. *Annual Review of Population Law 1982.* New York: UNFPA.

The World Bank. 1984. *The World Development Report 1984.* Washington, D.C.: The World Bank.

PART VI

Parental Leave
Policy Options

SEVENTEEN

The Legal Background of a Parental Leave Policy and Its Implications

MARY PICCIRILLO

One of the most important prerequisites to an infant-care-leave policy is a discussion of the existing law and the degree to which such law supports—or does not support—a comprehensive infant-care policy. The basis for this discussion is twofold: existing law not only provides a foundation for creating and enacting a national leave, but it also reveals the degree to which the law recognizes the need for such a leave and delineates the parameters of a legally permissible leave policy. The types of parenting needs affected by employment leave policies must be identified in order to determine the extent to which the law currently provides adequate protection for such needs.

Current law has emphasized only the physical requirements of pregnancy, childbirth, recovery from childbirth, and related medical conditions and then only insofar as employers already give medical leaves to other employees. Further, current law gives virtually no recognition to parenting demands beyond producing the child. The distinction between leave for childbirth and leave for childbearing—the two components of a comprehensive infant-care-leave policy—is central to a discussion of existing law. Although there are some legal standards that all leave policies must meet, the degree to which lawmakers recognize the separate needs and requirements of effective parenting largely determines the kinds of leave protection that exist or should exist.

The legal context for discussion of the options for infant care leave is comprised of the federal and state law as it pertains to the following four types of leave:

1. leaves of absence from work taken by women by choice or when unable to work due to pregnancy, childbirth, recovery from childbirth, and related medical conditions;

2. leaves of absence from work taken by mothers to care for their new-born infants;
3. leaves of absence from work taken by fathers to care for their newborn infants; and,
4. leaves of absence from work taken by parents to care for a newly-adopted infant or older child.

The first type of leave—for pregnancy, childbirth, recovery from child-birth and related conditions (or maternity)—is now provided to varying extents under disability leave laws and employer policies. Most relevant law now addresses only this type of leave. The last three types of leave—for maternal and paternal care of infants and for parental care of adopted infants or children—can be grouped together under the terms infant care leave, childcare leave, childrearing, parental, or parenting leave. Very little law governs these last three categories. Under the terms of the proposed Family and Medical Leave Act (earlier known as the Parental and Disability Leave Act), job protection and continuation of benefits (but not income replacement) are provided for all four categories of leave (H.R. 2020, 99th Cong., 1st Sess. [1985] [Parental and Disability Leave Act]; see also S. 2278, 99th Cong., 2nd Session [1986]; H. R. 4300, 99th Cong., 2nd Sess. [1986]; S. 249, 100th Cong., 1st Sess. [1987]; H.R. 925, 100th Cong., 1st Sess. [1987] [Family and Medical Leave Act]). In addition, the proposed act provides legal protection for leaves taken to care for the serious health condition of a dependent child or parent.

Understanding current legal treatment of childbearing and childrearing leaves is complicated by three factors: first, the law treats differently each of the kinds of leave that comprise a comprehensive leave policy; second, because no federal law requires all employers in all states to provide pregnancy disability leave or leave to care for infants, there is great variation in leave policies from state to state and from employer to employer; and third, because, as a general premise the law is subject to interpretation, there may be disagreement about what it requires.

In general, existing law does not squarely or comprehensively address either pregnancy disability leave or leave to care for infants. Rather, it is an amalgam of state and federal statutory and case law derived from such diverse areas as constitutional law, state and federal laws on civil rights and employment discrimination, state temporary disability insurance law, contract law, labor law, family law, and so on. Furthermore, evaluation of existing law and options for change must taken into account that the intent of a law and its practical effect can be contradictory.

Whether established constitutionally, by legislation (laws/statutes enacted by state legislatures or Congress), by regulation (promulgated by state or federal government administrative agencies like DHHS), or by case law (judicial/court decisions), law is susceptible to varying interpretations. Just as in conversations between people, questions arise about what is meant by the words used. A main function of courts is to interpret and apply law. For example, appellate courts often disagree with lower courts' constructions of statutes, as do courts of different states, or Congress. In turn, state legislatures or Congress may not like what a court has decided that a law means and thus enact another law to change it. Therefore, a general caveat is in order: while I will present the prevailing interpretation of law and point out controveries, other interpretations no doubt exist, and the law is subject to change.

An overview reveals that existing law by itself is not fully responsible for the development and practice of current leave provisions. Some people believe that law should not govern the provision of leave and that the protection of the family and parenting is a purely private matter best left to each individual family's needs and to arrangement between employer and employee. Pointing to the comprehensive parental leave policies of other countries, others believe that the law in this country is sadly obsolete and ignores the growing conflict between the demands of business and needs of families. While my purpose has been to focus on the origin and development of pregnancy disability and, to a very limited extent, infant-care-leave policies in the United States through public-sector legal initiatives, it should be noted that apart from the initiatives discussed below, development of such policies has been left to employers and employees in the private sector (Gladstone, et al. 1985; Williams 1984–85). Paradoxically, both of the above viewpoints have proved beneficial, for the individual employees and employers of private businesses have had much to do with the formulation of existing parental leave practices.

Contract and labor law, for example, have provided tools for management and labor to negotiate benefit packages that vary in their provisions for pregnancy disability and infant care leave, as well as for job guarantees, income replacement, and protection of fringe benefits. And although a study of private employment policies developed pursuant to labor and contract law is beyond the scope of this chapter, collective bargaining agreements and employment contracts constitute a significant source of pregnancy-related leave (Gladstone, et al. 1985; Association of Junior Leagues 1985). In particular, a 1984 study of the unionization of fringe benefits suggests that while unionization increases the changes of day-care availability and job guarantee following pregnancy leave, it also seems to decrease slightly the chance for leave with pay (Freeman and Medoff 1984; Gladstone, et al. 1985). Furthermore, the practices of individual businesses vary widely, may not be comprehensive, and, in some instances, may be discriminative against some employees (Kamerman, et al. 1986).

The issue is the status of existing legal provisions for development of an infant-care-leave policy. In the following discussion, I will look more closely at the law governing the four basic components of a comprehensive leave policy, and how the law (and its varying interpretations) now seems to provide for them. These components are leave itself; job and seniority protection; income replacement; and continuation of benefits, including health insurance and pension protection (Kamerman, et al. 1986).

ORIGIN AND DEVELOPMENT OF LEAVE POLICIES IN THE UNITED STATES

Women and men have historically been treated very differently and accorded different rights under the law. These distinctions have derived principally from the notion that men's natural social role is productive labor, while women's is reproductive labor (Williams 1984–85; Finley 1986). For example, during the late eighteenth and early nineteenth century, a woman's legal identity was merged into that of her husband (Williams 1982b). For all practical purposes, during that period married women were legally nonexistent; they could not own property, enter into contracts, or keep any wages earned (Olsen 1983; Williams 1982b). Time and progress were to change this system: industrialization increasingly absorbed women into the working world, and states began to adopt married women's property acts to give women more rights (Olsen 1983). The midnineteenth century seemed to promise greater recognition of women as equals.

Out of these beginnings, however, came in many respects increasing discrimination against women instead of increasing equality. Through the rise of protective legislation, the law in practice constrained rather than enhanced women's movement in the world of employment (Williams, 1984–85). Protective legislation, apparently well intentioned, was purportedly designed to protect women's childbearing abilities and to accommodate their special maternal needs in the working world (Williams, 1984–85). Such legislation backfired. Believing that women needed special treatment because of their maternal status, lawmakers prohibited them from night work, excluded them from "hazardous" work, and established minimum hourly wages (which were often kept to the minimum) (Harris 1982; Kamerman, et al. 1986; Finley 1986; Rothman 1978). Similarly, a few states prohibited the employment of women during a period before and following the birth of a child (Williams 1984–85). The laws of many states made women who were pregnant or had recently given birth ineligible for unemployment insurance (Williams 1984–85).

Instead of being protective, such limitations tended to perpetuate inequality. A sex-segregated labor market relegated women to "women's work"—less desirable, lower paying jobs held by women because employers, reflecting socioeconomic views reinforced in legislation, considered that motherhood made women less desirable workers. Underlying protective labor legislation was the notion that women's proper and separate sphere was childbearing and motherhood (Finley 1986; Williams 1984–85). Motherhood became a liability in the world of work; therefore, women had only considerably restricted employment opportunities.

In 1867, the first state policy concerning maternity and employment was passed in Wisconsin, restricting the hours of women's paid employment (Kamerman, et al. 1986; Gladstone, et al. 1985). During the twentieth century, many states adopted similar protective labor legislation restricting women's employment rights (Kamerman, et al. 1986). The first federal action concerning maternity and employment was the case of *Muller v. Oregon*, decided in 1908 (208 U.S. 412 [1908]). In that case, the Supreme Court upheld state laws specifying maximum working hours for women, explaining that a woman's "physical structure and a proper discharge of her maternal functions . . . justify legislation to protect here . . . " (208 U.S. 412 [1908]). Just three years before, the Supreme Court had ruled that similar regulations for men violated their freedom to contract (*Id.* Lochner v. New York, 198 U.S. 45 [1905]; Gladstone, et al. 1985). With these "protective" laws, the foundations for special treatment of women in employment were laid. Yet this special treatment was a two-edged sword, providing welcome relief to some working mothers while having as its effect inequality of both employment opportunity and outcome. In effect, protective labor legislation—enacted out of a professed concern for the health of women employees and their offspring—has historically operated to relegate women to a separate and subordinate private family sphere (Gladstone, et al. 1985; Finley, 1986).

These attitudes toward the limitations of women employees shaped employment and maternity practices for the next half-century. Women in general were considered to be marginal or temporary workers because of the demands of maternity. Married women were especially suspect; during the depression of the 1930s, many state legislatures considered bills to restrict the employment of married women (Gladstone, et al. 1985). Pregnant workers were usually either fired or allowed to resign (Gladstone et al. 1985). The demands of World War II gave only a brief, and paradoxical, respite to female employment restrictions. Due to a shortage of men, women were recruited to do their jobs, but following the war there was a reversion to the same sex-stratified employment (Rothman 1978). At the same time, the early 1940s saw the nascence of laws specifically addressing pregnancy (Williams 1984–85). Pursuant to recommendations made by the Women's Bureau of the Department of Labor, a number of states passed laws prohibiting the employment of women during a period before and after childbirth in order to protect maternal and child health. Such laws reinforced the employer practice of terminating pregnant employees (Williams, 1984–85). Laws also made women who were unemployed because of pregnancy or recent childbirth ineligible for unemployment insurance when they sought unsuccessfully to reenter the labor market. Pregnancy was either excluded or given limited coverage under four state temporary disability programs that were created to provide partial wage replacement to temporarily disabled workers (Williams 1984–85).

For the most part, however, development of policies concerning maternity and employment was left to employers or unions (Williams 1984–85). Before the 1970s, employers could choose with few legal constraints how to treat pregnancy in the workplace (Gladstone, et al. 1985). In the early 1960s, employers often fired women who became pregnant or provided unpaid leave, usually without job security, seniority rights, health insurance coverage (Williams, 1984–85). With women entering the work force in dramatically increasing numbers, the message was that women were not supposed to work when pregnant, especially when visibly so.

Thus, pregnancy has historically been given less favorable treatment than other conditions affecting an employee's ability to work (Williams 1984–85). This fact reflects an underlying assumption of our society that childbearing and employment are inherently incompatible. Judicial decisions are replete with this assumption (Finley 1986). Even today, this attitude is still apparent; women continue to be excluded from certain "hazardous" employments on the basis of "fetal risk" (Williams 1981). Moreover, in spite of the fact that legislation governs the provision of pregnancy leaves to some extent, no federal policy requires provision of any of the following benefits to working mothers or parents during the period before and after the birth of a child: income replacement, job guarantee, or continuation of benefits including health benefits (Gladstone, et al. 1985). Yet children, and their health and well-being, are essential to our society and its future.

FEDERAL LAW

Title VII and Related Court Cases

The law has yet to address either the socioeconomic reality of the two-worker family or the stress that families experience when parents must both work and raise their children. Yet the legal treatment of parental rights in the work force, specifically in terms of a national infant-care-leave policy, has its roots in action begun in the 1960s concerning sex discrimination. At that time, employers' practices with respect to pregnancy and time for childrearing began to be seen by some, particularly by members of the women's rights movement, as discrimination against women (Kamerman, et al. 1986). So, women began to challenge such policies using constitutional equal protection and due process claims and Title VII of the Civil Rights Act of 1964, a comprehensive federal law prohibiting, among other things, sex discrimination in employment.

As enacted in 1964, Title VII outlawed discrimination by private employers of fifteen or more employees. A 1972 amendment extended the prohibition to public employers (except military personnel) as well (Johnson v. Alexander, 572 F 2d 1219[8th] Cir. 1978). Congress also established an enforcement agency, the Equal Employment Opportunity Commission (EEOC), to administer and interpret the statute's provisions.

Title VII makes several types of sex discrimination unlawful. First, employer practices which mandate different treatment on the basis of sex violate Title VII unless the employer can establish that sex is a *bona fide occupational qualification* (BFOQ) "reasonably necessary to the normal operation of that particular business or enterprise" (Title VII of the Civil Rights Act of 1964 §703(e); 42 U.S.C. §2000 e–2(e) 1982). Second, employer actions motivated by a discriminatory intent violate Title VII. In such cases, the employee alleges that the employer refused to hire, failed to promote, fired, or took other adverse action because of the employee's sex. Employers may avoid liability by producing a nondiscriminatory explanation for the employment action, such as poor work performance or excess absenteeism (Burdine v. Texas Department of Community Affairs, 647 F. 2d 513 [5th Cir. 1981]; Williams 1984–85). Third, Title VII makes unlawful employment practices that have a disparate impact on one sex; rules which are neutral on their face but which have a disproportionately adverse effect on any protected group may violate Title VII (Williams 1984–85). An example might be a rule such as height and weight requirements for certain jobs which exclude or result in the termination of substantially more women than men (Williams 1984–85). If, however, an employer can show that a rule is a "business necessity," or related to job performance, the employment practice does not violate Title VII (Note 1985; see Dothard v. Rawlinson 433 U.S. 321 [1977]).

It was not clear at first to many, including employers, whether adverse employer policies or actions based on pregnancy constituted sex discrimination under Title VII. In 1972, the EEOC finally clarified its position with the issuance of guidelines on pregnancy (29 C.F.R. §1604 [1979]). The guidelines state unequivocally that an "employment policy or practice which excludes from employment applicants or employees because of pregnancy is in prima facie violation of Title VII" (*Guidelines*

on Discrimination Because of Sex, 37 Fed. Reg. 6836 [1972], 29 C.F.R. §1604
[1979]). The EEOC elaborated this basic principle by stating that work
disabilities resulting from "pregnancy, miscarriage, abortion, childbirth,
and recovery therefrom are, for all job-related purposes, temporary
disabilities," and benefits such as leave, medical and temporary disability
insurance, seniority policies, and reinstatement rights comparable to
those provided to male and nonpregnant employees must be provided
(37 Fed. Reg. 6836 [1972] [codified at 29 C.F.R. §1604 (1979)]; Gladstone, et al. 1985). In response to these guidelines, twenty-two states
and the District of Columbia passed legislation requiring that employers provide coverage for pregnancy-related disabilities comparable to
that which they provided for other temporary disabilities. The EEOC
guidelines also affected employer policy regarding mandatory, unpaid leave before and after childbirth. The guidelines required the
"commencement and duration" of maternity leave and the "availability of extensions" be provided on the same "terms and conditions" as
other disabilities. Consequently, most employers eliminated fixed limitations on the time women were allowed to work during pregnancy
(Gladstone, et al. 1985).

The EEOC guidelines, however, did not end the controversy over
employers' legal obligations under Title VII. While lower federal courts
fairly consistently adopted the interpretation of Title VII promulgated
by the EEOC in its pregnancy guidelines, many employers continued to
resist the guidelines, particularly the requirements with a price tag—
namely, the requirement that pregnancy-related disabilities be treated
like other disabilities under employer sick leave, disability and health
insurance provisions.

The question of how employer pregnancy policies should be treated
under Title VII did not reach the United States Supreme Court until
1976, in a case called *General Electric Co. v. Gilbert*. Prior to *Gilbert*, however, the Court had decided two cases, neither involving Title VII, that
presaged the result it reached in *Gilbert*.

In 1974, in the case of *Cleveland Board of Education v. LaFleur*, the
Supreme Court struck down school board regulations requiring every
teacher to take unpaid maternity leave at the end of the fourth or fifth
month (326 F. Supp. 1159 [E.D. Va 1971], *aff'd* 467 F. 2d 262 [7th Cir.
1972]; 414 U.S. 632 [1974]). Reasoning that inflexible cut-off dates constituted an irrebutable presumption of inability to work and that an
alternate means—individual determination—existed, the Court held that
such mandatory leaves violate the due process of law clause of the Fourteenth Amendment by impermissibly infringing on a woman's fundamental right to choose to bear a child (Williams, 1984–85). In so ruling,
the Court avoided the question, discussed in the lower court opinions,

of whether discrimination against pregnant women is sex discrimination, and therefore subject to a tougher constitutional standard of review in sex discrimination cases brought under the equal protection clause (Williams 1984–85). The fixed Cleveland rule prohibiting women from returning to their jobs until three months after the birth of their child was also held unconstitutional as violating due process (414 U.S. 632 [1974]).

In the second case, decided in 1974, the Supreme Court reached the question it had avoided in *LaFleur*—whether discrimination against pregnant employees on the basis of pregnancy is sex discrimination. This second case, *Geduldig v. Aiello*, was a case brought under the Equal Protection Clause of the Fourteenth Amendment to the United States Constitution (417 U.S. 484 [1974]). Unlike Title VII, the constitutional provision could only be invoked to challenge action by a state and thus could not be used against an employer. Nonetheless, the question whether pregnancy discrimination could be characterized as sex discrimination, and thus subject to constitutional challenge, was quite similar to the question of whether pregnancy discrimination was sex discrimination for purposes of Title VII.

The Supreme Court in 1974 rejected the equal protection challenge made in *Geduldig v. Aiello* that discrimination on the basis of pregnancy is sex discrimination, thus subject to an intermediate standard of review under the equal protection clause as a gender-based classification (Williams 1984–85; 417 U.S. 484 [1974]). In the majority's view, exclusion of pregnancy-related disabilities from California's otherwise comprehensive disability program did not discriminate against women *as women*, because it provided coverage for women's other disabilities. Because the program only excluded a particular risk (pregnancy disability) rather than women as a group, the provision did not discriminate on the basis of sex (417 U.S. at 496 n. 20 [1974]). Note that, as was true in *Cohen v. Chesterfield Board of Education*, the Court characterized pregnancy as unique among disabilities and therefore eligible for different treatment than other disabilities (Williams 1984–85; Williams 1982a).

When the Supreme Court finally addressed in *General Electric Co. v. Gilbert* the question whether discrimination based on pregnancy is sex discrimination within the meaning of Title VII, it relied on its reasoning in *Geduldig*, the equal protection case (429 U.S. 125 [1976]; Williams 1984–85). The Court held that exclusion of pregnancy-related disability from a private employer's otherwise comprehensive disability coverage did not constitute unlawful sex discrimination and was not a pretext for discrimination against females (Note 1985). Writing for the Court, Justice Rehnquist reasoned that pregnancy was an "*additional* risk, unique to women," and that a pregnancy classification distinguished between pregnant and nonpregnant persons, not between men and women (429

U.S. at 139 [emphasis in original]). Thus, the Court established male needs and risks as the norm (Williams 1984–85). Only females who did not differ from this same set of needs and risks—nonpregnant females— would be given the same protection as men (Williams 1984–85). In so ruling, the Supreme Court rejected previous interpretations of Title VII by the EEOC, seven federal appellate courts, and eighteen federal district courts (Kamerman, et al. 1986). While Supreme Court constitutional rulings, such as the equal protection decision on *Geduldig*, can only be changed by the Supreme Court itself or by constitutional amendment, Supreme Court interpretations of federal statutes, such as the *Gilbert* decision interpreting Title VII, can be changed by Congressional amend- ment of the federal legislation (Association of Junior Leagues 1985). Congress moved quickly in effect to reverse the Supreme Court decision; *Gilbert* provided the impetus for passage of the Pregnancy Discrimination Act (PDA) described in the next section of this chapter (Pub. L. No. 95– 555 §1, 92 Stat. 2076 [codified at 42 U.S.C. §2000 e[k] [1982]; Kamer- man, et al. 1986).

One more significant Supreme Court decision regarding pregnancy both preceded and instigated passage of the PDA. In *Nashville Gas v. Satty*, the denial of sick leave pay to pregnant employees, like the disability benefits at stake in *Gilbert*, was held not to be a violation of Title VII (434 U.S. 136 [1977]; Johnson and Higgins 1984). By contrast, the Court did find that the company's policy requiring forfeiture of all accrued seniority by employee's on maternity leave was not justified by business necessity and invalidated it under Title VII disparate impact analysis. The Court rejected the argument for inclusion of pregnancy in sick leave policies on the grounds that it would require provision of a special benefit to pregnant workers but accepted the challenge to the policy requiring forfeiture of seniority acquired before maternity leave on the ground that it imposed a burden on women—loss of seniority—that men would not suffer (see Gladstone, et al. 1985).

The Pregnancy Discrimination Act of 1978

The Pregnancy Discrimination Act of 1978 amended Title VII of the Civil Rights Act of 1964 to include discrimination on the basis of preg- nancy and pregnancy-related conditions in the definition of sex discrim- ination proscribed by Title VII. The PDA explains that "women affected by pregnancy shall be treated the same for all employment related pur- poses, including receipt of benefits under fringe benefit programs, as other persons not so affected but similar in their ability or inability to work" 42 U.S.C. §2000e[k][1982]. Thus the Act requires that physically able pregnant women not be subjected to leaves or terminations when other able-bodied workers would not and that when a women is disabled from working by pregnancy she receive the same sick pay, insurance coverage, and job protection as an employer's other disabled employees.

Although this set of requirements sounds promising, the PDA is not a cure for all the disadvantages pregnant workers face. First, as noted above, although the PDA, like Title VII, has generally been interpreted to apply to federal, state, and local governments as well as to private employers, it applies only to those private employers of fifteen or more workers, leaving many workers without protection (Title VII of the Civil Rights Act of 1964 §701[b], 42 U.S.C. §2000 e–2(e) [1982]). Second, because employers are not required to provide disability leaves or other benefits to *any* employees, disability leave is available to pregnant employees only to the extent that it is provided for other comparable disability (Association of Junior Leagues 1985; Krieger and Cooney 1983). Employers with inadequate leave policies are free to maintain such policies as long as they are equally disadvantageous to all workers (Krieger and Cooney 1983).

Third, disability leaves, when available, need only be applied to pregnant employees for the period of disability—that is, the period of physical inability to work—caused by pregnancy or childbirth (Gladstone, et al. 1985). This period, typically between four and eight weeks, addresses a woman's need for physical recovery but does not meet the need for a childcare leave extending beyond this brief recovery period (see Krieger and Cooney 1983). Employers, faced with the PDA's requirement that paid benefits be extended to many pregnant women, have often traded in longer, unpaid "maternity leaves," which included time for both childbearing and childrearing, for shorter, paid disability leaves (Association of Junior Leagues 1985).

Moreover, the PDA did not clear up all ambiguities in the law, in spite of interpretation by the EEOC. Some courts have taken an unduly narrow view of the protection offered by the PDA (29 C.F.R. 1604 [1979]; Gladstone, et al. 1985). For example, in a series of cases challenging airline policies that ground flight attendants or place them on mandatory leave as soon as their pregnancy is detected, the federal courts have upheld the policies. In these cases, courts have acknowledged that the policies discriminate on the basis of sex but have declared the discrimination justified under Title VII's bona fide occupational qualification (BFOQ) exception (Finley 1986; In re American Airlines, 582 F. 2d 1142 [7th Cir. 1978] *rev'd* 455 U.S. 385 [1982]). Several Courts of Appeals have held that airlines have stated viable BFOQ defenses because passenger safety necessitates such leaves (Levin v. Delta Airlines 730 F 2d 994 [5th Cir. 1984]). As was explained in one of the cases, "It is the inability to predict in advance which pregnant flight attendants will suffer [fatigue, nausea, or spontaneous abortion] that makes it so difficult . . . to deal with pregnant flight attendants on an individualized basis and thus justifies [the] blanket exclusion of pregnant attendants from flight duty..." (Levin v. Delta Air Lines, 730 F. 2d at 998 [5th Cir. 1984]). In striking contrast to the pregnancy cases, in which the flight attendant's pregnant state was held to be so dangerous to passenger safety that it constituted a BFOQ, the Supreme Court has, in the face of similar safety arguments based on old age, upheld a lower court decision that age is not a BFOQ for the position of flight engineer (Western Airlines, Inc. v. Criswell, 472 U.S. 400 [1985]). These cases illustrate that exceptions to the PDA rule that pregnancy-related disabilities be treated like other short-term disabilities have been and may be judicially created.

Other cases, however, strengthened the impact of the PDA. In *Newport News Shipbuilding & Dry Dock Co. v. EEOC*, for example, a health insurance plan which limited coverage for pregnancy-related expenses incurred by spouses of employees was held to violate Title VII by discriminating against male employees (462 U.S. 669 [1983]). The Supreme Court found that because spouses of female employees received full medical coverage while spouses of male employees were covered for all medical conditions except pregnancy, male employees were discriminated against. Thus, the employer failed to show that its plan came within the Title VII BFOQ exception (Williams 1984–85).

Although the PDA does not solve the problems of how to parent and work at the same time, it has had an effect on the environment in which women must work. Because employers are not allowed to assume that pregnancy will interfere with a woman's employment, a more equitable atmosphere exists in the workplace toward pregnant workers and pregnancy-related leave. Most public and private employers have formulated their own specific guidelines for providing leave and benefits to pregnant workers. In most cases, these provisions still fall short of a comprehensive policy that would require employer accommodation of parenthood. Further, what they often do not provide reveals that discrimination still exists against pregnant women, and in some cases, is extended to fathers who want time off to care for their infants or adopted children. Although unrepresentative of leave policies in general in terms of the extent of leave provided, guidelines governing leave for members of the federal civil service provide an example of policies developed pursuant to the PDA and Title VII (Gladstone et al. 1985; Kamerman et al. 1986). These guidelines apply to all federal employees, except where policies differ as a result of collective bargaining agreements. The guidelines must comply with Title VII and therefore require that agencies provide continued employment in the same or comparable position with continuation of seniority rights and pension benefits to women returning from pregnancy leave. Women employees may use accrued paid sick and annual leave; a minimum of five weeks is available for pregnancy disability leave. They may use accrued annual leave and leave without pay for childcare leave. A male employee may request annual leave or leave without pay for purposes of infant care. Authorization of such leaves and their length and timing are, however, a matter of individual agency administrative discretion (U.S. Office of Personnel Management 1976; Gladstone, et al. 1985).

Specific laws govern pension benefits. In terms of pension plan benefits, the Employee Retirement Income Security Act (ERISA) provides some protection against employer penalization of employees who take infant care leaves (Pub. L. No. 93–406, 88 Stat. 829 [1974] codified at 29 U.S.C. §1001 et seq. [1982]). Under ERISA, an employee who has completed a period of break-in service of one year normally becomes eligible for protection of pension benefits; that is, if she has completed one year of service, an employer cannot abridge her eligibility for pension benefits by imposing other eligibility requirements incompatible with infant care leave (Williams, March 1985). The Retirement Pension Act of 1984 protects the pension benefits of workers on extended childcare leave otherwise previously lost due to break-in service (Gladstone, et al. 1985; Pub. L. No. 98–397 [1984]). Under the Retirement Equity Act, pension benefits are protected for up to five years if a woman taking pregnancy-related leave is subsequently rehired by the same employer (Gladstone, et al. 1985).

As the principal federal law concerning employer treatment of pregnancy, the PDA has had beneficial effects but does not mandate any affirmative treatment of pregnancy, childbirth, and related medical conditions. Rather, it addresses pregnancy only as a physical, medical condition and, as an antidiscrimination provision, it requires only that pregnancy be treated the same as other physical conditions with similar employment effects. Moreover, as the flight attendant cases illustrate, exceptions to the antidiscrimination mandate may be judicially carved out, with latitude continuing to exist for judicial and employer stereotyping and assumptions to figure into the BFOQ calculus. Both Title VII and the Equal Protection Clause prohibit the granting of childcare leave to one sex only. Just as the PDA does not require that pregnancy leave be provided, there is no legal requirement that infant care leave be provided. The law only requires that, if infant care leave is provided at all, it must be available to parents on a gender-neutral basis.

STATE PROVISIONS

At this time, state law can provide protection for pregnant workers in four different forms: through nondiscrimination provisions like the PDA, through unemployment insurance, through temporary disability insurance, and through statutory mandates of minimum protection. Most of the fifty states, however, provide little, if any, protection. It should be noted that a number of states are currently considering enacting state maternity and infant-care-leave laws, which would enable pregnant women to take leave (whether they were provided with either of the two above forms of insurance). There are at least thirteen such states; their efforts parallel the current effort in Congress to create a national Family and Medical Leave Act (H.R. 925 100th Cong., 1st Sess. [1987].). Nondiscrimination provisions suffer from the deficiencies of the PDA, although they typically reach small employers not covered by Title VII.

Traditionally, state unemployment insurance across the nation is very limited in its application to pregnant women. In 1960, thirty-five states explicitly made otherwise eligible women ineligible for benefits if the cause of their unemployment was pregnancy (Kamerman, et al. 1986). The period of exclusion was between eight weeks and six months. In *Turner v. Dept. of Employment Security and Board of Review of the Industrial Commission of Utah*, the Supreme Court held these practices unconstitutional, but problems remain (423 U.S. 44 [1975]). In *Wimberly v. Labor and Industrial Relations Commission of Missouri*, a provision of the Federal Unemployment Tax Act, specifying that "no person shall be denied compensation solely on the basis of pregnancy or termination of pregnancy," was interpreted by the Supreme Court (688 S.W. 2d 344 [1985], *aff'd*, 107 S. Ct. 821 [1987]). In that case, a state provision making all disabled persons ineligible for unemployment insurance upon their recovery had been interpreted by the state to apply to women disabled by pregnancy and childbirth. The Court held that the federal provision only prohibited states from singling out pregnancy for especially disadvantageous treatment. Here, pregnancy disabilities were treated like all other disabilities, and thus the women were not denied benefits "solely" on the basis of pregnancy. The case highlights the deficiencies of the unemployment laws of the minority of states that impose obstacles to eligibility on temporarily disabled workers who have recovered—including those disabled by pregnancy—and may also highlight the need for more enlightened unemployment policies for parents unemployed because of childcare obligations when their attempt to reenter the work force does not meet with immediate success.

At this time, only five states—California, Hawaii, New Jersey, New York, Rhode Island—and Puerto Rico have enacted laws to create temporary disability insurance programs (Cal. Unemp. Ins. Code §2626 [Deering 1971]; N.J. Stat. Ann. §43: 21–29 [West 1962]; N.Y. Work. Comp. Law §200–242 [McKinney 1965]; R.I. Gen. Laws §§28–41–8 to

28–41–32 [1979]; Hawaii Rev. Stat. §392 [1976]). All of these programs now cover pregnant workers as well as those with other temporary disabilities, guaranteeing partial wage replacement during periods of inability to work (Kamerman, et al. 1986). Even so, no state program is comprehensive in its coverage: no state requires that employers provide job guarantees during periods of temporary disability, nor does any state require maternal or parental leaves for care of recently born infants or adopted children (Williams 1984–85).

None of these states' TDI programs are identical, but they all share some characteristics (Kamerman, et al. 1986; Gladstone, et al. 1985; Johnson and Higgins 1983). These TDI programs provide partial income to persons who are unable to work due to non-job-related injuries or illnesses (Gladstone, et al. 1985; Johnson and Higgins, 1983). Except in New Jersey, where state employees are also covered, private-sector workers contribute to and can draw upon the state TDI funds; the employers affected must comply with both the state TDI and federal Title VII requirements.

Coverage under the state TDIs is nearly universal. Four of the five statutes apply to employers of one of more employees. The New Jersey statute covers employers with an annual payroll of $1,000 or more (Gladstone, et al. 1985). The first four states to adopt TDI—California, New Jersey, New York, and Rhode Island—initially either excluded pregnancy-related disability coverage or provided restricted benefits (Williams 1984–85). By comparison, in conformity with the Pregnancy Discrimination Act of 1978, pregnancy and childbirth disabilities now are treated like other physical conditions of employees under the equality model (Gladstone, et al. 1985; Kamerman, et al. 1986).

Four states (Montana, California, Massachusetts, and Connecticut) have statutes that require employers to provide job-protected unpaid leaves to pregnant employees (Williams 1984–85; Cal. Code §12945(b) [West 1980]; Conn. Gen. Stat. Ann. §46a–60(7) [West 1984]; Mont. Code Ann. §49–2–310(i)–(2) [1983]; Mass. Gen. Laws Ann. ch. 149, §1050 [West 1982]). The relevant statutes of all four states prohibit an employer from firing a woman because she is pregnant. The most controversial provisions of these statutes require that employers provide unpaid pregnancy disability leave; in California the period must be *reasonable* (determined on the basis of disability) and up to four months; in Montana and Connecticut, the period must be reasonable; and in Massachusetts, with qualifications, there must be up to eight weeks for birth or adoption. With few exceptions, all four states require an employer to reinstate the employee to her original or an equivalent position with equivalent pay and accumulated seniority, retirement, fringe benefits, and other service credits unless changes in business circumstances make it impossible or unreasonable. Such leaves and reinstatement rights are not mandated for other disabled employees.

Two of these provisions—those of California and Montana—have been the subject of legal challenge by employers who claim that the state provisions are inconsistent with the federal PDA's apparent requirement that pregnancy-related disabilities and other disabilities be treated the same for all employment-related purposes, since similar protection was not afforded other disabled employees. One of these cases, *California Federal Savings and Loan v. Guerra*, has now been decided by the Supreme Court 33 Emp. Prac. Dec [CCH] ¶ 34, 227 [C. D. Cal. 1984], 758 F. 2d 390 [9th Cir. 1985], 107 S. Ct. 683 [1987]; *see also* The Miller-Wohl Co. v. Commissioner of Labor and Industry, 515 F. Supp. 1264 [D. Mont. 1981], *vacated*, 685 F. 2d. 1088 [9th Cir. 1982]). In that case, the Supreme Court declared that the California law providing job security for up to four months for women disabled by pregnancy did not conflict with Title VII and that the employer was therefore bound to comply with it. The Court explained that the PDA is "a floor beneath which pregnancy disability benefits may not drop—not a ceiling above which they may not rise" (55 U.S.L.W. 4077, quoting 758 F. 2d 390, 396 [9th Cir. 1985]). At the same time, the Court cautioned that state laws based on "archaic or stereotypical notions about pregnancy and the abilities of pregnant workers" rather than an actual physical disability, as the California legislation was, would be inconsistent with Title VII's (and the PDA's) goals. Presumably, an old-fashioned maternity leave which required a woman to leave work at a certain point in the pregnancy and extended the leave beyond the point of disability recovery could be attacked by pregnant women on the grounds that the requirement that leave commence at a fixed point is based on stereotypes concerning the capacities of pregnant women and by fathers asserting that to the extent the "maternity" leave encompasses time for child*rearing*, it must also be extended to them.

SPECIAL TREATMENT VS. EQUAL TREATMENT

The *Cal. Fed.* case spawned a debate among feminists about the preferable approach to pregnancy in the workplace, and this debate has significant policy implications. One feminist group defended the state statute, arguing that special accommodation to pregnancy is necessary to ensure women an equal right with men to both work and procreate. The other argued that Title VII and the PDA should be interpreted to preclude "special treatment" of pregnancy, contending instead either that the employer should be required to comply with both the state statute by providing disability leave to pregnant women and Title VII by extending similar leave to other disabled workers, or that Title VII should be held to conflict with the state law and that the court should impose, as a remedy, the extension of the state law to all disabled workers. (The employer, *Cal. Fed.*, took a third position, namely, that the state law was inconsistent with the PDA and should be struck down, depriving pregnant as well as nonpregnant workers of job-protected leaves.) Thus, the two feminist positions set forth two models for treating pregnancy. Under the special-treatment model, provisions singling out pregnancy for separate, favorable treatment should be upheld in the courts; under the equal treatment model, benefits made available to pregnant, disabled workers should be extended to nonpregnant, disabled workers. (In the *General Electric* case, they similarly had argued that benefits provided only to nonpregnant, disabled workers should be extended to pregnant workers as well.)

Although the two models at issue—the special and equal treatment models—are relevant to both pregnancy disability leave and either maternal or paternal leave to care for an infant (or adopted child), the special treatment statutes on which feminists disagree are only those that concern how pregnancy will be treated during the period of disability. Under the special treatment model, maternity, pregnancy, childbirth, and, at least to the extent that it encompasses breastfeeding, infant care, are viewed as unique to women and meriting *special* treatment to accommodate and protect working women.

By comparison, under the equality, equal (or comparative) treatment model, pregnancy, childbirth, and recovery from childbirth are treated like any other temporary physical disability that prevents an employee from performing his or her job. The PDA, as interpreted by the courts prior to the *Cal. Fed.* decision, was consistent with the equal treatment approach.

In discussing the special-versus-equal treatment debate and its analysis, a distinction must be made between the pregnancy/childbirth disability and infant/adopted childcare components of a comprehensive parental leave policy. The feminist legal community is in agreement that parents of both sexes should be entitled to leave to care for their infants or adopted children. Furthermore, because Title VII prohibits sex discrimination, employers cannot offer infant care leave to mothers only (Title VII of the Civil Rights Act of 1964 703(a)(2), 42 U.S.C. §2000e et seq., "terms, conditions, or privileges of unemployment;" Association of Junior Leagues 1985). To give only women childcare leave would be to treat male and female employees differently with respect to a shared characteristic—parenthood (cf. Phillips v. Marietta Corp., 400 U.S. 542 [1971]). Thus, if provided at all, childcare leaves must be provided to employees on a gender-neutral basis.

Feminist legal scholars also agree that job-protected pregnancy- and childbirth-related disability leaves should be available to working women. The feminist legal community is, however, divided about what strategies should be used to reach that goal. The special-versus-equal-treatment controversy is best understood by examining some of the arguments made by the parties and amici curiae in the *Miller Wohl* and *Cal. Fed.* cases. To some extent, the debate can be characterized as an effort to resolve a perceived inherent tension in Title VII and the PDA between its nondiscrimination or equal treatment mandate (represented by the disparate treatment case) and its disparate impact remedy.

Special-treatment advocates make the following case for their position. They argue that, because of pregnancy, women face job obstacles that men do not and that special treatment is responsive to a real sexual difference (Krieger and Cooney 1983). Positive treatment, they argue, is necessary for women to have equal opportunities or substantive as opposed to formal equality in the workplace (Krieger and Cooney, 1983; Finley 1986). It is also necessary in order to overcome the history of discrimination against women in the workplace and the consequent sex-stratification of employment (Taub 1985). Pregnancy leave guaranteed by special treatment is particularly important for low-income women (Association of Junior Leagues 1985). Furthermore, this approach recognizes pregnancy as having special and important societal value (Finley 1986).

In particular, two special-treatment views should be noted. Under a *bivalent view*, pregnant women should be provided disability leave by analogy to the disabled who, for example, need special means of access to buildings in order to have equal rights (Krieger & Cooney 1983; Wolgast 1980). Critics point out, however, that employers tend to consider the accommodated group to be more expensive and less desirable employees and that courts have interpreted such laws very narrowly (Williams, 1984–85). The *incorporationist approach* calls for different treatment only with regard to the sex-specific characteristics unique to women, that is, pregnancy, childbirth, and breastfeeding (Krieger & Cooney 1983; Scales 1981). This approach is, essentially, the special-treatment approach by different nomenclature.

There are a number of cogent criticisms of the special-treatment approach. As the history of protective labor legislation illustrates, special treatment of women allows disadvantageous as well as advantageous treatment (Williams 1982a; Williams, 1984–85). The incorporationist view attempts to mitigate the following two criticisms: special treatment promotes the assumption that woman is both childbearer and child-rearer, and that she is, therefore, a marginal member of the work force (Williams, 1982a; Williams 1984–85). In effect, special treatment reinforces the notion that woman's primary role is that of mother as opposed to worker (Taub 1985). This criticism is made against the backdrop that judicial decisions made within the past twenty years are replete with the assumption that special childbearing and childrearing roles are fundamentally incompatible with being a worker (Finley 1986).

As a practical matter, the special treatment of pregnancy- and childbirth-related disabilities potentially jeopardizes the desirability of hiring women because of the added cost, measured both financially and in terms of disruption of the workplace (Taub 1985; Williams 1984–85). Given a choice between hiring two equally qualified candidates, a woman in her childbearing years, or a man, employers may prefer to hire the man to avoid pregnancy-leave issues. Furthermore, opponents of the special treatment of pregnancy, often employers, have traditionally felt that pregnancy, unlike other disabilities, is voluntary and therefore that the woman, by choosing to be disabled, should bear the burden of any interference with employment. Although women can bring Title VII claims, such suits in practice may offer limited recourse because they are often difficult to win and are expensive (Williams 1982a). The danger is that, although it is intended to provide badly needed benefits for women, special treatment may, both theoretically and in practice, ossify traditional sex roles and perpetuate employment disadvantages. Giving pregnancy preferential treatment also may foster hostility among workers where leave for other disabilities is nonexistent or is relatively inadequate (Williams 1984–85).

Another criticism is that the defense of special treatment statutes involves a retrenchment in constitutional equal protection analysis that runs counter to the premise of PDA . One possible defense is the problematic *Geduldig* reasoning: classifications based on pregnancy, such as disability leaves, are not sex-based and therefore are subject only to minimal judicial scrutiny or, in other words, to the least stringent standard instead of to intermediate scrutiny applied to sex-based classifications. Proponents contend that such an argument need not be made because such statutes will not be invalidated under the equal protection clause if it can be shown that the classification serves important government objectives and is substantially related to achievement of those objectives (Krieger and Cooney 1983). The question remains whether special treatment statutes would survive such an equal protection challenge (Williams, 1984–85).

In making the case for equal treatment, analysts explain that, because maternity will be treated as a sex-based classification, relevant state action will be subject to an intermediate level of scrutiny, and employment practices cannot be justified under Title VII unless the employer can establish a bona fide occupational qualification defense (Williams 1984–

85; Krieger and Cooney 1983). In short, it is more difficult for a policy to withstand judicial scrutiny under the equal treatment approach.

Advocates also argue that equal treatment does not perpetuate traditional assumptions about sex-roles within the family, but rather it provides the greatest opportunity for choice in family roles (Williams 1982a). Equal treatment also emphasizes commonality rather than differences; special treatment advocates, of course, criticize the failure to recognize certain differences (Williams 1984–85).

Each group accuses the other of adherence to a male norm. Critics counter that equal treatment accepts maleness as "normal" or as the standard or norm, and the equal treatment of the sexes results in inequality for women (Williams 1984–85; Krieger and Cooney 1983). As the most articulate proponent of the equal treatment position admits, "[b]y definition, a nondiscrimination provision can only bring outsiders into the existing order" (Williams 1982a). Title VII, in fact, allows inadequate treatment of or no job protection at all for persons temporarily disabled (Williams, 1982a). Although framed in terms of treating *likes* alike, treatment is, in effect, dictated by a male reference point (Finley 1986). Since most women work in low-paying, sex-segregated jobs in the small business, service, or retail sectors typically having the least generous leave policies, they have limited bargaining power to induce employers to provide an overall higher level of disability coverage (Williams 1982a; Krieger and Cooney 1983; Kamerman, et al. 1986). Special-treatment advocates who believe that the social importance of childbearing should be recognized reject what they perceive to be an "assimilationist imperative of androgeny," with maleness as the standard (Krieger and Cooney 1983; Finley 1986).

Equal-treatment advocates respond that the special-treatment approach accepts the male norm in defining disability coverage and merely tacks on special provisions for women's differences rather than adopts a perspective encompassing and defined from inception by the needs of both men and women. They argue that the goal of the equal treatment approach is a comprehensive work disability program through general rather than special legislation, under which disability benefits and parental leave would be extended to all workers (Williams 1984–85). Requiring that equal leave and benefits be provided for comparable disabilities, it is argued, is a more value-neutral approach which does not encourage stereotyping by and biases of employers and judges (Krieger and Cooney 1983). Special-treatment advocates fear, however, that greater statutory protection of pregnancy would be eliminated rather than extended (Association of Junior Leagues 1985).

In summary, special-treatment proponents believe it is best to work incrementally toward the goal of eliminating barriers to women's equal opportunity to participate in the work force that are associated with childbearing and childrearing by seeking and defending special provisions for women (Finley 1986). The *Cal. Fed.* decision is consistent with their viewpoint. Equal-treatment advocates believe that the incremental approach may backfire in Pyrrhic victory, and that it is preferable to work to improve workplace protections for both men and women (Finley 1986). The equal-versus-special-treatment debate has in turn spawned provocative analyses of the debate itself and its predication on equality theory (Finley 1986). The Supreme Court, for the moment, has aligned itself with the special-treatment advocates.

Regardless of which approach is taken, a concern raised about any parental leave policy is that, in countries providing leaves to both parents, the vast majority of leaves are taken by women (Williams 1984–85). If this pattern is replicated in the United States, an incentive is created for employers to avoid hiring women of childbearing ages, especially in businesses that would be significantly disrupted by leaves. If employers respond in this way, women have the option of bringing sex-discrimination suits to challenge such action.

Equal-treatment feminists are pursuing their model approach in the form of federal legislation creating a right to return to work after medical leave of up to twenty-six weeks, including leaves for pregnancy-related conditions, and a right to a family leave of eighteen weeks for workers of both sexes upon the birth or adoption of a child or the serious illness of a child (proposed Parental and Medical Leave Act, S. 249). The bill includes a mandate to create a Congressional Commission to study mechanisms for providing paid leaves. And in the wake of *Cal. Fed.*, a number of states are considering legislation to provide special-treatment pregnancy leaves, like that upheld in the *Cal. Fed.* case, as well as parental childcare leaves. Given these state and federal legislative initiatives, it seems likely that a substantial number of states and perhaps the nation will have some form of maternity and childcare leave legislation in the coming years.

REFERENCES

Association of Junior Leagues. 1985. Parental Leave: Options for Working Parents. A Report of a Conference sponsored by the Association of Junior Leagues, March 1985.

Finley, L. *Maternity and the Workplace: Transcending Equality Theory.* 86 Columbia Law Review 1118 (October 1986).

Freeman, R. B., and Medoff, J. L. 1984. *What Do Unions Do?* New York: Basic Books.

Gladstone, L. W., Williams, J. D., and Belous, R. S. 1985. Maternity and Parental

Leave Policies: A Comparative Analysis. Congressional Research Service Report, no. 85–148. Washington, D.C.

Johnson and Higgins. 1983. Comparative analysis of non-occupational disability laws. January. Unpublished manuscript.

Johnson, T. *The Legal Background and Implications of Pregnancy Benefits.* Labor Law Journal 352 (June 1984).

Kamerman, S., Kahn, A., and Kingston, P. 1986. *Maternity Policies and Working Women.* New York: Columbia University Press.

Kessler-Harris, A. 1982. *Out to Work: A History of America's Wage-Earning Women in the United States.* New York: Oxford University Press.

Krieger, L. J., and Cooney, P. N. *The Miller-Wohl Controversy: Equal Treatment, Positive Action and the Meaning of Women's Equality.* 13 Golden Gate 513 (1983).

Note. *Employment Equality Under the Pregnancy Discrimination Act of 1978.* 94 Yale Law Journal 929 (1985).

Olsen, E. G. *The Family and the Market: A Study of Ideology and Legal Reform,* 96 Harvard Law Review 1497 (1983).

Rothman, S. 1978. *Woman's Proper Place.* New York: Basic Books.

Scales, A. C. *Towards a Feminist Jurisprudence,* 56 Indiana Law Journal 375 (1981).

Taub, N. *From Parental Leaves to Nurturing Leaves,* 13 New York University Review of Law and Social Change 381 (1985).

U.S. Office of Personnel Management. 1976. Federal Personnel Manual: Absence for Maternity Reasons. FPM Supplement. Washington, D.C.: U.S. Government Printing Office.

Williams, W. W. *Firing the Woman to Protect the Fetus: The Reconciliation of Fetal Protection with Employment Opportunity Goals under Title VII,* 69 Georgetown Law Journal 641 (1981).

————. 1982a (March 7). Remarks to a panel discussion on *Pregnancy: Special Treatment vs. Equal Treatment,* subsequently revised and published in *Responses,* 13 New York University Review of Law and Social Change 407–10 (1984–85).

————. 1982b. Remarks to the National Association for the Education of Young Children, November 11.

————. *Equality's Riddle: Pregnancy and the Equal Treatment/Special Treatment Debate,* 13 New York University Review of Law and Social Change 325 (1984–85).

————. 1985 (March). Personal Communication.

Wolgast, E. 1980. *Equality and the Rights of Women.* Ithaca, New York: Cornell University Press.

EIGHTEEN

Cost, Financing, and Implementation Mechanisms of Parental Leave Policies

MERYL FRANK

Other approaches to the need for an infant care leave have dealt with numerous social and psychological factors, both in policy formation and application, and with the substantial benefits such a policy would provide. However, it is also necessary to consider the economic cost of implementation and the factors that affect decisions about financing a leave policy. Yet the cost of a national infant care leave for both public and private employers raises serious questions about how to finance and implement such a leave. Who will pay for this leave? How much will it cost the nation at large? What are the options for financing such a leave? These questions, and many others, must be answered before the suggestions and concerns of the preceding chapters can be acted upon.

ARGUMENTS IN SUPPORT OF A FINANCED INFANT CARE LEAVE

In order to calculate the costs of an infant-care-leave policy and to evaluate some of the options available for financing, it is first necessary to identify three premises as essential to the policy options discussed:

A Leave Policy Would Deliver Substantial Public and Private Benefits. First and foremost is that the necessity of a leave be recognized. The point has been made that mothers are entering the work force in increasing numbers and that the trend shows no sign of reversing. Yet both mothers and fathers feel a conflict between their parenting and work roles. It has also been established that employed parents of infants desire leave policies, and that such policies would address many of the physical and psychological problems associated with the combination of work and parenting. Such a period of leave would allow time after birth for both

315

infant and parents to establish patterns of trust and interaction necessary to family effectiveness and stability. Family stability and employee satisfaction are both conducive to a stronger social system.

In Order for a Leave Policy to be Utilized, It Must Offer Some Income Replacement. Time alone is not enough for a new family, since many parents cannot affort to take a three- or four-month leave without financial support. An infant care leave without pay is limited in its utility and effect. Such a policy would essentially negate the opportunity to take leave for many low-income and single parents. Further, it would penalize parents for attending to that part of society for which they are uniquely responsible—the family—by making them lose substantial income during this leave time.

In Order for a Leave Policy To Be Utilized, It Must Provide Some Guarantee That Parents May Return to Their Jobs after the Leave Ends. Parents work to provide economic stability for the family. Although other reasons can also be involved, most dual-income families report that both parents work because they could not support their family otherwise. A leave that would *not* guarantee job security in effect penalizes parents for taking a leave, because they thus risk losing their hard-earned positions and seniority status.

Given these conditions, the cost factors discussed in this chapter are considered according to how much they support employed parents in meeting both sets of their obligations, those to their family and those to their employers.

COST CONSIDERATIONS

A cost estimate of a paid infant-care-leave policy is a necessary component in the evaluation of an economic commitment which will sustain the policy. Cost estimates, however, require the identification of several characteristics that describe the scope of the program: eligibility criteria, wage and benefit levels, and the length of leave.

Eligibility Criteria. Some eligibility criteria must be established for any public policy. A certain amount of time in the work force and the establishment of a contribution record might be two requirements for participation in an infant-care-leave policy. For our purposes, the year-long tenure with the employer recommended by the Yale Bush Center Advisory Committee is assumed.

Wage and Benefit Levels. Although it is clear that a paid leave is necessary if the benefits of the policy are to be meaningful to the nation's families,

Table 18.1.   Annual Cost of National Paid Leave
(1983 Dollars in Thousands)

Paid Weeks on Leave	@ 50% of Earnings	@75% of Earnings	@100% of Earnings
1	96,872	145,307	193,743
13	1,259,330	1,888,994	2,518,659
(3 months)			
17.3	1,675,877	2,513,816	3,351,754
(4 months)			
26	2,518,659	3,777,988	5,037,318
(6 months)			

Source: See table 18.2 for data underlying cost estimate.

the determination of the rate of pay is problematic. If compensation is 100% of salary, for example, parents who choose to return to work before the end of their available leave in effect suffer economic penalty. For low-income families on leave, a higher rate of compensation may be warranted, and for higher income families, a cap on weekly compensation. For the purposes of this cost estimate, however, only three rates of salary compensation have been calculated: 100%, 75%, and 50%.

The Length of Leave. The length of paid leave granted is subject to a trade-off between the physical and emotional needs of the parents and the infants, on one hand, and the economic concerns of employers and the public, on the other. While the productivity loss to the employer remains somewhat constant each week of the leave period, the benefit of the leave to the family and to society would theoretically decrease over time as the family physically recovers and adjusts to the new infant. Three distinct periods of leave are suggested: three months (sufficient for physical recovery from normal pregnancy and childbirth), four months (Brazelton's estimate of the period of time necessary for a healthy family adjustment), and six months (the stated preference of parents for leave length).

In determining the cost of a paid leave policy, the constraining characteristics of the leave policy have been combined with the estimated population expected to take leaves and the average weekly salary of that population (primarily women of childbearing age, as well as a small proportion of fathers). The estimated cost of the leave under different percentages of salary and leave period is shown in table 18.1. In table 18.2 the data and method used to develop the cost estimate are shown.

These cost calculations do not reflect the savings that are likely to

Table 18.2. Data Underlying Infant Care Leave Cost Estimate (1983 Dollars in Thousands)

Age Range	(1) Female Population in 1983	(2) % Female Participation in Labor Force	(3) % Female Labor Force Employed	(4) % Female Employed More Than 50 Weeks	(5) % Births per 1,000 Employed Females	(6) Female Average Weekly Wages (includes benefits)	(7) Male Average Weekly Wages (includes benefits)	(8) Female Earnings Replaced at 90% of Total	(9) Male Earnings Replaced at 10% of Total	(10) Total Earnings Replaced
16–19	9,404	50.8	79	48.7	46.8	201	223	15,560	1,918	17,478
20–24	10,780	69.9	87	49.1				27,251	3,359	30,610
25–29	10,562	68.9	91	60.3	72.8	263	405	68,810	11,774	80,584
30–34	9,600							21,220	3,631	24,851
35–39	8,243	68.7	93	65.7	24.7			20,230	3,461	23,691
40–44	5,751							14,114	2,415	16,529
Total								167,185	26,558	193,743

Source of data in each column: (1) *Statistical Abstract of the United States, 1985*, from U.S. Department of Commerce, Census Bureau; (2) *Supplement to Labor Force Statistics Derived for the Current Population Survey: A Databook*, vol. 2, U.S. Department of Labor, Bureau of Labor Statistics, Bulletin 2096–1, May 1985; (3) *Work Experience of the Population*, Bureau of Labor Statistics, Bulletin 2199, p. 12, June 1984; the data include women who are employed full- and part-time; (4) Census Population Reports, vol. 20, *Fertility of American Women*, June 1983, p. 395; only females are included because the difference between 90% female and 10% male leave takers is not sufficiently significant to affect outcome; (5) developed from Census Population Reports, *Child Care Arrangements of Working Mothers*, C.3.186, p. 23; (6) and (7) *Statistical Abstract of the United States, 1985*, Department of Commerce, Census Bureau; includes full-time and part-time workers; (8) the data in columns 1, 2, 3, 4, 5, and 6 have been multiplied, and this total has been multiplied by .9; it has been assumed that 90% of leave takers will be women; (9) the data in columns 1, 2, 3, 4, 5, and 7 have been multiplied, and this total has been multiplied by .1; it has been assumed that 10% of the leave takers will be men and that these men will be the husbands of employed females.

Note: Bracketed data are in the aggregate.

occur as a result of a paid leave policy. For example, the parent on leave will not require day care or substitute care, and will therefore save the cost of this care. In addition, the cost of training the replacement employee is offset by the fact that in the absence of a leave policy, many employees simply would not return to the same position. Recruiting and training new employees is often more costly than hiring and training temporary help.

CRITERIA FOR ASSESSING FINANCING MECHANISMS

Estimating the costs of an infant care leave is one exercise; determining who shall pay the costs and how they shall be financed is another. Assessing financing mechanisms for an infant-care-leave policy requires consideration of two different factors. Shortcomings in either of them would seriously undermine the effectiveness of a parent/infant-care-leave policy. First the financing method should be such that the income of any contributing party (be it the employer, the employee, or the government) is not disproportionately affected. A program which, for example, required that only participants pay the cost would in essence leave them no better off than parents are today. Second, the financing method should not create any unintended economic incentives. For example, a financing method that requires only the employer to contribute to the cost of employee leave might give an employer the incentive not to hire individuals who would most likely take the leave—women of childbearing age. The creation of a financing mechanism is difficult, for most "solutions" incur either one or the other of the above obstacles.

ASSESSMENT OF FINANCING METHODS

There are four potential sources of funding for a paid infant-care-leave policy: (1) the employee-participant (the parent); (2) all employees, regardless of participation; (3) the employer; or (4) the government (federal or state). I will consider, in turn, financing structure built around each of these sources, as well as their combinations, in order to determine the various options.

Employee-Participant-Based Financing

Family Financed. The greatest beneficiary of an infant leave care is the participating family. There are several different ways of structuring a financing mechanism supported by the participant. The first of these is for the individual on leave to forgo compensation during the leave period and to pay living expenses from savings and other income (for example, the salary of a spouse). Although upper-middle income, two employed parent families may be able to finance the leave, other families—lower income or single parent—cannot consider this a viable option.

Insured Leaves. Another method by which employee-participants can pay for the leave is through an insurance program. Public or private insurance programs could be designed so that an individual or couple who planned to become parents could pay premiums toward the time when one of the parents would not be employed and would care for the newborn infant. Insurance is economically justified when an individual is willing to pay a premium above the expected cost of an event in order to insure against the risk of greater cost. In other words, insurance is a prudent action by the consumer and a profitable one for the carrier when the potential for great loss exists. However, an insurance program of salary replacement for infant care leave fails to fit into this definition, and therefore would not provide additional benefit, because it would not be insuring against an event of unknown time and duration. That is, because those who purchase insurance would be presumed to be planning for pregnancy and childbirth, there is no risk against which to insure. In such a situation, insurance ceases to be insurance and simply becomes a savings account. As in the family-financed option, the individual retains sole responsibility for the family in a changing social structure. A more serious limitation of this option is that an unplanned child would find the parent without insurance and any leave would be unpaid.

In sum, an infant-care-leave policy, where the responsibility for income maintenance falls solely on the participant through savings or private insurance is not effective. Although it certainly allocates costs to the greatest beneficiary—the family with the leave-taker—it ignores all other beneficiaries. Moreover, with the strong negative income effect it would have on participants, it would surely create an incentive for parents to avoid leave time (as they do at present) and to continue to rely on the current hodge-podge system of infant care.

All-Employee-Based Financing

There are two examples of insurance being financed solely by the contributions of all employees. In two states, California and Rhode Island, temporary disability insurance that includes the physical recovery from pregnancy and birth is paid for by all employees. This type of financing provides comprehensive coverage; however, it puts the entire burden of the cost on employees, rather than spreading it across all beneficiary groups.

Employer-Based Financing

There are few instances of corporate or business contributions as the sole financial source of social or economic programs. Typically, employers are mandated to pay for programs for which the industry is directly responsible. The corporate contributions to the Superfund clean-up of toxic waste are one example of employer- and industry-based financing of programs. In the area of financing infant care leaves, a total employer contribution to a fund would create a negative incentive by failing to fulfill either of the assessment criteria. While employers would see some benefit from the leave in the form of a more stable work force, they would clearly not be the prime beneficiaries of such a policy. Levying the entire cost of the leave period on the employers would create a strong incentive to avoid employing the individuals who would be most likely to take a leave—women. Further, few employers provide a full salary to parents on leave, or, if they do, they create the "salary" out of disability pay and sick, annual, and personal leave days.

There is one circumstance when an employer-financed plan in feasible. A union-negotiated contract could provide for paid infant care leave as well as protection in hiring practices. Paid leave has been an issue in a limited number of labor negotiations. This approach toward implementation of a paid leave is heavily dependent on the economic health of the individual firm.

Employer- and Employee-Based Financing

Current programs designed to assist employees under various circumstances are financed by parent-employees, employees as a whole, and employers. All employees in the nation (except federal employees) pay into the social security insurance system to create a fund to finance payment to retirees, the disabled, and the blind. Similarly, employees contribute to state-administered unemployment programs, and, in five states, they contribute to a paid disability leave program. It is important to note that most of these programs are not private insurance systems, which are based on building a reserve of funds for payment when the insured event occurs. Instead, these programs are based on a *pay as you go annuity* in which payment rates are set to cover benefit payments over a substantial period of time.

Another important aspect of these benefit programs is that they are partially supported by the participating employee, along with other employees and employers who may never participate in the benefit program (in the case of unemployment or disability). The connection between employee payment and eventual benefit payment is an important characteristic. The payroll tax gives the employee the feeling that the benefit has been earned and is not charity.

A Federal Program. A payroll tax on the employer, with a matching employee contribution as part of the social security system is attractive as a financing method for salary replacement during infant care leaves. The principal beneficiary—the employee—makes a contribution while the employer matches the contribution.

Given the already frequent use of the payroll tax across the nation and the fact that this tax would be levied on the employer for all employees, expansion of this type of system would not create any incentive for employers to discriminate against one employee group. One shortcoming of the social security tax as a financing mechanism is that it is currently a regressive tax due to its income ceiling. An employer/ employee-based tax for an infant care leave should not have the regressive characteristics of the present social security tax. By embedding the cost of paid leave into the social security system, at some future time the costs of infant care leave may be viewed in the same manner as the costs of retirement, occupational safety, and environmental safeguards— a necessary cost of doing business.

From a purely political perspective, financing of paid leaves as part of the social security system carries an additional benefit. The fact that individuals of childbearing age would receive benefits for social security might make it more feasible to raise the payroll tax should it become necessary to increase the funds for retirement benefits, because those of childbearing age would have a current stake in the system. There is a final important factor supporting the concept of a mandatory infant-care-leave program with both employer and employee contribution. Requiring participation by all employees eliminates a major difficulty of policy implementation brought about when firms compete against one another. Under a voluntary program, any employer who offers a paid infant care leave may be at a competitive disadvantage to other employers who do not. A mandatory program removes the slower process of a market induced plan. Further, the mandatory program removes the discrimination that some employees may feel when their firm does not offer parenting benefits.

A State Program. Taxing mechanisms at the state level present an additional source for funding of paid infant care leave. At present, all states utilize the payroll tax for their employment insurance funds, and for paid disability where it exists. A state payroll tax built along lines similar to these taxes would imply the same degree of attractiveness as a social-security-based system on a federal level—with one potential drawback. If all else is held constant, the cost of employment in states with a paid leave policy might have the effect of deterring investment in that state. Alternatively, the creation of such a policy in a state could increase the quality of life in that state, which is an important factor for new business and industry in deciding where to locate. Given the recent interest in many states in developing innovative social and economic policy (right-to-know laws, toxic waste clean-up, urban enterprise zones, and the like), it may well be that individual states would move more quickly toward financing infant care leave than the federal government. The five states with paid disability insurance for all employees are the most likely candidates for a state leave policy. The disability pay may cover leave for the first six to eight weeks after childbirth. An infant-care-leave policy could build upon this disability program.

Participant and State or Federal Government Financing

Current tax law provides for an income tax credit for parents who must buy day care for their infants. In essence, the tax credit allows the federal government (in reality, all other taxpayers) to subsidize the cost of day care. A tax credit based on each month of infant care leave taken similarly would provide a partial reduction in tax burden to the leave-taker. From a purely economic perspective, this approach provides some income that leave-takers would not otherwise have, but nevertheless there are some deficiencies in this approach. First, the tax credit would not provide a sufficient amount of income replacement. In addition, expansion of the tax credit to include leave-takers is unlikely given the current legislative and executive office demands for deficit reduction and tax reform. Moreover, even if a reasonable tax credit could be developed, it may prove difficult for families to use, since the tax refund would be provided at the end of the tax year and not when it is needed by the family. On the whole, the tax-credit solution leaves too much of the cost of the infant care leave on the participating family.

General Revenue Financing

Financing of paid infant care leave by general tax revenue is the simplest means of financing the leave. As another line item in the state and/or federal budget, the cost of the program is not clearly distinguishable as being borne by any one interest group. The cost of the plan would be borne in proportion to each group's total tax contribution. Hence, while the method would not inordinately affect the income of any one party, certain important benefits of a payroll tax financed plan would not occur in this method. There is no relation between payment and beneficiary. Financing out of general revenue may mean that the participants would not feel that they earned the leave, but that they were entitled to it.

Conclusion

To be truly effective an infant care leave should not only be mandatory for all firms and guarantee a continuation of benefits, seniority, and job title, but it should also be *paid* at a reasonable percentage of salary. Only in this way can those most in need of the leave take advantage of it. Maintenance of salary will enable the parent to continue to meet both the economic and emotional needs of the child. Since adequate corporate or governmental policies of paid leaves for infant care are extremely rare in this country, a multifaceted approach to leave policies, made in accordance with the principles discussed above, will provide means of meeting financial obligation. The three preferred methods for implementing leave policies are described below.

First, there should be a national system of *paid, guaranteed* infant care leave for parents with the following characteristics:

- The individual must be employed in the firm for one year prior to the leave, in accordance with the recommendations of the Yale Bush Center Advisory Committee.
- The leave-taker's salary is maintained at less than 100% of the preleave salary during the duration of the leave.
- The leave lasts for up to six months after the birth of the child.
- The leave should be financed through systems similar to the employer/employee based social security tax and payment system. Such a system spreads the cost to all sectors of society, employer and employee, and will be neutral as an incentive on hiring practices.

Second, until such a policy is implemented at the federal level, individual states should be encouraged to take steps toward a paid leave policy. Such steps include:

- The five states that currently require paid disability insurance, which by federal law also applies to pregnancy leave, should legislate provisions which extend disability insurance to a disability and parental leave. The financing mechanism used for disability—a payroll deduction—should be extended accordingly to cover the cost of the leave. These states should also be encouraged to add a job guarantee to their present disability programs.
- Those states that do not require paid disability insurance must be encouraged to move toward required guaranteed disability at partial salary replacement, and to include some recognition of the need for parental leave as well.

Third, until a paid leave policy is mandated at the federal or state level, individual unions and employers should be encouraged to make the requirement of a paid leave an important item in contract negotiations. Inclusion of infant care leave as part of a benefit package would demonstrate that employers are sensitive to the needs of their employees, most of whom will desire a leave at some time in their lives.

NINETEEN

Parental Leave:
The Need for
a Federal Policy

REPRESENTATIVE PATRICIA SCHROEDER

In the past century, there have been attempts by the federal government to improve conditions of the American family, yet the United States has never been able to formulate a comprehensive policy directed to the needs of the family. Federal programs such as welfare and Social Security were formulated with a set notion of the American family that ignores the diversity and strength inherent in the American family unit. Changes in the demographics of the American family and the American work force demand that we renew our efforts to develop public policy initiatives to support families facing economic crises while respecting their strengths and diversity.

Many of the contributors to this book have defined the nature of the demographic revolution that is altering the American work force. Yet it is worth reemphasizing here that the most dramatic contrast affecting the labor force over the past forty years is not the large number of women who are working, but the growing number of mothers who are working. If demography is destiny, a closer look at working women reveals an even more striking picture of the future. Over 80% of women in the work force are of childbearing age; and 93% of these women are likely to become pregnant during their working careers. This means that three out of four women will experience pregnancy in their working lives.

But unlike the generation of women who bore children in the 1950s, the majority of these new mothers will be back at work within one year. The United States Census Bureau issued figures in June 1986 showing that the percentage of mothers returning to work in the first year after childbirth had increased significantly in the past decade, from 31% in

1976 to 48% in 1985. Moreover, the Joint Economic Committee of Congress recently found that the mothers joining the work force at the fastest rate are those from two-parent households. In the past, it was single or divorced mothers who led in this statistic.

And, economics is the driving force behind the massive entrance of women and especially mothers into the labor force. In 1985, it took two people working to maintain the standard of living their parents could have enjoyed in the 1950s on one income. The median income for American families, adjusted for inflation, has fallen by an average of $300 per year over the past eleven years. That means the average American family has $3,300 less today than in 1975 for housing, education, food, and clothing.

As Johanna Freedman showed in chapter 2, the typical American family painted by Norman Rockwell—father working outside the home while mother stays at home with the kids—is vanishing. Less than 10% of all American families fit this model. The majority of American parents are two-earner couples working outside the home. Over half of the 45.6 million children in two-parent families have both parents in the work force. In other words, today's American family is a working family. No matter how you divide or add up the demographic forecast for the 1990s, the numbers say one thing: the workplace must change to accommodate families and the care of children. It is time for the federal government to drag itself into the twentieth century and deal with these dramatic changes and the social and economic realities which underpin them.

No federal policy currently exists which addresses these changes in the American work force and family. As a result, the family is under enormous economic pressure, with both men and women facing new demands as they struggle to make a living and provide for their families. The absence of family-enhancing employment policies, such as child care, flextime, and work sharing, gives families few options. Consequently, many working parents are forced to choose between job security and parenting. As Secretary of Labor William Brock has pointed out, "It's just incredible that we have seen the feminization of the work force with no more adaption than we have had. It is a problem of sufficient magnitude that everybody is going to have to play a role: families, individuals, businesses, local governments..." The federal government is also going to have to play a significant role in helping families reconcile the demands of work and family responsibilities, because the absence of a national federal leave policy undervalues the critical importance of families and children to the nation's future. The United States can no longer afford to separate parenting from the everyday world of work; rather we must build a bridge from work to home that can carry the American family into a healthy and productive future.

In 1978, Congress took a significant step toward responding to the conflict between women, work, and family by passing the Pregnancy Discrimination Act (PDA). This law defines discrimination on the basis of pregnancy as sex discrimination. It requires that pregnancy-related serious health conditions be treated like other short-term serious health conditions. The PDA amends Title VII of the 1964 Civil Rights Act, which prohibits employment discrimination on the basis of sex. Thus, the PDA is an antidiscrimination law that explicitly states that employers must treat employees equally. Passage of the PDA sent a strong signal to the business community. No longer would a woman's role as a child-bearer be justification for discrimination against her as a worker. In adopting the standard of equal treatment for workers who are similar in their ability or inability to work, the PDA rejected the *special treatment* of women in the law, which has been the foundation for protectionist legislation that had restricted women's access to the workplace. The PDA has had a profound impact on the perception of women as wage earners and on the availability and nature of both parental and disability leave. It has extended benefits and protections to millions of women workers who were previously not covered. Yet the PDA remains primarily an antidiscrimination law. It only states that an employer must treat all employees equally; it is silent as to the standard of that treatment.

The PDA is limited in four ways. First, current federal law does not require employers to offer disability benefits for *any* employee for *any* reason. If an employer offers no disability program, a pregnant employee, like any other employee who is temporarily unable to work, risks losing her job, her seniority, and her health and pension benefits. The PDA applies to companies with fifteen or more employees that provide disability benefits. Only about 40% of women work for companies that offer disability insurance. Thus, the law applies to less than half of the country's employers and an even smaller proportion of those with a high concentration of female employees. Five states—New York, New Jersey, California, Rhode Island, and Hawaii—provide pregnancy disability benefits through a statewide temporary disability insurance (TDI) program. TDIs protect any worker who is unable to work because of a short-term medical condition. Although TDIs entitle workers to partial wage replacement, the programs do not guarantee workers their job on return from their disability leave.

Second, the PDA does not provide any job guarantee for workers who take their disability leave. Both men and women who take any available leave without job protection can lose their jobs, or be demoted. Even large corporations who are most likely to offer employees disability leave do not always guarantee an employee's job.

Third, the Pregnancy Disability Act does not take into account the time parents need to develop a relationship with a new child. Childrearing experts agree that the early months in the life of a natural or adopted infant, especially the first four months, provide an important opportunity for the new family to cement its relationship. Because the PDA deals only with the physical act of giving birth, it ignores the legitimate *childrearing* needs of all parents, both biological and adoptive.

Fourth, the Pregnancy Disability Act does not address the issue of the rights of fathers to take time off to be with their newborn or newly adopted children. Dr. T. Berry Brazelton has suggested in chapter 3 as well as in his testimony before a House subcommittee that a father's active role in his baby's first months will not only help the baby, but will also enhance the father's image of himself so that he will be more confident in his new role as father. The limited availability of paternity leaves prohibits fathers from playing an equal role rearing their children. It is encouraging that a report done by Catalyst, a New York organization that works with corporations on family issues, found in its survey of the top Fortune 1500 companies that the number of companies offering fathers parental leave jumped by 8.6% between 1980 and 1984. Although many companies have begun to respond to the increasing demand for paternity leave, too many private employers tend to limit parental leaves for fathers to a few days.

In spite of these shortcomings, compliance with the PDA has been a major reason why thousands of companies have reevaluated their personnel policies and implemented parental, maternity, and family leave. According to the Catalyst report, 95% of the country's 384 largest companies offer disability benefits for pregnancy. Of those companies, an overwhelming majority, 87%, cited the PDA as the reason for including pregnancy in their disability benefit program.

Current policy on parental leave, however, has not progressed since passage of the PDA. At present, national leave policy is merely an informal one that dependent upon the voluntarism and discretion of private, as well as, public employers. It is an ad hoc policy that subjects parents to arbitrary and inconsistent treatment. Some states such as New Jersey and Massachusetts are considering statewide parental leave policies. Commendable though these efforts are, a state-by-state approach to a national policy only exacerbates the disparity of current policy. More to the point, the federal government has both the authority and the obligation to take the lead in establishing uniform minimum standards for a family leave policy, providing states a model to build upon. Under the Constitution, Congress has the right to regulate interstate commerce and to set minimum standards to protect the health, safety, and welfare of workers. Historically, Congress has exercised its Constitutional powers in the areas of labor-management relations, wages, hours, use of child labor, safety and health standards, pensions, preference for veterans' reemployment, and the end of discrimination on the basis of race, color, sex, religion, national origin, and age. The courts have upheld the right of Congress to do so. Moreover, Congress has the obligation under the preamble of the Constitution to "promote the general Welfare" of the people. By promoting a minimum federal standard to which states must adhere, the federal government would protect all Americans equally. States and private employers would remain free, of course, to improve upon this basic right.

Such improvement is sorely needed. While women in large companies receive important disability and job protection benefits, it is women in smaller companies, who work in female-dominated jobs or who work part-time, who currently have the least protection. Small companies, while creating the largest percentage of new jobs, have been found to be least likely to provide employee benefits such as sick leave, pension coverage, health insurance, and disability. Yet almost a third of all American workers are employed by companies with fewer than 25 persons. Women make up 43% of this labor force.

Even for women working for the federal government, where maternity is covered under three separate types of leave (sick leave, leave without pay and annual leave) the length of time granted is a matter of administrative discretion. As a result of this practice, the amount of leave time permitted for parental leave varies widely from agency to agency and from supervisor to supervisor.

Many groups have proposed ways in which such standards could be formulated. For example, the Economic Policy Council of the United Nations Association of the United States of America, a group comprised of corporate executives, union presidents, and academics, released a study in 1985 calling for a national leave policy. The Economic Policy Council recommended a six- to eight-week job-protected maternity leave with partial wage replacement and a six-month, unpaid, job-protected parental leave. In response to studies outlining both the need for a national policy and the inadequacies of private and public leave policies, I introduced legislation which proposes a national leave policy providing an unpaid job-protected leave for workers to meet parental responsibilities and to deal with serious health conditions. This legislation, known as the Family and Medical Leave Act, would provide parents with four months of unpaid job-protected leave to care for a newborn, newly adopted, or seriously ill child or dependent parent. It would also provide all workers with a six-month unpaid leave for any serious illness that prevents them from working. Because of the political climate, the legislation does not include the partial wage replacement that experts consider to be a key component of a national leave policy model. The bill does, however, propose a commission to study existing and proposed family or medical leave policies that provide for wage replacement and to report to Congress within two years with legislative recommendations on the implementation of such a system.

The Family and Medical Leave Act fills the policy vacuum created by the PDA in three important ways. First, the legislation simultaneously creates a medical and parental leave. While medical leave would be provided for any worker who is temporarily unable to work because of a serious health condition (including pregnancy), family leave would also be available for any parent who needed to take time off from work to care for a newborn, newly-adopted, or seriously-ill child. Also, any worker could use the leave to care for a seriously ill, dependent parent. By combining the two types of leave in a comprehensive national leave policy, the bill underscores the equal treatment premise of the PDA and eliminates the risk of employment discrimination against pregnant women which is posed by legislation providing job protection only for pregnant women. By providing a right to medical leave, the legislation acknowledges the longstanding problem of workers who lose a job because of a serious health condition. Not only do these workers have to deal with their illness, but they also have to cope with the increase in the physical, emotional, and financial strains on their family.

Second, the legislation acknowledges that childbearing and childrearing are the emotional and economic responsibility of both parents, and it therefore makes fathers eligible for parental leave. Third, the legislation addresses the unique difficulties that face parents of adopted and seriously ill children. Job security is as much an issue for these families as it is for parents who are planning families. The emotional stress that accompanies the illness of a child or the adoption of a child compounds the economic pressure a family may already be experiencing. Families that adopt not only face uncertainty as to when the adoption will go through, but in many cases they also must be able to take leave from their jobs in order to meet the requirements for the adoption. Most adoption agencies require that one parent be at home with their newly-adopted child for a minimum six-month period, but few employers have policies that guarantee six-month leaves. The lack of adequate leave time forces many couples to choose between having a family and keeping their jobs. Few companies even acknowledge the need for time with adopted children. Caring for a seriously ill child is also trying for a family. Serious medical conditions require constant care, and parents feel that they are the ones who should provide that care. Yet, too few parents have the flexibility in the workplace to make this decision. Job-protected leave is critical in assisting families to survive such difficult times.

The Family and Medical Leave Act proposes a much needed federal policy that strikes a balance between the needs of employers and the needs of employees and their families. Employers who have parental leave policies have found that such leaves represent a low-cost benefit that increases morale and productivity and decreases absenteeism, tardiness, and employee turnover. Their experience also demonstrates that parental-leave policies are workable and cost-effective.

Finally, the Family and Medical Leave Act meets the requirements of a national leave policy and its passage would allow the United States to continue the American tradition of improving working conditions by addressing the needs of its new, diverse work force. In addition to expanding employment policies to meet the demands of the country's new demographics, the Family and Medical Leave Act would establish public policy that would shake loose the static model of the American family where the father works and the mother stays at home and replace it with a vibrant, dynamic model. American workers need more flexible work options if the gap between work and home is to be bridged. Public policy must no longer allow job security or economic security to be traded against the needs of the family. Instead, the public and private sector must work together to pass public policy such as family leave legislation that can support families in their effort to cope with economic pressures without sacrificing their family's stability.

TWENTY

The State's Role in the Implementation of Infant Care Leave

GOVERNOR THOMAS H. KEAN

New Jersey is what sociologists call a "Bellwether" state, in the forefront of the economic and social challenges facing the United States. Our high population density, location, and diverse economy force us to solve many problems before other states even become aware of them. In no area is this more true than in the area of family policy, and quality, accessible day care and flexible employment schedules are only two of the major issues in this area for the 1980s and 1990s. The overall goals of New Jersey family policy are very simple: to provide incentives to keep families together and growing and to promote flexibility and productivity in the workplace. Although we still have a way to go, I believe other states can learn from New Jersey's experience.

Maternity

Working women in New Jersey who are pregnant can approach childbirth secure in the knowledge that the state is trying to ease the initial financial crunch and emotional burden of leaving work to give birth. New Jersey is one of only five states which provide temporary disability benefits to employees who become disabled outside of the workplace. Under the New Jersey Temporary Disability Benefits Law, pregnancy is treated like any other medically justifiable condition that prevents an employee from performing his or her job. As a result, a pregnant employee is entitled to receive partial wage replacement.

Evolution of the Law

This law evolved in response to a combination of forces. When New Jersey first enacted the State Temporary Disability Benefits Law in 1948, pregnancy leave was treated as a unique category that provided minimum benefits. This law was amended to eliminate discrimination based on gender when the federal Pregnancy Discrimination Act (PDA) of 1978 was passed. The federal PDA required employers in every state that had temporary disability programs to extend short-term disabilty benefits to cover pregnancy or childbirth just as any other medically disabling condition. The PDA, however, did not require that short-term disability benefits be made available in states where it did not exist previously.

Although the PDA did little to change childbirth and childcare policies throughout the nation, it had an immediate impact on New Jersey's relatively generous disability policy. Prior to the enactment of this federal legislation, state law provided women with only eight-weeks for pregnancy disability. In order to comply with the PDA, pregnancy had to be treated like any other short-term illness, and a longer disability became available. In effect, pregnant women were to receive the same job consideration and cash benefits as male colleagues who suffered heart attacks or other disabling medical conditions.

Benefits Package

The maximum period for which employees may receive Temporary Disability Insurance (TDI) is twenty-six weeks, but an individual's eligibility period may be much shorter if her medical condition improves enough so that she is able to return to work before the end of twenty-six weeks. All claims for TDI are evaluated in terms of a medical doctor's diagnosis of the individual's disabling condition and prognosis for successfully returning to work.

In order to be eligible for TDI benefits, an employee must have worked at least twenty weeks and earned more than $76 each week during that year, or have earned a total of $4,300 for that year. Once a person is approved for TDI, she can receive two-thirds of her average weekly wage. The amount of the TDI benefit is determined by averaging the individual's weekly earning during the eight weeks immediately preceding the beginning of the disability. The maximum weekly benefit is set at $200, which equals approximately 53% of the statewide average weekly wage.

Temporary Disability Insurance Fund

This liberal benefits package is paid for by both employee and employer contributions. As with unemployment compensation, almost all organizations that employ one or more persons and that earn at least $1,000 annually must contribute to the state's TDI fund, or they must carry an approved private plan for temporary disability. Both employee and employer must contribute 0.5% of an individual's earnings, as long as the maximum individual contribution does not exceed $53.50. In essence,

Table 20.1.   Temporary Disability Insurance Trust Fund Data: 1980–1985
(Millions of Dollars)

Calendar Year	Balance at End of December	Net Contributions[a]	Assessments[b]	Interest Earned	Average Tax Rate[c]	Net Benefits Paid
1980	$ 94.3	$116.5	$20.9	$7.6	0.90%	$127.8
1981	107.8	127.6	19.1	4.9	0.86%	136.0
1982	116.3	137.0	20.0	5.9	0.93%	138.7
1983	127.1	150.0	16.8	4.3	0.90%	145.5
1984	124.6	174.6	3.1	4.0	0.93%	164.7
1985	75.1[d]	193.4	5.1	7.7	1.0 %	184.5

Source: New Jersey Department of Labor Division of Planning and Research, November 1986.

[a]Includes employer and employee contributions.
[b]State and private plan employers are assessed a percentage of taxable wages paid to cover the costs of program administration.
[c]Includes 0.5% employee tax and experience rated employer taxes.
[d]In April 1985, $50 million was transferred from the disability insurance to the unemployment insurance trust fund under the terms of P.L. 1984, Chapter 24.

the employer's contribution to the TDI fund is based on the first $10,700 earned by each employee.

All the evidence I have reviewed shows that the state mandate to require organizations employing one or more persons to participate in the TDI program has not caused a significant economic strain on employers. The maximum employer contribution of $53.50 per year is a small price to pay to guarantee an employee partial wage replacement in the event that she becomes physically unable to work. In fact, the employer contribution is considered an important investment in an employee's future well-being.

The State Treasurer has authority over the TDI fund. The Treasurer has the statutory authority to consult with the Secretary of State, the Labor Commissioner, the Director of the Division of Unemployment and Disability, and the State Comptroller to manage the fund to assure favorable growth, without jeopardizing cash reserves. The following chart illustrates that the steady growth of the TDI program has not adversely affected the fiscal stability of the TDI fund.

In addition to the State TDI program, private employers may opt to organize their own plans. Private TDI plans may be insured on their own, by an insurance company, a union welfare fund, or a labor-management welfare fund. The State Division of Unemployment and Disability Insurance must authorize all private plans. The Division has a commitment to employees to assure that they receive at least as many benefits as those provided by the state.

TDI Recipients: A Profile

The greatest number of women join the labor force between the ages of twenty and thirty-four, which is at the time in their life when they are most likely to become pregnant. According to the New Jersey Department of Labor, 31% of the women filing for TDI earn between $10,000 and $15,000 per year, and only 3% earn $25,000 or more. The partial wage replacement provided by the TDI program fosters the economic survival of low- and middle-income women who wish to bear children.

Over one-half of all women under the age of 35 who filed for TDI benefits claimed pregnancy or a related condition as the reason for their leave. Overall, 17% of all TDI claims paid by the state in fiscal year 1985 were pregnancy-related. In table 20.2 a complete breakdown of the distribution of claims according to morbitity, an average amount paid per claim in each medical category, and duration of the temporary disability is provided.

Among female TDI recipients, pregnancy claims paid higher benefits than other morbidities because it often takes women ten or more weeks before their medical condition has improved sufficiently to enable them to return to work. The *average* pregnancy claimant in 1985 is shown in table 20.3: someone who received weekly benefits of $133 over an average disability period of seventy-four days.

PARENTAL LEAVE

Even though New Jersey is generous in granting paid disability leave to virtually all working women who are physically unable to work after pregnancy, there is no state policy protecting women who are not ready to leave their infants and jump back into work after the physical toll of their pregnancy dissipates. To close this gap, legislation has been introduced in New Jersey to expand job protection to men and women who want to take time off from work to care for their young child.

Modeled after Congresswoman Patricia Schroeder's bill, the Parental Leave Act (New Jersey Senate Bill No. 2392) proposed by State Senator Donald DiFrancesco, would allow mothers and fathers to take a twenty-six-week leave to care for newly born, adopted, or seriously ill children. Under this Act, parents would be allowed to take paid, unpaid, or a combination of paid and unpaid leave, as long as the total leave does not exceed twenty-six weeks in any two-year period. The leave may also

Table 20.2

Morbidities	Distribution TDI Claims	Average Amount Paid Per Claim		Average Number of Days Per Claim	
		Male	Female	Male	Female
Infectious and Parasitic Disease	3%	$725	$721	34.2	36.4
Neoplasms	5	1,644	1,219	74.1	61.2
Allergic, Endocrine, Metabolic and Nutritional Diseases	2	836	892	36.6	45.2
Diseases of Blood and Blood Forming Organs	*	685	715	29.8	35.0
Mental, Psychoneurotic and Personality Disorders	4	1,133	1,178	55.8	60.1
Nervous System and Sense Organs	3	1,190	1,235	54.9	65.8
Circulatory System	9	1,685	1,221	76.4	65.0
Respiratory System	7	746	509	33.7	26.0
Digestive System	8	987	956	45.1	51.0
Genito-urinary System	4	1,039	751	49.5	38.8
Pregnancy and Complications of Childbirth	**17**	**–**	**1,367**	**–**	**70.9**
Skin and Cellular Tissue	1	789	631	37.9	33.7
Bones and Organs of Movement (including back problems)	7	1,434	1,296	65.6	68.3
Congenital Malformations	*	*	*	*	*
Other Ill-defined and Unknown Causes	6	1,359	1,076	62.7	55.3
Accidents, Poisoning, and Violence	24	1,096	1,170	58.6	58.9
Totals	100	$15,348	$14,937	55.5	58.9

Source: New Jersey Department of Labor.
*Less Than One Percent
Note: Data derived from sample selected in July 1984 and from the universe of claims paid between July 1983 and June 1984.

Table 20.3:   New Jersey Temporary Disability Insurance Program Claims for
              Pregnancy and Related Complications
              (State Plan)

	July 1983– June 1984	Calendar Year 1985
Number of Claims	19,652	19,851
Average Total Days Paid	70.9	70.8
Average Amount Paid Per Claim	$1,367	$1,491[a]
Average Weekly Benefit	$133.16	$147.62[a]

Source: New Jersey Department of Labor.
[a]The maximum weekly benefit rate was one-half of the statewide average weekly
wage (SAWW) in the second preceding calendar year prior to October 1, 1984.
Effective that date, it rose to fifty-three percent of the SAWW. The maximum
weekly benefit was $158 during 1983, $170 from January 1 to September 30,
1984, $180 between October 1, 1984 and December 31, 1984, $189 in 1985,
$200 for 1986 and will increase to $213 in 1987.

take the form of a reduced working schedule in which one or both
parents reduce their usual number of hours at the workplace.

The flexibility of this approach is promising. New Jersey's small businesses, which rely on women for almost half of their staffing needs and
can least afford to lose trained staff members, would be in a position to
craft a workable arrangement to accommodate the needs of both the
parents and the business. An employer and employee could arrange a
flexible work schedule and compensation package within the legislative
guidelines of S–2392.

Job Security

This legislation is vitally important because it communicates the concern
of public officials that the business community has failed, for the most
part, to respond to the needs of parents in the work force. Family policies,
nevertheless, are also part of the economic issue. American businesses
need to initiate company policies that promote employee productivity
and loyalty if they are to compete in the global economy.

This legislation is revolutionary because it requires an employer to
provide job security to employees on parental leave. Although the idea
of guaranteeing an employee who takes time off for infant care with an
equivalent position upon return to work is anathema to many American
employers, it is a widely accepted notion abroad. The proposed legislation would guarantee a person on leave an equivalent position—in
terms of seniority, benefits and pay—upon return. The key to the success

of this legislation is to devise workable enforcement mechanisms so that individuals who take parental leave are indeed offered equivalent positions when they reenter the workforce.

One example of the degree to which employee loyalty can be improved by providing job security to those on parental leave is demonstrated by the experience of New Jersey-based pharmaceutical giant, Merck Incorporated. Merck grants its employees two parental leave options: a six-month childcare leave with full job security, or eighteen-months leave with the chance to return to the same or similar position if an opening exists. Temporary workers are hired during some employees' parental leaves, while other divisions opt to pool an employee's responsibilities during her childcare leave. By providing this generous childcare leave, Merck shows an interest in the well-being of its employees. The job-security provision is cited by managers and employees as an important reason for Merck's reputation as a company with intense employee loyalty.

Need for Change

New Jersey, in fact, is home to some progressive corporate giants and smaller business ventures that have helped reduce the pressure on working parents to choose between career growth and having a family. But while many companies have been responsive to the needs of the changing work force, industry still has a long way to go before company policies accommodate all women's professional and personal needs. Developing new childcare programs, philosophies, and service networks to meet the needs of working parents and their families is indeed one of the foremost challenges of the coming decade.

DAY CARE

New Jersey has been a national leader in responding to the flood of employee demands for day care. In May 1986 we opened the Al Wurf Day Care Center, the first state-owned and operated day-care facility in the country. This model program serves thirty children. The projected cost for staffing and leasing the facility for the first year is $349,000, but this cost is expected to decrease to $200,000 in subsequent years as the center's start-up costs are absorbed. In spite of the high operational costs to open a first-rate center, I am convinced that employer-sponsored day care is a great investment. Indeed, I am encouraged by the initiative and care exhibited by this center's eight staff members. The price for these services is kept affordable. The amount an employee contributes is determined on a sliding fee basis, ranging from $25 to $50 per week. When one sees the difference in attitudes displayed by working parents and their children who are enrolled in a successful day-care operation, one realizes that the investment in quality day care far outweighs the cost.

Day Care in the Private Sector

Government-sponsored day care is not enough. The public and the private sector must work together to provide affordable, accessible, quality day care. The strength of the modern family, the health and welfare of children, and the ability of employers to retain skilled staff members all depend on child care. I am impressed by the growing number of employers who have built on-site childcare facilities, hired off-site facilities, or provided employees with vouchers. Tax incentives, greater employee loyalty, less absenteeism, tardiness, and turnover, and increased productivity have shown many executives that day care is a good investment. To aid businesses in starting to include child care as part of their benefits package, New Jersey has an officially appointed day-care liaison with industry.

Since I was elected to my first term (November 1981), the number of business-sponsored or supported childcare programs in New Jersey has increased by more than 325 percent. New Jersey-based Hoffman-La-Roche's day-care center is a model on-site corporate facility. Employees with children between the ages of two-and-a-half and seven years old can drop their children off on their way to work. The sixty participants are placed in one of five classrooms with other children in similar stages of social, emotional, and educational development. The center's staff reevaluates each child's language, cognitive, and self-help skills on a regular basis to ensure proper classroom placement. The children benefit from daily exposure to art, reading, math, and creative play that the center offers. Both parents and employers have expressed satisfaction with the arrangement. I hope the success of Hoffman-La-Roche and New Jersey's sixty other employer-sponsored day-care programs will spur other business organizations to follow suit.

Conclusion

For 200 years, the family has been the stable foundation of our country. Today we must adjust public and private policy to accommodate the changing needs of the modern family. Our policy must encourage families to stay together and provide a stable atmosphere for child rearing. We must keep pace with the changing needs and changing demographics of the work force by bringing issues like the need for child care and parental leave to the forefront of the agenda of public and private sector policymakers.

PART VII

Recommendations and the Future

TWENTY-ONE

Recommendations of the Yale Bush Center Advisory Committee on Infant Care Leave

In 1983, the Bush Center in Child Development and Social Policy at Yale University convened an Advisory Committee as part of its Infant Care Leave Project. Representing both the professional world as well as the scholarly one, the members of this committee were to evaluate the impact of the changing composition of the work force on families. In doing so, they would both influence research directions and examine research outcomes. After a two-year period during which ongoing research on the relevant issues was studied, the Committee was then in a position to make policy recommendations to government and business on the needs of working families with infants.

Because insights into the issues facing working families today are not to be found in academia alone, the members of the Advisory Committee were drawn from a wide range of disciplines involving various aspects of child development and family health. Those asked to serve were distinguished in their fields, whether in law or education, medicine or academics, government or industry. The field of child development was represented by such noted scholars as Professors Urie Bronfenbrenner of Cornell University, Jerome Kagan of Harvard University, and Edward Zigler of Yale University. The distinguished pediatricians T. Berry Brazelton of Harvard Medical School and Sally Provence of the Yale Child Study Center served as the Committee's experts on child and family health. Betty Caldwell, an authority on early childhood education from the University of Arkansas, provided insight into the condition of day care. Wilbur Cohen, formerly Secretary of the U.S. Department of Health, Education and Welfare and now at the University of Texas, and

Julius Richmond, formerly U.S. Surgeon General and now at Harvard University, provided the committee with their expertise in social policy development and implementation. Sheila Kamerman of the Columbia University School of Social Work contributed her extensive knowledge of family policy throughout the world. Insight into the circumstances and concerns of women and minorities and experience in the development of policy was provided by Blandina Cardenas Ramirez of the U.S. Commission on Civil Rights and Wendy Williams, an authority on gender law from Georgetown University. Jo Ann Gasper of the U.S. Department of Health and Human Services represented the government's perspective on family issues, and Irving Harris, Chairman of the Executive Committee of the Pittway Corporation, contributed his vast knowledge of the interests of the business community and of the action necessary to meet the needs of children and families. Each of the thirteen members brought a depth of experience and expertise to the committee's task: to discover what working families need and want in order to be able to function well in the context of rapidly changing social forces.

The members of the committee met three times during the course of its tenure, received summaries of research, and corresponded by mail. On November 26, 1985, the committee was convened in New Haven, Connecticut, to announce its policy recommendations. The recommendations were derived from a two-year review of the relevant research and days of intense discussion. At the outset, the committee members held disparate views about the causes and solutions to the problems of working parents of infants. After much debate, however, it became clear that there were several conclusions upon which all could agree. These conclusions make up the introduction to the committee's recommendations (see p. xix, Introduction).

Following a discussion of the conclusions, members were asked to provide written statements of their own perceptions of the issue and to consider each of the points prepared for recommendation. The members' individual statements were collected and discussed, and the following text represents their collective opinion.

RECOMMENDATIONS

The Yale Bush Center Advisory Committee on Infant Care Leave has considered the evidence and has concluded that the infant-care-leave problem in the United States is of a magnitude and urgency such as to require immediate national action.

The Committee recommends that policies be initiated to allow employees a leave of absence for a period of time sufficient to care for their newborn or newly-adopted infants. Such a leave should provide income replacement, benefit continuation, and job protection. The leave should be available for a minimum of six months, and it should include partial income replacement (75% of salary) for three months, up to a realistic maximum benefit, sufficient to assure adequate basic resources for the families who need them most. Benefit continuation and job protection should be available for the entire six-month leave period.

This Committee recommends that the federal government require a combination of employee-employer contributions toward an insurance fund, covering both short-term disability and infant care leave, as the most efficient and effective financing mechanism. Several options are available that meet these criteria. These include:

1. A federally managed insurance fund, modeled on state short-term disability insurance funds such as those operated by New York and New Jersey.
2. State managed insurance funds based on the New York and New Jersey disability models.
3. Employer selection of private insurance to fund such leaves. An example is provided by the State of Hawaii's disability insurance law which requires employers to obtain disability insurance coverage.

Until such time as a comprehensive national program is established, this Committee recommends that employers provide infant care leave for their employees.

In addition, the Committee recommends that employers assist parents of newborn and newly-adopted infants in other ways, consistent with the needs of the workplace and of the family. For example, employers should implement such policies as flexible work schedules, reduced work hours, job sharing, and childcare information and referral services.

The Advisory Committee on Infant Care Leave further recommends that steps be taken to improve the quality of out-of-home infant care, including strengthening state licensing requirements.

Conclusion

EDWARD ZIGLER
AND MERYL FRANK

TIME FOR PARENTING

The research presented in this volume brings to the forefront for the first time many points that our grandmothers could have told us: that mothers need time to recover physically and emotionally from pregnancy and childbirth; that families need time to adjust to the arrival of a new family member; and that infants need time in a stable, caring environment. Our grandmothers' intuitions are supported today by a multitude of medical and social science research that provides strong evidence for the need to enact an infant-care-leave policy in the United States.

In effect, medical science has provided the rationale for policies of the past, such as a disability leave after childbirth. Research in the field of obstetrics and gynecology has shown that women require between six and eight weeks to recover physically from pregnancy and childbirth following a normal, safe, vaginal delivery (Williams 1985). These six to eight weeks of postpartum recovery are necessary to allow the uterus to return to its normal size, and to allow the placental site to properly heal. A delivery that requires surgery, or is premature or abnormal, would require more recovery time. And given the high percentage of atypical births today, the average disability leave associated with pregnancy and childbirth is more likely to be approximately ten weeks (Kean, chapter 20). Yet even though medical science has provided a clear definition of the length of time needed for mothers to recover from their physical disablement, it would be wrong and even foolish to assume that the time needed for physical recovery alone also ensures a healthy and caring parent-infant relationship.

The evidence of social science adds to our understanding of the time parents need with newborn infants in addition to recovery time. Numerous studies in the field of psychology have concluded that time together in the first months of life is essential to the development of a healthy parent-infant relationship. Stern and Brazelton (1974; 1986), for example, demonstrate that parents and their infants need time to establish a pattern of interaction which will enable them to recognize and respond to each other's signals. This attunement to each other's rhythms provides an important foundation in the infant's developing sense of self. Through their interaction with their parents, infants come to realize that they can influence and affect their environment, and thus they begin to develop a sense of security and trust within the family relationship and environment.

In addition to the development of a general sense of security, time together during the early period of an infant's life is crucial to insure a secure attachment to the caregiver. This attachment, based upon the infant's trust in the continuity of physical care and positive emotional response, is essential if the infant is to feel comfortable enough to begin to explore and experience the world (Bretherton 1985; Parke 1981). The infant must be provided with an environment which is of good quality, one that is warm, nurturing, and stimulating. Although new parents may immediately cherish their infant, it takes time for them, as well as the infants, to develop the emotions that insure bonding and to learn how to establish the routines of continuity and security. All of these characteristics take time for parents to develop, and certainly additional time for parents to find and recognize in infant day-care arrangements.

Research on the family system has highlighted the period immediately following birth as vital for the redefinition of family roles (Belsky 1985; Goldberg and Easterbrook 1984; Minuchin 1985). During the first few months following birth, all family members—mothers, fathers, and siblings—need time to adjust to the presence of a new family member and to renegotiate their family relationships and roles. Each member of the family feels disruption at the entrance of the new baby. Time is necessary to allow for a comfortable transition and to regain family equilibrium. Although these relationships are dynamic and do continue to change, the period following the introduction of the newborn into the family is one of the most important transitional periods in a family's life, and therefore requires special attention.

It is also clear that families need infant care leave upon the birth of a new child. A large number of surveys report stressed, overburdened families who must contend with the conflicting pressures of work and family. Parents report guilt over leaving infants too early and in questionable care arrangements. These worries are not without foundation.

As Brazelton and others have shown, many parents who are unable to spend time with their infants begin to distance themselves emotionally from too great an attachment to the infant.

The lack of regulations and quality in infant day care adds to the stress of the family as well. As research presented in this volume and elsewhere suggests, little is known about the effects of placing newborn infants in day care of varying quality, and high quality infant day care is rare, and if it is available at all, it is costly (Belsky 1986). What research tells us, however, is that a comprehensive approach must be taken when evaluating the outcome of infants in day care. An infant's environment must be considered in terms of many factors, among them: levels of stress at home; maternal and parental attitudes about working; the support the mother receives from the community; and the infant's temperament and individual characteristics. All of these elements will affect the infant's experience in day care and all of these elements may be closely tied to the time, opportunity, and inclination parents have to establish a responsive environment and to recognize one in an infant day-care arrangement.

Research, surveys, and experience all independently lead to the same conclusion: parents and infants need time together to adjust to the many changes a family experiences at birth and to grow together into a strong family system. Grandma's knowledge has come full circle: as a society, we should support a period of family togetherness in the early months.

SOCIETY AND SUPPORT

When social structures and institutions support parents in their parenting role, especially with very young infants, the message is communicated that the development of the family is valuable to society, and that the family is essential to society's well-being. However, no current, truly national policy exists to support families when parents must work as well as care for and respond to a new infant. Research prepared for this volume presents a convincing case that the first year following the birth of a child is becoming an increasingly difficult period in a family's life. More and more parents of both genders must work outside the home to provide for their families. Without a recognition of the special needs parents and their infants have, families have little hope for relief. The working mother's recovery from childbirth, the parent's adjustment to the entrance of a newborn, the kind of day care the infant is receiving, and even the availability of such care is viewed mainly as a private concern, rather than a larger social concern. We, as a society, need to recognize the conflicts parents face between their work and their family, and we need to help to strengthen families by resolving these conflicts.

To date, the necessary support, both in terms of time and money, has not been provided to most American families. Even where it does exist, and then only for a minority of the population, it is often inadequate. Independently arranged leave policies, instituted by too few of our nation's employers, do little to address the overall problem of recognition and support for the role of the family on a national level. The uneven and haphazard adoption of leave policies has the effect of discrimination, both internally within a business and externally between businesses. A business may extend time only to a favored employee or to attract talented employees away from competitors. However, the opposite is equally true: some businesses are unwilling or unable to provide a leave, without the knowledge that competitors are doing the same. This type of competition may be efficient in the marketplace, but it does little to contribute to the stability of the family and the total work force in the long run. Yet the existing practices of individual businesses are too informal and haphazard to meet the needs of most families. Most families, especially low-income and single-parent families, still must struggle to meet all the demands being made on their time. Inevitably, when the financial survival of the family competes with attention to its emotional growth, survival takes precedence. Many families at this time have no other option than to put their family's development on hold while they earn the wages to provide for material support that is absolutely necessary.

As has been made clear in this volume, we are still far behind the other nations of the world, both in our recognition of the family-society relationship and in our efforts to strengthen that relationship. For many nations of the world, infant-care-leave policies were established to rebuild economic and human capital in the aftermath of war. These policies have been in existence for years and have proven viable through the test of time. Only the United States lags in its recognition of the importance of the family over short-term economic interests. Only the United States refuses to see that "it is in the best interest of society to support families and parenthood in whatever way possible" (Allen, chapter 15, above). American society is slow to become aware of how drastic and influential the changing demographics of the work force are. Although we may want to preserve the illusion that all mothers are at home with their young infants and that those who do work wait until their children are toddlers, statistics paint a much different and more realistic picture, as the chapters of this volume have made clear. There can be no illusion that we will return to a nostalgic past; a changed work force is here to stay.

WHAT WE CAN EXPECT FROM AN INFANT-CARE-LEAVE POLICY

As the Bush Center's Advisory Committee has emphasized, "The infant-care-leave problem in the United States is of a magnitude and urgency such as to require immediate national attention." Government has a responsibility to create and enforce an infant-care-leave system of support. Whereas some employers may be individually motivated to do so out of a concern for their work force, only a national policy mandated by the federal government can ensure that uniform support is available to all families working in all businesses, whether private or public. In calling for a recognition of the need for an infant care leave and its implementation on a national level, we are asking for increased responsibility by all who should be involved—parents, employers, and government.

Employers must acknowledge that employees are family members with responsibilities outside the workplace—responsibilities that will affect their performance as employees, especially at specific times in their lives. The strength of the American workplace and work force is directly related to the strength of the family. One way in which employers may be able to meet both their needs and the needs of their workers who are family members is to provide flexible working arrangements to help both employer and employee bridge the time between childbirth and reentry into the workplace.

Parents have the responsibility to determine what their family needs are and to communicate these needs to their employers. They will have to decide how they can model and structure their own lives as they address the needs of both their infants and their employers. Some parents may need to and be eager to return to work as soon as possible, and they may be fully capable of handling the multiple demands on their time. For those parents who need more time with their infants before resuming work responsibilities, however, the option for at least six-months leave should exist.

Day-care providers, too, have an increased responsibility in caring for an increasing number of infants. They need to address what the unique needs of infants are, and to develop day-care systems that provide quality care for infants. Further, government needs to act on the never-enforced Federal Interagency Day Care Requirements, which would provide a standard for quality care for infants and which would also strengthen licensing requirements. Finally, the need for more care and more available places for the increasing number of infants coming into care in the first six months must be addressed.

Currently, legislation has been introduced in Congress which would provide time for parents to meet a number of different needs, including the time immediately following birth. Several state governments are currently considering the implementation of a mandated parental leave time during the first few months of an infant's life. Although we applaud the efforts of legislators in both the state and federal governments, we must also caution that the unpaid leaves that are being advocated are not a panacea. In fact, this type of leave policy is a compromise and should be considered as only the first step toward a more comprehensive program sensitive to the needs of all American families. The lack of any salary replacement and the exemption of small businessess are compromises which exclude the most needy, single-parent, and low-income families. These families will be forced to make an unfair choice between economic stability and personal care for their newborn infants. Further, the small-business exemption removes the most important benefits many of these families would reap from such legislation—job protection for at least the amount of time they feel they can afford and continued medical insurance. Since a large proportion of the female and working-poor population is employed by small businesses the exemption is not an insignificant matter.

Mechanisms for financing a paid national leave policy are not out of reach. Employer-employee contributions toward an insurance fund to finance a leave policy could serve this purpose well. As Governor Kean of New Jersey has pointed out, the *maximum* employer contribution of $53.50 per year necessary to finance a system that provides wage replacement for all employees during a period of any physical disablement is a small investment that promises large returns. He concludes that that there is no evidence that such contributions, have caused "significant economic strain on employers."

Although infant care leaves may be aimed primarily at helping new parents integrate their family and career roles, it is not a benefit which is one-sided. Rather it is a part of the larger issue wherein society's well-being arises out of a more synergistic relationship between the family and the workplace. The ultimate benefit is a stable, dependable, and productive work force, supported by a strong American family system.

The leave policy recommended by the Yale Bush Center Advisory Committee on Infant Care Leave does not seek to side with the family over the workplace. Rather, it requires respect from each side for the needs of the other, and it requires compromises that need to be made by each. It calls upon employers to recognize that family concerns constitute a legitimate demand on an employee's time and attention. The workplace can benefit by respecting those demands and by helping the employee meet the responsibilities of both work and family. One responsibility should not displace the other. The Committee's work calls equally upon parent-employees to recognize the employers' demands on their time and commitment. An infant care leave does not mean that family concerns displace those of the workplace. Rather, the two concerns affect each other. An infant care leave would need to address the distinct character of the American workplace as well as of American families in order to find a balance between the needs of parents, of infants, and of employers.

The issue of a nationally mandated infant care leave addresses a concern central to society's very existence: the well-being of the family. It is an issue involving what the family needs in order to cope with the birth of a new child, and how parents who do work can meet obligations of both work and family. A society is only as strong as its components, who are family members. The family, in turn, is only as strong as the institutions of society permit it to be.

REFERENCES

Belsky, J. 1985. Experimenting with the family in the newborn period. *Child Development* 56:407–14.

Belsky, J. 1986. Infant day care: a cause for for concern? *Zero to Three* 6:1–7.

Brazelton, T. 1986. Issues for working parents. *American Journal of Orthopsychiatry* 56(1).

Bretherton, I. 1985. Attachment theory: retrospect and prospect. *Monographs of the Society for Research and Child Development* 50:3–35.

Goldberg, W. A., and Easterbrooks, M. A. 1984. Role of marital quality in toddler development. *Developmental Psychology* 20:504–14.

Minuchin, P. 1985. Families and individual development: provocations from the field of family therapy. *Child Development* 56:289–302.

Parke, R. 1981. *Fathers*. Cambridge: Harvard University Press.

Pritchard, J. A., MacDonald, C., and Gant, N. F. 1985. *Williams Obstetrics*. 17th Edition. Norwalk, Conn.: Appleton, Century, Crofts.

Stern, D. 1974. Mother and infant at play: The dyadic interaction involving facial, vocal and gaze behavior. M. Lewis and L. Rosenblum, eds. *The Effect of the Infant on the Caregiver*. New York: John Wiley & Sons.

Index